w many
ecies of
ogs are
here?
→ 68

When did
African countries
begin to win their
independence?
→ 306

W...the
!
SO-BBZ-532
→ 129

Where is
the world's
tallest
building?
→ 50

Where can
you ride the
world's
longest roller
coaster?
→ 101

hat
sident
ed two
ns but
t in a
w?
→ 257

If it's noon in
Washington, DC,
what time is it in
Alaska?
→ 53

How many
Americans
speak
Arabic?
→ 107

Which Williams
sister won the
1999 U.S. Open?
→ 235

If you were a
camel, which
Texas city
would you
avoid?
→ 110

o won
999
mmy
Best
song?
→ 187

Where does
your state
rank in
population?
→ 181

How many
zeros does
a septillion
have?
→ 172

Which rookie
led the NFL in
rushing in 1999?
→ 224

What's the
difference
between an
alligator and a
crocodile?
→ 30

hat
ens
ing
M
p?
→ 89

Who
invented
Lincoln
Logs?
→ 100

What's
the
coldest
planet?
→ 210

WORLD ALMANAC BOOKS
A Division of World Almanac Education Group, Inc.
A WRC Media Company

THE WORLD ALMANAC FOR KIDS 2001

EDITOR: Elaine Israel

CURRICULUM CONSULTANT:
Jean Craven, Director of Instructional Support
Albuquerque, NM, Public Schools

CONTRIBUTORS:
Matt Friedlander, Monica M. Gallen, Ann Hardy, Jane Havsy, Charles Hirsch,
Dr. Tom Hull, Randi Metsch-Ampel, Allen Mogol, Sean Price, Terry Simon
Consultants: Lee T. Shapiro, Ph.D. (Astronomy), Bernadette Fiscina, M.D. (Health)

KID CONTRIBUTORS: Ashley Bruggemann, Michelle Diaz, Shuana Dunton, Ana Dru Ellis,
Danielle Hilton, Ben Master, Elana Metsch-Ampel, Matthew Patrick, Ana-Maria Visoiu

DESIGN: Bill SMITH STUDIO
Art Directors: Jay Jaffe, Eric Hoffsten **Illustration Buying:** Marianne Tozzo
Cover Art Director: Brian Kobberger **Design:** Jeff Rutzky

WORLD ALMANAC BOOKS

**Vice President–
Sales and Marketing:**
James R. Keenley

**Editorial
Director:**
William McGeveran, Jr.

**Marketing
Manager:**
Jacqueline J. Ogle

Editorial Staff: Beth R. Ellis, Lori P. Wiesenfeld, Senior Editors;
Kelly Enright, Kevin Seabrooke, Associate Editors;
Elizabeth J. Lazzara, Desktop Publishing Associate;
Edward A. Thomas, Picture Research

WORLD ALMANAC EDUCATION GROUP
President: Alfred DeSeta
Publisher: Ken Park
Director of Editorial Production: Andrea J. Pitluk
Director–Purchasing and Production: Edward A. Thomas
Director of Indexing Services: Marjorie B. Bank; **Index Editor:** Walter Kronenberg
Desktop Publishing Assistant: Hana Shaki

CONTENTS

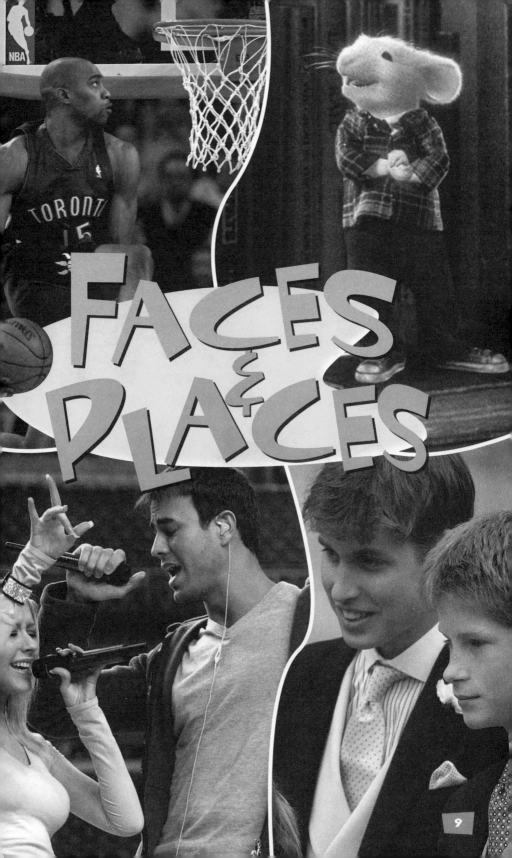

FACES & PLACES

MUSIC MAKERS

Christina AGUILERA & Enrique IGLESIAS

Each topped the charts in 1999. Now Christina is off on a U.S. tour, while Enrique makes sure to stay wired-in to his fans.

'N SYNC

Justin Timberlake, James Lance Bass, Chris Kirkpatrick, JC Chasez, and Joey Fatone—more popular than ever.

Ricky MARTiN

A world tour in 2000 didn't leave much time for Ricky's favorite activities—yoga, working out, and rock climbing.

SCREEN STARS

Haley Joel OSMENT

This little guy does big things. He's following up his Oscar nomination with three movies, including a role in Steven Spielberg's *A.I.*, planned for summer 2001.

©A.M.P.

Stuart **LiTTLE**

Stuart's like a lot of kids. He tries to fit in but there's a mean "cat" out to get him. The movie is based on a much-loved book by E. B. White.

m **ALLEN**
Tom **HANKS**

Buzz and Woody, the real stars of *Toy Story 2*, take time out from their busy schedules to pose with Tim and Tom.

13

BROTHERS & SISTERS

Venus & Serena WILLIAMS

"We're both really tough to beat when we're playing our best," Serena (right) told a reporter. That kind of attitude is filling the Williams's cup with success.

Princes
WILLIAM & HARRY

William (left) and Harry, who call the Queen of England "Granny," are said to be athletic, nice, totally cool boys. William just graduated from Eton, a high school that Harry still attends.

Coco & Kelly MILLER

They're tall, they're smiling, and they're the top amateur athletes in the U.S. The basketball-playing Miller twins from the University of Georgia shared the Sullivan Award for 1999, becoming the first co-winners ever.

UNREAL!

The ROCK

He's won and lost several wrestling titles. He's changed his name a few times. But to die-hard fans, this former college football star will always be "The People's Champ."

PEANUTS

Charles Schulz, who drew *Peanuts* for almost 50 years without ever showing a grown-up, died in 2000. There will be no more new strips. But long-suffering Charlie Brown, wise Snoopy, and sassy Lucy live on in books, on TV, and in our memories.

AND IT SAYS HERE THAT NO ONE HAS BEEN KNOWN TO HAVE BEEN STRUCK BY A FALLING METEORITE..

POKÉMON

Rarely has anything so small been so monstrous. Figures, cards, games, TV shows, and movies prove the power of Pokémon.

ALTHOUGH A DOG WAS KILLED IN EGYPT BY A METEORITE YEARS AGO..

WHAT DO THEY MEAN, "ALTHOUGH" A DOG?

© 1994 United Feature Syndicate, Inc.

3-31

SPORTS FAVES

Mia HAMM

The all-time leading scorer in women's soccer, Mia has helped the U.S. win Olympic gold and two World Cups.

Ken GRIFFEY Jr.

"Junior" is a ten-time All-Star and the youngest player ever to hit 400 home runs. In 2000 he was traded to Cincinnati, where he grew up watching his father play for the Reds.

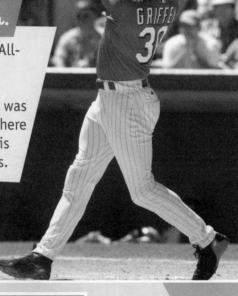

Tiger WOODS

He's been playing golf since he was two. Tiger's charisma and unprecedented achievements are bringing more and more fans and players to the sport.

SPORTS CHAMPS

Kurt **WARNER**

A few years ago he worked nights bagging groceries. Now he's a Super Bowl champion and MVP.

Vince CARTER

One of the most exciting players in the NBA, Vince was Slam Dunk champion in 2000 and led the Toronto Raptors to their first playoff appearance ever.

Marion JONES

A two-time world champion at 100 meters, this American Sprint Queen hoped to bring home plenty of gold— medals, that is—from the 2000 Olympics.

21

NEWS MAKERS

Al GORE

Vice President Al Gore and his wife, Tipper, are joined on the 2000 presidential campaign trail by family members—two daughters and a son-in-law.

George W. BUSH

George W. and his wife, Laura (far left), hoped to follow in the footsteps of his parents, former President George Bush and First Lady Barbara Bush.

Elián González, hiding in closet during raid by U.S. authorities.

Elián **GONZÁLEZ**

The plight of this shipwrecked Cuban boy captured the attention of the nation.

Elián reunited with his father, stepmother, and half brother.

23

Who Wants to be a **MILLIONAIRE**?

The final answer: tons of people. The show's high ratings were the surprise of the 2000 TV season.

J. K. **ROWLING**

Since childhood, the creator of Harry Potter had a wild imagination. Now millions of readers let her cast a spell on them as they follow Harry's adventures.

ANNIVERSARIES

IN 2001

50 YEARS AGO—1951

The *I Love Lucy* show, which is still in reruns, was first broadcast on television.

Richard Rodgers and Oscar Hammerstein's hit musical *The King and I* opened on Broadway.

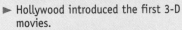

▶ Hollywood introduced the first 3-D movies.

▶ The first color TV program was broadcast by CBS. But color TVs remained rare for many years.

General Douglas MacArthur was fired from his command in Korea by President Harry Truman.

The Twenty-Second Amendment to the U.S. Constitution, restricting presidents to two terms in office, was ratified (approved).

The National Basketball Association's first All-Star game was played.

The New York Yankees' great centerfielder Joe DiMaggio retired from baseball.

100 YEARS AGO—1901

Great Britain's Queen Victoria died after reigning for 64 years. Her death brought the Victorian era to an end. She was succeeded by her son Edward VII.

President William McKinley was assassinated in Buffalo, New York. Vice President Theodore Roosevelt became president— the youngest ever, at the age of only 42.

The discovery of a gusher known as Spindletop launched the Texas oil industry.

The first Nobel Prizes were given out.

President Roosevelt invited African-American leader Booker T. Washington to the White House, angering many Southern whites.

Guglielmo Marconi sent and received the first transatlantic radio signals.

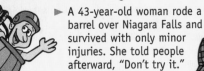

▶ A 43-year-old woman rode a barrel over Niagara Falls and survived with only minor injuries. She told people afterward, "Don't try it."

▶ Cartoonist Walt Disney was born.

IN 2002

50 YEARS AGO—1952

▶ Elizabeth II became queen of England after her father, George VI, died.

▶ The famous Western movie *High Noon* opened, starring Gary Cooper and Grace Kelly.

▶ At the Summer Olympic Games in Helsinki, Finland, the United States won 43 gold medals and 76 medals in all; the Soviet Union came in second with 22 gold medals and 71 in all.

▶ World War II General Dwight D. Eisenhower was elected president of the United States.

▶ Rocky Marciano won the world heavyweight boxing title from "Jersey" Joe Walcott.

▶ The United States set off the first hydrogen bomb (H bomb) at a test on a Pacific island.

▶ The classic children's story *Charlotte's Web*, by E. B. White, was published.

▶ McDonald's Golden Arches were created.

▶ *Mad* comic books were introduced. They eventually led to *Mad* magazine.

100 YEARS AGO—1902

▶ Michigan defeated Stanford, 49-0, in the first Rose Bowl.

▶ The United States gained control of the area where the Panama Canal was to be built.

▶ Jell-O became a hit product with U.S. kids.

▶ Helen Keller's *The Story of My Life*, recalling her struggle to overcome being both blind and deaf, became a best-seller.

▶ Beatrix Potter published the Peter Rabbit children's stories.

▶ Air conditioning was invented by Willis Carrier in Buffalo, New York.

▶ The first Cadillac was built in Detroit.

▶ Sir Arthur Conan Doyle's "The Hound of the Baskervilles," one of the most famous Sherlock Holmes stories, was published.

▶ A speedy new train called the 20th Century Limited made the run between New York and Chicago in just 16 hours.

▶ The Pepsi-Cola Company was founded.

BIRTHDAYS OF CELEBRITIES

Here are the birthdays of some favorite stars, along with famous sports heroes, writers, and public figures.

JANUARY

Mel Gibson	Jan. 3, 1956
A.J. McLean	Jan. 9, 1978
L.L. Cool J	Jan. 14, 1968
Jim Carrey	Jan. 17, 1962
Kevin Costner	Jan. 18, 1955
Beverley Mitchell	Jan. 22, 1981
Wayne Gretzky	Jan. 26, 1961
Vince Carter	Jan. 26, 1977
Joey Fatone	Jan. 28, 1977
Nick Carter	Jan. 28, 1980
Elijah Wood	Jan. 28, 1981
Oprah Winfrey	Jan. 29, 1954
Andrew Keegan	Jan. 29, 1979
Justin Timberlake	Jan. 31, 1981

FEBRUARY

Natalie Imbruglia	Feb. 4, 1975
Garth Brooks	Feb. 7, 1962
David Gallagher	Feb. 9, 1985
Sheryl Crow	Feb. 11, 1962
Jennifer Aniston	Feb. 11, 1969
Brandy	Feb. 11, 1979
Judy Blume	Feb. 12, 1938
Matt Groening	Feb. 15, 1954
Jaromir Jagr	Feb. 15, 1972
LeVar Burton	Feb. 16, 1957
Michael Jordan	Feb. 17, 1963
John Travolta	Feb. 18, 1954
Brian Littrell	Feb. 20, 1975
Jennifer Love Hewitt	Feb. 21, 1979
Drew Barrymore	Feb. 22, 1975
Erykah Badu	Feb. 26, 1971
Marshall Faulk	Feb. 26, 1973
Chelsea Clinton	Feb. 27, 1980

MARCH

Jake Lloyd	March 5, 1989
Shaquille O'Neal	March 6, 1972
Freddie Prinze, Jr.	March 8, 1976
James Van Der Beek	March 8, 1977
Billy Crystal	March 14, 1947
Mia Hamm	March 17, 1972
Ron Dayne	March 17, 1978
Rosie O'Donnell	March 21, 1962
Keri Russell	March 23, 1976
Mariah Carey	March 27, 1970
Celine Dion	March 30, 1968
Al Gore	March 31, 1948
Ewan McGregor	March 31, 1971

APRIL

Eddie Murphy	April 3, 1961
Maya Angelou	April 4, 1928
Haley Joel Osment	April 10, 1988
Beverly Cleary	April 12, 1916
Claire Danes	April 12, 1979
Rick Schroder	April 13, 1970
Sarah Michelle Gellar	April 14, 1977
Melissa Joan Hart	April 18, 1976
Tim Duncan	April 25, 1976
Andre Agassi	April 29, 1970

MAY

Lance Bass	May 4, 1979
Enrique Iglesias	May 8, 1975
George Lucas	May 14, 1944
Cher	May 20, 1946
Drew Carey	May 23, 1958
Jewel	May 23, 1974
Mike Myers	May 25, 1963
Lauryn Hill	May 25, 1975
Sally Ride	May 26, 1951
Clint Eastwood	May 31, 1930

JUNE

Morgan Freeman	June 1, 1937
Alanis Morissette	June 1, 1974
Scott Wolf	June 4, 1968
Liam Neeson	June 7, 1952
Michael J. Fox	June 9, 1961
Natalie Portman	June 9, 1981
Tara Lipinski	June 10, 1982
Tim Allen	June 13, 1953
Ashley Olsen	June 13, 1986
Mary-Kate Olsen	June 13, 1986
Courteney Cox-Arquette	June 15, 1964
Venus Williams	June 17, 1980
Prince William	June 21, 1982
Kurt Warner	June 23, 1971

JULY

Tom Cruise	July 3, 1962
George W. Bush	July 6, 1946
Michelle Kwan	July 7, 1980
Tom Hanks	July 9, 1956
Jessica Simpson	July 10, 1980
Bill Cosby	July 12, 1937
Harrison Ford	July 13, 1942
Matthew Fox	July 14, 1966
Carlos Santana	July 20, 1947
Robin Williams	July 21, 1952
Jennifer Lopez	July 24, 1970
Matt LeBlanc	July 25, 1967
Brad Renfro	July 25, 1982
Sandra Bullock	July 26, 1964
Arnold Schwarzenegger	July 30, 1947
Lisa Kudrow	July 30, 1963
J. K. Rowling	July 31, 1966

AUGUST

Edgerrin James	August 1, 1978
Jeff Gordon	August 4, 1971
David Duchovny	August 7, 1960
Joshua "JC" Chasez	August 8, 1976
Whitney Houston	August 9, 1963
Gillian Anderson	August 9, 1968
Ann Martin	August 12, 1955
Magic Johnson	August 14, 1959
Ben Affleck	August 15, 1972
Bill Clinton	August 19, 1946
Matthew Perry	August 19, 1969
Howie Dorough	August 22, 1973
Kobe Bryant	August 23, 1978
Shania Twain	August 28, 1965
Cameron Diaz	August 30, 1972

SEPTEMBER

Gloria Estefan	Sept. 1, 1957
Devon Sawa	Sept. 7, 1978
Adam Sandler	Sept. 9, 1966
Michelle Williams	Sept. 9, 1979
Prince Harry	Sept. 15, 1984
Marc Anthony	Sept. 16, 1969
Bill Murray	Sept. 21, 1950
Bruce Springsteen	Sept. 23, 1949
Kevin Sorbo	Sept. 24, 1958
Will Smith	Sept. 25, 1968
Serena Williams	Sept. 26, 1981
Gwyneth Paltrow	Sept. 28, 1972
Se Ri Pak	Sept. 28, 1977

OCTOBER

Mark McGwire	Oct. 1, 1963
Kevin Richardson	Oct. 3, 1972
Neve Campbell	Oct. 3, 1973
Alicia Silverstone	Oct. 4, 1976
Kate Winslet	Oct. 5, 1975
Matt Damon	Oct. 8, 1970
Brett Favre	Oct. 10, 1969
Luke Perry	Oct. 11, 1966
Usher	Oct. 14, 1978
Chris Kirkpatrick	Oct. 17, 1971
Monica	Oct. 24, 1980
Hillary Rodham Clinton	Oct. 26, 1947
Bill Gates	Oct. 28, 1955
Julia Roberts	Oct. 28, 1967

NOVEMBER

Sinbad	Nov. 10, 1956
Calista Flockhart	Nov. 11, 1964
Leonardo DiCaprio	Nov. 11, 1974
David Schwimmer	Nov. 12, 1966
Sammy Sosa	Nov. 12, 1968
Ryan Gosling	Nov. 12, 1980
Whoopi Goldberg	Nov. 13, 1949
Danny DeVito	Nov. 17, 1944
Jason Williams	Nov. 18, 1975
Calvin Klein	Nov. 19, 1942
Meg Ryan	Nov. 19, 1961
Ken Griffey, Jr.	Nov. 21, 1969

DECEMBER

Britney Spears	Dec. 2, 1981
Brendan Fraser	Dec. 3, 1967
Frankie Muniz	Dec. 5, 1985
Steven Spielberg	Dec. 18, 1947
Brad Pitt	Dec. 18, 1963
Katie Holmes	Dec. 18, 1978
Christina Aguilera	Dec. 18, 1980
Samuel L. Jackson	Dec. 21, 1948
Ricky Martin	Dec. 24, 1971
Denzel Washington	Dec. 28, 1954
Tiger Woods	Dec. 30, 1975

Animals

? Which animal has a sixth sense, and what is it?
You can find the answer below.

AMAZING ANIMAL FACTS

Facts about animals are often surprising. Here are a few.

While most insects and animals run away to try to escape from forest fires, jewel beetles, or fire beetles as they are sometimes called, actually fly into flames and smoldering trees, so that they can be the first to plant their eggs there.

If crocodile eggs are kept at a temperature below 84 degrees Fahrenheit, the baby crocodiles will be female!

Just as no two human thumbprints are alike, every gorilla has a unique set of lines around its nose. People who study gorillas use this noseprint to tell one from the other.

Only female mosquitoes eat blood. They need it to produce their eggs. Male mosquitoes can't even pierce the skin with their mouths. Instead of blood, they eat plant juice and sap.

Hummingbirds hold their nests together with spider silk. Robins use mud. Chimney swifts use their own saliva. Sparrows put trash in their nests. Male bowerbirds have a real sense of style. They try to attract mates by decorating their homes with shells, flowers, or shiny bits of glass.

Like most birds, macaws of South America eat seeds and berries. But they also eat clay. Clay contains minerals like calcium and potassium, but scientists think it may also help prevent the birds from getting sick from poisonous seeds and berries.

Through research, scientists have created "smart mice" that seem to know the difference between objects they have and objects they have not seen. In the future, results of their studies may help to improve human memory.

All About... SHARKS

Sharks are one of the oldest animals on Earth; they have ruled the seas for over 400 million years. They may be awesome predators, but they probably should fear humans more than we fear them. Sharks can see, hear, smell, taste, and feel. They also have a sixth sense. Through tiny pores in their heads, they can pick up electrical impulses that every animal emits. This ability, combined with strength and razor sharp teeth, makes them formidable undersea competitors.

But they have one big enemy: humans. People kill 30 to 70 million sharks every year. Their fins are churned into soup that is a big favorite in some parts of Asia; the soup can sell for up to $90 a bowl in Hong Kong. Other parts are used to make health and beauty aids. Some people also hunt sharks for sport. Because sharks reproduce slowly, these killings are a serious problem, and the future of the shark is threatened in many parts of the world.

CLASSIFYING ANIMALS

There are so many different types of animals that scientists had to find a way to organize them into groups. A Swedish scientist named Carolus Linnaeus (1707–1778) worked out a system for classifying both animals and plants. We still use it today.

ANIMAL KINGDOM

The animal kingdom is separated into two large groups—animals with backbones, called **vertebrates,** and animals without backbones, called **invertebrates.**

These large groups are divided into smaller groups called **phyla.** And phyla are divided into even smaller groups called **classes.** The animals in each group are classified together when their bodies are similar in certain ways.

VERTEBRATES: Animals With Backbones

FISH	Swordfish, tuna, salmon, trout, halibut
AMPHIBIANS	Frogs, toads, mud puppies
REPTILES	Turtles, alligators, crocodiles, lizards
BIRDS	Sparrows, owls, turkeys, hawks
MAMMALS	Kangaroos, opossums, dogs, cats, bears, seals, rats, squirrels, rabbits, chipmunks, porcupines, horses, pigs, cows, deer, bats, whales, dolphins, monkeys, apes, humans

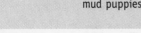

INVERTEBRATES: Animals Without Backbones

PROTOZOA	The simplest form of animals
COELENTERATES	Jellyfish, hydra, sea anemones, coral
MOLLUSKS	Clams, snails, squid, oysters
ANNELIDS	Earthworms
ARTHROPODS	
Crustaceans:	Lobsters, crayfish
Centipedes and Millipedes	
Arachnids:	Spiders, scorpions
Insects:	Butterflies, grasshoppers, bees, termites, cockroaches
ECHINODERMS	Starfish, sea urchins, sea cucumbers

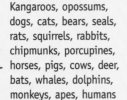

WHAT'S THE DIFFERENCE
Between...

A CROCODILE AND AN ALLIGATOR?

CROCODILE
Pointed snout

Fiercer

Fourth tooth on each side on the bottom sticks out over the upper lip

ALLIGATOR
Broad, flat snout

Less fierce

A LEOPARD, A JAGUAR, AND A CHEETAH?

LEOPARD
Lives in Africa and Asia

Spots are broken circles, no dot in the center

Black markings on the backs of the ears

JAGUAR
Lives in Central and South America

Spots are circles, with a dot in the center

Belly is white

CHEETAH
Lives in Africa and Arabian Peninsula

Spots are solid circles

Black mark from the nose to the eye

A RABBIT AND A HARE?

RABBIT
Shorter ears

Newborns are born blind

Newborns have no fur

Shorter hind legs

HARE
Larger than a rabbit

Newborns are born with eyes open

Newborns have fur

Longer hind legs

A FROG AND A TOAD?

FROG
Slim

Lighter skin, often green

Long back legs for jumping

Smooth skin

Spends most of its time in water

TOAD
Stout

Darker skin

Shorter back legs

Warty skin

Spends most of its time on land

A MOUNTAIN LION, A PUMA, AND A COUGAR?

Nothing! These are all names for the same large cats, *Felis concolor*, whose original range extended through North and South America. In some areas these animals are also called **panthers;** the name panther is also used for a leopard with a black coat.

The **LARGEST** and the **FASTEST** in the **WORLD**

WORLD'S LARGEST ANIMALS

LARGEST ANIMAL: blue whale (110 feet long, 209 tons)

LARGEST LAND ANIMAL: African bush elephant (13 feet high, 8 tons)

TALLEST ANIMAL: giraffe (19 feet tall)

LARGEST REPTILE: saltwater crocodile (16 feet long, 1,150 pounds)

LARGEST SNAKE: Heaviest: anaconda (27 feet, 9 inches long, 500 pounds)
Longest: reticulated python (26–32 feet long)

LONGEST FISH: whale shark (41 1/2 feet long)

LARGEST BIRD: ostrich (9 feet tall, 345 pounds)

LARGEST INSECT: stick insect (15 inches long)

WORLD'S FASTEST ANIMALS

FASTEST ANIMAL: peregrine falcon, a bird (100–200 miles per hour)

FASTEST MARINE ANIMAL: blue whale (30 miles per hour)

FASTEST LAND ANIMAL: cheetah (70 miles per hour)

FASTEST FISH: sailfish (68 miles per hour)

FASTEST BIRD: peregrine falcon (100–200 miles per hour)

FASTEST INSECT: dragonfly (36 miles per hour)

HOW FAST DO ANIMALS RUN?

Did you know that some animals can run as fast as a car can move or that a snail would need more than 30 hours just to go one mile? If you look at this table, you will see how fast some land animals can move.

	MILES PER HOUR
Cheetah	70
Lion	50
Cape hunting dog	45
Zebra	40
Rabbit	35
Grizzly bear	30
Cat (domestic)	30
Elephant	25
Squirrel	12
Pig (domestic)	11
Chicken	9
Snail	0.03

DiD YoU KNOW?

Humans at their fastest are still slower than many animals. In the 1996 Atlanta Olympics, U.S. sprinter Michael Johnson averaged 23.16 mph when he ran 200 meters in a record 19.32 seconds.

The area in nature where an animal lives is called its habitat. The table below lists some large habitats and some of the animals that live in them.

HABITAT	Some Animals That Live There
Deserts (hot, dry regions)	camels, bobcats, coyotes, kangaroos, mice, Gila monsters, scorpions, rattlesnakes
Tropical Forests (warm, humid climate)	orangutans, gibbons, leopards, tamandua anteaters, tapirs, iguanas, parrots, tarantulas
Grasslands (flat, open lands)	African elephants, kangaroos, Indian rhinoceroses, giraffes, zebras, prairie dogs, ostriches, tigers
Mountains (highlands)	yaks, snow leopards, vicunas, bighorn sheep, chinchillas, pikas, eagles, mountain goats
Polar Regions (cold climate)	polar bears, musk oxen, caribou, ermines, arctic foxes, walruses, penguins, Siberian huskies
Oceans (sea water)	whales, dolphins, seals, manatees, octopuses, stingrays, coral, starfish, lobsters, many kinds of fish

FOSSILS: CLUES TO ANCIENT ANIMALS

A fossil is the remains of an animal or plant that lived long ago. Most fossils are formed from the hard parts of an animal's body, such as bones, shells, or teeth. Some are large, like dinosaur footprints. Some are so tiny that you need a microscope to see them. Most fossils are found in rocks formed from the mud or sand that collects at the bottom of oceans, rivers, and lakes. Fossils offer scientists clues to ancient animals.

WHAT Do Fossils Tell Us?

Scientists study fossils to help them understand plant and animal life in ancient periods of the world's history. The age and structure of the rocks in which fossils are found can help scientists tell how long ago certain kinds of animals or plants lived. For example, dinosaurs lived millions of years ago, but people have known about dinosaurs only since the first dinosaur fossils were uncovered, less than 200 years ago.

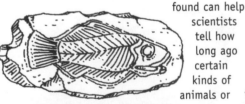

WHERE Are Fossils Found?

In eastern and southern Africa and other places, people have found fossils that are ancestors of early humans. Insects that lived millions of years ago are sometimes found preserved in amber (hardened tree sap). Fossils have also been found in ice and tar.

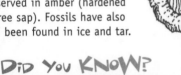

DID YOU KNOW?

In 1998, scientists reported finding a fossil that showed the intestines, liver, muscles, and windpipe of a baby meat-eating dinosaur. By comparing it to modern birds and reptiles, the scientists may be able to tell if today's birds are descendants of dinosaurs.

Box turtle	100 years
Human	70–80 years
Asian elephant	40 years
Grizzly bear	25 years
Horse	20 years
Gorilla	20 years
Polar bear	20 years
Rhinoceros (white)	20 years
Black bear	18 years
Lion	15 years
Lobster	15 years
Rhesus monkey	15 years
Rhinoceros (black)	15 years
Camel (Bactrian)	12 years
Cat (domestic)	12 years
Dog (domestic)	12 years
Leopard	12 years
Giraffe	10 years
Pig	10 years
Squirrel	10 years
Red fox	7 years
Kangaroo	7 years
Chipmunk	6 years
Rabbit	5 years
Guinea pig	4 years
Mouse	3 years
Opossum	1 year

HOW LONG DO ANIMALS LIVE?

Most animals do not live as long as human beings do. A monkey that is 14 years old is thought to be old. A person who is 14 is still considered young. The average life span of a human being today is 70 to 80 years. The average life spans of some animals are shown here. Only one of these animals lives longer than human beings.

BUNNIES, KIDS, AND OTHER ANIMAL BABIES

ANIMAL	MALE	FEMALE	YOUNG
bear	boar	sow	cub
pig	boar	sow	piglet
horse	stallion	mare	foal, filly (female), colt (male)
lion	lion	lioness	cub
cattle, elephant, giraffe, whale	bull	cow	calf
deer	buck	doe	fawn
goat	buck, billy goat	doe, nanny goat	kid
rabbit	buck	doe	bunny, kit
duck	drake	duck	duckling
goose	gander	goose	gosling
sheep	ram	ewe	lamb
tiger	tiger	tigress	cub

ENDANGERED SPECIES

A Few Endangered Species

Mammals: *Giant panda* in China; *humpback whale* in all oceans

Fish: *Sockeye (red) salmon* in North Pacific from the United States to Russia

Bird: *Piping Plover* along East Coast and Great Lakes region of the United States

Reptile: *American crocodile* from the southeastern United States to South America

When an animal becomes less and less plentiful on one part of the Earth or in the entire world, the animal is said to be endangered or threatened. The U.S. Department of the Interior keeps track of endangered and threatened animals. Throughout the world today, 1,035 species of animals are endangered or threatened. Among them are:

Mammals: 333 species	**Reptiles:** 115 species
Birds: 273 species	**Clams:** 71 species
Fish: 122 species	**Insects:** 41 species

HOW DO SPECIES BECOME ENDANGERED?

Animals and plants can become endangered for several reasons:

CHANGES IN CLIMATE. Animals are endangered when the climate of their habitat (where they live) changes in a major way. For example, if an area becomes very hot and dry and a river dries up, the fish and other plant and animal life in the river will die.

HABITAT DESTRUCTION. Sometimes animal habitats are destroyed when people need the land. Wetlands, for example, where many types of waterfowl, fish, and insects live, might be drained for new houses or a mall. The animals that lived there would either have to find a new home or else die out.

OVER-HUNTING. Bison or buffalo once ranged over the entire Great Plains of the United States, but they were hunted almost to extinction in the 19th century. Since then, they have been protected by laws, and their numbers are increasing. Sometimes, when an animal population is too large, controlled hunting may reduce the number of animals enough so that the surviving animals can live comfortably with the food available to them.

Do You Want a PET?

Pets can be lots of fun, but they may need a lot of care. This takes time, effort, and money. If you are thinking of getting a pet, these questions will help you choose the best kind for you and your family. Look for information on pets at a library, pet shelter, or veterinarian's office.

QUESTIONS TO ASK BEFORE YOU GET A PET

Why do you want a pet? Do you want an animal to cuddle or keep you company? Do you want to teach a bird to talk? Or watch fish swim?

How much space do you need for the pet you want?

What kind of shelter should it live in?

Does the animal like to be held or left alone?

What kind of food is best for the animal? How often and how much food does it eat? How much does the food cost?

What kind of exercise should the pet get? How often?

What kind of grooming does the animal need?

Is there a veterinarian nearby to meet your pet's health needs? Will this care be expensive?

Are you or is anyone in your family allergic to any animals?

TRAVELING WITH YOUR PET

With careful planning, traveling with your pet can be safe and fun. Think about these tips before you leave home. Share them with the adults going with you.

Ask your veterinarian for advice on how to prepare for your trip. Make sure your pet is up to making the trip.

Make reservations to stay somewhere that allows pets. Let the place know what kind of pet you'll be bringing and ask about any special rules and fees.

Just as you need a seat belt to travel safely in a car, animals should be restrained by an animal seat belt, car seat, or animal carrier.

During long car rides, stop often so your pet can get water and exercise.

If you must leave your pet alone in a car, be quick, keep a window open a crack, and make sure the car does not get too hot or too cold.

What Are Groups of Animals Called?

The next time you describe a group of animals, try using one of the expressions below.

BEARS: *sleuth* of bears	**KANGAROOS:** *mob* or *troop* of kangaroos
BIRDS: *flight* of birds	**KITTENS:** *kindle* or *kendle* of kittens
CATS: *chowder* or *clutter* of cats	**LEOPARDS:** *leap* of leopards
CATTLE: *drove* of cattle	**LIONS:** *pride* of lions
CROWS: *murder* of crows	**RHINOCEROSES:** *crash* of rhinoceroses
ELKS: *gang* of elks	
FOXES: *skulk* of foxes	**TOADS:** *knot* of toads
GEESE: *flock* or *gaggle* of geese	**TURTLES:** *bale* of turtles
HARES: *down* of hares	**WHALES:** *pod* or *gain* of whales
HAWKS: *cast* of hawks	**WOLVES:** *pack* of wolves

Animal Life on Earth

This time line shows how animal life developed on Earth and when land plants developed. The earliest animals are at the top of the chart. The most recent are at the bottom of the chart.

YEARS AGO	ANIMAL LIFE ON EARTH
PRECAMBRIAN 4.5 BILLION	Formation of the Earth. No signs of life.
2.5 BILLION	First evidence of life in the form of bacteria and algae. All life is in water.
570–500 MILLION	Animals with shells (called trilobites) and some mollusks. Some fossils begin to form.
500–430 MILLION	Jawless fish appear, oldest known animals with backbones (vertebrates).
PALEOZOIC 430–395 MILLION	Many coral reefs, jawed fishes, and scorpion-like animals. First land plants.
395–345 MILLION	Many fishes. Earliest known insect. Amphibians (animals living in water and on land) appear.
345–280 MILLION	Large insects appear. Amphibians increase in numbers. First trees appear.
280–225 MILLION	Reptiles and modern insects appear. Trilobites, many corals, and fishes become extinct.
225–195 MILLION	Dinosaurs and turtles appear. Many reptiles and insects develop further. Mammals appear.
MESOZOIC 195–135 MILLION	Many giant dinosaurs. Reptiles increase in number. First birds and crablike animals appear.
135–65 MILLION	Dinosaurs develop further and then become extinct. Flowering plants begin to appear.
CENOZOIC 65–2.5 MILLION	Modern-day land and sea animals begin to develop, including such mammals as rhinoceroses, whales, cats, dogs, apes, seals.
2.5 MILLION– 10,000	Earliest humans appear. Mastodon, mammoths, and other huge animals become extinct.
10,000– PRESENT	Modern human beings and animals.

36

All About...
DINOSAURS

Dinosaurs lived during the Mesozoic era, from 225 to 65 million years ago. The Mesozoic era is divided into the three periods shown below.

TRIASSIC PERIOD, from 225 to 195 million years ago

▶ **First dinosaurs** appeared during the **Triassic period**. Most early dinosaurs were small, rarely longer than 15 feet.

▶ **Early meat-eating dinosaurs** were called **theropods**.

▶ **Earliest-known dinosaurs** were meat-eaters, found in Argentina: **Eoraptor** (the most primitive dinosaur, only about 40 inches long) and **Herrerasaurus**.

▶ **Early plant-eating dinosaurs** were called **prosauropods. Plateosaurus** and **Anchisaurus** were two early plant-eating dinosaurs.

JURASSIC PERIOD, from 195 to 135 million years ago

▶ Dinosaurs that lived during the **Jurassic period** were gigantic.

▶ Jurassic dinosaurs included the **sauropods**, giant long-necked plant-eaters, the **largest land animals** ever. **Apatosaurus** and **Brachiosaurus** (70–80 feet) and **Diplodocus** (over 80 feet) were Sauropods.

▶ **Stegosaurus** (30 feet), a large plant-eater, had sharp, bony plates along its back.

▶ **Allosaurus** and **Megalosaurus**, two giant meat-eaters, fed on large plant-eating dinosaurs like the Apatosaurus and Stegosaurus. Megalosaurus grew to 30 feet in length; Allosaurus, 30-36 feet.

CRETACEOUS PERIOD, from 135 to 65 million years ago

▶ New dinosaurs appeared during the **Cretaceous period**, but by the end of this period, all dinosaurs had died out.

▶ New plant-eaters: **Triceratops** and other horned dinosaurs, **Anatosaurus** and other duckbilled dinosaurs, **Ankylosaurus** and other armored dinosaurs.

▶ New meat-eater: **Tyrannosaurus Rex**, one of the largest and fiercest meat-eaters, growing to 20 feet high and 40 feet long.

DiD You KNOW?

Using computer software designed to copy dinosaur movements, scientists have changed their ideas about how long-necked dinosaurs ate. Scientists used to think these huge animals munched on treetops as giraffes do. New evidence, however, suggests their necks were too stiff to reach up high, so the dinosaurs probably grazed on low shrubs, ferns, and water plants.

DEADLY DINOS DISCOVERED

One hundred million years ago there lived meat-eating dinosaurs that were probably more terrifying than any that came before or after. That's what scientists believe, based on bones they dug up in Argentina in 2000. The scientists say the newly discovered dinosaurs were probably about 45 feet in length with long, sharp snouts, long skulls, and razor-sharp teeth. And they apparently traveled in packs, unlike most other dinosaurs.

WHICH U.S. ZOOS HAVE THE LARGEST NUMBERS OF SPECIES?

Houston Zoological Gardens
Hermann Park
1513 North MacGregor
Houston, Texas 77030
Phone: (713) 523-5888
Number of Species: 800
Popular Exhibits: Wortham World of Primates, Mexican wolves, cheetahs

San Diego Zoo
2920 Zoo Drive
San Diego, California 92101
Phone: (619) 234-3153
Number of Species: 800
Popular Exhibits: Tiger River, Komodo dragons, koalas, Hippo Beach

Denver Zoo
City Park
Denver, Colorado 80205
Phone: (303) 376-4800
Number of Species: 715
Popular Exhibits: Tropical Discovery, Northern Shores, Primate Panorama

St. Louis Zoological Park
Forest Park
St. Louis, Missouri 63110
Phone: (314) 781-0900
Number of Species: 705
Popular Exhibits: Living World, Bear Pits, Jungle of the Apes

Cincinnati Zoo
3400 Vine Street
Cincinnati, Ohio 45220
Phone: (800) 94-HIPPO
Number of Species: 700+
Popular Exhibits: Gorilla World, white Bengal tigers, Jungle Trails

Columbus Zoo
9990 Riverside Drive
Powell, Ohio 43065-0400
Phone: (800) MONKEYS
Number of Species: 700
Popular Exhibits: Discovery Reef, Ohio Wetlands, Tidepool Touch Tank

Toledo Zoological Gardens
2700 Broadway
Toledo, OH 43609
Phone: (419) 385-5721
Number of Species: 659
Popular Exhibits: Hippoquarium, Primate Forest, aviary

Omaha's Henry Doorly Zoo
3701 South 10th Street
Omaha, Nebraska 68107
Phone: (402) 733-8401
Number of Species: 640
Popular Exhibits: Indoor rain forest, aquarium, cat complex

Cleveland Metroparks Zoo
3900 Brookside Drive
Cleveland, Ohio 44109
Phone: (216) 661-6500
Number of Species: 617
Popular Exhibits: Rain Forest with 600 animals and 7,000 plants

Bronx Zoo/Wildlife Conservation Park
Fordham Road and Bronx River Pkwy.
Bronx, New York 10460
Phone: (718) 367-1010
Number of Species: 600+
Popular Exhibits: Himalayan Highlands, Jungle World, endangered species

ANiMALS iN THE WORLD
WORD SEARCH

The words in the box below are hidden in this puzzle. The words go across, up, down, backward, and diagonally. Many letters are used in more than one word.

S	D	N	A	L	S	S	A	R	G
P	E	T	U	R	T	L	E	E	B
E	N	D	A	N	G	E	R	E	D
C	T	O	R	R	A	P	A	L	R
I	S	G	O	R	F	A	M	I	A
E	R	U	A	S	O	N	I	D	G
S	R	A	E	B	E	D	N	O	O
W	O	R	C	U	B	A	O	C	N
I	N	S	E	C	T	Z	I	O	F
X	O	D	I	K	R	A	L	R	L
E	K	O	Y	N	O	L	O	C	Y

WORD BOX

BEARS	DINOSAUR	KID	SEA
BEE	DOG	LARK	SPECIES
BUCK	DRAGONFLY	LION	TURTLE
COLONY	ENDANGERED	PANDA	YOKE
CROCODILE	FROGS	PARROT	ZOO
CROW	GRASSLANDS	PET	
CUB	INSECT	RAM	

MATCHING ANiMALS

Match each clue at left with the animal on the right that it describes. You can find all the descriptions in this chapter.

1. another name for mountain lion   a. frog
2. lives in a pod   b. crocodile
3. amphibian   c. camel
4. fastest insect   d. box turtle
5. one tooth sticks out   e. giraffe
6. female sheep   f. dragonfly
7. lives in the desert   g. gorilla
8. lives up to 100 years   h. cougar
9. tallest animal   i. ewe
10. has a noseprint   j. whale

Answers are on pages 317–320.

39

Art

What do soup cans and the head of a woman have in common?
You can find the answer on page 41.

THROUGH ARTISTS' EYES

Art may be realistic or unlike anything you usually see. It may be funny or sad, beautiful or disturbing. Here are some examples of different kinds of art, along with the names of some of their creators, the nationality of each artist, and the name of one of his or her works.

Look around. You'll notice art in many places, not only hanging on walls in museums. What kind of art have you seen today?

Looking at Places

A drawing or painting of nature is called a **landscape.** A picture of the sea is called a **seascape.** A picture of city buildings is called a **cityscape.**

Salomon van Ruysdael (about 1600–1670), Dutch: "River with Ferry-Boat"

J.M.W. Turner (1775–1851), British: "River Scene"

Claude Monet (1840–1926), French: "Haystacks"

▲ *A landscape*

Winslow Homer (1836–1910), American: "High Cliff, Coast of Maine, 1894"

Georgia O'Keeffe (1887–1986), American: "City Night"

Yoshitoshi Mori (1898–1992), Japanese: "Lantern Maker"

Portraying People

▲ *A portrait*

A **portrait** is a painting of one or more people. A **self-portrait** is a picture of the artist painted by that artist. Here are some painters and information about them.

Leonardo da Vinci (1452–1519), Italian: "Mona Lisa"

Rembrandt (1606–1669), Dutch: "A Scholar"

Thomas Gainsborough (1727–1788), British: "The Blue Boy"

John Singer Sargent (1856–1925), American: "The Wyndham Sisters"

Käthe Kollwitz (1867–1945), German: "Outbreak"

Norman Rockwell (1894–1978), American: "The Four Freedoms"

William H. Johnson (1901–1970), American: "Jitterbugs (I)"

SEEING THINGS

A picture of small objects—flowers, bottles, or fruit, for example—is a **still-life**. Some artists also have done paintings of rooms, called **interior paintings**.

Jan Jansz van den Uyl (about 1595–1640), Dutch: "Breakfast Still-Life"

Cornelis de Heem (1631–1695), Dutch: "Still-Life of Flowers in a Glass Vase"

Jean Simeon Chardin (1699–1779), French: "The Grace"

Henri Matisse (1869–1954), French: "Large Red Interior"

▲ *A still-life*

OTHER POINTS OF VIEW

Some artists, like those below, create pictures using shapes, colors, or textures in ways that do not look like anything in the real world. These abstract and pop artists created modern art.

Piet Mondrian (1872–1944), Dutch: "Composition with Red, Yellow and Blue"

Pablo Picasso (1881–1973), Spanish: "Head of a Woman"

Joan Miró (1893–1983), Spanish: "Dutch Interior"

Jackson Pollock (1912–1956), American: "Autumn Rhythm"

Andy Warhol (1928–1987), American: "Campbell's Soup Cans"

Helen Frankenthaler (born 1928), American: "Blue Causeway"

◀ *An abstract painting*

MORE THAN SNAPSHOTS

Photography, too, is a form of art. News photos inform us about current events. Other photos record both the familiar and the exotic. The works of the photographers listed here help prove that a picture can truly be worth a thousand words.

Matthew Brady (about 1823–1896), American: official photographer of the Civil War

Alfred Stieglitz (1864–1946), American: helped create acceptance of photography as art

Ansel Adams (1902–1984), American: photos of the Southwest

Margaret Bourke-White (1906–1971), American: photojournalist

Austin Hansen (1910–1996), American: photos of New York's Harlem and other city life

Gordon Parks (born 1912), American: photojournalist

Making ORIGAMI

THE ART OF ORIGAMI

Origami is the art of folding paper into different shapes. The name comes from the Japanese words for *ori,* which means "to fold" and *gami,* which means "paper."

Origami is not just a Japanese art, though many great origami artists are Japanese. The Chinese, inventors of paper, used beautiful folded paper shapes to decorate temples and shrines. Many origami shapes are of animals, especially the crane. It is said that folding 1,000 cranes ensures that you will have a long and prosperous life.

With practice, you can create a roomful of lovely origami creations. All you need is patience and squares of thin paper. Some stores sell special origami paper that is colored on one side and plain on the other, but it's not necessary to have it.

LEARNING MORE ABOUT ORIGAMI

You don't have to know special words to do origami, though it helps to know what the arrows and lines on diagrams stand for. Each of the books listed here gives complete instructions. The projects they include range from easy to complicated.

Visit your local library to look at some of the many books on origami. You can usually find them in the 700 section under 736.98.

Paperback Books

▶ *Easy Origami,* by Dokuohtei Nakano (Puffin Books)

▶ *Easy Origami,* by John Montrall (Dover Publications)

▶ *Folding Paper Toys,* by Shari Lewis and Lillian Oppenheimer (Stein and Day)

▶ *The Magic of Origami,* by Alice Gray and Kunihiko Kasahara with cooperation of Lillian Oppenheimer and Origami Center of America (Japan Publications)

▶ *Origami in Action/Paper Toys that Fly, Flap, Gobble, and Inflate,* by Robert J. Lang (St. Martin's Griffin)

▶ *Origami Made Easy,* by Kunihiko Kasahara (Japan Publications)

▶ *Origami, Plain and Simple,* by Thomas Hull with models by Robert Neale (St. Martin's Griffin)

▶ *Origami Treasure Chest,* by Keiji Kitamura (Japan Publications Trading Company)

▶ *Paper Pandas and Jumping Frogs,* by Florence Temko (China Books)

▶ *The World of Origami,* by Isao Honda (Japan Publications Trading Company)

For more information about origami, send a self-stamped (two first-class stamps), self-addressed business-size envelope to Origami USA, 15 West 77th Street, New York, NY 10024-5192.

AN ORIGAMI BOX

For a project, try making this box. You can use a sheet of 8½" x 11" paper. Before you begin folding, color a design on one side of the paper. Put that side face down.

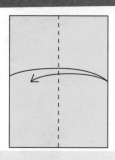

1 Fold the paper sharply in half in the long direction, and unfold.

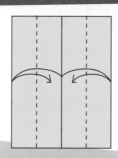

2 Now fold the sides to the center and unfold.

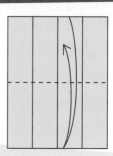

3 Then fold in half in the other direction and unfold.

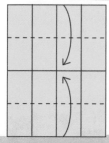

4 Now fold the top and bottom sides to the center, but this time leave them folded!

5 Can you see the crease lines from before? Fold the upper right corner alongside the nearest crease. (Look at the next picture to see how this should turn out.)

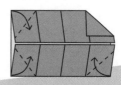

6 There should be a "gap" at the bottom of the triangle flap you just folded. Do the same thing to the other three corners.

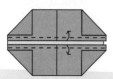

7 Now fold the long "lips" up and down to cover the triangle flaps you just folded.

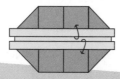

8 Finally, pull the two "lips" apart to open the box!

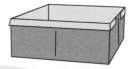

9 And here's the completed box!

Try making a slightly bigger box to be the lid. Or tape or staple a strip of paper to be a handle, and your box will become a basket!

43

Sculpture is a three-dimensional form made from clay, stone, metal, or other material. Many sculptures stand freely so that you can walk around them. Some are mobiles that hang from the ceiling. Sculptures can be large, like the Statue of Liberty, or small. Some sculpture is representational (looks like the person or animal it represents). Some modern sculpture is abstract and has no form that can be recognized.

A sculpture ▶

THE ART OF SCULPTURE

Below is a list of a few sculptors, when they lived, their nationality, and the name of one of their sculptures.

Michelangelo (1475–1564), Italian: "Pietà"
Augustus Saint-Gaudens (1848–1907), American: "Farragut"
Frederic Remington (1861–1909), American: "Bronco Buster"
Constantin Brancusi (1876–1957), Romanian-French: "Flying Turtle"
Alexander Calder (1898–1976), American: "Circus" mobiles
Louise Nevelson (1900–1986), American: "Black Chord"
Isamu Noguchi (1904–1988), American: "Kouros"

Where to Look at Art

There are art museums in many cities in the United States. Some of them are general art museums, where you can see art from many different countries and time periods—sometimes from early Egyptian art to modern art. Many cities also have museums of American art, museums of modern art, and other special collections. For museums that focus on ethnic art, culture, and history, such as African or Asian culture, see the section called Ethnic Museums, on page 126. A few general art museums are listed below.

Art Institute of Chicago	Denver Art Museum	Los Angeles County Museum of Art	North Carolina Museum of Art (Raleigh, NC)
Baltimore Museum of Art	Detroit Institute of Arts	Metropolitan Museum of Art (New York)	Philadelphia Museum of Art
Boston Museum of Fine Arts	Getty Center (Los Angeles, CA)	Minneapolis Institute of Arts	San Antonio Museum of Art
Cleveland Museum of Art	Houston Museum of Fine Arts	National Gallery of Art (Washington, D.C.)	San Francisco Museum of Art
Dallas Museum of Art	Kansas City (MO) Art Institute		Seattle Art Museum

Books

? What popular series of books about a wizard-in-training may soon be made into a movie?
You can find the answer on page 46.

Book AWARDS, 1999-2000

Are you in the mood for unforgettable characters? For exciting stories? For an experience that will make you think about life in a fresh way? Then read one of the following award-winning books.

Boston Globe-Horn Book Award

These are given every year.

1999 winners:
  Fiction: *Holes*, by Louis Sachar

  Nonfiction: *The Top of the World: Climbing Mount Everest*, by Steve Jenkins

  Picture Book: *Red-Eyed Tree Frog*, by Joy Cowley, illustrated by Nic Bishop

Caldecott Medal

This is the highest honor a picture book can receive.

2000 winner: *Joseph Had a Little Overcoat,* by Simms Taback

Newbery Medal

This is an award for writing. It is the highest honor for a children's book that is not a picture book.

2000 winner: *Bud, Not Buddy*, by Christopher Paul Curtis

Coretta Scott King Award

These are given to artists and authors whose works promote the cause of peace and world brotherhood.

2000 winners:
  Author Award: *Bud, Not Buddy,* by Christopher Paul Curtis

  Illustrator Award: *In the Time of the Drums,* illustrated by Brian Pinkney

Poetry Award

The Claudia Lewis Award is given every year by the Bank Street College of Education in New York for the best poetry book of the year for young readers.

1999 winner: *Stop Pretending: What Happened When My Big Sister Went Crazy,* by Sonya Jones

Hans Christian Andersen Awards

2000 winners:
  Author: Ana Maria Machado (Brazil)

  Illustrator: Anthony Browne (Great Britain)

▼ *The Newbery winner*

BEST NEW BOOKS of the Year
(Among those chosen in 2000 by the American Library Association)

▶*The Birchbark House,* by Louise Erdrich — The first of a series of books about Little Frog, an Ojibwa Indian girl who lives on an island in Lake Superior with her adopted family in the mid-1800s.

▶*The Firework-Maker's Daughter,* by Philip Pullman — Lila travels to Mount Merapi with her friend and his talking white elephant. She wants to find the royal sulphur she needs to become a great fireworks artist like her father.

▶*The Good Liar,* by Gregory Maguire — Three brothers in Nazi-occupied France during World War II fish, play pranks, and see who can make up the best lies. They are shocked when their mother wins the contest.

▶*Gypsy Rizka,* by Lloyd Alexander — A funny tale about a gypsy girl who uses magic and cleverness to outwit the dishonest leaders of the village.

▶*Skellig,* by David Almond — Michael finds Skellig, a mysterious creature covered with dead flies and spiderwebs, in a garage. As he and his friend Mina take care of Skellig, his dying baby sister recovers her health.

▶*They Saw the Future: Oracles, Psychics, Scientists, Great Thinkers and Pretty Good Guessers,* by Kathleen Krull — A beautifully illustrated book about twelve people who made accurate (and some not-so-accurate) predictions, including Black Elk, Nostradamus, and Jeane Dixon.

▶*Through My Eyes,* by Ruby Bridges and Margo Lundell — In 1960, when she was six, Ruby became the first African-American student ever at a school in New Orleans. Here she relates her powerful story.

▶*When the Beginning Began: Stories About God, the Creatures, and Us,* by Julius Lester — A colorfully illustrated collection of Jewish Bible stories, lovingly interpreted by an African-American storyteller.

▶*When Zachary Beaver Came to Town,* by Kimberly Willis Holt — At first Toby gawks at 600-pound Zachary Beaver, but he later realizes Zachary is more than just the fattest boy in the world.

▶*William Shakespeare & the Globe,* by Aliki — Using Shakespeare's writings and official documents, Aliki pieces together a lively account of his life, in the form of a five-act play, with illustrations.

THE MAGIC OF HARRY POTTER

He started out lonely and miserable, sleeping in a cupboard under the stairs of his mean aunt and uncle's house. But now Harry Potter is one of the most popular boys in the world—the world of magic, that is. Millions of people have read the first three books of the Harry Potter series by Scottish author J. K. Rowling: *Harry Potter and the Sorcerer's Stone, The Chamber of Secrets,* and *The Prisoner of Azkaban.*

Stories about owls that deliver mail, boa constrictors that wink, sports played on flying broomsticks, and jellybeans that taste like everything from strawberries to sardines have captivated the imaginations of girls and boys alike. A fourth book is scheduled to come out in the summer of 2000. There may soon be a Harry Potter movie and—surprise, surprise—stores sell lots of Harry Potter toys. Ms. Rowling plans to write seven Harry Potter books in all, one about each of Harry's years at Hogwart's School of Witchcraft and Wizardry, and each story a little scarier than the one before.

FOR YOUR BOOKSHELF

The books on this page and the next one have been praised by many people.

For more on children's books, go to **WEB SITE** *http://www.ala.org/ booklist/v96/002.html*

FICTION Fiction books are stories that come out of the writer's imagination. They are not true. Some fiction books are set in a world of fantasy. Others seem incredibly real.

On this list are new books and favorites from the past. If you read and like them, recommend the books to your friends. If you want to remember which ones you've read and what you thought of them, write your comments in a small notebook.

Bud, Not Buddy, **by Christopher Paul Curtis** Set in Michigan during the Great Depression, this is the story of spunky Bud Caldwell, who runs away from his nasty foster family in search of a famous jazz musician he believes is his father.

The Circuit: Stories From the Life of a Migrant Child, **by Francisco Jimenez** Twelve short stories about a migrant family that moves from one field to another, picking strawberries, cotton, or whatever is in season, doing backbreaking work for paltry pay, but never giving up hope for a better life.

Holes, **by Louis Sachar** An unusual and funny story about a boy who escapes from a juvenile detention center run by a warden who polishes her fingernails with rattlesnake venom.

Island of the Blue Dolphins, **by Scott O'Dell** After her younger brother dies, Karana manages to live alone on an evacuated island off the coast of California. A modern classic based on a true story.

Preacher's Boy, **by Katherine Paterson** The year is 1899. When the preacher's son Robbie hears another preacher predicting that 1900 will bring the end of the world, he decides to have as much fun as possible just in case it's true.

The Trolls, **by Polly Horvath** While their parents are in Paris, Aunt Sally comes to stay with Melissa, Amanda, and Frank and tells them stories about their father's childhood that he would rather forget.

Weslandia, **by Paul Fleischman** Taunted by his classmates for being different, Wesley creates a fascinating backyard civilization that even his former enemies can't resist.

When the Soldiers Were Gone, **by Vera W. Propp** In 1945, when World War II ends, eight-year-old Henk's real parents come to take him back, away from the family that protected him from the Nazis, the family he has come to love as his own.

Where the Red Fern Grows, **by Wilson Rawls** An all-time best-selling book about the adventures of a boy and his beloved hunting dogs.

A Wrinkle in Time, **by Madeleine L'Engle** Meg Murry travels through space with her brother and friend to find her father, a scientist who disappeared while working on a secret government project.

POETRY Poems use language in new and imaginative ways, sometimes in rhyme.

Daddy Poems, selected by John Micklos, Jr. Poets tell about fatherhood.

Laugh-eteria: Poems and Drawings, by Douglas Florian Silly rhymes and wordplays by the author of the popular *Bing Bang Boing.*

The Oxford Illustrated Book of American Children's Poems, edited by Donald Hall Some of the best poetry from the last two hundred years, including poems by Shel Silverstein, Jack Prelutsky, Nikki Giovanni, Robert Frost, and Langston Hughes.

My Man Blue, by Nikki Grimes Fourteen poems about the special friendship between an African-American boy whose father recently died and the man who treats him like his own son.

NONFICTION These books prove facts can be fascinating.

Angels of Mercy: The Army Nurses of World War II, by Betsy Kuhn Stories about the more than 59,000 women who risked their lives to care for the sick and wounded.

Black Hands, White Sails: The Story of African-American Whalers, by Pat McKissack, Fredrick L. McKissack, and Patricia C. McKissack In the 19th century, working on a whaling ship was brutally hard and dangerous, but many freed and runaway slaves seized the job as a chance to get ahead.

Honest Pretzels: And 64 Other Amazing Recipes for Cooks Ages Eight and Up, by Mollie Katzen Learn how to make yummy desserts and mouth-watering, meatless main dishes with this easy-to-follow, illustrated cookbook.

Kids on Strike!, by Susan Campbell Bartoletti Photographs from the late 1800s and early 1900s help tell the story of children who worked in factories and sweatshops and bravely fought for better conditions.

The Tiniest Giants: Discovering Dinosaur Eggs, by Lowell Dingus, Luis M. Chiappe, and Dingus Chiappe The fossil experts who found a huge dinosaur nesting ground in Argentina describe their work.

The Top of the World: Climbing Mount Everest, by Steve Jenkins Papercut collages and vivid descriptions help you imagine what it would be like.

What You Never Knew About Fingers, Forks, and Chopsticks, by Patricia Lauber A fun, fascinating, and sometimes disgusting history of table manners and eating utensils.

REFERENCE Many reference materials are stored on CD-ROMs and are also available on the Internet.

Almanac: A one-volume book of facts and statistics.

Atlas: A collection of maps.

Dictionary: A book of words in alphabetical order. It gives meanings and spellings of and shows how words are pronounced.

Encyclopedia: A place to go for information on almost any subject.

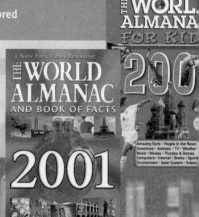

HOW WE MAKE THIS BOOK

Here's the inside scoop. Every year, we put together a new edition of *The World Almanac for Kids*, with tons of new facts, all-fresh puzzles, and colorful pictures of the year's people and events.

WHAT WE NEED

► **IDEAS AND DATA** Ideas come to us from readers' letters and e-mails, from our Kid Contributors, and from newspapers and magazines. We get new information from the government, different organizations, books, and the World Wide Web.

► **HARDWORKING PEOPLE**
- **Writers and contributors** put together new features and update old ones, using the latest information. The words they produce are called *copy*.
- **Editors** plan what the writers should do and look over the copy when it is done.
- **Consultants** help decide whether the information is correct and also interesting and important for kids.
- **Artists** do drawings to go in the book.
- **Designers** plan how each page will look. They put the copy and art in place, using a program called Quark XPress.
- **Indexers** create the index in the back to make stuff easy to find.

► **MACHINES AND MATERIALS** Machines at a printing plant print and bind the hundreds of thousands of books. Each book uses 1½ pounds of paper.

STEPS

1 Plan contents of book. The main editor and other editors help plan the book. What's hot? Which people, places, and events stood out in the past year? We have a limited number of pages, so it's important to include the information that will most interest readers and help them with their schoolwork.

2 Assign writing jobs and give deadlines. The main editor assigns work to writers who are experts on the subjects they're writing about. They are given deadlines that must be met. It takes about six months each year to create a new edition of *The World Almanac for Kids*.

3 Edit copy. Will kids find the copy clear and interesting? Are the facts correct? Are the spelling, punctuation, and grammar OK? These are the first questions the editors must answer.

4 Select illustrations and design pages. Editors and designers work together to select illustrations and photographs. The designers place the copy and art on each page.

5 Check the proofs and make changes. After pages are designed they are printed out on proofs. Editors look over the proofs and mark changes to be made. Some copy may be too long or short to fit, so editors may need to cut or add material. When the pages are ready, they go back to the designers.

6 Send the book to the printer. It's time to put together the whole book. There's one last chance to check for slip-ups. Are the *folios* (page numbers) correct? Is everything here that should be? Is the color right? When everything looks OK, a disk is sent to the printer, with electronic files that contain all the pages and art.

7 Print and bind the book, and distribute it to bookstores. This is the payoff time. In 1999 *The World Almanac for Kids* made the bestsellers list. We expect this to happen again. After the book is printed and bound, it is sent to bookstores all over the United States, mostly by truck.

If you were working on *The World Almanac for Kids*, what job would you like the most? Do you like to write? Are you an artist? Do you enjoy working with numbers? Do you have a good imagination? Do you like to work with other people?

Buildings, Bridges & Tunnels

? What is the longest suspension bridge in the U.S.?
You can find the answer on page 51.

TALLEST BUILDINGS IN THE WORLD

Here are the world's tallest buildings, with the year each was completed:

Petronas Towers 1 & 2 ▼

- ► **Petronas Towers 1 & 2**, Kuala Lumpur, Malaysia (1998) **Height:** each building 88 stories, 1,483 feet
- ► **Sears Tower**, Chicago, Illinois (1974) **Height:** 110 stories, 1,450 feet
- ► **Jin Mao Building**, Shanghai, China (1998) **Height:** 88 stories, 1,381 feet
- ► **World Trade Center 1** (1972) & 2 (1973), New York, New York **Height:** each building 110 stories; Building 1, 1,362 feet; Building 2, 1,368 feet
- ► **CITIC Plaza**, Guangzhou, China (1996) **Height:** 80 stories, 1,283 feet
- ► **Shun Hing Square**, Shenzhen, China (1996) **Height:** 81 stories, 1,260 feet
- ► **Empire State Building**, New York, New York (1931) **Height:** 102 stories, 1,250 feet
- ► **Central Plaza**, Hong Kong, China (1992) **Height:** 78 stories, 1,227 feet
- ► **Bank of China**, Hong Kong, China (1989) **Height:** 70 stories, 1,209 feet
- ► **Emirates Towers One**, Dubai, United Arab Emirates (2000) **Height:** 55 stories, 1,161 feet

LONGEST TUNNELS IN THE WORLD

A tunnel is a long underground passageway, dug through rock or earth or built underwater. Vehicular tunnels (on land and under water) are for automobiles, trucks, and the like. Railroad tunnels are for trains and subway traffic. Water tunnels are for water mains, drainage, sewage, mining, and storage. Here are the longest tunnels of each type:

TYPE OF TUNNEL	NAME	LOCATION	LENGTH
Land	St. Gotthard	Switzerland	10.1 miles
Underwater	Queensway Road	England	2.1 miles
Railroad	Seikan	Japan	33.5 miles
Water	Colorado River Aqueduct	California, U.S.	92.1 miles

The SEVEN WONDERS of the Ancient World

PYRAMIDS OF EGYPT At Giza, Egypt, built as royal tombs from 2700 to 2500 B.C. The largest is the Great Pyramid of Khufu (or Cheops).

HANGING GARDENS OF BABYLON Terraced gardens in Babylon (now Iraq) built by King Nebuchadnezzar II around 600 B.C. for his wife.

TEMPLE OF ARTEMIS At Ephesus (now part of Turkey), built mostly of marble around 550 B.C. in honor of a Greek goddess, Artemis.

COLOSSUS OF RHODES In the harbor on the island of Rhodes (Greece). A bronze statue of the sun god Helios, built during the 200s B.C.

STATUE OF ZEUS At Olympia, Greece. The statue, made about 457 B.C. by the sculptor Phidias from ivory and gold, showed the king of the gods.

MAUSOLEUM OF HALICARNASSUS (Now part of Turkey), built about 353 B.C. in honor of King Mausolus, a ruler of ancient Caria.

LIGHTHOUSE OF ALEXANDRIA, EGYPT Built about 270 B.C. during the reign of Ptolemy II. It was probably 200 to 600 feet tall.

LONGEST BRIDGES IN THE WORLD

← — *Main Span* — →

The **span** of a bridge is the distance between its supports. The bridges below, as measured by main spans, are the world's longest suspension bridges (those that hang from cables). The longest suspension bridge in the U.S. is the Verrazano-Narrows Bridge in New York (4,260 feet).

NAME OF BRIDGE	LOCATION	MAIN SPAN
Akashi Kaikyo	Japan	6,570 feet
Storebaelt	Denmark	5,328 feet
Humber	England	4,626 feet

Calendars & Time

If it is 11 A.M. in Memphis, Tennessee, what time is it in Honolulu, Hawaii?
You can find the answer on page 53.

CALENDARS

Calendars divide time into days, weeks, months, and years. Calendar divisions are based on movements of Earth and on the sun and the moon. A day is the average time it takes for one rotation of Earth on its axis. A year is the average time it takes for one revolution of Earth around the sun. Early calendars were based on the movements of the moon across the sky. The ancient Egyptians were probably the first to develop a calendar based on the movements of Earth around the sun.

ROMAN CALENDARS

THE JULIAN AND GREGORIAN CALENDARS

The ancient Romans had a calendar with a year of 304 days. In 46 B.C., the emperor Julius Caesar decided to use a calendar based on movements of the sun. This calendar, called the **Julian calendar**, fixed the normal year at 365 days and added one day every fourth year (leap year). It also established the months of the year and the days of the week.

In A.D. 1582, the Julian calendar was revised by Pope Gregory XIII, because it was 11 minutes and 14 seconds too long. This added up to three too many days every 400 years. To fix it, he made years ending in 00 leap years only if they can be divided by 400. Thus, 2000 is a leap year, but 1900 is not. The new calendar, called the **Gregorian calendar**, is the one used today in most of the world.

OTHER CALENDARS

JEWISH AND ISLAMIC CALENDARS

Other calendars are also used. The Jewish calendar, which began almost 6,000 years ago, is the official calendar of the State of Israel. The year 2001 is equivalent to the year 5761–5762 on the Jewish calendar, which starts at Rosh Hashanah. The Islamic calendar starts counting years in A.D. 622. The year 2001 is equivalent to 1421–1422 on the Islamic calendar, which begins with the month of Muharram.

BIRTHSTONES

MONTH	BIRTHSTONE
January	Garnet
February	Amethyst
March	Aquamarine
April	Diamond
May	Emerald
June	Pearl
July	Ruby
August	Peridot
September	Sapphire
October	Opal
November	Topaz
December	Turquoise

DID YOU KNOW?

Stonehenge, the ancient stone monument in Salisbury, England, is between 3,000 and 5,000 years old. Most scientists think it was used to predict the positions of the sun and moon—a kind of huge calendar.

What Are TIME ZONES?

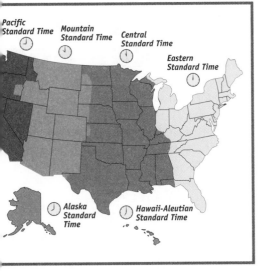

Pacific Standard Time

Mountain Standard Time

Central Standard Time

Eastern Standard Time

Alaska Standard Time

Hawaii-Aleutian Standard Time

A day is 24 hours long—the time it takes Earth to complete one rotation on its axis. The system we use to tell time is called standard time. In standard time, Earth is divided into 24 time zones. Each zone is 15 degrees of longitude wide and runs from the North to the South Pole.

Daylight Savings Time (DST) begins on the first Sunday in April and ends on the last Sunday in October. During DST, clocks are advanced one hour so that people can benefit from daylight in the evening rather than in the early morning. All states observe DST except Arizona, Hawaii, and parts of Indiana. Western parts of Indiana observe DST, while most of the eastern part only has Standard Time.

WHEN IT IS 12 NOON IN WASHINGTON, D.C., IT IS

12 noon Columbus, Ohio	11 A.M. Chicago, Illinois	11 A.M. Memphis, Tennessee	10 A.M. Santa Fe, New Mexico	9 A.M. Seattle, Washington	8 A.M. Anchorage, Alaska	7 A.M. Honolulu, Hawaii

TIME WILL TELL

Latitude and longitude combined tell ships exactly where they are on Earth (see page 77). Many centuries ago it was fairly easy to pinpoint a ship's latitude by observing the sun and stars. But it was almost impossible to find the exact longitude. For that, sailors needed to know the time difference between their home port and their position at sea. But clocks of that period could not keep accurate time on ships. For example, a rolling sea could make the pendulum in a clock slow down or speed up, so it showed the wrong time. Or changes in temperature could make the oil in a clock thinner or thicker and cause the metal parts to expand or contract. The mistakes that resulted killed thousands of sailors in shipwrecks.

Then in 1735, an English clockmaker named John Harrison invented the first chronometer. It was a highly accurate clock that could withstand the rigors of seafaring. Once it caught on, the chronometer made finding longitude a routine chore and saved many sailors' lives.

If you'd like to read more about John Harrison and his chronometer, try reading *Longitude: The True Story of a Lone Genius Who Solved the Greatest Scientific Problem of His Time,* by Dava Sobel.

Computers & the Internet

? In computer talk, what's the difference between a bit and a byte? *You can find the answer on page 55.*

WHAT DO COMPUTERS DO?

At first, computers were used to add, subtract, multiply, and divide big numbers. Today they can do much more. For example, a pizza shop owner might use a computer to keep track of the number and type of pizzas sold each day. This information, organized and stored in a database, helps the owner order new supplies more efficiently. A student can use a computer to send e-mail, get information from the Internet (see page 59), play games, or do homework.

COMPUTERS HELP PEOPLE CREATE.

► People use computers to create artwork and music or to design buildings.

► Computers are used to create special effects for movies and television.

COMPUTERS HELP PEOPLE COMMUNICATE.

► Computers can be used to write letters or stories or reports for school.

► Computers help create newspapers, magazines, and books.

► People use computers to send electronic mail (e-mail), sometimes across the continent or to other countries.

► People who cannot speak can type in messages that the computer translates into speech. People who cannot type can speak into a computer that translates their speech into text.

COMPUTERS HELP PEOPLE LEARN.

► Programs on computers help teach school subjects.

► Computer programs can keep track of students' progress.

► Pilots and astronauts use computer flight simulators.

COMPUTERS KEEP INFORMATION ORGANIZED.

► Many companies and organizations keep a database with information. The FBI has a database that police departments can use to find information about criminals or stolen goods from all around the United States.

COMPUTERS ARE USED TO MANUFACTURE PRODUCTS.

► Engineers use special software to create detailed drawings of an object and then test it to see how to make it stronger or cheaper.

► Computers can control machinery used to make the new product.

COMPUTERS HELP PREDICT THE FUTURE.

► Companies use computer programs to help them make decisions.

► Computer programs use data from satellites to help forecast weather.

COMPUTERS AREN'T JUST FOUND ON DESKS.

► Computers are used in automatic teller machines at the bank and with the price scanner at the supermarket checkout.

► Cars, VCRs, video games, calculators, and digital watches all have built-in computers.

COMPUTER TALK

artificial intelligence or AI
The ability of computers and robots to imitate human intelligence by learning and making decisions.

bit The smallest unit of data.

boot To turn on a computer.

browser A program to help get around the Internet.

bug or glitch An error in a program or in the computer.

byte An amount of data equal to 8 bits.

database A large collection of information organized so that it can be retrieved and used in different ways.

desktop publishing The use of computers for combining text and pictures to design and produce magazines, newspapers, and books.

download To transfer information from a host computer to a personal computer, often through a modem.

e-mail or electronic mail
Messages sent from one computer to another over a network.

gig or gigabyte (GB) An amount of information equal to 1,000 (or 1,024) megabytes.

hard copy Computer output printed on paper or similar material.

Internet A worldwide system of linked computer networks.

K This stands for *kilo*, or "thousands," in Greek. It is used to represent bytes of data or memory.

laptop or notebook A portable personal computer that can run on batteries.

megabyte (MB) An amount of information equal to 1 million (or 1,048,516) bytes.

multimedia Software that includes pictures, video, and sound. In multimedia software, you can see pictures move and hear music and other sounds.

network A group of computers linked together so that they can share information.

password A secret code that keeps people who do not know it from using a computer or software.

program Instructions for a computer to follow.

RAM or random access memory
The memory your computer uses to open programs and store your work until you save it to the hard drive or a disk. The information in RAM disappears when the computer is turned off.

ROM or read only memory
ROM contains permanent instructions for the computer and cannot be changed. The information in ROM remains after the computer is turned off.

scanner A device that can transfer words and pictures from a printed page into the computer.

upload To send information from a personal computer to a host computer.

virtual reality Three-dimensional images on a screen that are viewed using special equipment (like gloves and goggles). The user feels as if he or she is part of the image and can interact with everything around.

virus A program that damages other programs and data. It gets into a computer through telephone lines or shared disks.

Web site A place on the Internet's World Wide Web where text and pictures are stored. The contents are sent to computers when the correct World Wide Web address (which begins with http:// or www.) is entered.

HOW COMPUTERS

SOFTWARE

► Kinds of Software
To write a story (or letter or school report) you use a type of software called a word-processing program. This program can be selected by using the **keyboard** or a **mouse**.

Other common types of software include programs for doing mathematics, keeping records, playing games, and creating pictures.

► Entering Data
In a word processing program, you can input your words by typing on the **keyboard**. The backspace and delete keys are like electronic erasers. You can also press special keys (called **function keys**) or click on certain symbols (**icons**), to center or underline words, move words and sentences around, check your spelling, print out a page, and do other tasks. When you input a command, the word-processing program tells the computer what to do.

HARDWARE

► Inside the Computer
The instructions from the program you use are carried out inside the computer by the **central processing unit**, or **CPU**. The CPU is the computer's brain.

► Getting the Results
The **monitor** and **printer** are the most commonly used output devices in a computer system. When you type a story, the words appear on a **monitor**, which is similar to a television screen. Your story can then be printed on paper by using a **printer**.

If you print out a story, you can mail it to a friend. But if you and your friend both have **modems**, the story can be sent from your computer directly to your friend's computer. A **modem** allows information from a computer to travel over telephone lines.

Computers perform tasks by using programs called **software**. These programs tell the computer what to do when the user enters certain information or commands. This is called **input**.

The computer then processes the information and gives the user the results (**output**). The computer can also save, or **store**, the information so that it can be used again and again.

The machines that make up a computer system are kinds of **hardware**. The largest and most powerful computers are called **mainframes**. Scientists use them to perform calculations that would take years to do by hand. The computers most people are familiar with are personal computers (**PCs**). These can be used at a desk (**desktops**), carried around (**laptops**), even held in your hand (**palm computers**).

STORAGE

KEEPING DATA TO USE IT LATER A computer also stores information. You can save your work and return to it at your convenience. It is important to save as often as possible.

FLOPPY DISK

Information can be saved on a **"floppy" disk** that goes into a slot in the computer called a **disk drive.** If you use a disk to save your story, you can use the disk on another computer and your story will be there to work on. Disks today are usually stiff. Older computers used larger disks that were light and easy to bend, so people began calling them floppy disks.

ZIP DISK

Zip disks hold much more information than floppy disks. They are used in special zip drives. A **Jazz disk** holds a gigabyte of information, 10 times as much as a Zip disk.

HARD DISK

Most computers have a **hard drive**. The hard drive contains a **hard disk** that is not removed. It holds much more information than zip or floppy disks. It stores your software and information you have entered into the computer.

CD-ROMs

Many computers have a CD-ROM drive. This allows you to play special disks called **CD-ROMs**, similar to music CDs. A CD-ROM can hold a huge amount of information, including pictures and sound. Almanacs, games, encyclopedias, and many other types of information and entertainment are on CD-ROMs.

DVDs

Digital Versatile Disks look like CD-ROMs, but hold about eight times more information on a single side. DVDs are currently used to store movies, encyclopedias, and other products with lots of data.

Monitor · CPU · Printer · CD-ROM · Zip Drive · Modem · Keyboard · Mouse · Floppy Disk

The BINARY SYSTEM

A computer can do many impressive things, but one thing it cannot do is understand English. For a computer to do its work, every piece of information given to it must be translated into binary code. You are probably used to using 10 digits, 0 through 9, when you do arithmetic. When the computer uses the **binary code**, it uses only two digits, 0 and 1. Think of it as sending messages to the computer by switching a light on and off.

Each 0 or 1 digit is called a **bit**, and most computers use a sequence of 8 bits (called a **byte**) for each piece of data. Almost all computers use the same code, called ASCII (pronounced "askey"), to stand for letters of the alphabet, number digits, punctuation, and other special characters that control the computer's operation. Below is a list of ASCII bytes for the alphabet.

A	01000001	J	01001010	S	01010011
B	01000010	K	01001011	T	01010100
C	01000011	L	01001100	U	01010101
D	01000100	M	01001101	V	01010110
E	01000101	N	01001110	W	01010111
F	01000110	O	01001111	X	01011000
G	01000111	P	01010000	Y	01011001
H	01001000	Q	01010001	Z	01011010
I	01001001	R	01010010		

WHAT IS A PROGRAMMING LANGUAGE?

The first computer programs were written in binary code, which is slow to work with. Today, computer programmers use languages both humans and computers can understand. They are translated by the computer into binary code.

On the screen at right you can see a very simple program in a language called BASIC. It tells the computer to print the sum of 1 + 2, or 3. Some other programming languages you might hear about are FORTRAN, COBOL, Pascal, Java, and C++.

```
LET A=1
LET B=2
LET C=A+B
PRINT C
```

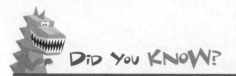

DID YOU KNOW?

If you want to use the Internet to write to The World Almanac for Kids, the e-mail address is: **Waforkids@waegroup.com**
Look for information from The World Almanac for Kids at **www.eplay.com**

THE INTERNET

What is the Internet?

The **Internet** (**"Net"**) connects computers from around the world so people can share information. You can play games on the Net, send electronic mail (e-mail), shop, and find information. The **World Wide Web (www)** is a part of the Internet that lets you see information using pictures, colors, and sounds. Most people just call it the Web. Information on the Web lives on a **Web site**. To get to the Web site you want, you need to use the right **Universal Resource Locator (URL)**, or address. If you know the address, just find the place for it on the screen and type it in carefully.

If you don't know the address, hit **Search**. You may have to pick a search engine, which is like a huge index. A few popular search engines are Yahoo, Infoseek, and Lycos. When you have the one you want, type in words that tell exactly what you're searching for. The result will be a list giving you a choice of sites. You can choose the site that seems most likely to have the information you want. Some sites have **links**—names of other sites on the same subject.

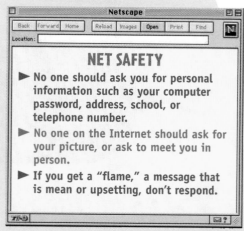

NET SAFETY

► No one should ask you for personal information such as your computer password, address, school, or telephone number.

► No one on the Internet should ask for your picture, or ask to meet you in person.

► If you get a "flame," a message that is mean or upsetting, don't respond.

Can you depend on information from the Internet?

Watch out when you use information from the Internet. Because anyone can create a Web site, you cannot always be sure the information is correct. An official Web site produced by a company, organization, or government agency may be more reliable than a site created by a fan or someone interested in the topic you are looking up. It often may be worth checking more than one source.

COMPUTER GAMES

Dr. Brain Thinking Games: Puzzle Madness
Knowledge Adventure, for Windows 95 and Mac
Chasing down Dr. Brain's evil clone is the goal of this virtual board game. But the real thrill comes from unlocking tricky puzzles along the way.

Imagynasium
SouthPeak Interactive, for Windows 95/98
This game unleashes your creativity. Special tools help you make music, create art, and write cool stories.

Road Adventures USA
The Learning Company, for Windows 95/98
Take a fun road trip from coast to coast. It's up to you to plan the trip—from where to stay for the night to where to munch down meals, all while keeping under your budget.

Star Wars Pit Droids
Lucas Learning, for Windows 95/98/Mac
Building cute little robots called Pit Droids isn't hard. The hard part is figuring out how to get them to go where you want them to go. This puzzle game is a real test of your ability to think ahead.

SMiLEYS

Smileys are typed letters and symbols that look like faces when you turn them sideways. They tell other things about yourself in messages you send. Here are a few, with what they mean.

:-)	Smile	:-O	Shout	:-&	Tongue-tied
:-(	Sad	;-)	Wink	:-()	Can't stop talking
:-D	Laugh	:-*	Kiss	[:-)	I wear headphones
:'(	Cry	{*}	Hug and kiss	:-#	I wear braces

FYI: Here's a BL

Smileys are just one quick way to express an idea or feeling on the Internet. People also use initials as a shorthand. For example, FYI stands for For Your Information. And BL means Belly Laugh. Here are some other common abbreviations. For each one, can you tell the real definition from the one we made up?

1. BG
a. Been Gone
b. Big Grin

2. CU
a. See You
b. Cracking Up

3. LOL
a. Laughing Out Loud
b. Lots O' Luck

4. WU?
a. Who You?
b. What's Up?

5. IMO
a. In My Opinion
b. I'm Movin' On

6. BTW
a. By The Way
b. Back To Work

7. LD
a. Like, Duh!
b. Later, Dude

8. FAQ
a. Frequently Asked Question
b. Funny Answer, Quick

You can find the answers on page 317-320.

COMPUTER MUSEUMS

Some museums have sections where you can learn about computers and use them to do many fascinating things. A few museums are devoted entirely to the computer. Here are three:

AMERICAN COMPUTER MUSEUM
234 East Babcock Street
Bozeman, MT 59715
Phone: (406) 587-7545
WEB SITE http://www.compustory.com
EMAIL americancomputermuseum@computer.org

THE COMPUTER MUSEUM AT THE MUSEUM OF SCIENCE
Science Park
Boston, MA 02114
Phone: (617) 723-2500
WEB SITE http://www.net.org

TECH MUSEUM OF INNOVATION
201 South Market Street
San Jose, CA 95113-2008
Phone: (408) 279-7150
WEB SITE http://www.thetech.org
EMAIL info@thetech.org

COMPUTER PUZZLES

FIND THE FACTS

The World Wide Web is full of facts. In this puzzle, you must locate some of those facts by visiting Web sites. Here's what to do.

1 Find the answer to each question below. The answer can be found at the Web site indicated.

2 Look at the formula that follows the questions and answers. When you find all the answers, replace the letters in the formula with the right numbers. We've done one to get you started.

3 Do the math to see what X equals.

a = According to *The Guinness Book of World Records*, the most skips ever made for a single stone-skipping toss is _____.
http://www.yeeha.net/nassa/a1.html
The answer is 38.

b = The average number of ounces an adult heart weighs is _____.
http://sln.fi.edu/biosci/heart.html

c = The number of areas protected by the National Parks Service is _____.
http://www.nps.gov

d = The number of states that entered the Union before New Mexico is _____.
http://www.state.nm.us

e = The date in 1998 that John Glenn's space shuttle flight landed is November _____.
http://www.nasa.gov/
The formula is: a x b − c + d − e = **X**
X equals _____.

Try This: On which page of *The World Almanac for Kids 2001* can you find the answer to this question: How deep is the Atlantic Ocean? *Hint: You already have the number!*

FIND THE WORDS

Each sentence below contains a computer-related word. But the words are hidden in the sentences. For example, here's a sentence with the word "net" hidden:

Are you going to frow**n et**ernally because your laptop broke?

The eight hidden words are: boot, input, printer, byte, scanner, program, monitor, and mouse. Can you find them?

1 That bug in the computer is actually a baby termite.

2 Is slo mo useless in watching TV sports? No way!

3 Turn your modem on. It ordinarily won't work until you do that.

4 If a ghost said boo to me, I'd run.

5 Hey, show-off typists, if you sprint, errors will appear on the screen.

6 My floppy disk fell in the dirty clothes bin. PU! Throw it away!

7 For a writing pro, grammar is the number one concern.

8 By sending e-mails, can nerds make more friends?

Answers are on pages 317-320.

Energy

? What fossil fuel is used to make bubble gum?
You can find the answer on page 65.

ENERGY Keeps Us Moving

You can't touch, smell or taste energy, but you can observe what it can do. You can feel that sunlight warms objects, and you can see that electricity lights up a light bulb, even if you can't see the heat or the electricity.

WHAT IS ENERGY? Things that you see and touch every day use some form of energy to work: your body, a bike, a basketball, a car. Energy enables things to move. Scientists define **energy** as the ability to do work.

WHY DO WE NEED ENERGY TO DO WORK? Scientists define **work** as a force moving an object. Scientifically speaking, throwing a ball is work, but studying for a test isn't! When you throw a ball, you use energy from the food you eat to do work on the ball. The engine in a car uses energy from gasoline to make the car move.

Are There Different Kinds of Energy?

POTENTIAL When we rest or sleep we still have the ability to move. We do not lose our energy. We simply store it for another time. Stored energy is called **potential energy**. When we get up and begin to move around, we are using stored energy.

KINETIC As we move around and walk, our stored (potential) energy changes into kinetic energy, which is the energy of moving things. A parked car has potential energy. A moving car has **kinetic energy**. A sled stopped at the top of the hill has potential energy. As the sled goes down the hill, its potential energy changes to kinetic energy.

HOW IS ENERGY CREATED? Energy cannot be created or destroyed, but it can be changed or converted into different forms. **Heat**, **light**, and **electricity** are forms of energy. Other forms of energy are **sound**, **chemical energy**, **mechanical energy**, and **nuclear energy**.

WHERE DOES ENERGY COME FROM? All of the forms of energy we use come from the energy stored in **natural resources**. Sunlight, water, wind, petroleum, coal, and natural gas are natural resources. From these resources, we get heat and electricity.

THE SUN AND ITS ENERGY

All of our energy really comes from the Sun. The Sun is a big ball of gases, made up mostly of hydrogen. Inside the Sun, hydrogen atoms join together (through a process called nuclear fusion) and become helium. During this process, large amounts of energy are released. This energy works its way to the Sun's surface and then radiates out into space in the form of waves. These waves give us heat and light. The energy from the Sun is stored in our food, which provides fuel for our bodies.

The Sun Stores Its ENERGY in FOSSIL FUELS

The Sun also provides the energy stored in fossil fuels. Coal, petroleum, and natural gas are **fossil fuels**. Fossil fuels come from the remains of ancient plants and animals over millions and millions of years. This is what happened:

1 Hundreds of millions of years ago, before people lived on Earth, trees and other plants absorbed energy from the Sun, just as they do today.

2 Animals ate plants and smaller animals.

3 After the plants and animals died, they slowly became buried deeper and deeper underground.

4 After millions of years, they turned into coal and petroleum.

Although the buried prehistoric plants and animals changed form over time, they still contained stored energy.

When we burn fossil fuels today, the stored energy from the Sun is released in the form of heat. The heat is used to warm our homes and other buildings and produce electricity for our lights and appliances.

From the Sun to You

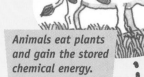

Plants absorb energy from the Sun (solar energy) and convert absorbed energy to chemical energy for storage.

Animals eat plants and gain the stored chemical energy.

People eat plants and meat.

Food provides the body with energy to work and play.

HOW ENERGY REACHES YOU

ENERGY FROM FOSSIL FUELS

Fossil fuels are a major source of energy. Your home may be heated with oil or natural gas. You may have a kitchen stove that uses natural gas. Your car needs gasoline to run. Here is how a power plant uses fossil fuel to make electricity, which is then sent by wires into homes and businesses.

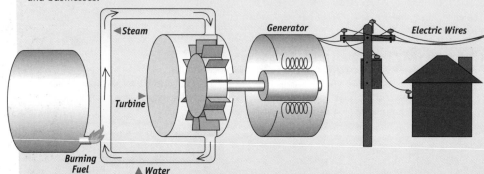

Steam • Generator • Electric Wires • Turbine • Burning Fuel • Water

1 The **fossil fuel,** usually coal, is taken to a furnace, where it is burned. The **heat** from the burning fuel heats up water that flows through pipes. When the water boils, it becomes **steam.**

2 The steam is sent to a **turbine** (a wheel with blades). The steam pushes against the blades of the turbine and causes it to spin.

3 A shaft (a long, round bar) attached to the turbine turns a **generator.** Inside the generator, a spinning **magnet** produces **electricity** in coils nearby.

4 The electricity is sent by **wires** to homes and businesses. It can then be used for lighting and for running appliances or machines.

ENERGY FROM WATER

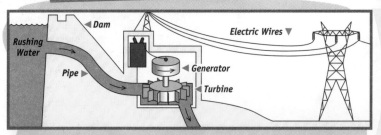

Dam • Rushing Water • Electric Wires ▼ • Pipe ▶ • Generator • Turbine

For centuries, people have been harnessing energy from rushing water. In a **hydroelectric plant,** water channeled through rivers or dams is used to drive machinery like a turbine. The turbine is connected to a generator, which produces electricity.

NUCLEAR ENERGY

In **nuclear reactors,** uranium atoms are split into smaller atoms to produce heat. The heat is then used to produce electricity, just as the heat from burning coal is used.

WHO PRODUCES AND USES THE MOST ENERGY?

The United States produces about 19 percent of the world's energy—more than any other country—but it uses 25 percent of the world's energy. The table at left lists the world's ten top energy-producers and the percent of the world's production that each was responsible for in 1997. The other table lists the world's top energy-users and the percent of the world's energy use that each was responsible for.

Countries That Produce the Most Energy

United States	19 percent
Russia	11 percent
China	9 percent
Saudi Arabia	6 percent
Canada	5 percent
Great Britain	3 percent
Iran	3 percent
Norway	3 percent
Venezuela	3 percent
India	2 percent

Countries That Use the Most Energy

United States	25 percent
China	10 percent
Russia	7 percent
Japan	6 percent
Germany	4 percent
Canada	3 percent
India	3 percent
Great Britain	3 percent
France	3 percent
Italy	2 percent

DID YOU KNOW?

▶ When you chew gum, you are really chewing petroleum! Bubble gum is one of many products made from crude oil. A few others are crayons, ink, heart valves, deodorant, dishwashing liquid, plastics, tires, ammonia, and eyeglasses.

▶ There are so many family vehicles in the United States, if you put them all in a straight line, they would reach the moon and back!

▶ For the first time since 1991, energy use in the U.S. went down slightly in 1997. We may see this trend continue in future years. The main reason is not that we are conserving better but that our winters are often warmer.

▶ Natural gas has no smell, but before it is sent through pipes to heat our homes, a chemical containing sulfur is added in. This gives the gas a smell like rotten eggs, which helps us to detect dangerous gas leaks.

WILL WE HAVE ENOUGH ENERGY?

WHERE DOES OUR ENERGY COME FROM?

In 1998, most of the energy used in the United States came from fossil fuels (about 38.8% from petroleum, 23.2% from natural gas, and 22.9% from coal). The rest came mostly from hydropower (water power) and nuclear energy. Fossil fuels are *nonrenewable* sources of energy. That means the amount of fossil fuel available for use is limited and that all this fuel will get used up after many years.

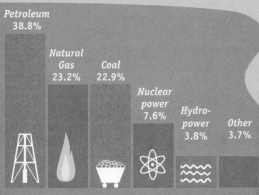

Petroleum 38.8%

Natural Gas 23.2%

Coal 22.9%

Nuclear power 7.6%

Hydro-power 3.8%

Other 3.7%

Looking for Renewable Resources

Scientists are trying to find more sources of energy that will reduce pollution and save some of the fossil fuels. People are using several types of **renewable resources**. Some of these forms of energy exist in an unlimited supply.

► **Solar power.** Solar power uses energy directly from sunlight. Solar panels can collect the sun's rays for heating. Solar cells can convert light energy directly into electricity.

► **Water from the ocean.** Ocean waves and tides can be used to drive generators to produce electricity.

► **The wind.** Windmills can be used to drive machinery. Today, some people are using wind turbines to generate electricity.

► **Biomass energy.** Biomass includes wood from trees and other plants, animal wastes, and garbage. When these are burned or allowed to decay, they produce natural gas. Biomass energy is widely available and used in some parts of the world.

► **Geothermal energy.** Geothermal energy is energy that comes from the hot, molten rock inside Earth. In certain parts of the world, such as Iceland and New Zealand, people use this kind of energy for electricity and to heat buildings.

SAVING ENERGY For Tomorrow

► Recycling reduces the number of new products that take energy to make.

► Riding buses and trains, car pooling, walking, and driving fuel-efficient cars reduces the use of fossil fuels.

► Using less heat, less hot water, and less air-conditioning also helps save energy.

► Some businesses save energy and reduce pollution by replacing old lighting, heating, cooling, and ventilation systems with newer, more efficient models.

Environment

? What common flower is used to make a drug for heart disease?
You can find the answer on page 68.

What Is the ENVIRONMENT?

Everything that surrounds us is part of the environment. Not just living things like plants and animals, but also beaches and mountains, the air we breathe, the sunlight that provides warmth, and the water that we use in our homes, schools, and businesses.

People and the Environment

People have lived on Earth for many thousands of years. For a long time people thought the Earth was so huge that it could easily absorb human wastes and pollution. And they thought that Earth's natural resources would never be used up.

In prehistoric times, people killed animals for food and built fires to cook food and keep themselves warm. They cut down trees for fuel, and their fires released gases into the air. But there were so few people that their activities had little impact on the environment.

In modern times, the world's population has been growing very fast. In 1850 there were around a billion people in the world. In 1950 there were around 2.5 billion, and in 2000, there were more than 6 billion. Their activities have a big impact on the environment.

SHARING THE EARTH

We share the planet with trees, flowers, insects, fish, whales, dogs, and many other plants and animals. Each species (type) of animal or plant has its place on Earth, and each one is dependent on the others. Plants give off oxygen that animals need to breathe. Animals pollinate plants and spread their seeds. Animals eat plants and are in turn eaten by larger animals. When plants and animals die, they become part of the soil in which new plants, in their turn, take root and grow.

Watching Over the Earth

People are becoming more aware that human activities can seriously damage the planet and the animals and plants on it. Sometimes this damage can be reversed or slowed down. But it is often permanent. On the following pages you'll learn about the damage, and about some things that can be done to help clean up and protect our planet.

You can learn more about the environment at:

WEB SITE *http://www.nwf.org/nwf/kids/index.html*

What Is BIODIVERSITY?

Our planet, Earth, is shared by millions of species of living things. The wide variety of life on Earth, as shown by the many species, is called "biodiversity" (*bio* means "life" and *diversity* means "variety"). Human beings of all colors, races, and nationalities make up just one species, *Homo sapiens.*

How Many Species Are There?
This list is just a sampling of how diverse Earth is.

BEETLES: 290,000 species
Fascinating Fact ▼ There are more species of beetles than any other animal on Earth.

FLOWERING PLANTS: 250,000 species
Fascinating Fact ► The 750,000 species of insects and the 250,000 species of flowering plants depend on one another. The insects need the plants for food, the plants need the insects for pollination.

ANTS: 20,000 species
Fascinating Fact ► If you were to weigh all the insects on Earth, ants would make up almost half of the total.

BIRDS: 9,000 species
Fascinating Fact ► More than 1,000 of these species are in danger of becoming extinct.

BATS: 1,000 species
Fascinating Fact ► There are more species of bats than of any other mammal.

PET DOGS: 1 species
Fascinating Fact ► Even though they can look very different, all dogs belong to the same species.

HUMAN BEINGS: 1 species
Fascinating Fact ► This one species holds the fate of all the other species in its hands. People can affect the environment more than any other form of living thing.

SOME THREATS TO BIODIVERSITY
Plants and animals are harmed by air, water, and land pollution, and their habitats are often destroyed by deforestation. For example, in recent years, large areas of rain forests have been cleared for wood, farmland, and cattle ranches, and people have become concerned that rain forests may be disappearing. Another threat is overharvesting, or the use of too many animals for food or other products. For example, the number of catfish, salmon, and trout has been declining, and some species could eventually be wiped out entirely.

PROTECTING BIODIVERSITY
Efforts to reduce pollutants in air, water, and soil, to preserve rain forests, and to limit other deforestation and overharvesting help to preserve biodiversity. A few species that were once endangered now will probably survive.

DiD You KNOW?

Many of our medicines come from plants found in tropical rain forests around the world. Rosy periwinkle, a wildflower, is used to create drugs that fight leukemia. The purple foxglove provides a powerful drug (digitalis) that controls heart disease.

ENVIRONMENT GLOSSARY

climate The ordinary pattern of weather in a region of the world.

compost heap A pile of food scraps and yard waste that is gradually broken down by worms and tiny insects. The result looks like plain dirt. It can be used to enrich the soil.

conservation The preservation and wise use of water, forests, and other natural resources so they will not be damaged or wasted.

deforestation The cutting down of most of the trees from forested land, usually so that the land can be used for farming and housing.

ecosystem A community of living things that depend on each other, in a particular place, such as a forest or pond.

environment The variety of plants, animals, and conditions (such as climate, soil, weather) that affects the growth of living things in an area.

extinction The disappearance of a type (species) of plant or animal from Earth. Some species become extinct because of non-human forces, but many others are becoming endangered or threatened with extinction because of the activities of people.

fossil fuel A source of energy (such as oil, gas, and coal) formed deep in the Earth from once-living matter.

global warming An increase in Earth's surface temperature due to a buildup of certain gases in the atmosphere.

greenhouse effect Warming of Earth caused by certain gases (called **greenhouse gases**) that form a blanket in the atmosphere high over Earth. Small amounts of these gases keep Earth warm so we can live here, but the larger amounts produced by factories, cars, and burning trees may hold in too much heat and cause global warming.

groundwater Water in the ground that flows in the spaces between soil particles and rocks. Groundwater supplies water for wells and springs.

habitat The natural home of an animal or a plant.

pollution Contamination of air, water, or soil by materials that can injure health, the quality of life, or the working of ecosystems.

recycling Using something more than once, either just the way it is, or reprocessed into something else.

reforestation Planting and growing new trees where other trees have been cut down.

soil erosion The washing away or blowing away of topsoil. Trees and other plants hold the soil in place and help reduce the force of the wind. Soil erosion happens when trees and plants are cut down.

RECYCLING GARBAGE

Most of the things around you will be replaced or thrown away someday. Skates, clothes, the toaster, furniture—they can break or wear out, or you may get tired of them. Where will they go when they are thrown out? What kinds of waste will they create, and how will it affect the environment?

LOOK AT WHAT IS NOW IN U.S. LANDFILLS

Metal
8%

Plastic
24%

Food and
Yard Waste
11%

Rubber
and Leather
6%

Other
Trash
21%

Paper
30%

DiD You KNOW?

What Happens to Things We Throw Away?

LANDFILLS

Most of our trash goes to places called landfills. A **landfill** (or dump) is a low area of land that is filled with garbage. Most modern landfills are lined with a layer of plastic or clay to try to keep dangerous liquids from seeping into the soil and ground water supply.

The Problem with Landfills

More than half of the states in this country are running out of places to dump their garbage. Because of the unhealthful materials many contain, landfills do not make good neighbors, and people don't want to live near them. Then, where can cities dispose of their waste? How can hazardous waste — material that can poison air, land, and water — be disposed of in a safe way? Those questions are facing officials in dozens of areas.

INCINERATORS

Another way to get rid of trash is to burn it. Trash is burned in a furnace-like device called an **incinerator**. Because incinerators can get rid of almost all of the bulk of the trash, some communities would rather use incinerators than landfills.

The Problem with Incinerators

Leftover ash and smoke from burning trash may contain harmful chemicals, called **pollutants**. They can harm plants, animals, and people.

Keeping a compost heap is a great way to reduce garbage. The pile can include grass clippings, fruit, vegetable peels, stale bread, eggshells, coffee grounds, and tea bags. But leave out meat, dairy, or oily leftovers. They can attract pests such as mice or rats.

Reduce, Reuse, Recycle

You can help reduce waste by reusing containers, batteries, and paper. You can also recycle newspaper, glass, and plastics to provide materials for making other products. At right are some of the things you can do.

WHAT IS MADE FROM RECYCLED MATERIALS?

► From **RECYCLED PAPER** we get newspapers, cereal boxes, wrapping paper, cardboard containers, and insulation.

► From **RECYCLED PLASTIC** we get soda bottles, tables, benches, bicycle racks, cameras, backpacks, carpeting, shoes, and clothes.

► From **RECYCLED STEEL** we get steel cans, cars, bicycles, nails, and refrigerators.

► From **RECYCLED GLASS** we get glass jars and tiles.

► From **RECYCLED RUBBER** we get bulletin boards, floor tiles, playground equipment, and speed bumps.

	To Reduce Waste	To Recycle
Paper	Use both sides of the paper. Use cloth towels instead of paper towels.	Recycle newspapers, magazines, comic books, catalogs, cardboard, and junk mail.
Plastic	Wash food containers and store leftovers in them. Reuse plastic bags.	Return soda bottles to the store. Recycle other plastics.
Glass	Keep glass bottles and jars to store other things.	Recycle glass bottles and jars.
Clothes	Give clothes to younger relatives or friends. Donate clothes to thrift shops.	Cut unwearable clothing into rags to use instead of paper towels.
Metal	Keep leftovers in storage containers instead of wrapping them in foil. Use glass or stainless steel pans instead of disposable pans.	Recycle aluminum cans and foil trays. Return wire hangers to the dry cleaner.
Food/Yard Waste	Cut the amount of food you throw out. Try saving leftovers for snacks or meals later on.	Make a compost heap using food scraps, leaves, grass clippings, and the like.
Batteries	Use rechargeable batteries for toys and games, radios, tape players, and flashlights.	Find out about your town's rules for recycling or disposing of batteries.

THE AIR WE BREATHE

All human beings and animals need air to survive. Without air we would die. Plants also need air to live. Plants use sunlight and the carbon dioxide in air to make food, and then give off oxygen. We all breathe the air that surrounds Earth. The air is made up mainly of gases: around 78% nitrogen, 21% oxygen, and 1% carbon dioxide, water vapor, and other gases. Human beings breathe more than six quarts of air every minute. Because air is so basic to life, it is very important to keep the air clean by reducing or preventing air pollution. Today, air pollution causes health problems and may bring about **acid rain, global warming,** and a breakdown of the **ozone layer.**

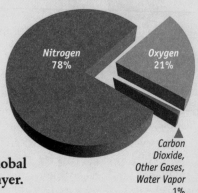

Nitrogen 78%

Oxygen 21%

Carbon Dioxide, Other Gases, Water Vapor 1%

What Is Air Pollution and Where Does It Come From?

Air pollution is a dirtying of the air caused by toxic chemicals or other materials. It can injure health, the enjoyment of life, or the working of ecosystems. The major sources of air pollution are cars, trucks and buses, waste incinerators, factories, and some electric power plants, especially those that burn fossil fuels.

What Is Acid Rain and Where Does It Come From? **Acid rain** is polluted rain or other precipitation that results from chemicals released into the air.

A factory on Lake Superior in northern Michigan ▼

The main sources of these chemicals are fumes from cars' exhaust pipes, and from power plants that burn coal, and from many kinds of factories. When these chemicals mix with moisture and other particles, they create sulfuric acid and nitric acid. The wind often carries these acids many miles before they fall to the ground in rain, snow, and fog, or even as dry particles.

Why Worry About Air Pollution and Acid Rain?

Air pollution and acid rain can harm people, animals, and plants. Air pollution can cause our eyes to sting and can even make some people sick. It can also damage crops and trees.

Air pollution (especially acid rain) is also harmful to water in lakes, often killing plants and fish that live there. Hundreds of lakes in the northeastern United States and thousands in Canada are so acidic that fish can no longer survive there. Acid rain has affected trees in U.S. national parks. In the Appalachian Mountains, for example, it has harmed spruce trees growing in the Shenandoah and Great Smoky Mountains National Parks. It can even turn buildings and statues black and damage them by eating away at metal, stone, and paint.

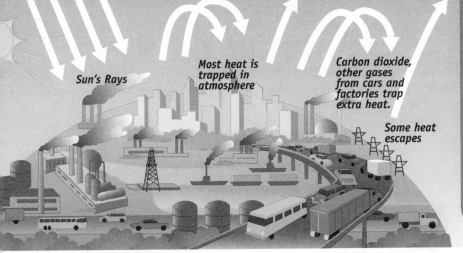

Sun's Rays

Most heat is trapped in atmosphere

Carbon dioxide, other gases from cars and factories trap extra heat.

Some heat escapes

▲ How the greenhouse effect happens

Global Warming and the Greenhouse Effect

Many scientists believe that gases in the air are causing Earth's climate to gradually become warmer. This is called **global warming**. The hottest year on record was 1998. The second hottest was 1997, and 1999 was the fifth hottest. The six hottest years were all in the 1990s. If the climate becomes so warm that a great deal of ice near the North and South Poles melts and more water goes into the oceans, many areas along the coasts may be flooded.

In Earth's atmosphere there are tiny amounts of gases called **greenhouse gases**. These gases let the rays of the sun pass through to the planet, but they hold in the heat that comes up from the sun-warmed Earth—in much the same way as the glass walls of a greenhouse hold in the warmth of the sun.

As cities have increased in size and population, factories and businesses have also grown. People have needed more and more electricity, cars, and other things that must be manufactured. As industries in the world have grown, more greenhouse gases have been added to the atmosphere. These increase the thickness of the greenhouse "glass," causing more heat to be trapped than in the past. This is called the **greenhouse effect.**

Good and Bad Ozone

Good Ozone. A layer in the atmosphere high above Earth, called the **ozone layer,** protects us from the harsh rays of the sun. When refrigerators, air conditioners, and similar items are thrown away, gases from them (called chlorofluorocarbons, or CFCs) rise into the air and destroy some of the ozone in this layer. The United States and many European countries banned the manufacture and use of CFCs after 1995.

Bad Ozone. Ozone forms near the ground when sunlight hits air pollutants from cars and smokestacks, causing smog. This ozone can cause breathing problems and contribute to the greenhouse effect.

What Are We Doing to Reduce Air Pollution?

Many countries are trying to reduce air pollution. In the United States, cars must have a special device to remove harmful chemicals from the exhaust before it comes out of the tailpipe. Many power plants and factories have devices on their smokestacks to catch harmful chemicals. Many people try not to use more electricity than they really need, so that less coal will have to be burned to produce it. And in some places, power companies use windmills or other equipment that does not pollute the air.

PROTECTING Our WATER

Every living thing needs water to live. Many animals also depend on water as a home. People not only drink water, but also use it to cook, clean, cool machinery in factories, produce power, and irrigate farmland.

WHERE DOES WATER COME FROM?

Although about two thirds of the Earth's surface is water, we are able to use only a tiny fraction of it. Seawater makes up 97% of Earth's water, and 2% is frozen in glaciers and ice around the north and south poles. **Freshwater** makes up only 1% of our water, and only part of that is close enough to Earth's surface for us to use.

The water we can use comes from lakes, rivers, reservoirs, and groundwater. **Groundwater** is melted snow or rain that seeps deep below the surface of the Earth and collects in pools called aquifers.

Overall, the world has enough freshwater, but sometimes it is not available exactly where it is needed. Extreme water shortages, or **droughts**, can occur when an area gets too little rain or has very hot weather over a long period of time, causing water supplies to dry up.

How Much Water Do We Use?

Average American's daily cooking, washing, flushing, and lawn care: 183 gallons

An average load of wash in a washing machine: 50 gallons

10-minute shower or a bath: 25–50 gallons

One load of dishes in a dishwasher: 12–20 gallons

One person's daily drinking and eating: 2 1/2 quarts

HOW WATER IS USED AT HOME

Bathroom 74%

Laundry and cleaning 21%

Kitchen 5%

WHAT IS THREATENING OUR WATER?

Water is polluted when it is not fit for its intended uses, such as drinking, swimming, watering crops, or serving as a habitat. Polluted water can cause disease and kill fish and other animals. Some major water pollutants include sewage, chemicals from factories, fertilizers and weed killers, and leakage from landfills. Water pollution is being reduced in some areas, such as Lake Erie, the Willamette River in Oregon, Boston Harbor, and the Hudson River in New York State. Companies continue to look for better ways to get rid of wastes, and many farmers are trying new ways to grow crops without using polluting fertilizers or chemicals.

The Importance of Forests

Trees and forests are very important to the environment. In addition to holding water, trees hold the soil in place. Trees use carbon dioxide and give off oxygen, which animals and plants need for survival. And they provide homes and food for millions of types of animals.

Cutting down trees—usually to use the land for something besides a forest—is called **deforestation.** Although people often have good reasons for cutting down trees, deforestation can have serious effects. In the Amazon rain forest in South America, for example, thousands of plants and animal species are being lost before scientists can even learn about them. (For more about rain forests, see page 178.) In the Pacific Northwest, there is a conflict between logging companies that want to cut down trees for lumber and people who want to preserve the ancient forests.

Why Do We Cut Down Trees? People cut down trees for many reasons. When the population grows, people cut down trees to clear space to build houses, schools, factories, and other buildings. People may clear land to plant crops and graze livestock. Sometimes all the trees in an area are cut and sold for lumber and paper.

What Happens When Trees Are Cut Down? Cutting down trees can affect the climate. After rain falls on a forest, mist rises and new rain clouds form. When forests are cut down, this cycle is disrupted, and the area eventually grows drier, causing a change in the local climate.

If huge areas of trees are cut down, the carbon dioxide they would have used builds up in the atmosphere and contributes to the greenhouse effect. And without trees to hold the soil and absorb water, rain washes topsoil away, a process called **soil erosion.** Farming on the poorer soil that is left can be very hard.

What Are We Doing to Save Forests? In many countries trees are being planted faster than they are being cut down. Foresting companies are working on more efficient methods of replacing and growing forests. In addition, communities and individuals are helping to save forests by recycling paper.

All About...
DEADLY BUGS FROM FAR AWAY

Six-legged killers are on the loose. They are bugs that have destroyed millions of trees across the United States. Such bugs are usually brought in from other countries, often by accident. With no natural enemies, the bugs multiply.

Asian long-horned beetles, for example, were sent to a hardware store in the U.S. in a shipment of wood from China. Before the beetle was discovered, it killed thousands of trees. So far, the best way to fight it has been to destroy its eggs by cutting down and burning infested trees.

Experts have found a less destructive way to combat another tree-killer, the woolly adelgid, also from Asia. Adelgids threaten to wipe out East Coast hemlock forests. Hundreds of thousands of these bugs attack a tree at once and suck out its juices. But tiny, black ladybugs from Japan feast on the adelgid. American tree experts went to Japan, gathered the ladybugs, and released thousands of them in hemlock forests in the eastern U.S. So far, the Japanese ladybugs seem to be reducing the population of adelgids.

ENViRONMENT PUZZLE

ACROSS

4 Many of our _____ come from rain forest plants and animals.

7 An extreme shortage of water is called a _____.

12 _____ is the ordinary pattern of weather in a region.

13 Putting meat leftovers in a compost heap can attract _____.

14 Recycling paper helps save _____.

15 An animal's natural home is its _____.

17 Too much heat trapped in the atmosphere is a result of the _____ effect.

DOWN

1 The animal with the largest number of species on Earth is the _____.

2 More than 1,000 species of _____may soon be extinct.

3 A word for the variety of life on Earth: _____.

5 Americans use the most water in this room: _____.

6 Tree experts hope to save _____ forests from alien bugs.

8 Plants give off _____, which helps people and animals breathe.

9 Both nitrogen and oxygen are a kind of _____ in the air.

10 Oil, gas, and coal are _____ fuels.

11 _____ rain damages lakes and trees.

16 Incinerators _____trash.

Answers are on pages 317-320

Geography

? If you were on the world's biggest island, where would you be? *You can find the answer on page 80.*

LOOKING at Our WORLD

Did you ever travel on a spaceship? In a way, you're traveling around the sun right now on a spaceship called Planet Earth.

HALF OF A GLOBE

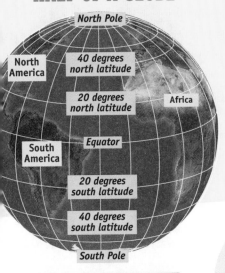

North Pole

North America

40 degrees north latitude

20 degrees north latitude

Africa

South America

Equator

20 degrees south latitude

40 degrees south latitude

South Pole

A **globe** is a small model of Earth. Like Earth, it is shaped like a ball or sphere. Earth isn't exactly a sphere because it gets flat at the top and bottom and bulges a little in the middle, but a globe gives us the best idea of what Earth looks like.

Because Earth is round, most flat maps that are centered on the equator do not show the shapes of the land masses exactly right. The shapes at the top and bottom usually look too big. For example, the island of Greenland, which is next to North America, may look bigger than Australia, though it is really much smaller.

Which Hemisphere Do You Live In?

Draw an imaginary line around the middle of Earth. This is the **equator**. It splits Earth into two halves called **hemispheres**. The part north of the equator is the **northern hemisphere**. The part south of the equator is the **southern hemisphere**.

You can also divide Earth into east and west. **North and South America** are in the **western hemisphere**. Africa, Asia, and most of Europe are in the **eastern hemisphere**.

LATITUDE AND LONGITUDE

Imaginary lines that run east and west around Earth, parallel to the equator, are called **parallels**. They tell you the **latitude** of a place, or how far it is from the equator. The equator is at 0 degrees latitude. As you go farther north or south, the latitude increases. The North Pole is at 90 degrees **north latitude**. The South Pole is at 90 degrees **south latitude**.

Imaginary lines that run north and south around the globe, from one pole to the other, are called **meridians**. They tell you the degree of **longitude**, or how far east or west a place is from an imaginary line called the **Greenwich meridian** or **prime meridian** (0 degrees). That line runs through the city of Greenwich in England.

READING A MAP

Physical maps mainly show features that are part of nature, such as rivers, mountains, oceans, and deserts. Political maps show features such as states and countries and the boundaries between them.

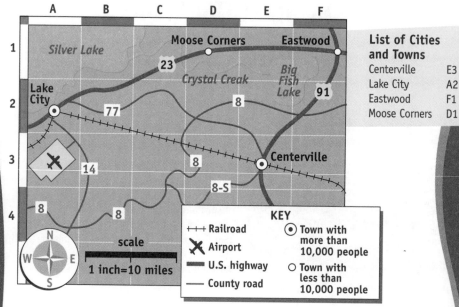

List of Cities and Towns

Centerville	E3
Lake City	A2
Eastwood	F1
Moose Corners	D1

KEY

+++ Railroad
✖ Airport
▬ U.S. highway
— County road

⊙ Town with more than 10,000 people
○ Town with less than 10,000 people

scale
1 inch=10 miles

DISTANCE Of course the distances on a map are much shorter than the distances in the real world. The **scale** shows you how to estimate the real distance. In the map above, every inch on paper stands for a real distance of 10 miles.

PICTURES Maps usually have little pictures or symbols. The map **key** tells what they mean. At the bottom of this map, you can see the symbols for towns, roads, railroad tracks, and airports. Can you tell which are the two biggest cities on the map? Can you find the airport? How would you get from the airport to Moose Corners by car?

DIRECTION Maps usually have a **compass rose** that shows you which way is north. On most maps, like this one, north is straight up. When north is up, south is down, east is right, and west is left.

FINDING PLACES To help you find places on a map, many maps have a list of places in alphabetical order, with a letter and number for each. In the map above, you can find the first city on the list, Centerville (E3), by drawing a straight line down from the letter E on top, and another line going across from the number 3 on the side. Straight lines from each letter and number on the side make a **grid.** Centerville should be near the place on the grid where the lines for E and 3 meet.

THE SEVEN CONTINENTS

Almost two-thirds of Earth's surface is made up of water. The rest is land. Oceans are the largest areas of water. Continents are the biggest pieces of land.

	Area	Population	Highest Point	Lowest Point
North America	9,400,000 square miles	476,000,000	Mount McKinley (Alaska), 20,320 feet	Death Valley (California), 282 feet below sea level
South America	6,900,000 square miles	343,000,000	Mount Aconcagua (Argentina), 22,834 feet	Valdes Peninsula (Argentina), 131 feet below sea level
Europe	3,800,000 square miles	727,000,000	Mount Elbrus (Russia), 18,510 feet	Caspian Sea (Russia, Azerbaijan; eastern Europe and western Asia), 92 feet below sea level
Asia	17,400,000 square miles	3,641,000,000	Mount Everest (Nepal, Tibet), 29,035 feet	Dead Sea (Israel, Jordan), 1,312 feet below sea level
Africa	11,700,000 square miles	778,000,000	Mount Kilimanjaro (Tanzania), 19,340 feet	Lake Assal (Djibouti), 512 feet below sea level
Australia & Oceania	3,300,000 square miles	30,000,000	Mount Kosciusko (New South Wales), 7,310 feet	Lake Eyre (South Australia), 52 feet below sea level
Antarctica	5,400,000 square miles	Zero	Vinson Massif, 16,864 feet	Bentley Subglacial Trench, 8,327 feet below sea level

The Four Oceans

The facts about the oceans include their size and average depth.

Pacific Ocean: 64,186,300 square miles; 12,925 feet deep

Atlantic Ocean: 33,420,000 square miles; 11,730 feet deep

Indian Ocean: 28,350,500 square miles; 12,598 feet deep

Arctic Ocean: 5,105,700 square miles; 3,407 feet deep

Longest River: Nile, in Egypt and Sudan (4,160 miles)
Highest Waterfall: Angel Falls, in Venezuela (3,212 feet)
Tallest Mountain: Mount Everest,
  in Tibet and Nepal (29,035 feet)
Deepest Lake: Lake Baykal, in Asia (5,315 feet)
Biggest Lake: Caspian Sea, in Europe and Asia
  (143,244 square miles)
Biggest Desert: The Sahara, in Africa
  (3,500,000 square miles)
Biggest Island: Greenland, in the Atlantic Ocean
  (840,000 square miles)

Mount Everest ▲

Some Important REGIONS

❶ **BALKANS** The Balkan region, in southeastern Europe, consists of Yugoslavia, Slovenia, Croatia, Bosnia and Herzegovina, Macedonia, and Albania. Bulgaria, southeastern Romania, northern Greece, and the portion of Turkey in Europe are also part of the Balkans. All the Balkan states were once part of the Ottoman Empire.

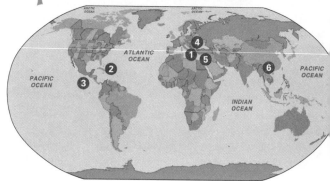

❷ **CARIBBEAN** This region is in the Caribbean Sea, an arm of the Atlantic Ocean between the U.S. and South America. The Caribbean has thousands of islands. The largest groups are the Greater Antilles and Lesser Antilles. Among countries in the Greater Antilles are Cuba, Haiti, Dominican Republic, Jamaica, and the U.S. commonwealth of Puerto Rico. The Lesser Antilles include Dominica, Barbados, Grenada, and Trinidad and Tobago.

❸ **CENTRAL AMERICA** Central America is the region between Mexico and South America. It consists of Belize, Guatemala, Honduras, El Salvador, Nicaragua, Costa Rica, and Panama.

❹ **EASTERN EUROPE** Countries of Eastern Europe include Poland, the Czech Republic, Slovakia, Hungary, Romania, and Bulgaria. Three other Eastern European countries (Estonia, Latvia, and Lithuania) form a region known as the Baltic States.

❺ **MIDDLE EAST** One of the most famous regions in the news is the Middle East. It includes Egypt and Libya (in northeast Africa), Israel, Jordan, Lebanon, Syria, and Iraq, and countries of the Arabian Peninsula: Saudi Arabia, Kuwait, Bahrain, Qatar, United Arab Emirates, Oman, and Yemen (all in southwest Asia). The term "Middle East" sometimes also includes the other Islamic countries of North Africa: Morocco, Algeria, and Tunisia.

❻ **SOUTHEAST ASIA** The region of Southeast Asia lies east of India and south of China. It consists of 10 independent countries: Myanmar (Burma), Thailand, Vietnam, Laos, Cambodia, Malaysia, Singapore, the Philippines, Indonesia, and Brunei.

SOME EUROPEAN AND AMERICAN EXPLORERS

THE AMERICAS

AROUND 1000 — **Leif Ericson,** from Iceland, explored "Vinland," which may have been the coasts of northeast Canada and New England.

1492-1504 — **Christopher Columbus** (Italian) sailed four times from Spain to America and started colonies there.

1513 — **Juan Ponce de León** (Spanish) explored and named Florida.

1513 — **Vasco Núñez de Balboa** (Spanish) explored Panama and reached the Pacific Ocean.

1519-36 — **Hernando Cortés** (Spanish) conquered Mexico, traveling as far west as Baja California.

1527-42 — **Alvar Núñez Cabeza de Vaca** (Spanish) explored the southwestern United States, Brazil, and Paraguay.

1532-35 — **Francisco Pizarro** (Spanish) explored the west coast of South America and conquered Peru.

1534-36 — **Jacques Cartier** (French) sailed up the St. Lawrence River to the site of present-day Montreal.

1539-42 — **Hernando de Soto** (Spanish) explored the southeastern United States and the lower Mississippi Valley.

1603-13 — **Samuel de Champlain** (French) traced the course of the St. Lawrence River and explored the northeastern United States.

1609-10 — **Henry Hudson** (English), sailing from Holland, explored the Hudson River, Hudson Bay, and Hudson Strait.

1682 — **Robert Cavelier, sieur de La Salle** (French), traced the Mississippi River to its mouth in the Gulf of Mexico.

1804-06 — **Meriwether Lewis** and **William Clark** (American) traveled from St. Louis along the Missouri and Columbia rivers to the Pacific Ocean and back.

ASIA AND THE PACIFIC

1271-95 — **Marco Polo** (Italian) traveled through Central Asia, India, China, and Indonesia.

1519-21 — **Ferdinand Magellan** (Portuguese) sailed from Spain around the tip of South America and across the Pacific Ocean to the Philippines, where he died. His expedition continued around the world.

1768-78 — **James Cook** (English) charted the world's major bodies of water and explored Hawaii and Antarctica.

AFRICA

1488 — **Bartolomeu Dias** (Portuguese) explored the Cape of Good Hope in southern Africa.

1497-98 — **Vasco da Gama** (Portuguese) sailed farther than Dias, around the Cape of Good Hope to East Africa and India.

1849-59 — **David Livingstone** (Scottish) explored Southern Africa, including the Zambezi River and Victoria Falls.

EARTHQUAKES

Earthquakes may be so weak that they are hardly felt, or strong enough to do great damage. There are thousands of earthquakes each year, but most are too small to be noticed. About 1 in 5 can be felt, and about 1 in 500 causes damage.

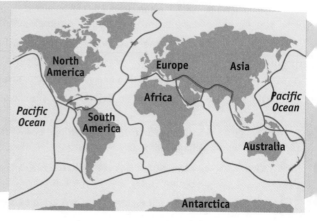

North America
Europe
Asia
Africa
Pacific Ocean
Pacific Ocean
South America
Australia
Antarctica

WHAT CAUSES EARTHQUAKES?
The Earth's outer layer, its **crust**, is divided into huge pieces called **plates** (see map). These plates, made of rock, are constantly moving—away from each other, toward each other, or past each other. A crack in Earth's crust between two plates is called a **fault**. Many earthquakes occur along faults where two plates collide as they move toward each other or grind together as they move past each other. Earthquakes along the **San Andreas Fault** in California are caused by the grinding of two plates.

MEASURING EARTHQUAKES

The Richter scale goes from 0 to more than 8. These numbers indicate the strength of an earthquake. Each number means the quake is 10 times stronger than the number below it. An earthquake measuring 6 on the scale is 10 times stronger than one measuring 5 and 100 times stronger than one measuring 4. Earthquakes that are 4 or above are considered major. (The damage and injuries caused by a quake also depend on other things, such as whether the area is heavily populated and built up.)

The strength of an earthquake, its magnitude, is registered on an instrument called a *seismograph* and is given a number on a scale called the *Richter scale.*

MAGNITUDE	EFFECTS
0-2	Earthquake is recorded by instruments but is not felt by people.
2-3	Earthquake is felt slightly by a few people.
3-4	People feel tremors. Hanging objects like ceiling lights swing.
4-5	Earthquake causes some damage; walls crack; dishes and windows may break.
5-6	Furniture moves; earthquake seriously damages weak buildings.
6-7	Furniture may overturn; strong buildings are damaged; walls and buildings may collapse.
7-8	Many buildings are destroyed; underground pipes break; wide cracks appear in the ground.
ABOVE 8	Total devastation, including buildings and bridges; ground wavy.

Major Earthquakes of the 20th Century

The earthquakes listed here are among the largest and most destructive recorded in the 1900s. The list begins with recent earthquakes.

DID YOU KNOW?

In 1692, the town of Port Royal, in the Caribbean nation of Jamaica, was pushed into the sea by a landslide caused by an earthquake. The town was buried under the ocean floor, and its homes frozen in time. In 1959 archaeologists uncovered a kettle still containing soup from the day of the quake.

YEAR	LOCATION	MAGNITUDE	DEATHS
1999	Taiwan (Taichung)	7.6	2,321
	Greece (Athens)	5.9	143
	Turkey (western)	7.4	16,700+
	Colombia (western)	6.0	1,185+
1998	Afghanistan (northeastern)	6.9	4,700+
	Afghanistan (northeastern)	6.1	2,323
1995	Sakhalin Island (Russia)	7.5	1,989
	Japan (Kobe)	6.9	5,502
1994	United States (Los Angeles area)	6.8	61
1993	India (southern)	6.3	9,748
1990	Iran (western)	7.7	40,000+
1989	United States (San Francisco area)	7.1	62
1985	Mexico (Michoacan)	8.1	9,500
1976	China (Tangshan)	8.0	255,000
	Guatemala	7.5	23,000
1970	Peru (northern)	7.8	66,000
1960	Chile (southern)	9.5	5,000
1939	Chile (Chillan)	8.3	28,000
1934	India (Bihar-Nepal)	8.4	10,700
1927	China (Nan-Shan)	8.3	200,000
1923	Japan (Yokohama)	8.3	143,000
1920	China (Gansu)	8.6	200,000
1906	Chile (Valparaiso)	8.6	20,000
	United States (San Francisco)	8.3	503

San Francisco earthquake, 1989

VOLCANOES

A volcano is a mountain or hill with an opening on top known as a **crater.** Every once in a while, hot melted rock (**magma**), gases, ash, and other material from inside the earth may blast out, or erupt, through the opening. The magma is called **lava** when it reaches the air. This red-hot lava may have a temperature of more than 2,000 degrees Fahrenheit. The hill or mountain is made of lava and other materials that come out of the opening, and then cool off and harden. Some islands are really the tops of undersea volcanoes. The Hawaiian islands developed when volcanoes erupted under the Pacific Ocean.

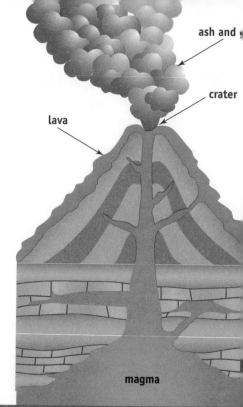

ash and

crater

lava

magma

Why Do Volcanoes Erupt?

More than 500 volcanoes have erupted over the centuries. Some have erupted many times. Volcanic eruptions come from pools of magma and other materials a few miles underground. The magma comes from rock far below. After the rock melts and mixes with gases, it rises up through cracks and weak spots in the mountain.

SOME FAMOUS VOLCANIC ERUPTION

YEAR	VOLCANO (PLACE)	DEATHS (approximate)
79	Mount Vesuvius (Italy)	16,000
1586	Kelut (Indonesia)	10,000
1792	Mount Unzen (Japan)	14,500
1815	Tambora (Indonesia)	10,000
1883	Krakatau or Krakatoa (Indonesia)	36,000
1902	Mount Pelée (Martinique)	28,000
1980	Mount St. Helens (U.S.)	57
1982	El Chichón (Mexico)	1,880
1985	Nevado del Ruiz (Colombia)	23,000
1986	Lake Nyos (Cameroon)	1,700
1991	Mt. Pinatubo (Philippines)	800

WHERE IS THE RING OF FIRE?

The hundreds of active volcanoes found on the land near the edges of the Pacific Ocean make up what is called the *Ring of Fire.* They mark the boundary between the plates under the Pacific Ocean and the plates under the continents around the ocean. (The plates of the Earth are explained on page 82, with the help of a map.) The Ring of Fire runs all along the west coast of South and North America, from the southern tip of Chile to Alaska. It includes the San Andreas Fault in California. The ring also runs down the east coast of Asia, starting in the far north in Kamchatka and continuing down past Australia.

GEOGRAPHY PUZZLE

MATCH THE SIGHT WITH THE SITE

Learn more about these sights on pages 79–80 and 84.

1. Mount McKinley
2. The Sahara Desert
3. Lake Baykal
4. Caspian Sea
5. Mount Vesuvius

a. Italy
b. Alaska
c. Africa
d. Asia
e. Europe and Asia

DISCOVER THE CONTINENTS

Change the spaces between the letters to find the names of the continents. *Hint:* They are arranged from smallest to largest. (Learn about the continents on page 79.)

A US TRA
LIAEU RO
PEA N TARC
TICA SO
UT HAM ERI
CAN OR THA
MER I CAA FRI
CAAS IA

EXPLORERS' PUZZLE

Complete the explorers' names below by filling in the blanks. Then, fit the names across the box so that the diagonal word spells **SAILORS**. Explorers' names are on page 81.

Henry _ _ _ _ _ _ _

_ _ _ _ _ _ _ _ de Champlain

Leif _ _ _ _ _ _ _ _

Francisco _ _ _ _ _ _ _ _

_ _ _ _ _ _ _ _ Cartier

Vasco Nunez de _ _ _ _ _ _ _

Hernando _ _ _ _ _ _ _

S						
	A					
		I				
			L			
				O		
					R	
						S

Answers are on pages 317-320.

DID YOU KNOW?

Canada's Northwest Territories broke in two as of April 1, 1999. The eastern part, a large area of Arctic wilderness that is one-fifth the size of Canada, became Canada's newest territory. It is known as Nunavut, which means "Our Land." Four out of five people in Nunavut are members of the Inuit native group.

Health

? Where are most of the bones in your body located?
You can find the answer on page 88.

Inside Your BODY

Your body is made up of many different parts that work together every minute of every day and night. Your body is more amazing than any machine or computer. Machines don't eat, run, have feelings, read and learn, or do other things that you do. Even though everyone's body looks different outside, people have the same parts inside.

DID YOU KNOW?

► Your body is made up of billions of tiny living units called **cells.** Different kinds of cells have different tasks to do in the body.

► Cells that do similar work form **tissue**, like nerve tissue or bone tissue.

► Tissues that work together form **organs**, like the heart, lungs, and kidneys.

► The **skin** is the body's largest organ. It protects the internal organs from infection, injury, and harmful sunlight. It also helps control body temperature.

► Organs work together as **systems**, and each system has a separate job to do.

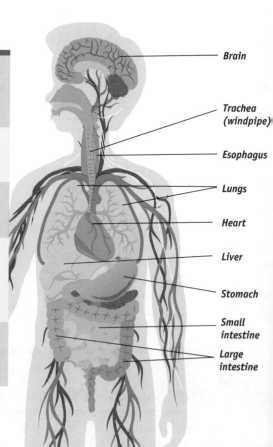

Brain

Trachea (windpipe)

Esophagus

Lungs

Heart

Liver

Stomach

Small intestine

Large intestine

What the Body's Systems Do

Each system of the body has its own job. Some of the systems also work together in teams to keep you healthy and strong.

Circulatory System

In the circulatory system, the **heart** pumps **blood**, which then travels through tubes, called **arteries**, to all parts of the body. The blood carries the oxygen and food that the body needs to stay alive. **Veins** carry the blood back to the heart.

Digestive System

The digestive system moves food through parts of the body called the **esophagus**, **stomach**, and **intestines**. As the food passes through, some of it is broken down into tiny particles called **nutrients**, which the body needs. Nutrients enter the bloodstream, which carries them to all parts of the body. The digestive system then changes the remaining food into waste that is eliminated from the body.

Endocrine System

The endocrine system includes **glands** that are needed for some body functions. There are two kinds of glands. **Exocrine** glands produce liquids such as sweat and saliva. **Endocrine** glands produce chemicals called **hormones**. Hormones control body functions, such as growth.

Muscular System

Muscles are made up of elastic fibers that help the body move. We use large muscles to walk and run, and small muscles to smile. Muscles also help protect organs.

Skeletal System

The skeletal system is made up of the **bones** that hold your body upright. Some bones protect organs, such as the ribs that cover the lungs.

Nervous System

The nervous system enables us to think, feel, move, hear, and see. It includes the **brain**, the **spinal cord**, and **nerves** in all parts of the body. Nerves in the spinal cord carry signals back and forth between the brain and the rest of the body. The brain tells us what to do and how to respond. The brain has three major parts. The **cerebrum** controls our thinking, speech, and vision. The **cerebellum** is responsible for physical coordination. The **brain stem** controls the body's respiratory, circulatory, and digestive systems.

Respiratory System

The respiratory system allows us to breathe. Air comes into the body through the nose and mouth. It goes through the **windpipe** (or **trachea**) to two tubes (called **bronchi**), which carry air to the **lungs**. Oxygen from the air is taken in by tiny blood vessels in the lungs. The blood then carries oxygen to the cells of the body.

Reproductive System

Through the reproductive system, adult human beings are able to create new human beings. Reproduction begins when a sperm cell from a man fertilizes an egg cell from a woman.

Urinary System

This system, which includes the **kidneys**, cleans waste from the blood and regulates the amount of water in the body.

SURPRISING FACTS ABOUT THE BODY

▶ More than half your bones are in the hands and feet.

▶ Red and white blood cells are made in bone marrow, the soft substance found inside bones.

▶ About eight million blood cells are made in the body every second. They replace eight million other blood cells that die every second.

▶ The surface area of the lungs is about the same size as a tennis court.

▶ Your right lung is a little larger than the left.

▶ We lose about a pint of water a day from breathing. You can see the water vapor when you breathe onto a mirror.

▶ Our bodies produce nearly two quarts of saliva every day.

▶ Muscles move in and out in waves to get food from your mouth to your stomach. That means food will get to your stomach even if you are standing on your head.

▶ During your lifetime, your heart will probably beat about three billion times.

▶ Hairs in your nose help to clean the air you breathe.

▶ Hair is dead. It is made of keratin, which is also what fingernails, cow hooves, and bird feathers are made of.

Stay Healthy with Exercise

Daily exercise is important for your good health, fitness, and appearance. Exercise makes you feel good. It helps you think better. And, believe it or not, it helps you sleep better and feel more relaxed. Once you start exercising regularly, you will feel stronger and keep improving at physical activities.

When you exercise, you breathe more deeply and get more oxygen into your lungs with each breath. Your heart pumps more oxygen-filled blood to all parts of your body with each beat. Your muscles and joints feel more flexible. Exercise also helps you to stay at a healthy weight.

Here are some types of exercise and the number of calories each burns up in one hour:

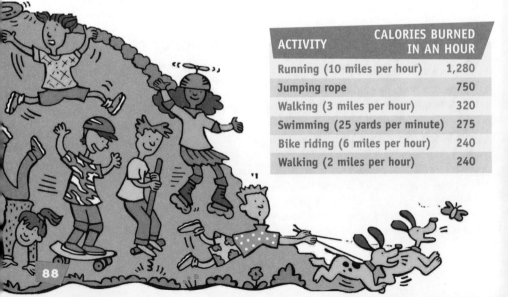

ACTIVITY	CALORIES BURNED IN AN HOUR
Running (10 miles per hour)	1,280
Jumping rope	750
Walking (3 miles per hour)	320
Swimming (25 yards per minute)	275
Bike riding (6 miles per hour)	240
Walking (2 miles per hour)	240

All About...
DREAMS AND DREAMING

We spend about one-third of our lives sleeping and usually dream every night, for about one-fourth of the time we are asleep. Dreams are generally in color. The time when we do most of our dreaming is called REM, which stands for rapid eye movement. It is a busy time. Even though our eyes are closed, they are constantly moving under our eyelids. REM sleep happens three or four times during the night.

Many books have been written about the meanings of dreams. And it's possible that some dreams mean the same to everyone. But most sleep experts believe that our dreams are individual; they reflect our own thoughts and feelings.

"I had the best dream last night!" a friend may say to you. But you may not remember any of your own dreams from that night. We often forget our dreams the moment we wake up, if not before. If you remember a dream when you wake up, write it down before you think about anything else. If you keep a journal of your dreams, you may see a pattern that could help you figure out what they mean.

Every once in a while, many children (and some adults) have nightmares. These are scary or unhappy dreams. Nightmares are believed to be a way people have of dealing with normal fears and problems. Talking to an adult about your nightmares may help you feel less afraid about them.

A DREAM REPORT

Try keeping track of your dreams every day in a journal. Be patient. You may often not be able to remember anything you dreamed.

After a while, make a report on your dreams. It could answer questions such as these:

▶ Did what you ate, or watched on TV, or played before bedtime often influence your dreams?

▶ Did you dream about things you were afraid of?

▶ Did you dream about exciting things that happened?

▶ Did you dream about people you saw the day before?

We are what we eat

Have you ever noticed the labels on the packages of food you and your family buy? The labels provide information people need to make healthy choices about the foods they eat. Below are some terms you may see on labels.

NUTRIENTS ARE NEEDED

Nutrients are the parts of food the body can use. The body needs nutrients for growth, for energy, and to repair itself when something goes wrong. Carbohydrates, fats, proteins, vitamins, minerals, and water are different kinds of nutrients found in food. **Carbohydrates** and **fats** provide energy. **Proteins** aid growth and help maintain and repair the body. **Vitamins** help the body to use food, help eyesight and skin, and aid in fighting off infections. **Minerals** help build bones and teeth and aid in such functions as muscle contractions and blood clotting. **Water** helps with growth and repair of the body. It also helps the body digest food and get rid of wastes.

CALORIES COUNT

A **calorie** is a measure of how much energy we get from food. The government recommends the number of calories that should be taken in for different age groups. The number of calories recommended for children ages 8 to 10 is about 1,900 a day. For ages 11 to 14, the government recommends around 2,200 calories a day for girls and 2,400 for boys.

To maintain a **healthy weight**, it is important to balance the calories in the food you eat with the calories used by the body every day. Every activity uses up some calories. The more active you are, the more calories your body burns. If you eat more calories than your body uses, you will gain weight.

A LITTLE FAT GOES A LONG WAY

SOME LOWER-FAT FOODS:

chicken or turkey hot dog

broiled chicken breast

tuna fish canned in water

pretzels

low-fat or nonfat frozen yogurt

plain popcorn (with no butter)

skim milk or 1% or 2% milk

SOME FATTY FOODS:

beef or pork hot dog

fried hamburger

tuna fish canned in oil

potato chips

ice cream

buttered popcorn

whole milk

A **little bit of fat** is important for your body. It keeps your body warm. It gives the muscles energy. It helps keep the skin soft and healthy. But the body needs only a small amount of fat to do all these things—less than one-third of your calories should come from fat, if you're over two years old.

Cholesterol. Eating too much fat can make some people's bodies produce too much **cholesterol** (ko-LESS-ter-all). This waxy substance can build up over the years on the inside of arteries. Too much cholesterol keeps blood from flowing freely through the arteries and can cause serious health problems such as heart attacks.

To eat less fat, try eating lower-fat foods instead of fatty foods.

WHICH FOODS ARE THE RIGHT FOODS?

To stay healthy, it is important to eat the right foods and to exercise. To help people choose the right foods for good health and fitness, the U.S. government developed the food pyramid shown below. The food pyramid shows the groups of foods that kids seven to twelve years old should eat every day.

FOOD PYRAMID
A Guide to Daily Food Choices

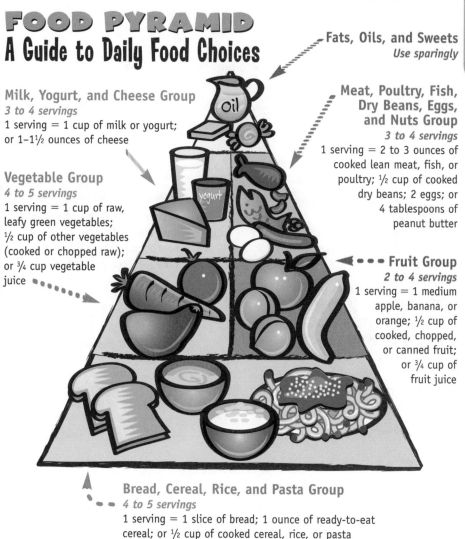

Fats, Oils, and Sweets
Use sparingly

Milk, Yogurt, and Cheese Group
3 to 4 servings
1 serving = 1 cup of milk or yogurt; or 1–1½ ounces of cheese

Meat, Poultry, Fish, Dry Beans, Eggs, and Nuts Group
3 to 4 servings
1 serving = 2 to 3 ounces of cooked lean meat, fish, or poultry; ½ cup of cooked dry beans; 2 eggs; or 4 tablespoons of peanut butter

Vegetable Group
4 to 5 servings
1 serving = 1 cup of raw, leafy green vegetables; ½ cup of other vegetables (cooked or chopped raw); or ¾ cup vegetable juice

Fruit Group
2 to 4 servings
1 serving = 1 medium apple, banana, or orange; ½ cup of cooked, chopped, or canned fruit; or ¾ cup of fruit juice

Bread, Cereal, Rice, and Pasta Group
4 to 5 servings
1 serving = 1 slice of bread; 1 ounce of ready-to-eat cereal; or ½ cup of cooked cereal, rice, or pasta

The foods at the bottom (the widest part) of the pyramid are the ones everyone needs to eat in the largest amounts. At the top are the foods to be eaten in the smallest amounts. The number of servings a person should eat depends on the person's age and body size. Younger, smaller people may eat fewer servings. Older, larger people may eat more.

THE TRUTH ABOUT COLDS

Colds are the most common illnesses we get. Schoolchildren often catch colds from one another—usually about five to eight colds a year. Here are some mistakes, and some facts, about colds.

FICTION: In low temperatures, you can catch a cold by going outside without a coat.

FACT: It's smart to dress warmly when it's cold out. But colds are caused by viruses, and not cold weather. Washing your hands is a good way to avoid catching many viruses.

FICTION: Some vitamins and medicines cure colds.

FACT: While some vitamins and medicines may make you feel better for a while, there is no cure for the cold. It usually lasts about one or two weeks.

FICTION: You can cure a cold by staying home.

FACT: There is no cure for the cold. Enough sleep, drinking juices, and eating well will help you feel better.

Take Care of Your Teeth

If you want to chew food properly and speak clearly, it is important to keep your teeth healthy. These tips will help you do that.

Brush your teeth at least twice a day—*after every meal if you can.*

Floss. *Use dental floss regularly to clean between your teeth.*

Eat healthful foods. *Eating too many sweets causes cavities.*

Visit your dentist *for a checkup and cleaning every six months.*

What Causes Cavities in Your Teeth? Cavities are caused by tiny pieces of food left on or between the teeth after eating. These pieces of food combine with the natural bacteria in your mouth t form an acid. The acid slowly eats away the tooth's enamel and causes tooth decay, or cavities.

WHICH DOCTOR DOES WHAT?

A *DENTIST* is a doctor who takes general care of your teeth.

An *ORTHODONTIST* is a doctor who straightens teeth.

A *PEDIATRICIAN* is a doctor who takes care of children.

An *ORTHOPEDIST* is a doctor who fixes broken bones.

A *DERMATOLOGIST* is a doctor who treats skin problems and diseases.

A *CARDIOLOGIST* is a doctor who treats people who have heart problems.

A *PSYCHIATRIST* is a doctor who helps people with emotional problems.

ALLERGIES: *Wheezes and Sneezes*

Ah-choo! That's your umpteenth sneeze today. Your nose is running. Your eyes itch. Your head aches. You feel yucky. Do you have a cold? Or, like 50 million other Americans, do you have an allergy? Usually, people with allergies don't get fevers, and people with colds don't feel itchy. But only a doctor can tell you for sure what your symptoms mean.

What is an allergy?

A person with an allergy is super-sensitive to something that is normally harmless. It could be animal dander, traces of hair, feathers, or skin shed by pets. It could be mold spores, dust in the air, or pollen from plants. It could be something you touch (such as poison ivy, which affects many people). It could be something you ate. Just because a person is allergic to one thing doesn't mean he or she is allergic to the others. Different kinds of allergies have different names, causes, and symptoms.

What is hay fever?

This is one of the most common allergies that affects sinuses. It is a reaction to pollen, from trees, grass, and weeds, which is in the air at certain times of the year. The pollen may come from the plants in your backyard. It could even come on air currents from places hundreds of miles away.

What is asthma?

It is a disease that can cause difficulty in breathing. Pollen and dust mites, as well as tobacco smoke, cold air, and certain foods can trigger an asthma attack.

What are hives?

Hives are big itchy blotches, bumps, or red spots. They come from an allergy that is often caused by certain foods.

How can you protect yourself against allergies?

You should see a doctor to find out more about your allergy and what to do about it.

You can also do some things to help yourself. If you're sensitive to pollens and molds, try not to stay outside long when they're at their highest levels. Grass pollen, for example, is strongest between 6 and 10 a.m. Pollens are high on windy days, so those are good times to stay indoors.

People who have allergies to dust mites and molds must sometimes avoid using wall-to-wall carpeting in their homes because it holds in these things.

Drugstore shelves are filled with medicines to fight allergies or slow down their symptoms. Allergy shots can help, too. Have a parent or guardian talk to your doctor.

TiCKLES

Question: What kind of teeth are smart? *Answer:* Wisdom teeth.

Question: Why isn't your nose 12 inches long? *Answer:* Because then it would be a foot.

Here's a sign from an optometrist's office.
If you don't see what you're looking for, you've come to the right place.

Question: What part of the body do you think an optometrist treats? *Answer:* The eyes.

UNDERSTANDING AIDS

What Is AIDS? AIDS is a disease that is caused by a virus called HIV. AIDS attacks the body's immune system. The immune system is important because it helps the body fight off infections and diseases.

How Do Kids Get AIDS? A mother with AIDS may give it to her baby before the baby is born. Sometimes children (and adults, too) get AIDS from blood transfusions. But this happens less often, because blood banks now test all donations of blood for the AIDS virus.

How Do Adults Get AIDS? Adults get AIDS in two main ways: Having sex with a person who has AIDS, or sharing a needle used for drugs with a person who has AIDS.

How Kids and Adults Don't Get AIDS. People don't get AIDS from everyday contact with infected people at school, at home, or other places. People don't get AIDS from clothes, telephones, or toilet seats, or from food prepared by someone with AIDS. Children don't get AIDS from sitting near AIDS victims or from shaking hands with them.

Is There a Cure for AIDS? There is no cure for AIDS. But researchers are working to develop a vaccine to prevent AIDS or a drug to cure it. And new treatments are beginning to increase the lifespan of many people with AIDS.

 **to Drugs, Alcohol, and Cigarettes**

Drugs, alcohol, and cigarettes can do serious damage to people's bodies and minds. Most kids keep away from them. But some kids have a tough time saying "no" when they are offered harmful substances. Here are some ways to say "no." They're suggested by DARE, a U.S. government program. Add your own ideas to this list.

Say "No thanks." (Say it again and again if you have to.)

Give reasons. ("I don't like cigarettes" or "I'm going to soccer practice" or "I have asthma.")

Change the subject or offer a better suggestion.

Walk away. (Don't argue, don't discuss it. Just leave.)

Avoid the situation. (If you are asked to a party where kids will be drinking, smoking, or using drugs, make plans to do something else instead.)

Find strength in numbers. (Do things with friends who don't use harmful substances.)

Stay SAFE, Prevent Accidents

NEWS FLASH! More than 8,500 students are injured in school bus accidents in the United States each year, according to the National Highway Traffic Safety Administration. Could seat belts have helped? No one knows for sure, but Florida officials say they might have. Starting in 2001, all new school buses there must be equipped with seat belts. New York and New Jersey already have that requirement.

Even without seat belts, you can still look out for your own safety.

Tips for School Bus Safety

▶ Make sure the driver sees you when you walk in front of a school bus to get on the bus or cross the street. Get at least 10 feet (five giant steps) in front so the driver has a clear view of you.

▶ Be careful about your bookbag straps, shoelaces, drawstrings on clothing. They could get caught in the doors when you get off the bus.

▶ Don't stand behind a bus. Don't even think of walking there.

▶ Tell the driver if you drop something under or near the bus. Never try to retrieve it unless the driver knows what you're doing.

▶ Don't get up while the bus is still moving—even if it is very close to your stop.

BE READY FOR ANY EMERGENCY

Tape a list of emergency numbers near the phone or on the refrigerator. Numbers to include are:

▶ your parents' or guardians' telephone numbers at work

▶ the telephone number of a relative or other adult who lives nearby

▶ the numbers of your family doctor, a nearby hospital, the fire department, and the police department

Emergency phone numbers can often be found inside the front cover of your local telephone book.

Remember 911.

The number 911 is a special phone number for emergencies only.

When a person who needs help right away calls 911, the operator asks the caller for his or her name and address and what the emergency is. Then the operator quickly sends the police, an ambulance, and, if needed, the fire department. Dial 0 (Operator) if your town doesn't have 911, and ask the operator for help.

Holidays

? Why is the number 11 important on Veterans Day?
You can find the answer below.

HOLIDAYS in the United States

There are no official holidays for the whole United States. The U.S. government decides which days will be federal holidays. (These are really just for Washington, D.C.) Each state picks its own holidays, but most states celebrate the ones listed here. On these holidays, most banks and schools are closed, and so are many offices. Washington's Birthday (or Presidents' Day), Memorial Day, and Columbus Day are usually celebrated on Mondays so that people can have a three-day weekend.

 NEW YEAR'S DAY Countries the world over celebrate the new year, although not always on January 1. The Chinese New Year falls between January 21 and February 19. In ancient Egypt, the New Year began around mid-June, when the Nile River overflowed and watered the crops.

MARTIN LUTHER KING, JR., DAY Observed on the third Monday in January, this holiday marks the birth (January 15, 1929) of the African-American civil rights leader Rev. Martin Luther King, Jr.

WASHINGTON'S BIRTHDAY or PRESIDENTS' DAY On the third Monday in February, Americans often celebrate the births of both George Washington (born February 22, 1732) and Abraham Lincoln (born February 12, 1809).

 MEMORIAL DAY or DECORATION DAY Memorial Day, observed on the last Monday in May, is set aside to remember all those who died while serving in the United States military.

 FOURTH OF JULY or INDEPENDENCE DAY July 4 is the anniversary of the day in 1776 when the American colonies signed the Declaration of Independence. Kids and grownups celebrate the event with bands and parades, picnics, barbecues, and fireworks.

LABOR DAY Labor Day, the first Monday in September, honors the workers of America. It was first celebrated in 1882.

COLUMBUS DAY Celebrated on the second Monday in October, Columbus Day is the anniversary of October 12, 1492, the day when Christopher Columbus was traditionally thought to have arrived in America.

ELECTION DAY Election Day, the first Tuesday after the first Monday in November, is a holiday in some states.

VETERANS DAY Veterans Day, November 11, honors veterans of wars. First called Armistice Day, it marked the armistice (agreement) that ended World War I. This was signed on the 11th hour of the 11th day of the 11th month of 1918.

THANKSGIVING Thanksgiving was first observed by the Pilgrims in 1621 as a harvest festival and a day for thanks and feasting. In 1863, Abraham Lincoln revived the tradition and made Thanksgiving the fourth Thursday in November.

CHRISTMAS Christmas is both a religious holiday and a legal holiday. (See p. 192.)

Some Other SPECIAL HOLIDAYS

VALENTINE'S DAY February 14 is a day for sending cards or gifts to people you love.

ARBOR DAY We plant trees on Arbor Day to remind us of how they protect the environment. Each state observes the day at different times in the spring, depending on the state's climate.

MOTHER'S DAY AND FATHER'S DAY Mothers are honored on the second Sunday in May. Fathers are honored on the third Sunday in June.

HALLOWEEN In ancient Britain, Druids wore grotesque costumes on October 31 to scare off evil spirits. Today, "trick or treating" children collect candy and other sweets. Some also collect money for UNICEF, the United Nations Children's Fund.

KWANZAA This seven-day African-American festival begins December 26. It celebrates seven virtues: unity, self-determination, collective work and responsibility, cooperative economics, purpose, creativity, and faith. Kwanzaa means "first fruits" in Swahili, an African language.

HOLIDAYS IN 2001

NEW YEAR'S DAY
January 1 • Monday

MARTIN LUTHER KING, JR., DAY
January 15 • Monday

WASHINGTON'S BIRTHDAY
February 19 • Monday

MEMORIAL DAY
May 28 • Monday

INDEPENDENCE DAY
July 4 • Wednesday

LABOR DAY
September 3 • Monday

COLUMBUS DAY
October 8 • Monday

ELECTION DAY
November 6 • Tuesday

VETERANS DAY
November 11 • Sunday

THANKSGIVING
November 22 • Thursday

CHRISTMAS
December 25 • Tuesday

HOLIDAYS AROUND THE WORLD

BASTILLE DAY On July 14, the French celebrate the fall of the Bastille, a prison in Paris, in 1789. This was the start of the French Revolution.

CHINESE NEW YEAR China's biggest holiday falls between January 21 and February 19 every year. Celebrations include lively parades, fireworks, and traditional family meals.

INDEPENDENCE DAY Mexico celebrates September 16 as its national holiday.

MIDSUMMER EVE After a long dark winter, people in Scandinavia celebrate the coming of summer and of light, usually around June 22.

UNIVERSAL CHILDREN'S DAY The United Nations has set aside November 20 to celebrate the world's children and to seek better lives for them.

Inventions

Who invented Lincoln Logs?
You can find the answer on page 100.

INVENTIONS Change Our Lives

Some of the world's most important inventions were developed before history was written. These include tools and the wheel, pottery, and the ability to make and control fire. More recent inventions help us to travel faster, communicate better, and live longer.

INVENTIONS TAKE US FROM ONE PLACE TO ANOTHER

YEAR	INVENTION	INVENTOR	COUNTRY
1785	parachute	Jean Pierre Blanchard	France
1807	steamboat	Robert Fulton	U.S.
1829	steam locomotive	George Stephenson	England
1852	elevator	Elisha G. Otis	U.S.
1885	bicycle	James Starley	England
1885	motorcycle	Gottlieb Daimler	Germany
1891	escalator	Jesse W. Reno	U.S.
1892	automobile (gasoline)	Charles E. Duryea & J. Frank Duryea	U.S.
1894	submarine	Simon Lake	U.S.
1895	diesel engine	Rudolf Diesel	Germany
1903	propeller airplane	Orville & Wilbur Wright	U.S.
1939	helicopter	Igor Sikorsky	U.S.
1939	jet airplane	Hans von Ohain	Germany
1980	Rollerblades	Scott Olson	U.S.
1983	minivan	Chrysler	U.S.

INVENTIONS HELP US LIVE HEALTHIER AND LONGER LIVES

YEAR	INVENTION	INVENTOR	COUNTRY
1780	bifocal lenses for glasses	Benjamin Franklin	U.S.
1819	stethoscope	René T.M.H. Laënnec	France
1842	anesthesia (ether)	Crawford W. Long	U.S.
1895	X ray	Wilhelm Roentgen	Germany
1922	insulin	Sir Frederick G. Banting	Canada
1929	penicillin	Alexander Fleming	Scotland
1954	antibiotic for fungal diseases	Rachel F. Brown & Elizabeth L. Hazen	U.S.
1955	polio vaccine	Jonas E. Salk	U.S.
1973	CAT scanner	Godfrey N. Hounsfield	England
1987	meningitis vaccine	Connaught Lab	U.S.

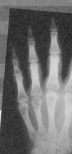

INVENTIONS HELP US COMMUNICATE WITH ONE ANOTHER

YEAR	INVENTION	INVENTOR	COUNTRY
A.D. 105	paper	Ts'ai Lun	China
1447	movable type	Johann Gutenberg	Germany
1795	modern pencil	Nicolas Jacques Conté	France
1837	telegraph	Samuel F.B. Morse	U.S.
1845	rotary printing press	Richard M. Hoe	U.S.
1867	typewriter	Christopher L. Sholes, Carlos Glidden & Samuel W. Soulé	U.S.
1876	telephone	Alexander G. Bell	U.S.
1888	ballpoint pen	John Loud	U.S.
1913	modern radio receiver	Reginald A. Fessenden	U.S.
1937	xerography copies	Chester Carlson	U.S.
1942	electronic computer	John V. Atanasoff & Clifford Berry	U.S.
1944	auto sequence computer	Howard H. Aiken	U.S.
1947	transistor	William Shockley, Walter H. Brattain, & John Bardeen	U.S.
1955	fiber optics	Narinder S. Kapany	England
1965	word processor	International Business Machines Corp.	U.S.
1979	cellular telephone	Ericsson Company	Sweden
1987	laptop computer	Sir Clive Sinclair	England

INVENTIONS MAKE OUR LIVES EASIER

YEAR	INVENTION	INVENTOR	COUNTRY
1800	electric battery	Alessandro Volta	Italy
1827	matches	John Walker	England
1831	lawn mower	Edwin Budding & John Ferrabee	England
1834	refrigeration	Jacob Perkins	England
1846	sewing machine	Elias Howe	U.S.
1851	cylinder (door) lock	Linus Yale	U.S.
1879	first practical electric light bulb	Thomas A. Edison	U.S.
1886	dishwasher	Josephine Cochran	U.S.
1891	zipper	Whitcomb L. Judson	U.S.
1901	washing machine	Langmuir Fisher	U.S.
1903	windshield wipers	Mary Anderson	U.S.
1907	vacuum cleaner	J. Murray Spangler	U.S.
1911	air conditioning	Willis H. Carrier	U.S.
1924	frozen packaged food	Clarence Birdseye	U.S.
1947	microwave oven	Percy L. Spencer	U.S.
1948	Velcro	Georges de Mestral	Switzerland
1963	pop-top can	Ermal C. Fraze	U.S.
1969	cash machine (ATM)	Don Wetzel	U.S.
1971	food processor	Pierre Verdon	France
1980	Post-its	3M Company	U.S.
1981	Polartec fabric	Malden Mills	U.S.

INVENTIONS ENTERTAIN US

YEAR	INVENTION	INVENTOR	COUNTRY
1709	piano	Bartolomeo Cristofori	Italy
1877	phonograph	Thomas A. Edison	U.S.
1877	microphone	Emile Berliner	U.S.
1888	portable camera	George Eastman	U.S.
1893	moving picture viewer	Thomas A. Edison	U.S.
1894	motion picture projector	Charles F. Jenkins	U.S.
1899	tape recorder	Valdemar Poulsen	Denmark
1923	television*	Vladimir K. Zworykin*	U.S.
1963	audiocassette	Phillips Corporation	Netherlands
1963	steel tennis racquet	René Lacoste	France
1969	videotape cassette	Sony	Japan
1972	compact disc (CD)	RCA	U.S.
1972	video game (Pong)	Noland Bushnell	U.S.
1979	Walkman	Sony	Japan

*Others who helped invent television include Philo T. Farnsworth (1926) and John Baird (1928).

INVENTIONS HELP US EXPAND OUR UNIVERSE

YEAR	INVENTION	INVENTOR	COUNTRY
1250	magnifying glass	Roger Bacon	England
1590	2-lens microscope	Zacharias Janssen	Netherlands
1608	telescope	Hans Lippershey	Netherlands
1714	mercury thermometer	Gabriel D. Fahrenheit	Germany
1926	rocket engine	Robert H. Goddard	U.S.
1930	cyclotron (atom smasher)	Ernest O. Lawrence	U.S.
1943	Aqua Lung	Jacques-Yves Cousteau & Emile Gagnan	France
1953	bathyscaphe	August Piccard	France
1977	space shuttle	NASA	U.S.

SCHOOLGIRL HAS BRIGHT IDEA

Ashley Kling, a ninth-grader from Ohio, created a battery-powered flashing light for the soles of firefighters' boots. It makes it easier to see firefighters in dark, smoky places.

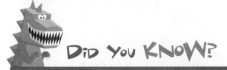

DID YOU KNOW?

In 1916 John Lloyd Wright, son of the famous architect Frank Lloyd Wright, designed the popular toy Lincoln Logs. The idea came to him in Tokyo while he and his dad were watching workers build the foundation of the Imperial Hotel, an earthquake-proof building designed by the older Wright.

NATIONAL INVENTORS HALL OF FAME

To learn more about inventions and the people who created them, or to make your own invention, visit

Inventure Place
National Inventors Hall of Fame
221 S. Broadway St., Akron, Ohio
44308 Phone: (330) 762-4463.
E-mail: info@invent.org
http://www.invent.org/book

All About...
ROLLERCOASTERS

Close your eyes. You are in a chair on top of a tall mountain. You come rushing down at top speed. Your heart beats wildly. The wind whips back your hair and pins you to your seat. Your stomach drops and you let out a shriek! Does this sound like fun to you? If so, you are not alone. People have found ways to whoosh down hills since the 1400s, when ice slides were built in Russia. In the late 1700s, Catherine the Great, Russia's ruler, placed wheels on sleds so that she could coast during the summer.

The first roller coaster came to the United States in 1827. "Gravity Road," in the mountains of Pennsylvania, was 18 miles long and dropped more than 1,200 feet. The highest, longest roller coaster ever built, it was made to carry coal from a mountaintop mine to boats along the canal below. But fascinated crowds clamored for rides.

In 1884, La Marcus A. Thompson built the "Switchback Railway" at Coney Island in Brooklyn, New York. This was the first roller coaster built purely for fun. Since then, hundreds more have been built. They are made of steel as well as wood, and some have loops that turn riders upside down. Today, roller coaster popularity seems to be at an all-time high! Here are some of the world's biggest and best.

WORLD'S FASTEST ROLLER COASTERS

RANK/NAME	SPEED	LOCATION
1. Millennium Force	92 mph	Sandusky, Ohio
2. Fujiyama	86 mph	Yamanashi, Japan
3. Desperado	85 mph	Primm, Nevada
4. Goliath	85 mph	Valencia, California
5. Steel Phantom	80 mph	West Mifflin, Pennsylvania

WORLD'S LONGEST ROLLER COASTERS

RANK/NAME	LENGTH	LOCATION
1. The Ultimate	7,498 ft	North Yorkshire, England
2. The Beast	7,392 ft	Cincinnati, Ohio
3. Son of Beast	7,032 ft	Cincinnati, Ohio
4. Millennium Force	6,595 ft	Sandusky, Ohio
5. Desperado	5,843 ft	Primm, Nevada

WORLD'S HIGHEST ROLLER COASTERS

RANK/NAME	HEIGHT	LOCATION
1. Millennium Force	310 ft	Sandusky, Ohio
2. Fujiyama	259 ft	Yamanashi, Japan
3. Goliath	255 ft	Valencia, California
4. Son of Beast	218 ft	Cincinnati, Ohio
5. Pepsi Max Big One	214 ft	Lancashire, England

WEB SITE See http://www.rollercoaster.com for more information.

Language

? What language gives us the English words *mosquito*, *alligator*, and *guitar*? You can find the answer on page 105.

SHORT and SHORTER
ABBREVIATIONS and ACRONYMS

An abbreviation is a short form of a word or phrase used to save time or space. Here are some abbreviations:

PTA	Parent-Teacher Association
Org.	Organization
Inc.	Incorporated
TLC	Tender, loving care
A.M./P.M.	*ante meridiem* (before noon)/ *post meridiem* (afternoon)
B.C./A.D.	before Christ/*anno Domini* (in the year of the Lord)

An acronym is a kind of abbreviation. It is a word you can pronounce, formed from the first letters, or other parts, of a group of words. These words you see every day are acronyms.

laser	**l**ight **a**mplification by **s**timulated **e**mission of **r**adiation
Lego	**le**s **go**dt (Danish for "play well")
Velcro	**vel**our + **cro**chet
yuppie	**y**oung **u**rban **p**rofessional

DID YOU KNOW?

In the 1600s Italian mathematicians took syllables from the ancient Arabic phrase "ilm-al-jebrw'al-mug-abalah" (meaning "reductions and comparison by equations") to add up to the acronym **algebra**. The Arabs had made important contributions to algebra in the Middle Ages.

TECHNICAL TALK
Special fields have their own abbreviations.

Internet. Abbreviations are a part of the everyday language of the Internet and e-mail (electronic mail). **FYI** (for your information), **URL** stands for Uniform Resource Locator, which is the official name for an Internet address. There's much more, but **TTFN** (ta-ta for now). See page 59 for more about the Internet.

Computers. To use your personal computer **(PC)**, you start, or boot up, the system. The computer works by using a central processing unit **(CPU)** that reads and writes using random access memory **(RAM)**. **BTW** (by the way), to find the answers to frequently asked questions **(FAQs)**, check with your computer manufacturer's online services.

Sports. Most college teams play in the **NCAA** (National Collegiate Athletic Association). Men's professional football, basketball, and hockey teams all belong to national leagues (the **NFL**, **NBA**, and **NHL**). There is also a women's professional basketball league — the **WNBA** (Women's National Basketball Association). Baseball has two leagues, the National League **(NL)** and the American League **(AL)**. The abbreviations **NL** and **AL** are used in giving baseball **stats** (statistics).

Words That SOUND ALIKE or Almost Alike

When words sound similar, sometimes their spellings and meanings are confusing. Words that sound alike are called homophones.

CLOTHES or CLOSE
Clothes are what we wear. To close means to shut something.

COMPLEMENT or COMPLIMENT
Complement is to make complete, or something that completes. A compliment is praise for someone.

FIND or FINED
To find means to come upon something you were looking for. Fined means having to pay for doing something wrong.

HAIR or HARE
Hair is what grows on the top of your head if you are not bald. A hare is similar to a rabbit.

ITS or IT'S
Its is the possessive form of "it" (the bird flapped its wings). It's is a contraction of (short form for) "it is."

LOAN or LONE
A loan is something that you lend or someone borrows. Lone means single or alone.

PRINCIPAL or PRINCIPLE
A principal is the person in charge of a school. Principal also means first in importance. A principle is a basic belief that a person strongly holds.

ROSE or ROWS
A rose is a sweet-smelling flower. Rows are groups of objects lined up.

STATIONARY or STATIONERY
When something is stationary it does not move. Stationery is special paper for writing letters.

THEIR, THEY'RE, or THERE
Their is the possessive form of "they." They're is short for "they are." There means at or in that place. (They're going to put their packages there on the table.)

WEEK or WEAK
The seven days from Sunday to Saturday are a week. Weak means not strong.

NEW WORDS

The English language is always changing. New words become part of the vocabulary, while other words become outdated. Many new words come from the field of electronics and computers, from the media, even from slang.

4x4 • (pronounced four by four) • a four-wheel-drive vehicle. (We loaded up the 4x4 with camping equipment and headed off to our vacation at the Grand Canyon.)

megaplex • a group of theaters showing different movies under one roof. (The seven-story megaplex in our neighborhood has fifteen theaters.)

spam • e-mail sent in bulk to a large number of e-mail addresses, usually to advertise something. (I often get as much spam e-mail as I get e-mail from people I know.)

screen saver • a computer program that usually displays various images on the screen of a computer that is on but not in use, to prevent damage to the screen. (Ana's soccer screen saver was really cool to look at.)

In Other Words:
IDIOMS

Idioms are groups of words (phrases) or sentences that cannot be understood just by knowing the meaning of each of the words. They may often be slang. Idioms may be confusing to people learning a new language. Here are some common idioms, with their meanings.

ALL WASHED UP

all wet: no good

my cup runneth over: I have everything I could possibly want

raining cats and dogs: raining very hard

shed crocodile tears: cry insincerely

CONNECTIONS

joined at the hip: always together

like two peas in a pod: very similar

on the same wavelength: thinking the same thing

get with the program: follow the rules

TRAVELING ON

hit the ground running: start a project immediately

flew the coop: left or departed, often secretly or guiltily

caught the wave: followed the latest trend

on the right track: heading for the right conclusion

made a beeline: went somewhere fast

off da hook: really cool

I got your back: I'm here for you

COLORFUL PHRASES

in the red: not having enough money

out of the blue: seemingly from nowhere

green thumb: very good at growing plants, vegetables, flowers.

white elephant: something of little or no value

PICTURE THIS

Use the picture to figure out these other idioms.

1   2   3

Answers are on pages 317-320.

BITTERSWEET and Other Oxymorons

A time that is bitter is sad. A time that is sweet is usually happy. So how can an occasion be described as bittersweet? It's an oxymoron, a pair of words that seem to contradict each other, or just look silly together. Here are some oxymorons you may come across.

OXYMORON	WHAT IT MAY MEAN
clearly confused	obviously mixed up
genuine imitation	not the real thing, but a lot like it
guest host	temporary star of a TV talk show or game show
jumbo shrimp	large shrimp
war games	exercises by the armed forces preparing troops for battle
open enclosed garden	a fenced-in garden that is open to the public

Where Do ENGLISH WORDS Come From?

Words from many other languages have become part of the English language. Here are some words and where they come from.

from French: antique, beret, boulevard, camouflage, carousel, casserole, corsage, deluxe, fatigue, intrigue, menu, omelette, reservoir, souvenir, surgeon

from German: frankfurter, hamburger, kindergarten, knapsack, pretzel, snorkel

from Hindi: cheetah, guru, jungle, pajamas, shampoo

from Italian: broccoli, macaroni, pasta, piano, pizza, prima donna, violin

from Japanese: haiku, judo, karate, kimono, sushi, tofu

from Spanish: alligator, bonanza, cafeteria, canyon, chocolate, guitar, mosquito, mustang, rodeo, patio, stampede, tomato, tornado, tortilla, vanilla

from Yiddish: chutzpah, klutz, kvetch, nosh, oy vay, schlemiel, schlep, shtick, tchotchke

Names From People

Some words we use come from place names. Others, called eponyms, are based on people's names.

bobbies: In 1850, Sir Robert Peel, a British politician, organized a police force in London.

Braille: This system of writing for the blind was named after Louis Braille, a Frenchman who invented it to teach his blind students.

cardigan: This sweater was first worn by the Earl of Cardigan in Great Britain.

cologne: This form of perfume was created in Cologne, Germany.

Derby: This stiff felt hat with a dome shape was popularized by Edward Stanley, twelfth Earl of Derby. Now it's favored by many rap singers.

guillotine: In 1789, Dr. Joseph Guillotin of France suggested beheading as a more humane way to execute people than hanging. The machine that resulted from his idea was designed by another doctor, who was actually guillotined during the French Revolution.

leotards: These tight-fitting clothes, worn by dancers and acrobats, were designed by Julius Leotard, a French gymnast, in the 1800s.

Writing a Letter

Did you know there are different kinds of letters?

Joe Consumer
P.O. Box 88
Oak Bluff, NY 10000

January 15, 2001

Customer Service
The Shop in the Swamp
101 Marsh Street
New Orleans, LA 70000

To whom it may concern:

When I was visiting New Orleans, I bought a sweatshirt at your store. It was a size XXL, but since I washed it, my sweatshirt is extra, extra small.

I feel bad. My friends thought the shirt was really cool. I really liked the alligators printed on the front, doing the swamp stomp. Now that it's shrunk, those alligators look like little salamanders.

Rather than get my money back, I'd like a new sweatshirt. How do I know that my new one won't shrink? Please advise me on your return policy.

Sincerely yours,

Joe Consumer
Joe Consumer

WRITING A BUSINESS LETTER
A letter to an official person—say, to your mayor or the head of a company—is a formal letter, and it should include your name and address, the date, the address of the person you're writing to, and an ending such as "Sincerely yours" or "Yours truly."

Dear Jenny,
My trip to Birdland today was amazing. If it flies, it's here. And I'm learning so much. I always thought birds grew from birdseeds. Wrong.
Wish you were here.
Your friend,
Polly

Jenny Lyons
354 Katz St.
Somewhere, ID
83000

	Send Money!		
Send	**Compose**	**Send Later**	**Delete**

Date: 3 July 01 13:04:17
From: Otis<otis@camp.com>
Subject: Dollar$ and cent$
To: Mom and Dad<myfamily@home.org>

Gue$$ what? I need $ome $$$. Can you $end $ome $oon?

Love and Be$t wi$he$,

Oti$:-(

WRITING TO A FRIEND
A letter to a relative or friend is informal, and you can write it any way you like. The same is true of a friendly postcard or e-mail.

TOP TEN Languages

Would you have guessed that Mandarin, the principal language of China, is the most common spoken language in the world? You may find more surprises in the chart below, which lists languages spoken in 1999 by at least 100,000,000 native speakers (those for whom the language is their first language, or mother tongue) and some of the places where each one is spoken.

LANGUAGE	WHERE SPOKEN	NATIVE SPEAKERS
Mandarin	China, Taiwan	885,000,000
Hindi	India	375,000,000
Spanish	Spain, Latin America	358,000,000
English	U.S., Canada, Britain	347,000,000
Arabic	Arabian Peninsula	211,000,000
Bengali	India, Bangladesh	210,000,000
Portuguese	Portugal, Brazil	178,000,000
Russian	Russia	165,000,000
Japanese	Japan	125,000,000
German	Germany, Austria	100,000,000

HELLO! (English)

¡HOLA! (Spanish)

KONNICHI WA! (Japanese)

LANGUAGE USED AT HOME	SPEAKERS OVER 5 YEARS OLD
1. English only	198,601,000
2. Spanish	17,339,000
3. French	1,702,000
4. German	1,547,000
5. Italian	1,309,000
6. Chinese	1,249,000
7. Tagalog	843,000
8. Polish	723,000
9. Korean	626,000
10. Vietnamese	507,000
11. Portuguese	430,000
12. Japanese	428,000
13. Greek	388,000
14. Arabic	355,000
15. Hindi, Urdu, related languages	331,000
16. Russian	242,000
17. Yiddish	213,000
18. Thai	206,000
19. Persian	202,000
20. French Creole	188,000

Which LANGUAGES Are SPOKEN in the UNITED STATES?

Since the beginning of American history, immigrants have come to the United States from all over the world and brought their native languages with them.

The table at left lists the most frequently spoken languages in the United States, as of the 1990 census, starting with English. The number for English is the number of people who speak only English at home.

PICTURE THESE

1
going in a circle

2 O / M.D. / Ph.D. / D.D.S.

3 ECNALG

4 Far   Home

5
one kind	another
one kind	another
one kind	another
one kind	another
one kind	another
one kind	another

6 DELAWARE / WASHINGTON

7 OOO CIRCUS

8 E O / C F / I F

9 HE'S/HIMSELF

10 DKI

11 R / ROADS / A / D / S

12 FRIENDS JUST FRIENDS

13 YOUR HAT / KEEP IT

14 ✔ YOUR WORK

15 HEAD / HEELS

16 LEFT / CHICKEN

Try arranging these words to make a picture puzzle: **SPLIT LEVEL**

Answers are on pages 317–320.

Law

? Where was it against the law to slurp soup?
You can find the answer on page 110.

Why Do We Need LAWS?

Did you ever wonder what your day would be like if there weren't any rules to follow? What if you could go to school any time you wanted? And what if there were no traffic lights or stop signs?

Life would be difficult and confusing without rules. We all need them.

The rules that a government makes are called laws. The government has the power to punish people who break laws. Laws vary from state to state. But all U.S. laws assume that people are innocent until proven guilty in the courts and that guilt has been proven beyond a reasonable doubt.

Laws are made to:

- Protect people from getting hurt
- **Help people do their jobs properly**
- Help people to be treated fairly
- **Help people know how to act in public**
- Protect animals, the environment, and property

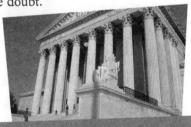

WHAT HAPPENS WHEN YOU BREAK THE LAW?

KIDS When children under 18 years old are arrested by the police, what happens next varies from state to state. Usually, they must appear in **juvenile court**, which has no jury. A judge decides whether or not there is strong enough evidence against the child and how the child should be punished or helped. Sometimes the judge lets the child go home, but still under the watch of authorities. This is called **probation**.

In other cases, a judge may decide a child should be tried as an adult in criminal court. This usually happens when a child who is at least 14 years old and has broken the law in the past is accused of a very serious crime, such as murder, robbery, arson, or gun possession. In recent years, children have been tried as adults more frequently.

ADULTS When an adult breaks the law, the offense may be minor or it may be serious. An adult who gets a parking ticket, a minor crime, may admit guilt and pay a fine or may go to court to argue against the ticket.

An adult arrested for a serious crime has to appear in court. A trial may result if the evidence against the person seems strong enough. At the trial, a government lawyer, called a **prosecutor**, presents the case against the accused person (the **defendant**) and must prove he or she is guilty "beyond a reasonable doubt." A person who is **acquitted**, or found not guilty, is free to go home. If the defendant is **convicted**, or found guilty, he or she will get a punishment, or a **sentence**, such as going to prison for a certain length of time. For very serious crimes, 38 U.S. states allow people to be sentenced to death.

LAWS that HAVEN'T STOOD the TEST of TIME

Laws change over the years. Sometimes laws that once made sense become silly. Here are some laws that have either been removed from the books or probably should be!

▶ In Mesquite, Texas, children may not wear strange haircuts.

▶ In New Jersey, slurping soup in public is forbidden.

▶ In Galveston, Texas, camels cannot freely roam the streets.

▶ In Marshalltown, Iowa, horses must not eat fire hydrants.

▶ In Oregon, dead people cannot be made to serve on a jury.

The Rights and Responsibilities of ADULTS and CHILDREN

The Constitution is the basis of all laws in the United States. Some specific rights are listed in the Bill of Rights, the first ten amendments of the Constitution. Among other rights, the Bill of Rights grants Americans freedom of religion and freedom of speech, and the right of anyone who is arrested to have a lawyer and a fair trial.

The United States is a democracy; its citizens are free to disagree with one another and with their government. This is not true in many other countries and is a great privilege. But with it comes the responsibility of being a good citizen. Adults' responsibilities include voting in elections and obeying laws, even those they disagree with. Children's responsibilities include going to school and obeying laws.

When CHILDREN Don't Have Rights:
CHILD LABOR

Like many kids, you probably have chores to do. You must go to school, just as adults go to jobs. And you have to do homework. This is all within the law and not an abuse of children's rights.

But in some parts of the world, many children between the ages of five and fifteen do not attend school. Instead, millions work in factories and fields. They may do backbreaking, often dangerous, work from early morning to late at night. The International Labor Organization (ILO) estimates that 250 million children around the world work. This is most common in Asia, Africa, and Latin America. Even in the United States, from $2\frac{1}{2}$ to $3\frac{1}{2}$ million children work. These are usually the children of migrant workers, people who move from place to place depending on the season, picking fruits and vegetables.

The families of many child laborers could not survive without the money children bring home. This poverty is a big obstacle to stopping child labor.

◀ Child worker in Peru

Money & Business

When is a mint not a candy?
You can find the answer on page 112.

HISTORY OF MONEY

WHY DID PEOPLE START USING MONEY? People first started using money in order to trade. A farmer who had cattle might want to have salt to preserve meat or cloth to make clothing. For this farmer, a cow became a "medium of exchange"—a way of getting things the farmer did not make or grow. Cattle became a form of money. Whatever people agreed to use for trade became the earliest kinds of money.

WHAT OBJECTS HAVE BEEN USED AS MONEY THROUGHOUT HISTORY? You may be surprised by some of the items that people have used every day as money. What does the form of money tell you about a society and its people?

► knives, rice, and spades in China around 3000 B.C.

► cattle and clay tablets in Babylonia around 2500 B.C.

► wampum (beads) and beaver fur by American Indians of the northeast around A.D. 1500

► tobacco by early American colonists around 1650

► whales' teeth by the Pacific peoples on the island of Fiji, until the early 1900s

WHY DID GOVERNMENTS GET INTERESTED IN ISSUING MONEY? The first government to make coins that looked alike and use them as money is thought to be the Greek city-state of Lydia in the 7th century B.C. These Lydian coins were actually bean-shaped lumps made from a mixture of gold and silver.

The first government in Europe to issue paper money that looked alike was France in the early 18th century. Governments were interested in issuing money because the money itself had value. If a government could gain control over the manufacture of money, it could increase its own wealth—often simply by making more money.

Today, money throughout the world is issued only by governments. In the United States, the Department of the Treasury and the U.S. Mint make all the paper money and coins we use. Nowadays, we also use checks and credit cards to pay for things we buy. These are not thought of as real money but more as "promises to pay."

The First Paper Money

By the time of the Middle Ages (about A.D. 800-1100), gold had become a popular medium for trade in Europe. But gold was heavy and difficult to carry, and the cities and the roads of Europe at that time were dangerous places to carry large amounts of gold. So merchants and goldsmiths began issuing notes promising to pay gold to the person carrying the note. These "promissory notes" were the beginning of paper money in Europe. Paper money was probably also invented in China, where the explorer Marco Polo saw it in the 1280s.

Making Money: THE U.S. MINT

What Is the U.S. Mint? The U.S. Mint makes all U.S. coins. It also safeguards the Treasury Department's stored gold and silver at Fort Knox, KY. The U.S. Mint was founded in 1792 and today is a part of the U.S. Treasury Department. The U.S. Mint's headquarters are in Washington, D.C. Another division of the Treasury Department—the Bureau of Engraving and Printing, also in Washington, D.C—designs and prints all U.S. paper money.

What Kinds of Coins Does the Mint Make? The U.S. Mint makes all the pennies, nickels, dimes, quarters, half dollars, and dollar coins that Americans use each day. These coins are made of a mixture of metals. For example, dimes, quarters, and half dollars look like silver but are a mixture of copper, nickel, and silver.

Where Can I Get Information About the Mint? Write to the United States Mint, Customer Service Center, 10003 Derekwood Lane, Lanham, MD 20706. Telephone: (202) 283-COIN.

Whose Portraits Are on Our Money? On the front of all U.S. paper money are portraits of presidents and other famous Americans. Presidents also appear on the most commonly used coins. Starting in 1999, five new quarters were coined each year, a practice that was scheduled to last ten years. Each quarter will feature the design of a different state on the back, with George Washington on the front. The quarters are being introduced in the same order as states entered the Union, starting with Delaware.

In January 2000, the Golden Dollar coin was issued. It features the likeness of Sacagawea, the young Shoshone woman who helped Lewis and Clark during their exploration of the Louisiana Purchase, on the front of the coin. The back shows a soaring Bald Eagle and 17 stars (one for each state in the Union at the time of the Lewis and Clark expedition).

DENOMINATION	PORTRAIT
1¢	**Abraham Lincoln**, 16th U.S. President
5¢	**Thomas Jefferson**, 3rd U.S. President
10¢	**Franklin Delano Roosevelt**, 32nd U.S. President
25¢	**George Washington**, 1st U.S. President
$1 (bill)	**George Washington**, 1st U.S. President
$1 (coin)	**Sacagawea**, Native American woman
$2	**Thomas Jefferson**, 3rd U.S. President
$5	**Abraham Lincoln**, 16th U.S. President
$10	**Alexander Hamilton**, 1st U.S. Treasury Secretary
$20	**Andrew Jackson**, 7th U.S. President
$50	**Ulysses S. Grant**, 18th U.S. President
$100	**Benjamin Franklin**, colonial inventor and U.S. patriot

PAPER MONEY In 1996 the U.S. Treasury printed a new $100 bill with many features to help prevent counterfeiting. A new $50 bill was printed in 1997, and a new $20 bill was issued in 1998. In 2000, new $10 and $5 bills were to be issued.

Read more about money at
WEB SITE *http://www.ustreas.gov/kids*

How Much MONEY Is in CIRCULATION?

As of March 31, 1999, the total amount of money in circulation in the United States came to $492,220,636,866 (about 492 billion dollars). Over 25 billion dollars was in coins, the rest in paper money. The chart below shows the number of bills of each kind in circulation.

Kind (Denomination)	Number of Bills in Circulation	Value of Money in Circulation
$1 bills	6,723,236,225	$6,723,236,225
$2 bills	584,608,768	$1,169,217,536
$5 bills	1,546,663,467	$7,733,317,335
$10 bills	1,353,493,806	$13,534,938,060
$20 bills	4,351,869,983	$87,037,399,660
$50 bills	998,342,803	$49,917,140,150
$100 bills	3,257,894,018	$325,789,401,800
$500 bills	287,515	$143,757,500
$1,000 bills	167,033	$167,033,000
$5,000 bills	351	$1,755,000
$10,000 bills	344	$3,440,000

What Are EXCHANGE RATES?

When one country exports goods to another, the payment from the country buying the goods must be changed into the currency of the country selling them. An exchange rate is the price of one currency in terms of another. For example, 1 U.S. dollar could buy about 6½ French francs in 2000.

WHAT A DOLLAR BOUGHT		
COUNTRY	IN 1970	IN 2000
France	6 francs	6½ francs
Germany	3⅗ marks	2 marks
Great Britain	⅖ pound	⅗ pound
Italy	600 lire	1,900 lire
Japan	350 yen	102 yen

The chart at right compares the exchange rates in 1970 and 2000 between the U.S. dollar and the currency of five of the country's biggest trading partners. The more foreign money the dollar can buy, the better the exchange rate for Americans.

$5 — United States

510 Yen — Japan

DID YOU KNOW?

In early February 2000, the U.S. economy set a new record for uninterrupted expansion—107 months. That broke the old record of 106 months, set in the 1960s.

Why BUDGETS Are Helpful

A budget is a plan that estimates how much money a person, a business, or a government will receive during a particular period of time, how much money will be spent and what it will be spent on, and how much money will be left over (if any).

A Family Budget

Does your family have a budget? Do you know what your family spends money on? Do you know where your family's income comes from? The chart below shows some sources of income and typical yearly expenses for a family's budget.

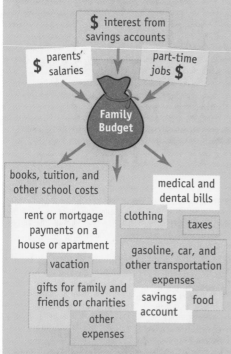

$ interest from savings accounts

$ parents' salaries

part-time jobs $

Family Budget

books, tuition, and other school costs

medical and dental bills

rent or mortgage payments on a house or apartment

clothing

taxes

vacation

gasoline, car, and other transportation expenses

gifts for family and friends or charities

savings account

food

other expenses

A Balanced Budget

A budget is **balanced** when the amount of money you receive equals the amount of money you spend. A budget is **in deficit** when the amount of money you spend is greater than the amount of money you have.

Making Your Own Budget

Imagine that you are given a weekly allowance of $10. With this money you must pay for things like snacks and magazines and also try to save up for special things. A budget will help you plan how to do this. Here are examples of items you might want to put in your budget:

Possible Purchases and Cost:
Snacks: $.75 each
Video movie rental: $3.00
Magazine: $2.00

Savings:
For gifts: $.50–$3.00
For something special for yourself
(like a basketball, a compact disc, a computer game, or concert tickets): $1.00 or more.

On the lines below, list the items you want along with their price. You may also add any other items that interest you—and their prices. And don't forget to include any money you want to save.

Item   **Amount**

_____

_____

_____

Savings _____

Now total all your
purchases and savings: _____

Is your budget balanced? Is the amount you plan to spend and save equal to the amount of your "income" ($10)? If not, try to reduce your planned savings or spending to make your budget balance.

THE U.S. BUDGET

The U.S. government also has a budget. It gets, and spends, lots of money.

WHERE DOES THE U.S. GOVERNMENT GET MONEY?

Here is how the U.S. government got its money in the 1999 budget year.

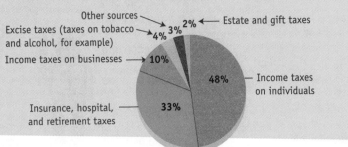

Other sources
Excise taxes (taxes on tobacco and alcohol, for example) — 4%
Income taxes on businesses → 10%
Other sources — 3% 2% ← Estate and gift taxes
48% — Income taxes on individuals
Insurance, hospital, and retirement taxes — 33%

WHERE DOES THE U.S. GOVERNMENT SPEND MONEY?

Here is how the U.S. government spent its money in the 1999 budget year.

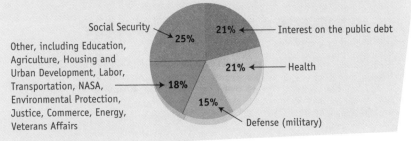

Social Security — 25%
21% ← Interest on the public debt
Other, including Education, Agriculture, Housing and Urban Development, Labor, Transportation, NASA, Environmental Protection, Justice, Commerce, Energy, Veterans Affairs → 18%
21% ← Health
15%
Defense (military)

FROM DEFICIT TO SURPLUS

Every year from 1969 to 1997 the government spent more money than it took in. This gap is called the **budget deficit.** Most economists say that paying interest on a large debt hurts the economy. Fortunately, the budget deficit has been going down since 1993. This is partly because people and companies have been making more money and thus paying more taxes. In 1998, the U.S. began to have a **budget surplus—it took in more than it spent.** In 1999 it had the biggest surplus since 1951.

YEAR	$ TAKEN IN	$ SPENT	DEFICIT
1993	$1.153 trillion	$1.408 trillion	$–255 billion
1994	$1.257 trillion	$1.460 trillion	$–203 billion
1995	$1.350 trillion	$1.514 trillion	$–164 billion
1996	$1.453 trillion	$1.560 trillion	$–107 billion
1997	$1.579 trillion	$1.602 trillion	$–23 billion
1998	$1.721 trillion	$1.651 trillion	$70 billion (surplus)
1999	$1.827 trillion	$1.705 trillion	$122 billion (surplus)

What Do AMERICANS BUY?

The chart below shows how Americans spent their money in 1998.

CATEGORY	AMOUNT SPENT
Medical and dental care	$1,032,300,000,000
Food and tobacco	$907,400,000,000
Housing	$855,900,000,000
Transportation expenses (such as cars, gasoline, and train, bus, and plane tickets)	$647,400,000,000
Household expenses (such as telephone, furniture, electricity, kitchen supplies)	$646,500,000,000
Personal business expenses (such as bank charges, lawyers)	$528,600,000,000
Recreation (such as books, magazines, toys, videos, sports events, amusement parks)	$494,700,000,000
Clothing and jewelry	$367,900,000,000
Religious and charitable contributions	$163,500,000,000
School tuition and other educational expenses	$139,200,000,000
Personal care (such as haircuts, health clubs)	$80,500,000,000

WHO OWNS WHAT?

During the 1990s, many companies bought other companies.

THIS COMPANY	BOUGHT THIS COMPANY	IN	MAIN TYPE OF BUSINESS
MCI WorldCom	Sprint	1999	telecommunications
Viacom	CBS	1999	entertainment
Daimler-Benz	Chrysler	1998	automobiles
British Petroleum	Amoco	1998	petroleum
Bell Atlantic	NYNEX	1997	telecommunications
Boeing	McDonnell Douglas	1997	airplanes
Walt Disney	Capital Cities/ABC	1996	entertainment
Time	Warner Communications	1990	magazines/entertainment

WHAT DO BUSINESSES TAKE IN?

Here is what some leading businesses took in during 1999.

AIRPLANES
Boeing, $57,993,000,000

BANKS
Bank of America, $51,392,000,000

BEVERAGES
PepsiCo, $20,367,000,000

CARS, MOTOR VEHICLES
General Motors, $189,058,000,000

CLOTHING
Nike, $8,777,000,000

COMPUTERS AND OFFICE EQUIPMENT
IBM, $87,548,000,000

ENTERTAINMENT
Time Warner, $27,333,000,000

FOOD AND DRUG STORES
Kroger, $45,352,000,000

INDUSTRIAL AND FARM EQUIPMENT
Caterpillar, $19,702,000,000

MEDICINES AND DRUGS
Merck, $32,714,000,000

RETAIL STORES
Wal-Mart Stores, $166,809,000,000

SOAPS AND COSMETICS
Procter & Gamble, $38,125,000,000

TELECOMMUNICATIONS
AT&T, $62,391,000,000

TOYS, SPORTING GOODS
Mattel, $5,515,000,000

What Do You Want to Be?

The way we work has been changing. Some people, for example, never go into an office. They work at home with the help of computers, fax machines, and telephones. Other people, including some teachers, share jobs. And still others have the same job they've always had—but with new or different responsibilities.

Here are just a few of the new or changing jobs reported by the U.S. Department of Labor. Do you think any of them will interest you when you're ready to start your career? What skills do you think you'll need?

ADMINISTRATIVE ASSISTANTS

Administrative assistants (AAs) typically have more responsibilities than secretaries, and provide a high level of support to executive staff. AAs may have office management functions (working with payroll, budget, or personnel records), may also work independently on research and other projects, and may supervise or assign tasks to clerks and others.

Bankruptcy Specialists

Many individuals and companies declare bankruptcy when they owe more money than they earn. These specialists may work for banks or companies to whom money is owed, or for lawyers, or they may represent the bankrupt party.

COMPUTER MANAGERS

Just about any job to do with computers is hot—and likely to stay that way. Managers help companies set up computer networks, train employees, keep systems secure, and last but not least, come to the rescue of those whose machines have crashed.

Consumer Credit Counselors

These are the people to see for advice on how to save money and budget for the future, how to help pay for a new home or business, or how to repay money that is owed.

CONVENTION MANAGERS

They arrange meetings and conferences. They deal with vendors, people whose products and services are needed to make a meeting work.

Development Directors

The U.S. government has cut back on the amount of money it gives to non-profit organizations, so these professional fundraisers are badly needed.

ENVIRONMENTAL ENGINEERS

As laws to clean up the environment become more important and more complicated, experts are needed to make sure companies are following them. These engineers and scientists may also be involved in finding ways to get rid of dangerous materials or watching out for the safety of people at work.

JOB COACHES

People who were on welfare and are going to work need training. So do some people who have disabilities. Coaches teach job duties, give advice, and solve job-related problems for the people with whom they work.

Web Masters

Who writes the computer codes needed to publish or update the content of Internet Web sites? Web masters do. They also design Web sites and keep them up-to-date.

What the U.S. Buys and Sells

When companies or countries buy and sell their products or services to other companies or countries, we call this trade. Exports are goods that one country **sells** to another country. Imports are goods that one country **buys** from another country. The United States trades with many other countries, both importing and exporting goods.

EXPORTS ◄ 🇺🇸

Electrical machinery	$65.6 billion
Motor vehicles	$53.5 billion
Farm products	$50.7 billion
Airplanes and parts	$50.3 billion
Computers and office machinery	$40.7 billion

IMPORTS ► 🇺🇸

Motor vehicles	$119.7 billion
Electrical machinery	$79.4 billion
Computers and office machinery	$76.8 billion
Clothing	$53.7 billion
Crude oil	$37.3 billion

WHAT DOES THE UNITED STATES SELL TO OTHER COUNTRIES? The chart above shows some of the major products that the United States exported in 1999. In 1999, the total value of all U.S. exports was $682.1 billion.

WHAT DOES THE UNITED STATES BUY FROM OTHER COUNTRIES? The chart above shows some of the major products that the United States imported in 1999. Note that the United States exports *and* imports motor vehicles. In 1999, the total value of all U.S. imports was $991.9 billion.

WHO ARE AMERICA'S LEADING TRADING PARTNERS? In 1999, the countries with which the United States traded most were: Canada, Japan, Mexico, Germany, China, and Great Britain.

WHY DO AMERICANS BUY FOREIGN-MADE PRODUCTS? Americans buy products from abroad that they do not make for themselves or that are less expensive or better made than products made in the United States. For example, the United States imports most of its clothing partly because foreign-made products are less costly.

WHAT HAPPENS IF A COUNTRY IMPORTS MORE THAN IT EXPORTS? When the United States sells to other countries (or exports), other countries pay the United States for the goods. When the United States buys from other countries (or imports), it makes payments to them. It is best for a country to export more than it imports, or to export and import an equal amount. When a country imports more than it exports, it has what is called a **trade deficit**. The United States imports more than it exports and has a trade deficit. That means it is spending more money abroad for foreign-made products than it is getting from selling American-made products overseas.

MONEY TALK
AN ECONOMICS GLOSSARY

bear market a time when the value of most stocks goes down.

bubble economy an economy in which certain possessions, such as real estate or stocks, are valued for more than they're worth. This can lead to temporary increases in wealth, then sharp decreases.

bull market a time when the value of most stocks goes up.

cost of living the average cost of the basic needs of life, including food, clothing, housing, medical care, and other services.

inflation an increase in the level of prices.

interest money a borrower pays to borrow money. When you open a savings account, the bank borrows from you and pays you interest.

labor union a group of workers in one company, industry, or area who agree to act together to increase wages and improve working conditions. Labor unions sometimes hold strikes to try to make an employer meet their demands.

mutual fund an investment fund that pools the money of many investors to buy shares in a variety of companies.

salary the payment an employer gives an employee for the work he or she performs.

stock a share in a corporation, representing partial ownership. A corporation sells shares to individuals or other companies to raise money. The shares may increase or decrease in value. When the company makes a profit, it may pay stockholders a "dividend," or part of its earnings.

strike stopping of work, by employees of a company, as a way of forcing their employer to meet their demands. Workers often strike for higher salaries or more job security.

taxes money that a government collects from people to pay for the programs and services it provides.

trade barriers obstacles put in place to limit how many goods come into a country from other countries (imports) or leave a country (exports). Two barriers that are often used are:

▶ tariffs, which are a tax on imports

▶ quotas, which are a set limit on goods that can be traded

unemployment being without a job. People who lose or quit their jobs, or who are unable to find jobs, are unemployed.

unemployment rate percentage of the work force that is looking for, but cannot find, work.

Movies, Videos & TV

? What recent movie has the voices of both Tom Hanks and Jodi Benson? You can find the answer on page 121.

Haley Joel Osment and Bruce Willis in The Sixth Sense ▶

20 MOVIE HITS of 1999-2000

Toy Story 2 (G)
Tarzan (G)
Pokémon: The First Movie (G)
The Straight Story (G)
The Cup (G)
Star Wars: Episode I—
The Phantom Menace (PG)
Stuart Little (PG)
Inspector Gadget (PG)
You've Got Mail (PG)
Bicentennial Man (PG)
My Favorite Martian (PG)
October Sky (PG)
The Iron Giant (PG)
Dudley Do-Right (PG)
A Dog of Flanders (PG)
Runaway Bride (PG)
Notting Hill (PG-13)
Never Been Kissed (PG-13)
Music of the Heart (PG-13)
The Sixth Sense (PG-13)

20 Popular KIDS' VIDEOS of 1999

Lion King II: Simba's Pride
Mulan
Lady and the Tramp
Mary-Kate & Ashley: Billboard Dad
Pokémon : I Choose You, Pikachu
The Rugrats Movie
101 Dalmatians
The Little Mermaid: The Special Edition
Pokémon: Pokey Friends
Batman Beyond
The King and I
Scooby-Doo on Zombie Island
Anastasia
Hercules
The Best of the Simpsons: Vol. 4
A Bug's Life
Antz
Dr. Dolittle
The Prince of Egypt
The Parent Trap

Some Popular MOVIES

Frankenstein (1931) Boris Karloff's scary makeup started a new era of horror movies.

King Kong (1933) Sixty years before *Jurassic Park*, King Kong, a giant ape, fought dinosaurs on a mysterious island. Captured by humans, he ended up battling civilization in New York City.

The Wizard of Oz (1939) As color was introduced into movies, Dorothy, played by Judy Garland, met a scarecrow, a tin woodsman, and a cowardly lion in the colorful land of Oz.

Gone With the Wind (1939) A massive movie set was destroyed to re-create the burning of Atlanta during the Civil War.

Anchors Aweigh (1945) Gene Kelly, a human actor, delighted audiences by dancing with Jerry, a famous cartoon mouse.

20,000 Leagues Under the Sea (1954) Giant squid were among the scary features of this sci-fi film. It was shown on a larger, wider movie screen that film producers used to lure audiences away from a new small-screen invention: television.

Tron (1982) For the first time, computer-generated images were used to create pictures in a movie.

Jurassic Park (1993) Computer-generated dinosaurs looked and sounded very real as they thrilled audiences around the world.

TOY STORY 2

NEW ADVENTURES FOR BUZZ AND WOODY

Toy Story was a big hit at the movies and went on to sell more than 22 million videocassettes in the United States alone. So it's no surprise that *Toy Story 2*, a sequel, was made.

The original *Toy Story*, released in 1995, was produced entirely on computer and was the first animated movie to be nominated for best screenplay written directly for the screen. Animation for a movie like this takes a lot of patience: a week of efforts by animators may result in just four or five seconds of usable film. But the work paid off.

In *Toy Story 2*, Andy, the boy who owns Buzz Lightyear, Woody, and the other toys, goes away to camp. While he's gone, Woody is kidnapped by a toy collector who knows he is a valuable toy from a 1950s TV show. Buzz, Mr. Potato Head, and Andy's other toys race to rescue Woody before Andy returns.

Some of the actors who provided the voices of the toys in the first *Toy Story* are back in the sequel. Tom Hanks again plays Woody, and Tim Allen is back as Buzz Lightyear. Among the new actors is Jodi Benson, the voice of the Little Mermaid, as Barbie. Wayne Knight, who played Newman on *Seinfeld* and now appears on *3rd Rock From the Sun*, is Al, the toy collector.

TELEVISION RATINGS

Since 1997 the television industry has used ratings to help parents choose programs that are OK for kids to watch. The ratings shown here may be followed by another letter such as (V) for violence or (L) for bad language.

TV-Y For all children—including those age 6 or younger.

TV-Y7 For children over age 6, especially those who can tell the difference between what is real and what is make-believe.

TV-G General audience—suitable for all ages. Program has little or no violence.

TV-PG Parental guidance suggested. Program may contain violence or bad language.

TV-14 Parents strongly warned. Program contains very violent or adult material.

TV-M For adults—program may not be suitable for children under 17.

Popular TV SHOWS in 1999-2000

(Source: Nielsen Media Research)

AGES 6-11

1. Wonderful World of Disney
2. Sabrina, the Teenage Witch
3. Malcolm in the Middle
4. Who Wants to Be a Millionaire (Sun.)
5. Odd Man Out

AGES 12-17

1. Malcolm in the Middle
2. The Simpsons
4. WWF Smackdown!
4. Who Wants to Be a Millionaire (Sun.)
5. Sabrina, the Teenage Witch

POPULAR VIDEO GAMES IN 1999

Pokémon Blue—Game Boy
Pokémon Red—Game Boy
Pokémon Yellow—Game Boy
Donkey Kong 64—Nintendo 64
Pokémon—Pinball-Game Boy

Pokémon Snap—Nintendo 64
Gran Turismo—Playstation
Super Smash Brothers—Nintendo
Driver—Playstation
Spyro the Dragon—Playstation

 DiD You KNOW?

Linwood Boomer, the creator of *Malcolm in the Middle,* acted on the TV series *Little House on the Prairie.* He played Adam Kendall, Mary Ingalls's husband. Before he created *Malcolm in the Middle,* Boomer wrote episodes of *3rd Rock From the Sun.*

PEOPLE TO KNOW

FRANKIE MUNIZ

For Frankie Muniz, 2000 was a big year, the year his career took off. As the star of *Malcolm in the Middle* on Fox, he's had rave reviews for playing the genius son in an oddball family. A TV magazine called him a "TV heavyweight." A news magazine said he's "irresistible" in "one of those rare shows that appeal equally to kids and parents."

When Frankie starred in the movie *My Dog Skip*, one newspaper review said he might become "the first child media sensation of the new century." The reviewer even said Frankie is almost as hard to resist as Skip is. (Skip is one *very* cute dog, so that's a real compliment!)

Born on December 5, 1985, in Ridgewood, New Jersey, Frankie Muniz spent his childhood performing in local productions of plays like *A Christmas Carol, The Sound of Music,* and *The Wizard of Oz.* He also appeared in TV movies, feature films, commercials, and TV series such as *Spin City* and *Sabrina the Teenage Witch.*

Frankie knows being a successful child actor may have its problems. "I know that some kids who are on TV and stuff wind up in trouble, but I'm not gonna be like that," he told one person interviewing him. He keeps his fame in perspective by hanging out with neighborhood friends, skateboarding, and playing basketball and baseball.

NATALIE PORTMAN

Who is Natalie Portman? That's not so easy to find out. She doesn't give a lot of interviews. In fact, she values her privacy so much she changed her last name for her work as an actress, and isn't telling her real name. Here's what the *WAK 2001* learned about this secretive star.

Although Natalie Portman started out as a pre-teen clothes model, she really wanted to be an actress. She got her wish. She's been in several movies, but the highlight of her career—for her—was to play Anne Frank in a famous Broadway play, *The Diary of Anne Frank.* It was her dream role. To have the time to do it, she turned down a movie offer from Robert Redford. To most of her fans, though, Natalie is probably best known as Queen Amidala in *Star Wars: Episode One—The Phantom Menace.* She plans to return in the next two Star Wars movies. In the meantime, Natalie is concentrating on her studies at Harvard University.

Born in Jerusalem, Israel, on June 9, 1981, Natalie has lived in Washington, D.C., and Connecticut. She went to high school in New York, where she earned a straight-A average. Even then she knew what was most important to her. "I'm going to college," she said. "I don't care if it ruins my career. I'd rather be smart than a movie star." It looks as if Natalie will continue to be both.

Museums

? What kind of museum has life-size models of dinosaur fossils, coal mines, and whales?
You can find the answer on page 125.

"TEMPLES of the MUSES"

Museums are great places to learn new things and have fun at the same time. The word *museum* comes from a Greek word that means "temple of the Muses." The Muses were the goddesses of art and science.

The oldest museum in the U.S. is The Charleston Museum, founded in South Carolina in 1773. The U.S. now has more than 8,300 museums. A few are listed here. For others, see the Index.

KIDS' MUSEUMS

The *Official Museum Directory* lists thousands of museums. You can also check out the Association of Youth Museums on the Internet at
WEB SITE *http://www.aym.org*

The Children's Museum, Boston, Massachusetts. Has a full-size Japanese house, a Latino market, plus displays on Native Americans.
WEB SITE *http://www.bostonkids.org*

The Children's Museum of Indianapolis, Indianapolis, Indiana. Has natural science exhibits, including a walk-through limestone cave; computer center; and an old-fashioned railway depot with a 19th-century locomotive.
WEB SITE *http://www.childrensmuseum.org*

Children's Museum of Los Angeles, Los Angeles, California. Exhibits on health and city life; has a TV studio.
WEB SITE *http://www.lacm.org*

Children's Museum of Manhattan, New York, New York. Hands-on displays of interest to kids on natural history, science, and art.
WEB SITE *http://www.cmom.org*

Children's Museum, Portland, Oregon. Hands-on displays allow kids 10 and under to shop for dinner, prepare a feast, or create with clay.
WEB SITE *http://www.pdxchildrensmuseum.org*

Museums of Natural History

Museums of natural history contain exhibits of things found in nature. These include animals, rocks, and fossils. Natural history museums allow you close-up looks at life-size models of coal mines, dinosaurs, desert and prairie life, or even whales.

The Academy of Natural Sciences, Philadelphia, Pennsylvania

American Museum of Natural History, New York, New York

Carnegie Museum of Natural History, Pittsburgh, Pennsylvania

Denver Museum of Natural History, Denver, Colorado

The Field Museum, Chicago, Illinois

Harvard Museum of Natural History, Cambridge, Massachusetts

Museum of the Rockies, Bozeman, Montana

National Museum of Natural History, Smithsonian Institution, Washington, D.C.

New Mexico Museum of Natural History and Science, Albuquerque, New Mexico

University of Nebraska State Museum, Lincoln, Nebraska

Historic Restorations

These houses or parts of cities or towns have been restored to look the way they did many years ago.

California Indian Museum & Cultural Center
San Francisco, California — A look at Indian history; opened in 1996 on the site of land taken from local tribes.

Lower East Side Tenement Museum
New York City — See how immigrants lived in the mid-1800s.

Colonial Williamsburg
Williamsburg, Virginia — A restored 18th-century capital (see photo above).

Mystic Seaport
Mystic, Connecticut — Re-creation of a New England whaling village, including ships and a museum.

Plimoth Plantation
Plymouth, Massachusetts — Re-creation of the Pilgrims' first settlement in the New World.

St. Augustine Historic District
St. Augustine, Florida — Includes the Oldest House (Gonzalez-Alvarez House), from the 1600s.

Museums of the Performing Arts

Contemporary Arts Center, New Orleans, Louisiana • Home to plays, music and dance performances, art, video, sculpture.

Country Music Hall of Fame and Museum, Nashville, Tennessee • Celebrates country music's history and stars.

Museum of Television & Radio, New York, New York • Contains more than 100,000 TV and radio programs from the 1920s to the present.

Rock and Roll Hall of Fame and Museum, Cleveland, Ohio • Chronicles rock's influence.

The Music House Museum, Acme, Michigan • A collection of musical instruments, juke boxes, radios, and other music machines from the past.

ETHNIC MUSEUMS

These museums show the culture and history of different groups.

Freer Gallery of Art and Arthur M. Sackler Gallery, Washington, D.C. • Displays art from China, Japan, India, and other Asian countries.

California African American Museum, Los Angeles, California • Displays art, books, and photographs on African-American culture.

The Heard Museum, Phoenix, Arizona • Displays art by Native Americans, primarily from the Southwestern U.S.

The University of Texas Institute of Texan Cultures, San Antonio, Texas • Shows material from 27 ethnic groups.

The Jewish Museum, New York, New York • Has exhibits covering 40 centuries of Jewish history and culture.

Museum of African American History, Detroit, Michigan • Features a large model of a slave ship, inventions by African Americans, music by black composers, and the space suit worn by the first U.S. black female astronaut.

National Museum of the American Indian, New York, New York • Has displays on the ways of life and the history of Native Americans.

DID YOU KNOW?

Find out about many of the pioneers who built the American West at the **National Cowboy Hall of Fame & Western Heritage Center**. It's at 1700 NE 63rd Street in Oklahoma City, Oklahoma.

WEB SITE http://www.cowboyhalloffame.org

American Museum of Natural History

New York, New York

The American Museum of Natural History, the largest of its kind in the world, recently expanded in a big way by opening the Rose Center for Earth and Space. The expanded Hayden Planetarium inside shows three-dimensional images of the Milky Way galaxy pulled from a database of more than two billion stars. The Rose Center also has a Hall of the Universe and a Hall of Planet Earth. They help explain how our galaxy evolved and how life formed on this planet. The museum also has more than 600 fossils of vertebrate animals, including the world's biggest exhibit of dinosaur fossils.

? **What kind of music did Muddy Waters play?**
You can find the answer on page 128.

MUSICAL INSTRUMENTS

There are many kinds of musical instruments. Instruments in an orchestra are divided into four groups, or sections: string, woodwind, brass, and percussion.

PERCUSSION INSTRUMENTS

Percussion instruments make sounds when they are struck. The most common percussion instrument is the drum. Others include cymbals, triangles, gongs, bells, and xylophone. Keyboard instruments, like the piano, are sometimes thought of as percussion instruments.

BRASSES

Brass instruments are hollow inside. They make sounds when air is blown into a mouthpiece shaped like a cup or a funnel. The trumpet, French horn, trombone, and tuba are brasses.

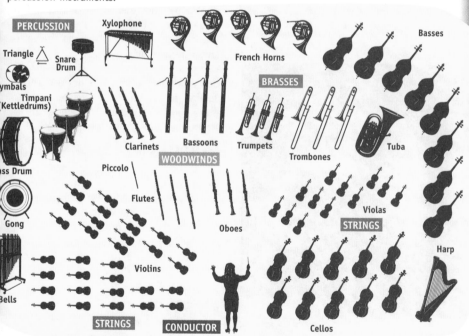

WOODWINDS

Woodwind instruments are long and round and hollow inside. They make sounds when air is blown into them through a mouth hole or a reed. The clarinet, flute, oboe, bassoon, and piccolo are woodwinds.

STRINGS

Stringed instruments make sounds when the strings are either stroked with a bow or plucked with the fingers. The violin, viola, cello, bass, and harp are used in an orchestra. The guitar, banjo, and mandolin are other stringed instruments.

MUSIC and MUSIC MAKERS

▶**POP** Pop music (short for popular music) puts more emphasis on melody (tune) than does rock and has a softer beat.
Famous pop singers: Frank Sinatra, Barbra Streisand, Whitney Houston, Madonna, Michael Jackson, Mariah Carey, Boyz II Men, Brandy, Celine Dion.

▶**RAP AND HIP-HOP** In rap, words are spoken or chanted at a fast pace, backed by hip-hop music that emphasizes rhythm rather than melody. Rap was created by African-Americans in inner cities. The lyrics show strong feelings and may be about anger and violence. Hip-hop includes "samples," which are pieces of music from other songs.
Famous rappers: Coolio, LL Cool J, TLC, The Fugees, Snoop Dogg, Will Smith.

▶**JAZZ** Jazz has its roots in the work songs, spirituals, and folk music of African-Americans. It began in the South in the early 1900s.
Famous jazz artists: Louis Armstrong, Fats Waller, Jelly Roll Morton, Duke Ellington, Benny Goodman, Billie Holiday, Sarah Vaughan, Ella Fitzgerald, Dizzy Gillespie, Charlie Parker, Miles Davis, John Coltrane, Thelonious Monk, Wynton Marsalis.

▶**ROCK** (ALSO KNOWN AS ROCK 'N' ROLL) Rock music, which started in the 1950s, is based on black rhythm and blues and country music. It often uses electronic instruments and equipment. Folk rock, punk, heavy metal, and alternative music are types of rock music.
Famous rock musicians: Elvis Presley, Bob Dylan, Chuck Berry, The Beatles, Janis Joplin, The Rolling Stones, Joni Mitchell, Bruce Springsteen, Pearl Jam, Alanis Morissette, Jewel, Kid Rock, Smash Mouth.

▶**BLUES** The music called "the blues" developed from work songs and religious folk songs (spirituals) sung by African-Americans. It was introduced early in the 1900s by African-American musicians. Blues songs are usually sad. (A type of jazz is also called "the blues.")
Famous blues performers: Ma Rainey, Bessie Smith, Billie Holiday, Buddy Guy, B. B. King, Muddy Waters.

Britney Spears ▼

TOP ALBUMS OF 1999

1 *Millennium,* Backstreet Boys

2 *. . . Baby One More Time,* Britney Spears

3 *Come on Over,* Shania Twain

4 *'N Sync,* 'N Sync

5 *Ricky Martin,* Ricky Martin

6 *Double Live,* Garth Brooks

7 *Americana,* The Offspring

8 *Wide Open Spaces,* Dixie Chicks

9 *Significant Other,* Limp Bizkit

10 *Fanmail,* TLC

►**COUNTRY** American country music is based on Southern mountain music. Blues, jazz, and other musical styles have also influenced it. Country music became popular through the *Grand Ole Opry* radio show in Nashville, Tennessee, during the 1920s.
Famous country artists: Hank Williams, Dolly Parton, Willie Nelson, Garth Brooks, Vince Gill, Reba McEntire, Shania Twain.

►**CLASSICAL** Often more complex than other types of music, classical music is based on European musical traditions that go back several hundred years. Common forms of classical music include the symphony, chamber music, opera, and ballet music.
Famous early classical composers: Johann Sebastian Bach, Ludwig van Beethoven, Johannes Brahms, Franz Joseph Haydn, Wolfgang Amadeus Mozart, Franz Schubert, Peter Ilyich Tchaikovsky.
Famous modern classical composers: Aaron Copland, Virgil Thomson, Charles Ives, Igor Stravinsky.

►**OPERA** An opera is a play whose words are sung to music. The music is played by an orchestra. The words of an opera are called the libretto, and a long song sung by one character (like a speech in a play) is called an aria.
Famous operas: *Madama Butterfly* (Giacomo Puccini); *Aida* (Giuseppe Verdi); *Porgy and Bess* (George Gershwin).

SYMPHONY
A symphony is music written for an orchestra. The parts of a symphony are called movements.

Rock and Roll
HALL OF FAME
The Rock and Roll Hall of Fame and Museum, located in Cleveland, Ohio, honors rock-and-roll musicians with exhibits and multi-media presentations. Musicians cannot be included until 25 years after their first record. Eric Clapton, Bonnie Raitt, and James Taylor were among the performers to be added in 2000.

►**CHAMBER**
Chamber music is written for a small group of musicians, often only three (a trio) or four (a quartet), to play together. In chamber music, each instrument plays a separate part. A **string quartet** (music written for two violins, viola, and cello) is an example of chamber music. Other instruments, such as a piano, are sometimes part of a chamber group.

VOICE
Human voices have a range in pitch from low to high. For men, the low end is called the bass (pronounced like base), followed by baritone, and tenor. The range for women goes from alto (the lowest) up to mezzo-soprano and soprano. The next time you listen to a singer, try to figure out his or her range.

MUSICAL NOTATION
These are some of the symbols composers use when they write music.

treble clef	𝄞
bass clef	𝄢
sharp	♯
flat	♭
natural	♮
whole note	𝅝
half note	𝅗𝅥
quarter note	♩
eighth note	♪
sixteenth note	𝅘𝅥𝅯
whole rest	𝄻
half rest	𝄼

DANCE

Dancers perform patterns of movement, usually to music or rhythm. Dance may be a form of art, or part of a religious ceremony. Or it may be done just as entertainment.

▶**BALLET** Ballet is a kind of dance based on formal steps. The movements are often graceful and flowing. Ballets are almost always danced to music. They are performed for an audience and often tell a story. In the 15th century, ballet was part of the elaborate entertainment performed for the rulers of Europe. In the 1600s, professional dance companies existed, but without women; women's parts were danced by men wearing masks. In the 1700s dancers wore bulky costumes and shoes with high heels. Women danced in hoopskirts— and so did men! In the 1800s ballet steps and costumes began to look the way they do now. Many of the most popular ballets today date back to the middle or late 1800s.

▶**BALLROOM DANCING**
Ballroom, or social, dancing involves dances done for fun by ordinary people. Social dancing has been around since at least the Middle Ages, when it was popular at fairs and festivals. In the 1400s social dance was part of fancy court pageants. It developed into dainty ballroom dances like the minuet and the waltz during the 1700s. More recent new dances include the Charleston, lindy, twist, and tango, as well as disco dancing, break dancing, line dancing, and dances such as the macarena and electric slide.

SOME FAMOUS BALLETS

Swan Lake. First danced in St. Petersburg, Russia, in 1895. Perhaps the most popular ballet ever, *Swan Lake* is the story of a prince and his love for a maiden who was turned into a swan by an evil magician.

The Nutcracker. When this ballet was first performed in St. Petersburg in 1892, it was a flop. It has since become so popular that it is danced in many places every year at holiday time in December.

Jewels. This ballet by the American choreographer George Balanchine was first performed in New York City in 1967. In *Jewels*, the dancers do not dance to a story. They explore patterns and movement of the human body.

The River. This 1970 ballet by Alvin Ailey is danced to music by the jazz musician Duke Ellington. It has been described as a celebration of life.

▶**MODERN DANCE** Modern dance differs from classical ballet. It is often less concerned with graceful, flowing movement and with stories. Modern dance steps are often not performed in traditional ballet. Dancers may put their bodies into awkward, angular positions and turn their backs on the audience. Many modern dances are based on ancient art, such as Greek sculpture, or on dance styles found in Africa and Asia.

▶**FOLK DANCE** Folk dance is the term for a dance that is passed on from generation to generation and is part of the culture or way of life of people from a particular country or ethnic group. Virginia reel (American), czardas (Hungarian), jig, and the Israeli hora are some folk dances.

American Musicals

American musicals are plays known for their lively music, dancing and singing, comedy, colorful costumes, and elaborate stage sets. Tony (Antoinette Perry) Awards are given every year to outstanding Broadway plays. (Broadway is the theater district of New York City, which includes the street named Broadway and several blocks around Times Square.) Some famous Broadway musicals are listed below. The date after the name of the play is the year it opened on Broadway.

Annie (1977), by Charles Strouse and Martin Charnin. Tony Award 1977.

Annie Get Your Gun (1946), by Irving Berlin.

Anything Goes (1930), by Cole Porter.

Beauty and the Beast (1994), by Alan Menken, Howard Ashman, and Tim Rice.

Bring in 'da Noise, Bring in 'da Funk (1996), by George C. Wolfe, Savion Glover, Daryl Waters, Zane Mark, and Ann Duquesnay.

Carousel (1945), by Richard Rodgers and Oscar Hammerstein II.

Cats (1982), by Andrew Lloyd Webber. Tony Award 1983.

A Chorus Line (1975), by Marvin Hamlisch and Edward Kleban. Tony Award 1976.

Evita (1979), by Andrew Lloyd Webber and Tim Rice. Tony Award 1980.

Fiddler on the Roof (1964), by Jerry Bock and Sheldon Harnick. Tony Award 1965.

Grease (1972), by Jim Jacobs and Warren Casey.

Hello, Dolly! (1964), by Jerry Herman. Tony Award 1964.

The King and I (1952), by Richard Rodgers and Oscar Hammerstein II. Tony Award 1952.

Kiss Me Kate (1948), by Cole Porter. Tony Award 1949.

The Lion King (1997), by Elton John, Tim Rice, Mark Mancina, Roger Allers, and Irene Meechi. Tony Award 1998.

The Music Man (1957), by Meredith Willson. Tony Award 1958.

My Fair Lady (1956), by Alan Jay Lerner and Frederick Loewe. Tony Award 1957.

Oklahoma! (1943), by Richard Rodgers and Oscar Hammerstein II.

The Pajama Game (1954), by Richard Adler and Jerry Ross. Tony Award 1955.

Rent (1996), by Jonathan Larson. Tony Award 1996.

Show Boat (1927), by Jerome Kern and Oscar Hammerstein II.

The Sound of Music (1959), by Richard Rodgers and Oscar Hammerstein II. Tony Award 1960.

South Pacific (1949), by Richard Rodgers and Oscar Hammerstein II. Tony Award 1950.

West Side Story (1957), by Leonard Bernstein and Stephen Sondheim.

Nations

? If you had 543,000 lira in Turkey, how many dollars would they be worth?
You can find the answer on page 151.

NATIONS of the WORLD

There are 193 nations in the world (including East Timor, formerly part of Indonesia, now on the way to full independence). The information for each of them goes across two pages. The left page gives the **name** and **capital** of each nation, its **location**, and its **area**. On the right page, the **population** column tells how many people lived in each country in 1999. The **currency** column shows the name of each nation's money and how much one United States dollar was worth there at the start of 2000. This column also shows which countries in Europe now use the euro, a shared currency, for some purposes. One euro was worth about one U.S. dollar in early 2000. The **language** column gives official languages or other commonly spoken languages.

COUNTRY	CAPITAL	LOCATION OF COUNTRY	AREA
Afghanistan	Kabul	Southern Asia, between Iran and Pakistan	250,000 sq. mi. (647,500 sq. km.)
Albania	Tiranë	Eastern Europe, between Greece and Yugoslavia	11,100 sq. mi. (28,750 sq. km.)
Algeria	Algiers	North Africa on the Mediterranean Sea, between Libya and Morocco	919,600 sq. mi. (2,381,740 sq. km.)
Andorra	Andorra la Vella	Europe, in the mountains between France and Spain	170 sq. mi. (450 sq. km.)
Angola	Luanda	Southern Africa on the Atlantic Ocean, north of Namibia	481,400 sq. mi. (1,246,700 sq. km.)
Antigua and Barbuda	St. John's	Islands on eastern edge of the Caribbean Sea	170 sq. mi. (440 sq. km.)
Argentina	Buenos Aires	Fills up most of the southern part of South America	1,068,300 sq. mi. (2,766,890 sq. km.)
Armenia	Yerevan	Western Asia, north of Turkey and Iran	11,500 sq. mi. (29,800 sq. km.)
Australia	Canberra	Continent south of Asia, between Indian and Pacific Oceans	2,967,900 sq. mi. (7,686,850 sq. km.)
Austria	Vienna	Central Europe, north of Italy	32,378 sq. mi. (83,858 sq. km.)
Azerbaijan	Baku	Western Asia, north of Iran	33,400 sq. mi. (86,600 sq. km.)

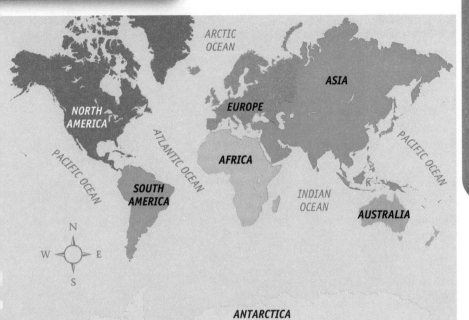

POPULATION	CURRENCY	LANGUAGE	COUNTRY
25,824,882	Afghani $1 = 4,750 afghanis	Afghan Persian (Dari), Pashtu	Afghanistan
3,364,571	Lek $1 = 134 leks	Albanian, Greek	Albania
31,133,486	Dinar $1 = 70 dinars	Arabic, French	Algeria
65,939	French franc or Spanish peseta	Catalan, French	Andorra
11,177,537	Readjusted kwanza $1 = 5³⁄₅ kwanzas	Portuguese	Angola
64,246	East Caribbean dollar $1 = 2²⁄₃ EC dollars	English	Antigua and Barbuda
36,737,664	Peso $1 = 1 peso	Spanish, English	Argentina
3,409,234	Dram $1 = 500 drams	Armenian	Armenia
18,783,551	Australian dollar $1 = 1½ Australian dollars	English	Australia
8,139,299	Schilling, also euro $1 = 13²⁄₃ schillings	German	Austria
7,908,224	Manat $1 = 4,275 manats	Azeri, Russian	Azerbaijan

COUNTRY	CAPITAL	LOCATION OF COUNTRY	AREA
The Bahamas	Nassau	Islands in the Atlantic Ocean, east of Florida	5,400 sq. mi. (13,940 sq. km.)
Bahrain	Manama	In the Persian Gulf, near the coast of Qatar	240 sq. mi. (620 sq. km.)
Bangladesh	Dhaka	Southern Asia, nearly surrounded by India	55,600 sq. mi. (144,000 sq. km.)
Barbados	Bridgetown	Island in the Atlantic Ocean, north of Trinidad	170 sq. mi. (430 sq. km.)
Belarus	Minsk	Eastern Europe, east of Poland	80,200 sq. mi. (207,600 sq. km.)
Belgium	Brussels	Western Europe, on the North Sea, south of the Netherlands	11,800 sq. mi. (30,510 sq. km.)
Belize	Belmopan	Central America, south of Mexico	8,900 sq. mi. (22,960 sq. km.)
Benin	Porto-Novo	West Africa, on the Gulf of Guinea, west of Nigeria	43,500 sq. mi. (112,620 sq. km.)
Bhutan	Thimphu	Asia, in the Himalaya Mountains, between China and India	18,000 sq. mi. (46,620 sq. km.)
Bolivia	La Paz	South America, in the Andes Mountains, next to Brazil	424,200 sq. mi. (1,098,580 sq. km.)
Bosnia and Herzegovina	Sarajevo	Southern Europe, on the Balkan Peninsula, west of Yugoslavia	19,781 sq. mi. (51,233 sq. km.)
Botswana	Gaborone	Southern Africa, between South Africa and Zambia	231,800 sq. mi. (600,370 sq. km.)
Brazil	Brasília	Occupies most of the eastern part of South America	3,286,478 sq. mi. (8,511,965 sq. km.)
Brunei	Bandar Seri Begawan	On the island of Borneo, northwest of Australia in the Pacific Ocean	2,200 sq. mi. (5,770 sq. km.)
Bulgaria	Sofia	Eastern Europe, on the Balkan Peninsula, bordering the Black Sea	42,800 sq. mi. (110,910 sq. km.)
Burkina Faso	Ouagadougou	West Africa, between Mali and Ghana	105,900 sq. mi. (274,200 sq. km.)
Burundi	Bujumbura	Central Africa, northwest of Tanzania	10,700 sq. mi. (27,830 sq. km.)
Cambodia	Phnom Penh	Southeast Asia, between Vietnam and Thailand	69,900 sq. mi. (181,040 sq. km.)
Cameroon	Yaoundé	Central Africa, between Nigeria and Central African Republic	183,600 sq. mi. (475,440 sq. km.)
Canada	Ottawa	Occupies the northern part of North America, north of the United States	3,851,800 sq. mi. (9,976,140 sq. km.)

POPULATION	CURRENCY	LANGUAGE	COUNTRY
283,705	Bahamas dollar Same value as U.S. dollar	English, Creole	The Bahamas
629,090	Dinar $1 = 3/8 dinars	Arabic, English	Bahrain
127,117,967	Taka $1 = 51 takas	Bangla, English	Bangladesh
259,191	Barbados dollar $1 = 2 Barbados dollars	English	Barbados
10,401,784	Ruble $1 = 32,000 rubles	Byelorussian, Russian	Belarus
10,182,034	Franc, also euro $1 = 40 francs	Flemish (Dutch), French	Belgium
235,789	Belize dollar $1 = 2 Belize dollars	English, Spanish	Belize
6,305,567	CFA franc $1 = 650 CFA francs	French, Fen	Benin
1,951,965	Ngultrum $1 = 43 1/2 ngultrums	Dzongkha, Tibetan	Bhutan
7,982,850	Boliviano $1 = 6 Bolivianos	Spanish, Quechua, Aymara	Bolivia
3,482,495	Mark $1 = 2 mark	Serbo-Croatian	Bosnia and Herzegovina
1,464,167	Pula $1 = 4 5/8 pula	English, Setswana	Botswana
171,853,126	Real $1 = 1 4/5 real	Portuguese, Spanish, English	Brazil
322,982	Brunei dollar $1 = 1 2/3 Brunei dollars	Malay, English	Brunei
8,194,772	Lev $1 = 2 leva	Bulgarian, Turkish	Bulgaria
11,575,898	CFA franc $1 = 650 CFA francs	French, Sudanic tribal languages	Burkina Faso
5,735,937	Franc $1 = 610 francs	Kirundi, French	Burundi
11,626,520	Riel $1 = 3,900 riels	Khmer, French	Cambodia
15,456,092	CFA franc $1 = 650 CFA francs	English, French	Cameroon
31,006,347	Canadian dollar $1 = 1 1/2 Canadian dollars	English, French	Canada

COUNTRY	CAPITAL	LOCATION OF COUNTRY	AREA
Cape Verde	Praia	Islands off the western tip of Africa	1,600 sq. mi. (4,030 sq. km.)
Central African Republic	Bangui	Central Africa, south of Chad	240,500 sq. mi. (622,980 sq. km.)
Chad	N'Djamena	North Africa, south of Libya	496,000 sq. mi. (1,284,000 sq. km.)
Chile	Santiago	Along the western coast of South America	292,300 sq. mi. (756,950 sq. km.)
China	Beijing	Occupies most of the mainland of eastern Asia	3,705,400 sq. mi. (9,596,960 sq. km.)
Colombia	Bogotá	Northwestern South America, southeast of Panama	439,700 sq. mi. (1,138,910 sq. km.)
Comoros	Moroni	Islands between Madagascar and the east coast of Africa	800 sq. mi. (2,170 sq. km.)
Congo, Democratic Republic of the	Kinshasa	Central Africa, north of Angola and Zambia	905,600 sq. mi. (2,345,410 sq. km.)
Congo, Republic of the	Brazzaville	Central Africa, east of Gabon	132,000 sq. mi. (342,000 sq. km.)
Costa Rica	San José	Central America, south of Nicaragua	19,700 sq. mi (51,100 sq. km.)
Côte d'Ivoire (Ivory Coast)	Yamoussoukro	West Africa, on the Gulf of Guinea, west of Ghana	124,500 sq. mi. (322,460 sq. km.)
Croatia	Zagreb	Southern Europe, south of Hungary	21,829 sq. mi. (56,538 sq. km.)
Cuba	Havana	In the Caribbean Sea, south of Florida	42,800 sq. mi. (110,860 sq. km.)
Cyprus	Nicosia	Island in the Mediterranean Sea, off the coast of Turkey	3,600 sq. mi. (9,250 sq. km.)
Czech Republic	Prague	Central Europe, south of Poland, east of Germany	30,387 sq. mi. (78,703 sq. km.)
Denmark	Copenhagen	Northern Europe, between the Baltic Sea and North Sea	16,639 sq. mi. (43,094 sq. km.)
Djibouti	Djibouti	North Africa, on the Gulf of Aden, across from Saudi Arabia	8,500 sq. mi. (22,000 sq. km.)
Dominica	Roseau	Island in the Caribbean Sea	300 sq. mi. (750 sq. km.)
Dominican Republic	Santo Domingo	On an island, along with Haiti, in the Caribbean Sea	18,800 sq. mi. (48,730 sq. km.)
East Timor	Dili	Part of an island in the South Pacific Ocean, north of Australia	5,744 sq. mi. (14,876 sq. km.)

POPULATION	CURRENCY	LANGUAGE	COUNTRY
405,748	Escudo $1 = 110 escudos	Portuguese, Crioulo	Cape Verde
3,444,951	CFA franc $1 = 650 CFA francs	French, Sangho	Central African Republic
7,557,436	CFA franc $1 = 650 CFA francs	French, Arabic	Chad
19,973,843	Peso $1 = 500 pesos	Spanish	Chile
1,246,871,951	Renminbi (yuan) $1 = 8¼ renminbis	Mandarin	China
39,309,422	Peso $1 = 1,875 pesos	Spanish	Colombia
562,723	Franc $1 = 490 francs	Arabic, French, Comorian	Comoros
50,481,305	Congolese franc $1 = 4½ Congolese francs	French, Lingala	Congo, Democratic Republic of the
2,716,814	CFA franc $1 = 650 CFA francs	French	Congo, Republic of the
3,674,490	Colon $1 = 300 colones	Spanish	Costa Rica
15,818,068	CFA franc $1 = 650 CFA francs	French, Diowa	Côte d'Ivoire (Ivory Coast)
4,676,865	Kuna $1 = 7⅔ kunas	Croatian	Croatia
11,096,395	Peso $1 = 1 peso	Spanish	Cuba
754,064	Pound $1 = 1¾ pound	Greek, Turkish	Cyprus
10,280,513	Koruna $1 = 35¾ koruny	Czech, Slovak	Czech Republic
5,356,845	Krone $1 = 7⅖ kronor	Danish, Faroese	Denmark
447,439	Djibouti franc $1 = 180 Djibouti francs	French, Arabic	Djibouti
64,881	East Caribbean dollar $1 = 2⅔ EC dollars	English, French patois	Dominica
8,129,734	Peso $1 = 16⅕ pesos	Spanish	Dominican Republic
800,000	U.S. dollar, rupiah, escudo, or Australian dollar	English, Portuguese, Bahasa Indonesia, Tetum	East Timor

COUNTRY	CAPITAL	LOCATION OF COUNTRY	AREA
Ecuador	Quito	South America, on the equator, bordering the Pacific Ocean	109,500 sq. mi. (283,560 sq. km.)
Egypt	Cairo	Northeastern Africa, on the Red Sea and Mediterranean Sea	386,700 sq. mi. (1,001,450 sq. km.)
El Salvador	San Salvador	Central America, southwest of Honduras	8,100 sq. mi. (21,040 sq. km.)
Equatorial Guinea	Malabo	West Africa, on the Gulf of Guinea, off the west coast of Cameroon	10,800 sq. mi. (28,050 sq. km.)
Eritrea	Asmara	Northeast Africa, north of Ethiopia	46,800 sq. mi. (121,320 sq. km.)
Estonia	Tallinn	Northern Europe, on the Baltic Sea, north of Latvia	17,462 sq. mi. (45,226 sq. km.)
Ethiopia	Addis Ababa	East Africa, east of Sudan	435,185 sq. mi. (1,127,127 sq. km.)
Fiji	Suva	Islands in the South Pacific Ocean, east of Australia	7,100 sq. mi. (18,270 sq. km.)
Finland	Helsinki	Northern Europe, between Sweden and Russia	130,100 sq. mi. (337,030 sq. km.)
France	Paris	Western Europe, between Germany and Spain	211,200 sq. mi. (547,030 sq. km.)
Gabon	Libreville	Central Africa, on the Atlantic coast, south of Cameroon	103,300 sq. mi. (267,670 sq. km.)
The Gambia	Banjul	West Africa, on the Atlantic Ocean, surrounded by Senegal	4,400 sq. mi. (11,300 sq. km.)
Georgia	Tbilisi	Western Asia, south of Russia, on the Black Sea	26,900 sq. mi. (69,700 sq. km.)
Germany	Berlin	Central Europe, northeast of France	137,800 sq. mi. (356,910 sq. km.)
Ghana	Accra	West Africa, on the southern coast	92,100 sq. mi. (238,540 sq. km.)
Great Britain (United Kingdom)	London	Off the northwest coast of Europe	94,500 sq. mi. (244,820 sq. km.)
Greece	Athens	Southern Europe, in the southern part of the Balkan Peninsula	50,900 sq. mi. (131,940 sq. km.)
Grenada	Saint George's	Island on the eastern edge of the Caribbean Sea	130 sq. mi. (340 sq. km.)
Guatemala	Guatemala City	Central America, southeast of Mexico	42,000 sq. mi. (108,890 sq. km.)
Guinea	Conakry	West Africa, on the Atlantic Ocean, north of Sierra Leone	94,900 sq. mi. (245,860 sq. km.)

POPULATION	CURRENCY	LANGUAGE	COUNTRY
12,562,496	Sucre $1 = 19,800 sucres	Spanish, Quechua	Ecuador
67,273,906	Pound $1 = 3²/₅ pounds	Arabic, English	Egypt
5,839,079	Colon $1 = 8³/₄ colones	Spanish	El Salvador
465,746	CFA franc $1 = 650 CFA francs	Spanish, French	Equatorial Guinea
3,984,723	Nakfa $1 = 8 nakfa	Tigrinya, Tigre, Kunama	Eritrea
1,408,523	Kroon $1 = 15³/₅ kroons	Estonian, Russian	Estonia
59,680,385	Birr $1 = 8¹/₈ birr	Amharic, Tigrinya	Ethiopia
812,918	Fiji dollar $1 = 2 Fiji dollars	English, Fijian	Fiji
5,158,372	Markka, also euro $1 = 6 markka	Finnish, Swedish	Finland
58,978,172	Franc, also euro $1 = 6¹/₂ francs	French	France
1,225,853	CFA franc $1 = 650 CFA francs	French, Bantu dialects	Gabon
1,336,320	Dalasi $1 = 11³/₅ dalasi	English, Mandinka	The Gambia
5,066,499	Lavi $1 = 1⁴/₅ lavis	Georgian, Russian	Georgia
82,087,361	Mark, also euro $1 = 2 marks	German	Germany
18,887,626	Cedi $1 = 3,500 cedis	English, Akan	Ghana
59,113,439	Pound $1 = ³/₅ pound	English	Great Britain (United Kingdom)
10,707,135	Drachma $1 = 330 drachmas	Greek	Greece
97,008	East Caribbean dollar $1 = 2²/₃ EC dollars	English, French patois	Grenada
12,335,580	Quetzal $1 = 7²/₃ quetzals	Spanish, Mayan languages	Guatemala
7,583,953	Franc $1 = 1,380 francs	French, tribal languages	Guinea

COUNTRY	CAPITAL	LOCATION OF COUNTRY	AREA
Guinea-Bissau	Bissau	West Africa, on the Atlantic Ocean, south of Senegal	13,900 sq. mi. (36,120 sq. km.)
Guyana	Georgetown	South America, on the northern coast, east of Venezuela	83,000 sq. mi. (214,970 sq. km.)
Haiti	Port-au-Prince	On an island, along with Dominican Republic, in the Caribbean Sea	10,700 sq. mi. (27,750 sq. km.)
Honduras	Tegucigalpa	Central America, between Guatemala and Nicaragua	43,300 sq. mi. (112,090 sq. km.)
Hungary	Budapest	Central Europe, north of Yugoslavia	35,900 sq. mi. (93,030 sq. km.)
Iceland	Reykjavik	Island off the coast of Europe, in the North Atlantic Ocean	40,000 sq. mi. (103,000 sq. km.)
India	New Delhi	Southern Asia, on a large peninsula on the Indian Ocean	1,269,300 sq. mi. (3,287,590 sq. km.)
Indonesia	Jakarta	Islands south of Southeast Asia, along the equator	735,360 sq. mi. (1,904,560 sq. km.)
Iran	Tehran	Southern Asia, between Iraq and Pakistan	636,000 sq. mi. (1,648,000 sq. km.)
Iraq	Baghdad	In the Middle East, between Syria and Iran	168,754 sq. mi. (437,072 sq. km.)
Ireland	Dublin	Off the coast of Europe, in the Atlantic Ocean, west of Great Britain	27,100 sq. mi. (70,280 sq. km.)
Israel	Jerusalem	In the Middle East, between Jordan and the Mediterranean Sea	8,000 sq. mi. (20,770 sq. km.)
Italy	Rome	Southern Europe, jutting out into the Mediterranean Sea	116,300 sq. mi. (301,230 sq. km.)
Jamaica	Kingston	Island in the Caribbean Sea, south of Cuba	4,200 sq. mi. (10,990 sq. km.)
Japan	Tokyo	Four big islands and many small ones, off the east coast of Asia	145,882 sq. mi. (377,835 sq. km.)
Jordan	Amman	In the Middle East, south of Syria, east of Israel	34,445 sq. mi. (89,213 sq. km.)
Kazakhstan	Astana	Central Asia, south of Russia	1,049,200 sq. mi. (2,717,300 sq. km.)
Kenya	Nairobi	East Africa, on the Indian Ocean, south of Ethiopia	225,000 sq. mi. (582,650 sq. km.)
Kiribati	Tarawa	Islands in the middle of the Pacific Ocean, near the equator	277 sq. mi. (717 sq. km.)
Korea, North	Pyongyang	Eastern Asia, in the northern part of the Korean Peninsula	46,500 sq. mi. (120,540 sq. km.)

POPULATION	CURRENCY	LANGUAGE	COUNTRY
1,234,555	CFA franc $1 = 650 CFA francs	Portuguese, Crioulo	Guinea-Bissau
705,156	Guyana dollar $1 = 180 Guyana dollars	English, Amerindian dialects	Guyana
6,884,264	Gourde $1 = 17½ gourdes	Haitian Creole, French	Haiti
5,997,327	Lempira $1 = 14⅗ lempiras	Spanish	Honduras
10,186,372	Forint $1 = 253 forints	Hungarian (Magyar)	Hungary
272,512	Krona $1 = 72 kronor	Icelandic (Islenska)	Iceland
1,000,848,550	Rupee $1 = 43½ rupees	Hindi, English	India
215,308,345	Rupiah $1 = 7,025 rupiah	Bahasa Indonesia	Indonesia
65,179,752	Rial $1 = 1,759 rials	Persian (Farsi)	Iran
22,427,150	Dinar $1 = ⅓ dinar	Arabic, Kurdish	Iraq
3,632,944	Punt, also euro $1 = ⅚ punt	English, Gaelic	Ireland
5,749,760	New shekel $1 = 4⅛ new shekels	Hebrew, Arabic	Israel
56,735,130	Lira, also euro $1 = 1,900 lire	Italian	Italy
2,652,443	Jamaican dollar $1 = 40 Jamaican dollars	English, Creole	Jamaica
126,182,077	Yen $1 = 102 yen	Japanese	Japan
4,561,147	Dinar $1 = ¾ dinar	Arabic, English	Jordan
16,824,825	Tenge $1 = 140 tenges	Kazakh, Russian	Kazakhstan
28,808,658	Shilling $1 = 73 shillings	Swahili, English	Kenya
85,501	Australian dollar $1 = 1½ Australian dollars	English, Gilbertese	Kiribati
21,386,109	Won $1 = 2⅕ won	Korean	Korea, North

COUNTRY	CAPITAL	LOCATION OF COUNTRY	AREA
Korea, South	Seoul	Eastern Asia, south of North Korea, on the Korean Peninsula	38,000 sq. mi. (98,480 sq. km.)
Kuwait	Kuwait City	In the Middle East, on the northern end of the Persian Gulf	6,900 sq. mi. (17,820 sq. km.)
Kyrgyzstan	Bishkek	Western Asia, between Kazakhstan and Tajikistan	76,600 sq. mi. (198,500 sq. km.)
Laos	Vientiane	Southeast Asia, between Vietnam and Thailand	91,400 sq. mi. (236,800 sq. km.)
Latvia	Riga	On the Baltic Sea, between Lithuania and Estonia	24,700 sq. mi. (64,100 sq. km.)
Lebanon	Beirut	In the Middle East, between the Mediterranean Sea and Syria	4,000 sq. mi. (10,400 sq. km.)
Lesotho	Maseru	Southern Africa, surrounded by the nation of South Africa	11,700 sq. mi. (30,350 sq. km.)
Liberia	Monrovia	Western Africa, on the Atlantic Ocean, southeast of Sierra Leone	43,000 sq. mi. (111,370 sq. km.)
Libya	Tripoli	North Africa, on the Mediterranean Sea, to the west of Egypt	679,400 sq. mi. (1,759,540 sq. km.)
Liechtenstein	Vaduz	Southern Europe, in the Alps between Austria and Switzerland	60 sq. mi. (160 sq. km.)
Lithuania	Vilnius	Northern Europe, on the Baltic Sea, east of Poland	25,200 sq. mi. (65,200 sq. km.)
Luxembourg	Luxembourg	Western Europe, between France and Germany	998 sq. mi. (2,586 sq. km.)
Macedonia	Skopje	Southern Europe, north of Greece	9,781 sq. mi. (25,333 sq. km.)
Madagascar	Antananarivo	Island in the Indian Ocean, off the east coast of Africa	226,700 sq. mi. (587,040 sq. km.)
Malawi	Lilongwe	Southern Africa, south of Tanzania and east of Zambia	45,700 sq. mi. (118,480 sq. km.)
Malaysia	Kuala Lumpur	Southeast tip of Asia and the north coast of the island of Borneo	127,300 sq. mi. (329,750 sq. km.)
Maldives	Male	Islands in the Indian Ocean, south of India	100 sq. mi. (260 sq. km.)
Mali	Bamako	West Africa, between Algeria and Mauritania	479,000 sq. mi. (1,240,000 sq. km.)
Malta	Valletta	Island in the Mediterranean Sea, south of Italy	120 sq. mi. (320 sq. km.)
Marshall Islands	Majuro	Chain of small islands in the middle of the Pacific Ocean	70 sq. mi. (181 sq. km.)

POPULATION	CURRENCY	LANGUAGE	COUNTRY
46,884,800	Won $1 = 1,100 won	Korean	Korea, South
1,991,115	Dinar $1 = ⅓ dinar	Arabic, English	Kuwait
45,546,055	Som $1 = 45 soms	Kyrgyz, Russian	Kyrgyzstan
5,407,453	Kip $1 = 6,550 kip	Lao, French	Laos
2,353,874	Lat $1 = ⅗ lat	Lettish, Lithuanian	Latvia
3,562,699	Pound $1 = 1,500 pounds	Arabic, French	Lebanon
2,128,950	Maloti $1 = 6⅛ maloti	English, Sesotho	Lesotho
2,923,725	Liberian dollar Same as U.S. dollar	English, tribal languages	Liberia
4,992,838	Dinar $1 = ½ dinar	Arabic, tribal languages	Libya
32,057	Swiss franc $1 = 1⅗ Swiss francs	German	Liechtenstein
3,584,966	Litas $1 = 4 litas	Lithuanian, Polish	Lithuania
429,080	Franc, also euro $1 = 40 francs	French, German	Luxembourg
2,022,604	Denar $1 = 60 denar	Macedonian, Albanian	Macedonia
14,873,387	Franc $1 = 5,200 francs	Malagasy, French	Madagascar
10,000,416	Kwacha $1 = 46 kwacha	English, Chichewa	Malawi
21,376,066	Ringgit $1 = 3⅘ ringgits	Malay, English	Malaysia
300,220	Rufiyaa $1 = 11¾ rufiyaas	Divehi	Maldives
10,429,124	CFA franc $1 = 650 CFA francs	French, Bambara	Mali
381,603	Maltese lira $1 = 2⅖ Maltese lira	Maltese, English	Malta
65,507	U.S. dollar	English, Marshallese	Marshall Islands

COUNTRY	CAPITAL	LOCATION OF COUNTRY	AREA
Mauritania	Nouakchott	West Africa, on the Atlantic Ocean, north of Senegal	398,000 sq. mi. (1,030,700 sq. km.)
Mauritius	Port Louis	Islands in the Indian Ocean, east of Madagascar	700 sq. mi. (1,860 sq. km.)
Mexico	Mexico City	North America, south of the United States	761,600 sq. mi. (1,972,550 sq. km.)
Micronesia	Palikir	Islands in the western Pacific Ocean	271 sq. mi. (702 sq. km.)
Moldova	Chisinau	Eastern Europe, between Ukraine and Romania	13,000 sq. mi. (33,700 sq. km.)
Monaco	Monaco	Europe, on the Mediterranean Sea, surrounded by France	3/4 of a sq. mi. (2 sq. km.)
Mongolia	Ulaanbaatar	Central Asia between Russia and China	604,000 sq. mi. (1,565,000 sq. km.)
Morocco	Rabat	Northwest Africa, on the Atlantic Ocean and Mediterranean Sea	172,400 sq. mi. (446,550 sq. km.)
Mozambique	Maputo	Southeastern Africa, on the Indian Ocean	309,500 sq. mi. (801,590 sq. km.)
Myanmar (Burma)	Yangon (Rangoon)	Southern Asia, to the east of India and Bangladesh	262,000 sq. mi. (678,500 sq. km.)
Namibia	Windhoek	Southwestern Africa, on the Atlantic Ocean, west of Botswana	318,695 sq. mi. (825,418 sq. km.)
Nauru	Yaren	Island in the western Pacific Ocean, just below the equator	8 sq. mi. (21 sq. km.)
Nepal	Kathmandu	Asia, in the Himalaya Mountains, between China and India	54,400 sq. mi. (140,800 sq. km.)
Netherlands	Amsterdam	Northern Europe, on the North Sea, to the west of Germany	16,033 sq. mi. (41,526 sq. km.)
New Zealand	Wellington	Islands in the Pacific Ocean east of Australia	103,700 sq. mi. (268,680 sq. km.)
Nicaragua	Managua	Central America, between Honduras and Costa Rica	49,998 sq. mi. (129,494 sq. km.)
Niger	Niamey	North Africa, south of Algeria and Libya	489,000 sq. mi. (1,267,000 sq. km.)
Nigeria	Abuja	West Africa, on the southern coast between Benin and Cameroon	356,700 sq. mi. (923,770 sq. km.)
Norway	Oslo	Northern Europe, on the Scandinavian Peninsula	125,200 sq. mi. (324,220 sq. km.)
Oman	Muscat	On the Arabian Peninsula, southeast of Saudi Arabia	82,000 sq. mi. (212,460 sq. km.)

POPULATION	CURRENCY	LANGUAGE	COUNTRY
2,581,738	Ouguiya $1 = 216 ouguiya	Wolof, Arabic	Mauritania
1,182,212	Mauritian rupee $1 = 25$2/5$ Mauritian rupees	English, French, Creole	Mauritius
100,294,036	New peso $1 = 9$1/2$ new pesos	Spanish, Mayan dialects	Mexico
131,500	U.S. dollar	English, Trukese	Micronesia
4,460,838	Leu $1 = 11 lei	Moldovan, Russian	Moldova
32,149	French franc $1 = 6$1/2$ francs	French, English	Monaco
2,617,379	Tugrik $1 = 1,000 tugriks	Khalkha Mongolian	Mongolia
29,661,636	Dirham $1 = 10 dirhams	Arabic, Berber dialects	Morocco
19,124,335	Metical $1 = 13,300 meticals	Portuguese, indigenous dialects	Mozambique
48,081,302	Kyat $1 = 6$1/3$ kyats	Burmese	Myanmar (Burma)
1,648,270	Rand $1 = 6$1/8$ rand	Afrikaans, English	Namibia
10,605	Australian dollar $1 = 1$1/2$ Australian dollars	Nauruan, English	Nauru
24,302,653	Rupee $1 = 69 rupees	Nepali	Nepal
15,807,641	Guilder, also euro $1 = 2$1/5$ guilders	Dutch	Netherlands
3,662,265	New Zealand dollar $1 = 1$7/8$ NZ dollars	English, Maori	New Zealand
4,717,132	Gold cordoba $1 = 12$1/3$ gold cordobas	Spanish	Nicaragua
9,962,242	CFA franc $1 = 650 CFA francs	French, Hausa, Djerma	Niger
113,828,587	Naira $1 = 100 nairas	English, Hausa, Yoruba	Nigeria
4,438,547	Krone $1 = 8 kroner	Norwegian	Norway
2,446,645	Rial Omani $1 = $3/8$ rial Omani	Arabic	Oman

COUNTRY	CAPITAL	LOCATION OF COUNTRY	AREA
Pakistan	Islamabad	South Asia, between Iran and India	310,400 sq. mi. (803,940 sq. km.)
Palau	Koror	Islands in North Pacific Ocean, southeast of Philippines	177 sq. mi. (458 sq. km.)
Panama	Panama City	Central America, between Costa Rica and Colombia	30,200 sq. mi. (78,200 sq. km.)
Papua New Guinea	Port Moresby	Part of the island of New Guinea, north of Australia	178,700 sq. mi. (462,840 sq. km.)
Paraguay	Asunción	South America, between Argentina and Brazil	157,000 sq. mi. (406,750 sq. km.)
Peru	Lima	South America, along the Pacific coast, north of Chile	496,200 sq. mi. (1,285,220 sq. km.)
Philippines	Manila	Islands in the Pacific Ocean, off the coast of Southeast Asia	116,000 sq. mi. (300,000 sq. km.)
Poland	Warsaw	Central Europe, on the Baltic Sea, east of Germany	120,700 sq. mi. (312,683 sq. km.)
Portugal	Lisbon	Southern Europe, on the Iberian Peninsula, west of Spain	35,672 sq. mi. (92,391 sq. km.)
Qatar	Doha	Arabian Peninsula, on the Persian Gulf	4,416 sq. mi. (11,437 sq. km.)
Romania	Bucharest	Southern Europe, on the Black Sea, north of Bulgaria	91,700 sq. mi. (237,500 sq. km.)
Russia	Moscow	Stretches from Eastern Europe across northern Asia to the Pacific Ocean	6,592,800 sq. mi. (17,075,200 sq. km.)
Rwanda	Kigali	Central Africa, northwest of Tanzania	10,200 sq. mi. (26,340 sq. km.)
Saint Kitts and Nevis	Basseterre	Islands in the Caribbean Sea, near Puerto Rico	104 sq. mi. (269 sq. km.)
Saint Lucia	Castries	Island on eastern edge of the Caribbean Sea	240 sq. mi. (620 sq. km.)
Saint Vincent and the Grenadines	Kingstown	Islands on eastern edge of the Caribbean Sea, north of Grenada	130 sq. mi. (340 sq. km.)
Samoa (formerly Western Samoa)	Apia	Islands in the South Pacific Ocean	1,100 sq. mi. (2,860 sq. km.)
San Marino	San Marino	Southern Europe, surrounded by Italy	20 sq. mi. (50 sq. km.)
São Tomé and Príncipe	São Tomé	In the Gulf of Guinea, off the coast of West Africa	400 sq. mi. (960 sq. km.)
Saudi Arabia	Riyadh	Western Asia, occupying most of the Arabian Peninsula	756,983 sq. mi. (1,960,582 sq. km.)

POPULATION	CURRENCY	LANGUAGE	COUNTRY
138,123,359	Rupee $1 = 51¾ rupees	Urdu, English	Pakistan
18,467	U.S. dollar	English, Palauan	Palau
2,778,526	Balboa Same value as U.S. dollar	Spanish, English	Panama
4,705,126	Kina $1 = 2⅔ kinas	English, Motu	Papua New Guinea
5,434,095	Guarani $1 = 3,300 guarani	Spanish, Guarani	Paraguay
26,624,582	New sol $1 = 3½ new soles	Spanish, Quechua	Peru
79,345,812	Peso $1 = 40 pesos	Pilipino, English	Philippines
38,608,929	Zloty $1 = 4⅛ zlotys	Polish	Poland
9,918,040	Escudo, also euro $1 = 200 escudos	Portuguese	Portugal
723,542	Riyal $1 = 3⅔ riyals	Arabic, English	Qatar
22,334,312	Leu $1 = 18,200 lei	Romanian, Hungarian	Romania
146,393,569	Ruble $1 = 27½ rubles	Russian	Russia
8,154,933	Franc $1 = 336 francs	French, Kinyarwanda	Rwanda
42,858	East Caribbean dollar $1 = 2⅔ EC dollars	English, French patois	Saint Kitts and Nevis
154,020	East Caribbean dollar $1 = 2⅔ EC dollars	English, French patois	Saint Lucia
120,519	East Caribbean dollar $1 = 2⅔ EC dollars	English	Saint Vincent and the Grenadines
229,979	Tala $1 = 3 tala	English, Samoan	Samoa (formerly Western Samoa)
25,061	Italian lira $1 = 1,900 lire	Italian	San Marino
154,878	Dobra $1 = 2,390 dobras	Portuguese	São Tomé and Príncipe
21,504,613	Riyal $1 = 3¾ riyals	Arabic	Saudi Arabia

COUNTRY	CAPITAL	LOCATION OF COUNTRY	AREA
Senegal	Dakar	West Africa, on the Atlantic Ocean, south of Mauritania	75,700 sq. mi. (196,190 sq. km.)
Seychelles	Victoria	Islands off the coast of Africa, in the Indian Ocean	176 sq. mi. (455 sq. km.)
Sierra Leone	Freetown	West Africa, on the Atlantic Ocean, south of Guinea	27,700 sq. mi. (71,740 sq. km.)
Singapore	Singapore	Mostly on one island, off the tip of Southeast Asia	250 sq. mi. (648 sq. km.)
Slovakia	Bratislava	Eastern Europe, between Poland and Hungary	18,859 sq. mi. (48,845 sq. km.)
Slovenia	Ljubljana	Eastern Europe, between Austria and Croatia	7,821 sq. mi. (20,256 sq. km.)
Solomon Islands	Honiara	Western Pacific Ocean	11,000 sq. mi. (28,450 sq. km.)
Somalia	Mogadishu	East Africa, east of Ethiopia	246,200 sq. mi. (637,660 sq. km.)
South Africa	Pretoria (admin.) Cape Town (legisl.)	At the southern tip of Africa	471,009 sq. mi. (1,219,912 sq. km.)
Spain	Madrid	Europe, south of France, on the Iberian Peninsula	194,880 sq. mi. (504,750 sq. km.)
Sri Lanka	Colombo	Island in the Indian Ocean, southeast of India	25,300 sq. mi. (65,610 sq. km.)
Sudan	Khartoum	North Africa, south of Egypt, on the Red Sea	967,500 sq. mi. (2,505,810 sq. km.)
Suriname	Paramaribo	South America, on the northern shore, east of Guyana	63,000 sq. mi. (163,270 sq. km.)
Swaziland	Mbabane	Southern Africa, almost surrounded by South Africa	6,700 sq. mi. (17,360 sq. km.)
Sweden	Stockholm	Northern Europe, on the Scandinavian Peninsula	173,732 sq. mi. (449,964 sq. km.)
Switzerland	Bern (admin.) Lausanne (judicial)	Central Europe, in the Alps, north of Italy	15,900 sq. mi. (41,290 sq. km.)
Syria	Damascus	In the Middle East, north of Jordan and west of Iraq	71,500 sq. mi. (185,180 sq. km.)
Taiwan	Taipei	Island off southeast coast of China	13,900 sq. mi. (35,980 sq. km.)
Tajikistan	Dushanbe	Asia, west of China, south of Kyrgyzstan	55,300 sq. mi. (143,100 sq. km.)
Tanzania	Dar-es-Salaam	East Africa, on the Indian Ocean, south of Kenya	364,900 sq. mi. (945,090 sq. km.)
Thailand	Bangkok	Southeast Asia, south of Laos	198,500 sq. mi. (514,000 sq. km.)

POPULATION	CURRENCY	LANGUAGE	COUNTRY
10,051,930	CFA franc $1 = 650 CFA francs	French, Wolof	Senegal
79,164	Rupee $1 = 5⅓ rupees	English, French	Seychelles
5,296,651	Leone $1 = 1,900 leones	English, Mende	Sierra Leone
3,531,600	Singapore dollar $1 = 1⅔ Singapore dollars	Chinese, Malay, Tamil, English	Singapore
5,396,193	Koruna $1 = 42 koruny	Slovak, Hungarian	Slovakia
1,970,570	Tolar $1 = 200 tolars	Slovenian, Serbo-Croatian	Slovenia
445,429	Solomon Islands dollar $1 = 5 Solomon dollars	English, Melanesian	Solomon Islands
7,140,643	Shilling $1 = 2,620 shillings	Somali Arabic, Italian	Somalia
43,426,386	Rand $1 = 6⅛ rand	Afrikaans, English, Ndebele, Sotho	South Africa
39,167,744	Peseta, also euro $1 = 166 pesetas	Castilian Spanish	Spain
19,144,875	Rupee $1 = 72 rupees	Sinhala, Tamil	Sri Lanka
34,475,690	Pound/Dinar $1 = 2,600 pounds or $1 = 260 dinars	Arabic, Nubian, Ta Bedawie	Sudan
431,156	Guilder $1 = 810 guilders	Dutch, Sranan Tongo	Suriname
985,335	Lilangeni $1 = 6⅛ emalangeni	English, siSwati	Swaziland
8,911,296	Krona $1 = 8½ kronor	Swedish	Sweden
7,275,467	Franc $1 = 1⅗ francs	German, French, Italian, Romansch	Switzerland
17,213,871	Pound $1 = 52 pounds	Arabic, Kurdish, Armenian	Syria
22,113,250	New Taiwan dollar $1 = 31⅖ new Taiwan dollars	Mandarin Chinese	Taiwan
6,102,854	Tajik ruble $1 = 1,650 Tajik rubles	Tajik, Russian	Tajikistan
31,270,820	Shilling $1 = 800 shillings	Swahili, English	Tanzania
60,609,046	Baht $1 = 37½ bahts	Thai	Thailand

COUNTRY	CAPITAL	LOCATION OF COUNTRY	AREA
Togo	Lomé	West Africa, between Ghana and Benin	21,900 sq. mi. (56,790 sq. km.)
Tonga	Nuku'alofa	Islands in the South Pacific Ocean	289 sq. mi. (748 sq. km.)
Trinidad and Tobago	Port-of-Spain	Islands off the north coast of South America	2,000 sq. mi. (5,130 sq. km.)
Tunisia	Tunis	North Africa, on the Mediterranean, between Algeria and Libya	63,200 sq. mi. (163,610 sq. km.)
Turkey	Ankara	On the southern shore of the Black Sea, partly in Europe and partly in Asia	301,400 sq. mi. (780,580 sq. km.)
Turkmenistan	Ashgabat	Western Asia, north of Afghanistan and Iran	188,500 sq. mi. (488,100 sq. km.)
Tuvalu	Funafuti Atoll	Chain of islands in the South Pacific Ocean	10 sq. mi. (26 sq. km.)
Uganda	Kampala	East Africa, south of Sudan	91,100 sq. mi. (236,040 sq. km.)
Ukraine	Kiev	Eastern Europe, south of Belarus and Russia	233,100 sq. mi. (603,700 sq. km.)
United Arab Emirates	Abu Dhabi	Arabian Peninsula, on the Persian Gulf	32,000 sq. mi. (82,880 sq. km.)
United States	Washington, D.C.	In North America, most of the country (48 of 50 states) between Canada and Mexico	3,717,796 sq. mi. (9,629,091 sq. km.)
Uruguay	Montevideo	South America, on the Atlantic Ocean, south of Brazil	68,000 sq. mi. (176,220 sq. km.)
Uzbekistan	Tashkent	Central Asia, south of Kazakhstan	172,700 sq. mi. (447,400 sq. km.)
Vanuatu	Port-Vila	Islands in the South Pacific Ocean	5,700 sq. mi. (14,760 sq. km.)
Vatican City		Surrounded by the city of Rome, Italy	1/5 sq. mi. (1/2 sq. km.)
Venezuela	Caracas	On the northern coast of South America, east of Colombia	352,100 sq. mi. (912,050 sq. km.)
Vietnam	Hanoi	Southeast Asia, south of China, on the eastern coast	127,200 sq. mi. (329,560 sq. km.)
Yemen	Sanaa	Asia, on the southern coast of the Arabian Peninsula	203,800 sq. mi. (527,970 sq. km.)
Yugoslavia	Belgrade	Europe, on Balkan Peninsula, west of Romania and Bulgaria	39,500 sq. mi. (102,350 sq. km.)
Zambia	Lusaka	Southern Africa, east of Angola	290,600 sq. mi. (752,610 sq. km.)
Zimbabwe	Harare	Southern Africa, south of Zambia	150,800 sq. mi. (390,580 sq. km.)

POPULATION	CURRENCY	LANGUAGE	COUNTRY
5,081,415	CFA franc $1 = 650 CFA francs	French, Ewe, Kabre	Togo
109,082	Pa'anga $1 = 1³/₅ pa'angas	Tongan, English	Tonga
1,102,096	Trinidad and Tobago dollar $1 = 6¼ Trinidad dollars	English, Hindi, French	Trinidad and Tobago
9,513,603	Dinar $1 = 1¼ dinar	Arabic, French	Tunisia
65,599,206	Turkish lira $1 = 543,000 Turkish liras	Turkish, Kurdish, Arabic	Turkey
4,366,383	Manat $1 = 5,200 manats	Turkmen, Russian	Turkmenistan
10,588	Tuvaluan dollar $ 1= 1½ Tuvaluan dollars	Tuvaluan, English	Tuvalu
22,804,973	Shilling $1 = 1,500 shillings	English, Luganda	Uganda
49,811,174	Hryvna $1 = 5⅕ hryvna	Ukrainian, Russian	Ukraine
2,344,402	Dirham $1 = 3⅔ dirhams	Arabic, Persian	United Arab Emirates
272,690,813	U.S. dollar	English, Spanish	United States
3,308,523	Peso $1 = 11³/₅ pesos	Spanish	Uruguay
24,102,473	Som $1 = 170 soms	Uzbek, Russian	Uzbekistan
189,036	Vatu $1 = 129 vatus	French, English, Bislama	Vanuatu
860	Vatican lira, Italian lira $1 = 1,900 lire	Italian, Latin	Vatican City
23,203,466	Bolivar $1 = 650 bolivares	Spanish	Venezuela
77,311,210	Dong $1 = 14,000 dong	Vietnamese, French, Chinese	Vietnam
16,942,230	Rial $1 = 160 rials	Arabic	Yemen
11,206,847	New dinar $1 = 11⅔ new dinars	Serbo-Croatian, Albanian	Yugoslavia
9,663,535	Kwacha $1 = 2,800 kwacha	English, indigenous languages	Zambia
11,163,160	Zimbabwe dollar $1 = 38 Zimbabwe dollars	English, Shona, Sindebele	Zimbabwe

A Quick Visit to Some
COUNTRIES OF THE WORLD

Suppose you got a free round-trip ticket to visit any spot in the whole world. Where would you like to go? Here are a few sights you might want to see.

AUSTRALIA **Ayers Rock** is the biggest exposed rock in the world. Located in a remote desert, it is about 1½ miles long and shines bright red when the sun sets. Australia's first people, the Aborigines, thought it was sacred.

CANADA Want to feel like you're in France without leaving North America? Visit **Quebec City**. You'll see a high, walled fortress (the Citadel), a hotel that looks like a French castle (Château Frontenac), and people who speak French. In **Toronto**, however, English is the main language. You can get a view of that fast-growing city by going to the top of the **CN Tower**, the tallest free-standing structure in the world.

CANADA–UNITED STATES On the border between Canada and the United States is the famous waterfall **Niagara Falls**. About 20,000 bathtubs of water pour over the falls every second. You can put on a raincoat and look at the falls from an observation deck—or ride by in a boat.

CHINA Some 2,400 years ago, workers started putting up the **Great Wall**. It became the world's longest structure, with a main section 2,150 miles long. It was built to keep out invaders, but it didn't stop Genghis Khan from conquering much of China in the 1200s.

DENMARK One of the world's oldest and most charming amusement parks is Denmark's **Tivoli Gardens**. There you will find everything from a mouse circus to the world's oldest roller coaster.

ECUADOR The **Galapagos Islands**, which belong to Ecuador, are remote islands in the Pacific Ocean, about 600 miles off South America. They are filled with wildlife (such as cormorants and penguins, giant tortoises and lizards) and odd plants.

EGYPT In Egypt you can see the **Great Sphinx**, a stone figure with a man's head and a lion's body. Carved in the desert 4,500 years ago, it's still there, despite wear and tear. Nearby are the great **pyramids** of ancient Egyptian pharaohs.

FRANCE A high point of a trip to France would be the **Eiffel Tower**. You get to the top of this open, cast-iron tower in four elevators, one after another. Then you can look down 1,000 feet on the beautiful city of Paris below.

GERMANY Though it was built in the 1800s, the mad King Ludwig II planned **Neuschwanstein Castle** to look just like a fairy-tale castle from the Middle Ages, complete with turrets and drawbridges.

◀ The Great Sphinx, Egypt

◄ *Taj Mahal, India*

You can stop at the **Western Wall**, where Jews pray; it is said to contain stones from Solomon's Temple. And you can see the **Church of the Holy Sepulcher**, built where it is said that Jesus was crucified and buried.

ITALY The **Leaning Tower of Pisa** is proof that kids aren't the only ones who make mistakes. Long before it was finished, the bell tower began sinking into the soft ground and leaning to one side. Every year, it leans one twentieth of an inch more.

KENYA Here and in other countries of East Africa, you can visit **National Parks**. You can go on safaris to see lions, zebras, giraffes, elephants, and other animals in their natural home.

MEXICO On the Yucatán peninsula, you can visit remains of the city of **Chichén Itzá**, where the Mayan people settled in the sixth century. Abandoned before the Spanish came, it's now partly rebuilt. You can see stone pyramids and temples and a Mayan ballfield.

RUSSIA A famous place to visit here is the **Kremlin**, a walled fortress in Moscow, with old churches, palaces, and towers with onion-shaped gold domes, dating back to the Middle Ages. Today the Kremlin is the headquarters for the Russian government.

SOUTH AFRICA Think of southern Africa and you probably think of wildlife like the elephant, lion, leopard, and rhino. You can see them up close at the **Kruger National Park,** a huge nature reserve, home to 137 species of mammals.

GREAT BRITAIN The regular London home of the queen of England is **Buckingham Palace**. When she's there a royal flag is flying. Outside you can see the Changing of the Guard. Another attraction is the **Tower of London**, where many famous people were jailed, tortured, and killed. The crown jewels are shown there.

GREECE On the **Acropolis**, you will find the ruins of the **Parthenon** and other public buildings from ancient Athens. The remains of the buildings, some partly rebuilt, stand high on a hill overlooking the city.

INDIA One of the world's biggest and richest tombs is the **Taj Mahal**, which took about 20,000 workers to build. A ruler of India had the Taj Mahal built for his wife after her death in 1631.

IRELAND If you kiss the **Blarney Stone**, which is in the tower of Blarney Castle, legends say you'll be able to throw words around and get people to agree with you—even if what you say is nonsense.

ISRAEL In Israel you can visit **Jerusalem**—a Holy City for three faiths. You can see the **Dome of the Rock**, built over the rock where Muhammad, founder of Islam, is said to have risen to heaven.

Chichén Itzá, Mexico ►

NATIONS PUZZLE

ACROSS

2. The name of this Caribbean nation begins with Saint and its capital is Kingstown.
5. The people of this North African nation south of Libya speak French and Arabic.
7. An Asian nation comprised of four big islands and many small ones.
8. Its capital is Madrid.
9. You'd expect to see kangaroos here.
12. The currency of this African nation is the kwacha; its capital is Lusaka.
13. A nation on the Black Sea, it has the same name as a U.S. state.
17. If you'd like to visit Nuku'alofa, this is where you'd go.
18. Jerusalem, a Holy City for three faiths, is here.
19. This coastal African nation is on the equator; its people speak French.
20. In Southern Africa; its capital is Lilongwe, and many of its people speak English.

DOWN

1. Suva is the capital of these South Pacific islands.
2. Don't forget to change your money to rupees when you visit this island nation in the Indian Ocean.
3. This chain of South Pacific islands covers 10 square miles.
4. This North American nation has many French-speaking natives.
6. Come here to see a mouse circus at the Tivoli Gardens.
9. This nation fills up most of the southern part of South America.
10. This European nation is tucked between Austria and Croatia.
11. Visit western Asia, north of Iran, and see this nation.
14. Its language is English and its capital is Georgetown.
15. A central European nation, it spends schillings and euros.
16. If you're in Rome, you're here.

Answers are on pages 317-320.

MAPS and FLAGS of the NATIONS of the WORLD

Maps showing the continents and nations of the world appear on pages 155 through 166. Flags of the nations appear on pages 167 through 170.

A map of the United States appears on pages 268–269.

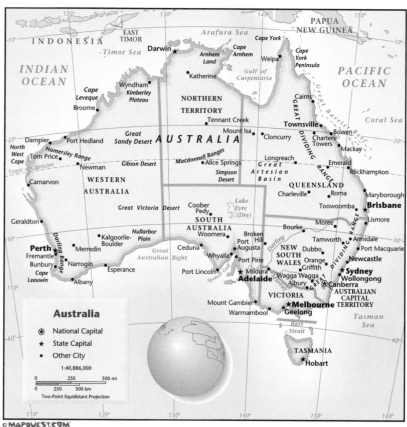

©MAPQUEST.COM

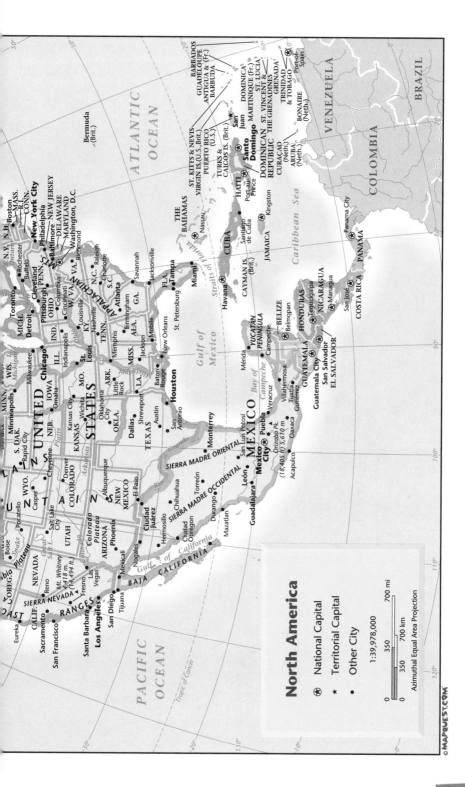

North America

⊛ National Capital
★ Territorial Capital
• Other City

1:39,978,000

| 0 | 350 | 700 mi |
| 0 | 350 | 700 km |

Azimuthal Equal Area Projection

© MAPQUEST.COM

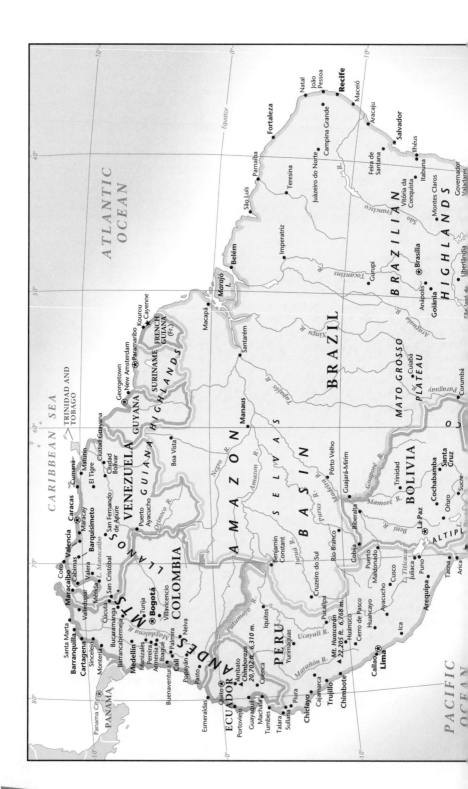

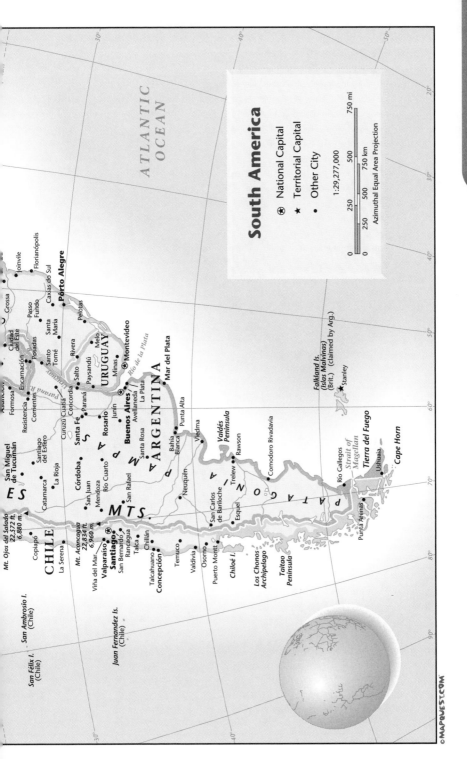

South America

⊛ National Capital
★ Territorial Capital
• Other City

1:29,277,000

| 0 | 250 | 500 | 750 mi |
| 0 | 250 | 500 | 750 km |

Azimuthal Equal Area Projection

ATLANTIC
OCEAN

Joinvile
Florianópolis
Porto Alegre
Caxias do Sul
Grossa
Passo Fundo
Santa Maria
Pelotas
Ciudad del Este
Posadas
Santo Tomé
Rivera
Santo
Melo
URUGUAY
⊛ **Montevideo**
Minas
Río de la Plata
Formosa
Encarnación
Corrientes
Resistencia
Paraná R.
Concordia
Salto
Paysandú
Santa Fe
Paraná
Buenos Aires ⊛
La Plata
Avellaneda
Mar del Plata
Curuzú Cuatiá
Rosario
Junín
Santiago del Estero
San Miguel de Tucumán
ARGENTINA
Santa Rosa
Punta Alta
Bahía Blanca
Viedma
Valdés Peninsula
Rawson
Falkland Is.
(Islas Malvinas)
(Brit.) (claimed by Arg.)
★ Stanley
Comodoro Rivadavia
Río Gallegos
Strait of Magellan
Tierra del Fuego
Ushuaia
Cape Horn
Punta Arenas
Juan Fernandez Is.
(Chile)
San Félix I.
San Ambrosio I.
(Chile)
Mt. Ojos del Salado
22,572 ft.
6,880 m.
Copiapó
La Serena
CHILE
Catamarca
La Rioja
Córdoba
San Juan
Mendoza
Río Cuarto
San Rafael
Mt. Aconcagua
22,834 ft.
6,960 m.
Viña del Mar
Valparaíso ⊛
Santiago ⊛
San Bernardo
Rancágua
Talca
Chillán
Talcahuano
Concepción
Temuco
Valdivia
Osorno
Puerto Montt
Chiloé I.
Los Chonos Archipelago
Taitao Peninsula
San Carlos de Bariloche
Esquel
Neuquén
Trelew
PATAGONIA
M T S.
A N D E S
Chuy

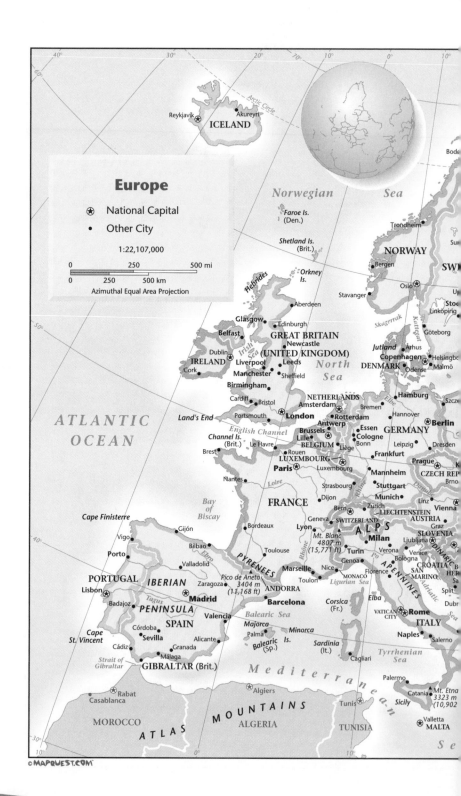

Europe

⊛ National Capital

● Other City

1:22,107,000

0	250		500 mi
0	250	500 km	

Azimuthal Equal Area Projection

ATLANTIC

OCEAN

Arctic Circle

Reykjavík ● ● Akureyri

ICELAND

Norwegian *Sea*

Faroe Is.
(Den.)

Trondheim ●

Shetland Is.
(Brit.)

NORWAY

Bergen ● **SW**

Hebrides

Orkney
Is.

Stavanger ● Oslo ⊛

U●

Sto●

Linköping ●

● Aberdeen

Glasgow ● ● Edinburgh *Skagerrak* *Kattegat* Göteborg ●

Belfast ● **GREAT BRITAIN** *Jutland* Århus ●

Newcastle ●

Dublin ● **(UNITED KINGDOM)** Copenhagen ⊛ ● Helsingbe

IRELAND ⊛ Liverpool ● Leeds ● **DENMARK** ● Odense ● Malmö

Cork ● Manchester ● ● Sheffield *North*

Birmingham ● *Sea*

Cardiff ● ● Bristol Hamburg ● Szcz●

NETHERLANDS Bremen ● *Elbe*

Amsterdam ⊛ Hannover ●

Land's End Portsmouth ● **London** ⊛ ● Rotterdam ●Berlin⊛

Antwerp ● Essen **GERMANY**

English Channel Brussels ● Cologne ●

Channel Is. Lille ● Bonn ● Leipzig ● Dresden

(Brit.) Le Havre ● **BELGIUM** Liège ●

Brest ● ● Rouen Frankfurt ●

LUXEMBOURG Prague ⊛ K

Paris ⊛ Luxembourg ● Mannheim ● **CZECH REP**

Brno ●

Nantes ● *Loire* Strasbourg ● Stuttgart ● *Danube*

Dijon ● Munich ●

FRANCE Bern ⊛ Zürich ● Linz ● Vienna ⊛

● **LIECHTENSTEIN** **AUSTRIA**

Bay Geneva ● **SWITZERLAND** Graz ●

of Lyon ● Mt. Blanc **SLOVENIA**

Cape Finisterre *Biscay* 4807 m **Milan** Ljubljana ⊛

Gijón ● Bordeaux ● (15,771 ft) Turin ● Verona ● Venice ● A L P S

Vigo ● Toulouse ● Genoa ● Bologna ● *DINAR*

Porto ● Bilbao ● *Rhône* Marseille ● Nice ● Florence ● A P **CROATIA**

Valladolid ● *Ebro* *Po* E **SAN**

P Y R E N E E S Monaco ⊛ N **MARINO**

PORTUGAL *IBERIAN* Pico de Aneto Toulon ● *Ligurian Sea* N Sa●

Zaragoza ● 3404 m **ANDORRA** I Split ●

Lisbon ⊛ (11,168 ft) Corsica Elba N Dubr●

Badajoz ● *Tagus* **Madrid** ⊛ **Barcelona** (Fr.) E

PENINSULA VATICAN ⊛●**Rome** S

Valencia ● *Balearic Sea* CITY **ITALY**

Cape Córdoba ● **SPAIN** Majorca ● Naples ● ● Salerno

St. Vincent Sevilla ● Alicante ● Palma ● Minorca Sardinia

Cádiz ● Granada ● *Balearic Is.* (It.) *Tyrrhenian*

Strait of ● Málaga (Sp.) Cagliari ● *Sea*

Gibraltar **GIBRALTAR (Brit.)** M e d i t e r r

Palermo ●

Rabat ⊛ ● Algiers Catania ● Mt. Etna

Casablanca ● Tunis ⊛ *Sicily* 3323 m

Valletta ⊛ (10,902

MOROCCO M O U N T A I N S **MALTA**

A T L A S **ALGERIA** **TUNISIA** S e

Bode ●

NORWAY

Su●

40° *30°* *20°* *70°* *10°* *0°* *10°*

60°

50°

40°

30°

10° *0°* *10°*

ATLANTIC OCEAN

IRELAND

PORTUGAL

GREAT
BRITAIN

SPAIN

NORWAY

Barents
Sea

MOROCCO

FRANCE

BEL. NETH. DEN.

SWEDEN

Murmansk

GERMANY

FINLAND

SWITZ.

CZECH
REP.

ESTONIA

Arkhangel'sk

ALGERIA

E U R O P E

AUS.

POLAND

LITH.

LAT.

St. Petersburg

ITALY

HUNG.

BELARUS

TUNISIA

Moscow

R U S S

ALB. YUG. ROM. MOL.

UKRAINE

Yekaterinburg

BUL.

UR AL MOUNTAINS

GREECE

Istanbul

Chelyabinsk

Irtysh

Izmir

Black
Sea

Volgograd

Volga

Magnitogorsk

Oms

LIBYA

Ankara

TURKEY

GEORGIA

Astrakhan'

Astana

Nov

T'bilisi

Caspian
Sea

KAZAKHSTAN

CYPRUS

Nicosia

ARMENIA

Aral
Sea

Qaraghandy

Sen

LEBANON

Beirut

Yerevan

AZERBAIJAN

Lake
Balkhash

CHAD

Tel Aviv

SYRIA

Damascus

Tabriz

Baku

TURKMENISTAN

UZBEKISTAN

Bishkek

Alm

Jerusalem

Amman

EGYPT

ISRAEL

JORDAN

IRAQ

Tehran

Ashgabat

Tashkent

KYRGYZST

Sinai

Baghdad

Dushanbe

Kashi

T

SAUDI

Al-Basrah

Mashhad

TAJIKISTAN

A F R I C A

ARABIA

Esfahan

Kuwait City

IRAN

AFGHANISTAN

Red

KUWAIT

Shiraz

Kabul

Islamabad

Srinagar

Jeddah

Manama

Kerman

Qandahar

Amritsar

SUDAN

Riyadh

BAHRAIN

Mecca

QATAR

Doha

Abu Dhabi

PAKISTAN

Lahore

Delhi

Sea

UNITED ARAB

Sukkur

NEP

ERITREA

EMIRATES

Muscat

Karachi

New Delhi

Kath

Nile

Sanaa

OMAN

Hyderabad

Jaipur

Kanpur

YEMEN

Ahmadabad

I N D I A

ETHIOPIA

DJI.

Aden

Nagpur

Gulf of Aden

Socotra
(Yemen)

Arabian
Sea

Mumbai

Hydera

SOMALIA

Equator

KENYA

Bangalore

Mad
(Che

Lakshadweep
(India)

Madurai

Kochi

SRI I

Colombo

Male

MALDIVES

Asia

⊛ National Capital

★ Territorial Capital

• Other City

1:51,084,000

0   500   1,000 mi

0   500   1,000 km

Two-Point Equidistant Projection

INDIAN

OC

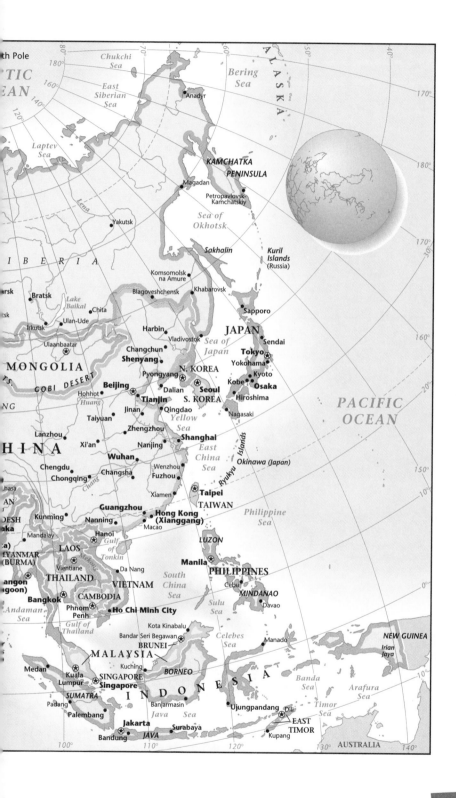

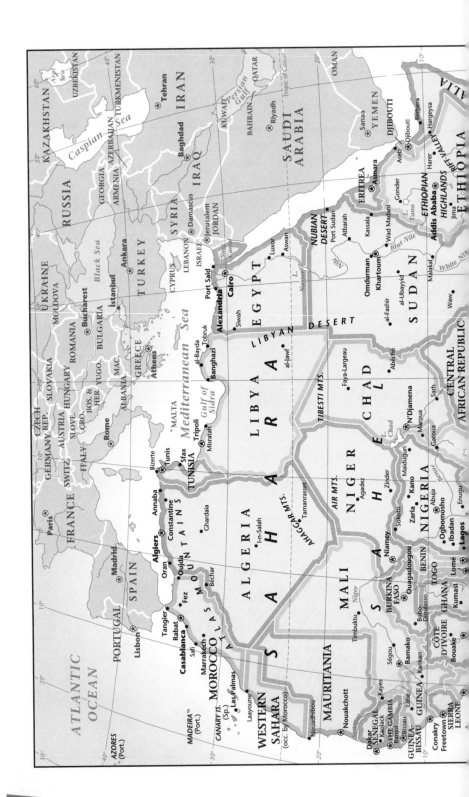

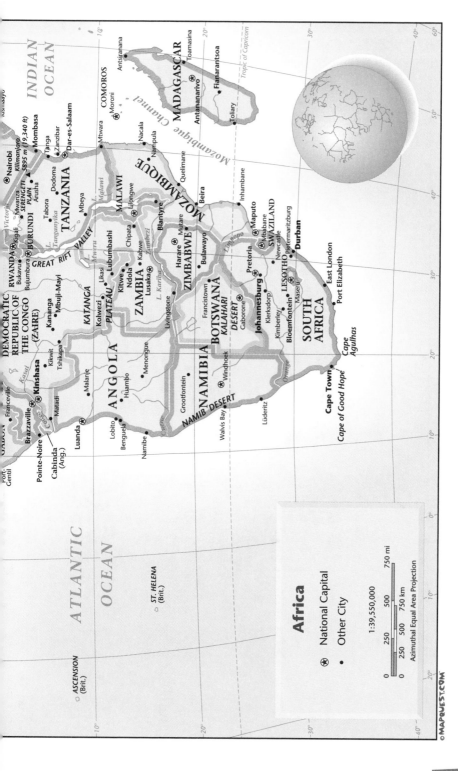

INDIAN OCEAN

ATLANTIC OCEAN

ASCENSION (Brit.)

ST. HELENA (Brit.)

Mozambique Channel

MADAGASCAR

Antsiranana
Toamasina
Antananarivo ✵
Flanararitsoa
Toliary

COMOROS
Moroni ✵

Tropic of Capricorn

Port-Gentil

Francisville

Brazzaville ✵
Pointe-Noire
Cabinda (Ang.)

Luanda ✵
Lobito
Benguela
Namibe

DEMOCRATIC REPUBLIC OF THE CONGO (ZAIRE)

Kinshasa ✵
Matadi
Kikwit
Kananga
Tshikapa
Mbuji-Mayi

Malanje
Huambo
Menongue

ANGOLA

KATANGA PLATEAU

Kolwezi
Likasi
Lubumbashi

GREAT RIFT VALLEY

RWANDA
Kigali ✵
Bukavu
BURUNDI
Bujumbura ✵

L. Kivu
L. Tanganyika
L. Mweru

Kabwe
Kitwe
Ndola
Lusaka ✵
ZAMBIA

Livingstone

L. Kariba

Grootfontein

Windhoek ✵
NAMIBIA

NAMIB DESERT

Walvis Bay
Lüderitz

Nairobi ✵
Kilimanjaro
5895 m (19,340 ft)
SERENGETI PLAIN
Arusha
Mwanza
Tabora
Mbeya
TANZANIA
Dodoma ✵

L. Victoria

Mombasa
Tanga
Zanzibar
Dar-es-Salaam ✵
Mtwara
Nacala
Nampula

MALAWI
Lilongwe ✵
L. Malawi

MOZAMBIQUE

Harare ✵
Mutare
Bulawayo
ZIMBABWE

Chipata
Chipinge

Zambezi

Blantyre
Beira
Quelimane
Inhambane

Maputo ✵
Pretoria ✵
Johannesburg ✵
Mbabane ✵
SWAZILAND
Pietermaritzburg
Durban

BOTSWANA

Gaborone ✵
Francistown

KALAHARI DESERT

LESOTHO
Maseru ✵
Newcastle

Klerksdorp
Kimberley
Bloemfontein ✵

SOUTH AFRICA

Port Elizabeth
East London
Cape Agulhas

Cape Town ✵
Cape of Good Hope

Limpopo
Orange

Africa

✵ National Capital
• Other City

1:39,550,000

0   250   500   750 mi
0   250   500   750 km

Azimuthal Equal Area Projection

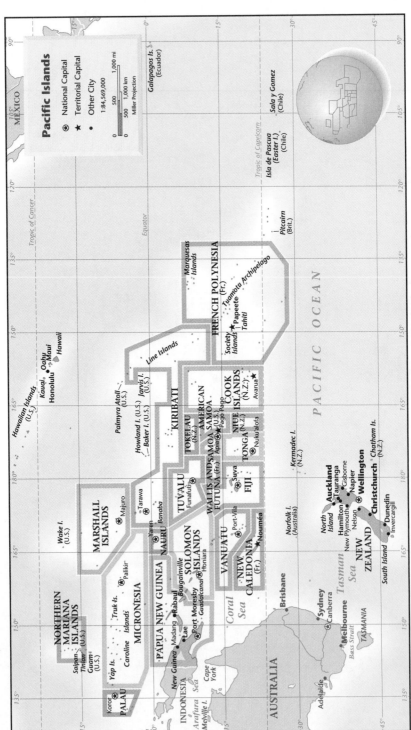

Pacific Islands

- ⊛ National Capital
- ★ Territorial Capital
- • Other City

1:84,569,000

0   500   1,000 mi
0   500   1,000 km
Miller Projection

MEXICO

Galapagos Is.
(Ecuador)

Tropic of Capricorn

Isla de Pascua
(Easter I.)
(Chile)

Sala y Gomez
(Chile)

Tropic of Cancer

Equator

Pitcairn
(Brit.)

MARQUESAS
Islands

FRENCH POLYNESIA
(Fr.)

Tuamotu Archipelago

Society
Islands ★ Papeete
Tahiti

PACIFIC OCEAN

Hawaiian Islands
(U.S.)

Kauai Oahu Maui
Honolulu Hawaii

Line Islands

Palmyra Atoll
(U.S.)

Howland I. (U.S.)
Baker I. (U.S.)

Jarvis I.
(U.S.)

KIRIBATI

TOKELAU
(N.Z.)

AMERICAN
SAMOA

COOK
ISLANDS
(N.Z.)

Avarua ★

NIUE
(N.Z.)

Wake I.
(U.S.)

MARSHALL
ISLANDS

Majuro ⊛

Tarawa

Banaba

Yaren

NAURU

TUVALU
Funafuti

WALLIS AND SAMOA
FUTUNA (Fr.) Apia ⊛ Pago Pago

TONGA (N.Z.)

Nuku'alofa ⊛

NORTHERN
MARIANA
ISLANDS

Saipan (U.S.)
Tinian (U.S.)
Guam
(U.S.)

Truk Is.
Palikir

Caroline Islands

MICRONESIA

Suva
⊛
FIJI

Port-Vila

Kermadec I.
(N.Z.)

Norfolk I.
(Australia)

North
Island

Auckland
Hamilton Tauranga
New Plymouth Napier
Nelson ⊛ Wellington
Christchurch

Chatham Is.
(N.Z.)

Gisborne

Korror ⊛
PALAU

Yap Is.

PAPUA NEW GUINEA

Madang Rabaul
New Guinea Lae Bougainville

Port Moresby ⊛
Guadalcanal ⊛ Honiara

SOLOMON
ISLANDS

VANUATU
⊛

NEW
CALEDONIA
(Fr.)

Nouméa ★

South Island

Dunedin
Invercargill

INDONESIA

Arafura
Sea

Melville I.

Cape
York

Coral
Sea

Tasman
Sea

Brisbane

Sydney
Canberra ⊛

Melbourne

TASMANIA

AUSTRALIA

Adelaide

Bass Strait

©MAPQUEST.COM

FLAGS of the NATIONS of the WORLD
(Afghanistan–Dominican Republic)

 AFGHANISTAN
 ALBANIA
 ALGERIA
 ANDORRA
 ANGOLA

 ANTIGUA AND BARBUDA
 ARGENTINA
 ARMENIA
 AUSTRALIA
 AUSTRIA

 AZERBAIJAN
 THE BAHAMAS
 BAHRAIN
 BANGLADESH
 BARBADOS

 BELARUS
 BELGIUM
 BELIZE
 BENIN
 BHUTAN

 BOLIVIA
 BOSNIA AND HERZEGOVINA
 BOTSWANA
 BRAZIL
 BRUNEI

 BULGARIA
 BURKINA FASO
 BURUNDI
 CAMBODIA
 CAMEROON

 CANADA
 CAPE VERDE
 CENTRAL AFRICAN REPUBLIC
 CHAD
 CHILE

 CHINA
 COLOMBIA
 COMOROS
 CONGO, DEM. REP. OF THE
 CONGO, REP. OF THE

 COSTA RICA
 CÔTE D'IVOIRE
 CROATIA
 CUBA
 CYPRUS

 CZECH REPUBLIC
 DENMARK
 DJIBOUTI
 DOMINICA
 DOMINICAN REPUBLIC

FLAGS of the NATIONS of the WORLD
(Ecuador–Lithuania)

ECUADOR	EGYPT	EL SALVADOR	EQUATORIAL GUINEA	ERITREA
ESTONIA	ETHIOPIA	FIJI	FINLAND	FRANCE
GABON	THE GAMBIA	GEORGIA	GERMANY	GHANA
GREECE	GRENADA	GUATEMALA	GUINEA	GUINEA-BISSAU
GUYANA	HAITI	HONDURAS	HUNGARY	ICELAND
INDIA	INDONESIA	IRAN	IRAQ	IRELAND
ISRAEL	ITALY	JAMAICA	JAPAN	JORDAN
KAZAKHSTAN	KENYA	KIRIBATI	NORTH KOREA	SOUTH KOREA
KUWAIT	KYRGYZSTAN	LAOS	LATVIA	LEBANON
LESOTHO	LIBERIA	LIBYA	LIECHTENSTEIN	LITHUANIA

FLAGS of the NATIONS of the WORLD
(Luxembourg–Senegal)

LUXEMBOURG

MACEDONIA

MADAGASCAR

MALAWI

MALAYSIA

MALDIVES

MALI

MALTA

MARSHALL ISLANDS

MAURITANIA

MAURITIUS

MEXICO

MICRONESIA

MOLDOVA

MONACO

MONGOLIA

MOROCCO

MOZAMBIQUE

MYANMAR (BURMA)

NAMIBIA

NAURU

NEPAL

NETHERLANDS

NEW ZEALAND

NICARAGUA

NIGER

NIGERIA

NORWAY

OMAN

PAKISTAN

PALAU

PANAMA

PAPUA NEW GUINEA

PARAGUAY

PERU

PHILIPPINES

POLAND

PORTUGAL

QATAR

ROMANIA

RUSSIA

RWANDA

ST. KITTS AND NEVIS

ST. LUCIA

ST. VINCENT AND THE GRENADINES

SAMOA

SAN MARINO

SÃO TOMÉ AND PRÍNCIPE

SAUDI ARABIA

SENEGAL

FLAGS of the NATIONS of the WORLD
(Seychelles–Zimbabwe)

 SEYCHELLES

 SIERRA LEONE

 SINGAPORE

 SLOVAKIA

 SLOVENIA

 SOLOMON ISLANDS

 SOMALIA

 SOUTH AFRICA

 SPAIN

 SRI LANKA

 SUDAN

 SURINAME

 SWAZILAND

 SWEDEN

 SWITZERLAND

 SYRIA

 TAIWAN

 TAJIKISTAN

 TANZANIA

 THAILAND

 TOGO

 TONGA

 TRINIDAD AND TOBAGO

 TUNISIA

 TURKEY

 TURKMENISTAN

 TUVALU

 UGANDA

 UKRAINE

 UNITED ARAB EMIRATES

 UNITED KINGDOM (GREAT BRITAIN)

 UNITED STATES

 URUGUAY

 UZBEKISTAN

 VANUATU

 VATICAN CITY

 VENEZUELA

 VIETNAM

YEMEN

YUGOSLAVIA

ZAMBIA

 ZIMBABWE

Numbers

? If a building is called the Pentagon, how many sides does it have? *You can find the answer on page 173.*

NUMERALS IN ANCIENT CIVILIZATION

People have been counting since the earliest of times. This is what some early numerals looked like.

Modern	1	2	3	4	5	6	7	8	9	10	20	50	100
Egyptian	I	II	III	IIII	‖	⦀	⦀I	⦀II	⦀III	∩	∩∩	∩∩∩∩∩	9
Babylonian	𒁹	𒈫	𒐲	𒐰	𒐳	𒐴	𒐵	𒐶	𒐷	<	≪	≪≪	𒐏≪
Greek	A	B	Γ	Δ	E	F	Z	H	θ	I	K	N	P
Mayan	•	••	•••	••••	—	—	••	•••	••••	=	⊙	⊙	⊙
Chinese	一	二	三	四	五	六	七	八	九	十	二十	五十	百
Hindu	I	2	3	8	y	ς	)	(	ξ	10	20	yo	100
Arabic	/	2	3	ڡ	6	٧	v	٨	9	/o	2o	8o	/oo

ROMAN NUMERALS

Roman numerals are still used today. The symbols used for different numbers are the letters I (1), V (5), X (10), L (50), C (100), D (500), and M (1,000). If one Roman numeral is followed by a larger one, the first is subtracted from the second. For example, IX means 10 − 1 = 9. Think of it as "one less than ten." On the other hand, if one Roman numeral is followed by another that is equal or smaller, add them together. Thus, VII means 5 + 1 + 1 = 7. Can you put your age in Roman numerals?

1	I	14	XIV	90	XC
2	II	15	XV	100	C
3	III	16	XVI	200	CC
4	IV	17	XVII	300	CCC
5	V	18	XVIII	400	CD
6	VI	19	XIX	500	D
7	VII	20	XX	600	DC
8	VIII	30	XXX	700	DCC
9	IX	40	XL	800	DCCC
10	X	50	L	900	CM
11	XI	60	LX	1,000	M
12	XII	70	LXX	2,000	MM
13	XIII	80	LXXX	3,000	MMM

Can you write the year on the front cover of this book in Roman numerals? The answer can be found on pages 317–320.

The PREFIX Tells the Number

Each number listed below has one or more prefixes used to form words that include that number. Knowing which number the prefix stands for may help you to understand the meaning of the word. For example, a unicycle has one wheel. A triangle has three sides. An octopus has eight tentacles. Next to the prefixes are some examples of words that use these prefixes.

1	uni-, mon-, mono-	unicycle, unicorn, monarch, monotone
2	bi-	bicycle, binary, binoculars, bifocals
3	tri-	tricycle, triangle, trilogy, triplet
4	quadr-, tetr-	quadrangle, quadruplet, tetrahedron
5	pent-, quint-	pentagon, pentathlon, quintuplet
6	hex-, sext-	hexagon, sextuplet
7	hept-, sept-	heptathlon, septuplet
8	oct-	octave, octet, octopus, octagon
9	non-	nonagon
10	dec-	decade, decibel, decimal
100	cent-	centipede, century
1000	kilo-	kilogram, kilometer
million	mega-	megabyte, megahertz
billion	giga-	gigabyte, gigawatt

READING AND WRITING
LARGE NUMBERS

Below are the words for some numbers, plus the number of zeros needed when each number is written out.

ten:	1 zero	10
hundred:	2 zeros	100
thousand:	3 zeros	1,000
ten thousand:	4 zeros	10,000
hundred thousand:	5 zeros	100,000
million:	6 zeros	1,000,000
ten million:	7 zeros	10,000,000
hundred million:	8 zeros	100,000,000
billion:	9 zeros	1,000,000,000
trillion:	12 zeros	1,000,000,000,000
quadrillion:	15 zeros	1,000,000,000,000,000
quintillion:	18 zeros	1,000,000,000,000,000,000
sextillion:	21 zeros	1,000,000,000,000,000,000,000
septillion:	24 zeros	1,000,000,000,000,000,000,000,000

Look below to see how numbers larger than those above would be written:

octillion has 27 zeros   decillion has 33 zeros
nonillion has 30 zeros   googol has 100 zeros

HOW MANY SIDES AND FACES DO THEY HAVE?

When a figure is flat (two-dimensional), it is a **plane** figure. When a figure takes up space (three-dimensional), it is a **solid figure**. The flat surface of a solid figure is called a **face**. Plane and solid figures come in many different shapes.

TWO-DIMENSIONAL			
square	circle	triangle	

THREE-DIMENSIONAL

cube   sphere   tetrahedron (pyramid)

The flat surface of a cube is a square.

WHAT ARE POLYGONS?

A polygon is a two-dimensional figure with three or more straight sides (called line segments). A square is a polygon. Polygons have different numbers of sides—and each has a different name. If the sides are all the same length and all the angles between the sides are equal, the polygon is called regular. If the sides are of different lengths or the angles are not equal, the polygon is called irregular. Below are some regular and irregular polygons.

NAME AND NUMBER OF SIDES	REGULAR	IRREGULAR
triangle — 3		
quadrilateral or tetragon — 4		
pentagon — 5		
hexagon — 6		
heptagon — 7		
octagon — 8		
nonagon — 9		
decagon —10		

WHAT ARE POLYHEDRONS?

A polyhedron is a three-dimensional figure with four or more faces. Each face on a polyhedron is a polygon. Below are some polyhedrons with many faces.

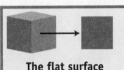
tetrahedron
4 faces

hexahedron
6 faces

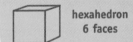
octahedron
8 faces

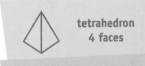
dodecahedron
12 faces

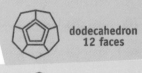
icosahedron
20 faces

NUMBERS PUZZLES

The Speedy Letter Carrier

To collect the mail, June, the letter carrier, needs to visit every mailbox on each street corner in her town. Help her find a way to visit every mailbox without visiting the same one twice, so that she returns to where she started.

June starts here

Toothpicks and Triangles

It takes three toothpicks to make one triangle. It's not too hard to use four toothpicks to make two triangles.
Can you find a way to make 16 triangles using only 12 toothpicks?

What comes next?

In each of the following series, what numbers should come next?

A 1, 3, 5, 7, _____, _____, _____, ...

B 1, 3, 6, 10, 15, 21, _____, _____, _____, ...

C 1, 1, 2, 3, 5, 8, 13, _____, _____, _____, ...

Answers are on pages 317–320.

CLIP and GUESS

Guess how many paper clips are on this page. Do this with a friend and compare answers. Did you both arrive at them in the same way?

Hint: You don't have to count all the paper clips to estimate the answer.

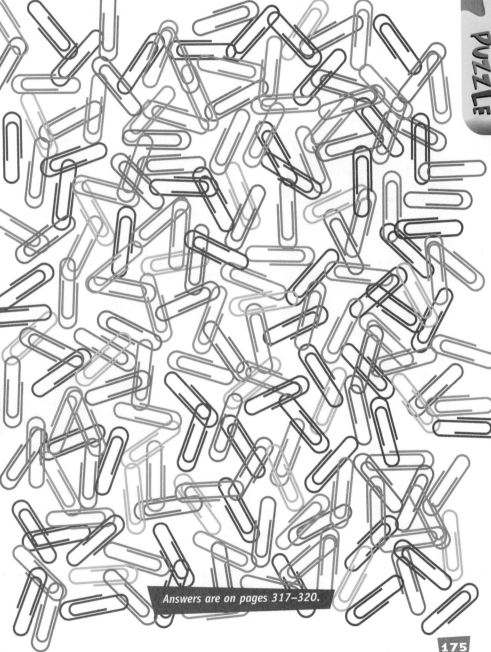

Answers are on pages 317–320.

Plants

? What would you need to make a terrarium?
You can find the answer on page 177.

What Makes a Plant a Plant?

Plants were the first living things on Earth. The first plants, called algae, appeared around three billion years ago and grew in or near water. About 300 or 400 million years ago, the first land plants appeared. These were ferns, club mosses, and horsetails. After these came plants that had cones (conifers) and trees that were ancestors of the palm trees we see today.

RECORD BREAKERS

WORLD'S OLDEST LIVING PLANTS: Bristlecone pine trees in California (4,700 years old)

WORLD'S TALLEST PLANTS: The tallest tree ever measured was a eucalyptus tree in Victoria, Australia, measuring 435 feet in 1872. The tallest tree now standing is a giant sequoia tree in Redwood National Park, California, standing at 365 feet.

Flowers, grass, weeds, oak trees, palm trees, and poison ivy are all plants. This means:

▶ *They can create their own food from air, sunlight, and water in a process called photosynthesis.*

▶ *They are rooted in one place—don't move around*

▶ *Their cells contain cellulose, a substance that keeps them standing upright.*

All plants need some air, water, light, and warmth. But they can grow in different kinds of conditions. A cactus plant needs lots of heat and light but not much water, while a fir tree will grow in a northern forest where it is cold much of the year and light is limited.

All About... GROWING GREAT GREENS

You can grow many kinds of plants in your house. Before you start, here are some basic rules for green thumbs.

❶ Give plants room to grow.

❷ Plants grow best in temperatures between 55 and 75 degrees Fahrenheit.

❸ Most plants love sunlight and could use seven to twelve hours of direct light every day.

❹ Roots need just the right amount of water—not too much and never too little. Some plants need to be watered from the bottom.

❺ Give plants room to breathe through their roots and leaves.

❻ Use soil that has nutrients plants like, such as nitrogen, phosphorus, and potassium.

❼ Plants need time to grow. Be patient and caring.

PLANT TALK

agronomy The growing of plants for food.

annual A plant that grows, flowers, and dies in one year. Most annuals produce seeds that can be planted the following spring.

biennial A plant that takes two years to mature. The first year the plant produces a stem and leaves, and the second year it produces flowers and seeds and then dies.

deciduous A tree that loses its leaves in autumn and gets new ones in the spring.

evergreen A tree that keeps its leaves or needles all year long.

fertilizer A natural or chemical substance applied to the soil to help plants grow bigger and faster.

herb A plant used for flavoring or seasoning, for its scent, or as medicine. Mint, lavender, palmetto, and rosemary are all herbs.

horticulture The growing of plants for beauty.

house plant A plant that is grown indoors. Many plants that are grown outdoors in tropical and desert regions have become popular as house plants.

hybrid A plant that has been scientifically combined with another plant or has been changed to make it more beautiful, larger, stronger, or better in some other way. Many roses are hybrids.

hydroponics A way of growing plants in a nutritional liquid rather than in soil.

mulch A covering of bark, compost (decomposed garbage), hay, or other substance used to conserve water and control weeds. Mulch can also provide nutrients for plants and keep plants warm in winter.

native A plant that has always grown in a certain place, rather than being brought there from somewhere else. Corn is native to North America.

perennial A plant that stops growing and may look dead in the fall, but comes back year after year.

photosynthesis The process that allows plants to make their own food from air, sunlight, and water.

phototropism The turning of plants toward the light.

propagation The reproduction of plants. Plants can be reproduced from seeds, or by dividing the roots of a plant, or sometimes by simply placing a piece of the leaf on soil.

terrarium A glass box containing small plants and animals, such as moss, ferns, lizards, and turtles.

transplant A plant that is dug up and moved from one place to another.

wildflower A flowering plant that grows on its own in the wild, rather than being planted by a person.

Where Do Plants Grow?

Plants grow nearly everywhere except near the South and North Poles.

Forests

WHERE EVERGREENS GROW. Forests cover about one-third of Earth's land surface. Evergreens, such as pines, hemlocks, firs, and spruces, grow in the cool forest regions farthest from the equator. These trees are called **conifers** because they produce cones.

TEMPERATE FORESTS. Temperate forests have warm, rainy summers and cold, snowy winters. Here **deciduous trees** (which lose their leaves in the fall and grow new ones in the spring) join the evergreens. Temperate forests are home to maple, oak, beech, and poplar trees, and to wildflowers and shrubs. These forests are found in eastern United States, southeastern Canada, northern Europe and Asia, and southern Australia.

TROPICAL RAIN FORESTS. Still closer to the equator are the tropical rain forests, home to the greatest variety of plants on Earth. The temperature never falls below freezing except on the mountain slopes. About 60 to 100 inches of rain fall each year. Tropical trees stay green all year. They grow close together, shading the ground. There are several layers of trees. The top, **emergent layer** has trees that can reach 200 feet in height. The **canopy,** which gets lots of sun, comes next, followed by the **understory.** The **forest floor,** covered with roots, gets little sun, and many plants cannot grow there.

Tropical rain forests are found mainly in Central America, South America, Asia, and Africa. They once covered more than 8 million square miles. Today, because of destruction by humans, fewer than 3.4 million square miles remain. More than half the plant and animal species in the world live there. Foods such as bananas and pineapples first grew there. Woods such as mahogany and teak also come from rain forests. Many kinds of plants there are used to make medicines.

When rain forests are burned, carbon dioxide is released into the air. This adds to the greenhouse effect (see page 73). As forests are destroyed, the precious soil is easily washed away by the heavy rains.

EMERGENT LAYER

CANOPY

UNDERSTORY

FOREST FLOOR

A rain forest ▼

Tundra and Alpine Region

In the northernmost regions of North America, Europe, and Asia surrounding the Arctic Ocean are plains called the **tundra.** The temperature rarely rises above 45 degrees Fahrenheit, and it is too cold for trees to grow there. Most tundra plants are mosses and lichens that hug the ground for warmth. A few wildflowers and small shrubs also grow where the soil thaws for about two months of the year. This kind of climate and plant life also exists on top of the highest mountains (the Himalayas, Alps, Andes, Rockies), where small Alpine flowers also grow.

What Is the Tree Line? On mountains in the north (such as the Rockies) and in the far south (such as the Andes), there is an altitude above which trees will not grow. This is the **tree line** or **timberline.** Above the tree line, you can see low shrubs and small plants, like Alpine flowers.

Deserts

The driest areas of the world are the **deserts.** They can be hot or cold, but they also contain an amazing number of plants. Cactuses and sagebrush are native to dry regions of North and South America. The deserts of Africa and Asia contain plants called euporbias. Dates have grown in the deserts of the Middle East and North Africa for thousands of years. In the southwestern United States and northern Mexico, there are many types of cactuses, including prickly pear, barrel, and saguaro.

Grassland

The areas of the world that are too dry to have green forests, but not dry enough to be deserts, are called **grasslands.** The most common plants found there are grasses. Cooler grasslands are found in the Great Plains of the United States and Canada, in the steppes of Europe and Asia, and in the pampas of Argentina. The drier grasslands are used for grazing cattle and sheep. In the **prairies,** where there is a little more rain, important grains, such as wheat, rye, oats, and barley are grown. The warmer grass-lands, called **savannas,** are found in central and southern Africa, Venezuela, southern Brazil, and Australia. Most savannas have moist summers and cool, dry winters.

FASCINATING PLANTS

PLANTS THAT EAT BUGS Bugs sometimes eat plants. But did you know that some plants trap insects and eat them? These are "carnivorous plants." The pitcher plant, Venus's-flytrap, and sundew are three examples. Most carnivorous plants live in poor soils, where they don't get enough nourishment. They digest their prey very slowly over a long period of time.

FLOWERING STONES Plants have ways of protecting themselves. For example, Lithops (or flowering stones) are plants in the South African desert that look like small, gray stones. They are much less likely to be eaten by animals than something that looks green and delicious.

Population

? How did American Indians become U.S. citizens?
You can find the answer on page 183.

WHERE DO PEOPLE LIVE?

Our planet is growing—not in size, but in population. In 1999, the number of people on Earth hit six billion. Just forty years ago, in 1959, Earth had five billion people. By 2050, the world population is expected to grow to more than nine billion people. Much of that growth will be in the world's poorest nations.

> According to UN estimates, the world population reached 6 billion on October 12, 1999.

LARGEST COUNTRIES
(Most People)

POPULATION	COUNTRY
1,246,872,000	China
1,000,849,000	India
272,691,000	United States
216,108,000	Indonesia
171,853,000	Brazil
146,394,000	Russia
138,123,000	Pakistan
127,118,000	Bangladesh
126,182,000	Japan
113,829,000	Nigeria
100,294,000	Mexico
82,087,000	Germany
79,346,000	Philippines
77,311,000	Vietnam
67,274,000	Egypt
65,599,000	Turkey
65,180,000	Iran
60,609,000	Thailand
59,680,000	Ethiopia
59,113,000	Great Britain
58,978,000	France
56,735,000	Italy
50,481,000	Congo Republic
49,811,000	Ukraine
48,081,000	Myanmar

LARGEST CITIES
(Most People)

Here are the 10 cities in the world that have the most people, as of 1995. Numbers include people from the whole built-up area around each city (the metropolitan area).

CITY, COUNTRY	POPULATION
Tokyo, Japan	26,959,000
Mexico City, Mexico	16,562,000
São Paulo, Brazil	16,533,000
New York City, U.S.	16,332,000
Mumbai (Bombay), India	15,138,000
Shanghai, China	13,584,000
Los Angeles, U.S.	12,410,000
Kolkata (Calcutta), India	11,923,000
Buenos Aires, Argentina	11,802,000
Seoul, South Korea	11,609,000

SMALLEST COUNTRIES
(Fewest People)

POPULATION	COUNTRY
860	Vatican City
10,588	Tuvalu
10,605	Nauru
18,467	Palau
25,061	San Marino
32,057	Liechtenstein
32,149	Monaco

DID YOU KNOW?

One out of every five people on Earth lives in China.

POPULATION
OF THE
NITED STATES

otal Population of the United States
in July 1999: 272,690,813

Population of the STATES and DISTRICT OF COLUMBIA in 1999

RANK & STATE NAME	POPULATION	RANK & STATE NAME	POPULATION
❶ California	33,145,121	㉗ Oklahoma	3,358,044
❷ Texas	20,044,141	㉘ Oregon	3,316,154
❸ New York	18,196,601	㉙ Connecticut	3,282,031
❹ Florida	15,111,244	㉚ Iowa	2,869,413
❺ Illinois	12,128,370	㉛ Mississippi	2,768,619
❻ Pennsylvania	11,994,016	㉜ Kansas	2,654,052
❼ Ohio	11,256,654	㉝ Arkansas	2,551,373
❽ Michigan	9,863,775	㉞ Utah	2,129,836
❾ New Jersey	8,143,412	㉟ Nevada	1,809,253
❿ Georgia	7,788,240	㊱ West Virginia	1,806,928
⓫ North Carolina	7,650,789	㊲ New Mexico	1,739,844
⓬ Virginia	6,872,912	㊳ Nebraska	1,666,058
⓭ Massachusetts	6,175,169	㊴ Maine	1,253,040
⓮ Indiana	5,942,901	㊵ Idaho	1,251,700
⓯ Washington	5,706,361	㊶ New Hampshire	1,201,134
⓰ Tennessee	5,483,535	㊷ Hawaii	1,185,497
⓱ Missouri	5,468,338	㊸ Rhode Island	990,819
⓲ Wisconsin	5,250,446	㊹ Montana	882,779
⓳ Maryland	5,171,634	㊺ Delaware	753,538
⓴ Arizona	4,778,332	㊻ South Dakota	733,133
㉑ Minnesota	4,775,508	㊼ North Dakota	633,666
㉒ Louisiana	4,372,035	㊽ Alaska	619,500
㉓ Alabama	4,369,862	㊾ Vermont	593,740
㉔ Colorado	4,056,133	㊿ District of Columbia	519,000
㉕ Kentucky	3,960,825	51 Wyoming	479,602
㉖ South Carolina	3,885,736		

LARGEST CITIES IN THE UNITED STATES

Cities grow and shrink in population. At right is a list of the largest cities in the United States in 1998 compared with their populations in 1950. Which six cities increased in population? Which four decreased?

RANK & CITY	1998	1950
❶ New York, NY	7,420,166	7,891,957
❷ Los Angeles, CA	3,597,556	1,970,358
❸ Chicago, IL	2,802,079	3,620,962
❹ Houston, TX	1,786,691	596,163
❺ Philadelphia, PA	1,436,287	2,071,605
❻ San Diego, CA	1,220,666	334,387
❼ Phoenix, AZ	1,198,064	106,818
❽ San Antonio, TX	1,114,130	408,442
❾ Dallas, TX	1,075,894	434,462
❿ Detroit, MI	970,196	1,849,568

TAKING THE CENSUS: EVERYONE COUNTS

Were you counted during Census 2000? It took place on April 1. The United States takes a census every ten years. It tries to count everyone. But it is believed that in every census some people get missed. In Census 2000, census-takers tried to track down and count people who did not send back forms, so that this census would be as accurate as possible.

WHY IS THE CENSUS NEEDED?

▶ The population of a state determines how many representatives it has in the U.S. House of Representatives.

▶ Census information helps the federal government in Washington, DC, decide which public services must be provided and where.

▶ In numbers, the census provides a picture of people living in the United States. Where do we live? How old are we? What do we do? How much money do we earn? How many children do we have?

WHEN WAS THE FIRST CENSUS TAKEN?
It was in 1790 just after the American Revolution. That year 3,929,200 people lived in what was then the United States. Most of the people lived on farms or in small towns. (Today, three out of every four Americans live in cities.)

WHAT WILL CENSUS 2000 SHOW?
The population in the western U.S. is growing faster than in any other area of the country. That means, in part, that more people are moving there. Nevada is the fastest-growing state. The population of the South is also growing steadily. But the Northeast and the Midwest are growing more slowly.

Even though the West is growing, it still has wide-open spaces. If you like room, lots of room, you might like living in Alaska, the most thinly populated state. It has only one resident for each square mile. Wyoming and Montana come next. But if you like to be surrounded by people, New Jersey is the most crowded, followed by Rhode Island and Massachusetts. New Jersey has more than 1,000 people per square mile.

WHO ARE WE?
Here are some other facts that the Census Bureau has gathered, or estimated, about people in the United States.

▶ About one out of every four people in the U.S. is now under 18 years old.

▶ People are living longer. In 1990, about 36,000 people in the U.S. were at least 100 years old. By 2050, more than 800,000 Americans will be 100 or older.

▶ About one out of every four children lives with a mother but not a father. About one out of every 17 lives with grandparents.

▶ Education pays off. On the average, people who went to college earn about twice as much as people who didn't graduate from high school.

The list below shows how many Americans considered themselves white, black, Asian, American Indian, and Hispanic in 1999. The percentages add up to more than 100% because Hispanics may count themselves as any race.

White, 225,000,000 . . . . 82%

Black, 35,000,000 . . . . 13%

Asian, 11,000,000 . . . . 4%
(including the Pacific Islands)

American Indian, 2,000,000. . . . 1%
(including Eskimo, or Aleut)

Hispanic, 31,000,000 . . . . 12%

 DID YOU KNOW?

In 1900, the most popular names were Mary, Helen, Anna, and Margaret for girls and John, William, James, and George for boys. Today's most popular names are Emily, Samantha, Madison, and Ashley for girls and Michael, Jacob, Matthew, and Christopher for boys.

Counting the FIRST AMERICANS

WHERE DID AMERICAN INDIANS COME FROM? American Indians, also called Native Americans, lived in North and South America long before the first European explorers arrived. Their ancestors are thought to have come from northeast Asia more than 20,000 years ago. American Indians are not one people, but many different peoples, each with their own traditions.

HOW MANY AMERICAN INDIANS WERE HERE IN THE 1400s? About 850,000 Native Americans lived in what is now the United States before Columbus arrived.

HOW MANY AMERICAN INDIANS ARE IN THE U.S. NOW? During the 17th, 18th, and 19th centuries, disease and wars with white settlers and soldiers caused the deaths of thousands of American Indians. By 1910 there were only about 220,000 left in the United States. Since then, the American Indian population has increased dramatically. By 1998, the total number of Native Americans was over two million.

WHEN DID AMERICAN INDIANS BECOME U.S. CITIZENS? In 1924, the U.S. Congress approved a law giving citizenship to all Native Americans.

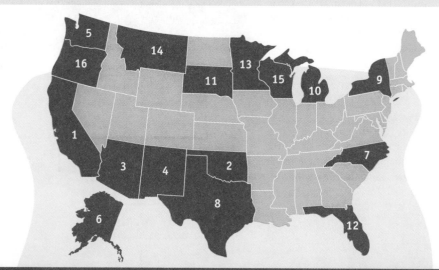

Where Do Native Americans Live?

Below are the states with the largest Native American populations. The states are numbered in the map above.

1. California	308,571		9. New York	75,886
2. Oklahoma	263,360		10. Michigan	59,601
3. Arizona	256,183		11. South Dakota	59,292
4. New Mexico	162,686		12. Florida	58,070
5. Washington	102,940		13. Minnesota	57,522
6. Alaska	99,603		14. Montana	55,615
7. North Carolina	97,507		15. Wisconsin	46,304
8. Texas	95,682		16. Oregon	44,998

THE MANY FACES OF AMERICA: IMMIGRATION

You have probably heard it said that America is a nation of immigrants. Many Americans are descended from Europeans, Africans, or Asians.

COMING TO AMERICA

Millions of people have immigrated to the United States from all over the world—over 40 million since 1820. They chose to come for various reasons, such as to live in freedom, to practice their religion freely, to escape poverty or oppression, and to make better lives for themselves and their children. But some people were brought here by force. In the 1600s, the British began shipping Africans to the American colonies to work as slaves. One out of every three people living in the southern colonies in the 1700s was an African slave.

What Countries Do Immigrants Come From?

Immigrants come to the United States from many countries. Below are some of the countries immigrants came from in 1998. The name of the country is followed by the number of immigrants. In 1998, immigration from all countries to the United States totaled 660,477.

Mexico	131,575
China	36,884
India	36,482
Philippines	34,466
Dominican Republic	20,387
Vietnam	17,649
Cuba	17,375
Jamaica	15,146
El Salvador	14,590
North and South Korea	14,268
Haiti	13,449
Pakistan	13,094
Colombia	11,836
Russia	11,529
Canada	10,190
Peru	10,154

Where Do Immigrants Settle?

California
170,126

New York
96,559

Florida
59,965

Texas
44,428

New Jersey
35,091

Illinois
33,163

The bar chart shows the states that received the highest number of immigrants in 1998.

More than two-thirds of the immigrants from Mexico went to live in California or Texas, while over half of the immigrants from China went to two states: California and New York. About 85 percent of the immigrants from Cuba went to live in Florida.

Becoming an AMERICAN CITIZEN

When a foreign-born person becomes a citizen of the United States, we say the person has become naturalized. To apply for American citizenship, a person:

- ▶ Must be at least 18 years old.
- ▶ Must have lived legally in the United States for at least five years.
- ▶ Must be able to understand English if under the age of 55.
- ▶ Must be of good moral character.
- ▶ Must show knowledge of the history and form of government of the United States.

A CITIZENSHIP TEST

When immigrants wanting to be United States citizens are interviewed, they may be asked any of 100 questions. Here are some of them. How many can you answer correctly?

1. What are the colors of our flag?
2. What do the stripes on the flag mean?
3. What are the duties of Congress?
4. How many senators are there in Congress?
5. Who helped the Pilgrims in America?
6. Which president freed the slaves?
7. Who is the chief justice of the Supreme Court?
8. Name one benefit of becoming a citizen of the United States.
9. What are the 49th and 50th states of the Union?
10. How many changes or amendments are there to the Constitution?

Answers are on pages 317-320.

THE STATUE OF LIBERTY

Many of the immigrants who crossed the Atlantic Ocean and steamed into New York Harbor passed by the Statue of Liberty. Set on her own island, the "Lady With the Lamp" was given to the United States by France and has served as a welcome to Americans-to-be since she was erected in 1886. In 1903, a poem by the U.S. poet Emma Lazarus was inscribed at the base of the statue. Two of its lines read: "Give me your tired, your poor, your huddled masses yearning to breathe free...."

Prizes, Awards, & Contests

Who won the Grammy for Best New Artist of 1999?
You can find the answer on page 187.

ENTERTAINMENT AWARDS

If you are interested in the movies, you probably know that an Oscar is a golden statuette that is awarded for the year's best actor, best actress, best movies, and so on. The Oscar presentations are watched on TV by millions of people all over the world. Among other awards given every year for the best in entertainment are the Grammys, the Emmys, and the Tonys.

ACADEMY AWARDS: THE OSCARS

The Oscars are given every year by the Academy of Motion Picture Arts and Sciences for the best in movies. Here are some of the films and people that won Oscars for 1999.

Best Picture: *American Beauty*
Best Actor: Kevin Spacey in *American Beauty*
Best Actress: Hilary Swank in *Boys Don't Cry*
Best Supporting Actor: Michael Caine in *The Cider House Rules*
Best Supporting Actress: Angelina Jolie in *Girl, Interrupted*
Best Director: Sam Mendes for *American Beauty*

▲ *Haley Joel Osment*

Best Original Screenplay: Alan Ball for *American Beauty*
Best Original Song: Phil Collins for "You'll Be in My Heart," from *Tarzan*
Best Original Musical Score: *The Red Violin*
Best Visual Effects: *The Matrix*
Best Costume Design: *Topsy-Turvy*
Best Makeup: *Topsy-Turvy*

DID YOU KNOW?

▶ For his role in The Sixth Sense, Haley Joel Osment was nominated in 2000 for a Best Actor Oscar. He was only eleven years old at the time. He had lots of fun at the Oscar ceremonies, but he didn't win. Osment was just a little older than Tatum O'Neal was when she won an Academy Award as Best Supporting Actress in 1974 at the age of ten, becoming the youngest person ever to win an acting Oscar.

▶ During his career, Walt Disney was nominated for 64 Oscars, more than anyone else ever. John Williams, who wrote the music for Star Wars and Jaws, has been nominated for 38 Oscars, the record for a living person.

▶ Katharine Hepburn and Meryl Streep are tied for the most acting nominations—12. Ms. Hepburn holds the record for the most wins, with four Oscars for Best Actress.

THE EMMYS

The Emmy Awards are given each year by the Academy of Television Arts and Sciences. Here are some of the major winners for the 1998–1999 season for primetime (the evening from 8 PM to 11 PM).

Best Drama Series: *The Practice* (ABC)

Best Actor in a Drama Series: Dennis Franz in *NYPD Blue* (ABC)

Best Actress in a Drama Series: Edie Falco in *The Sopranos* (HBO)

Best Comedy Series: *Ally McBeal* (FOX)

Best Actor in a Comedy Series: John Lithgow in *3rd Rock From the Sun* (NBC)

Best Actress in a Comedy Series: Helen Hunt in *Mad About You* (NBC)

Best Miniseries: *Horatio Hornblower* (A&E)

▲ *Carlos Santana, with Rob Thomas*

THE GRAMMYS

Grammys are awards given out each year by the National Academy of Recording Arts and Sciences. Some of the winners for 1999:

Best Record and Best Song: "Smooth," Santana, featuring Rob Thomas.

Best Album: *Supernatural,* Santana

Best New Artist: Christina Aguilera

Best Performance by a Rock Group: Santana, featuring Everlast

Best Rock Album: *Supernatural,* Santana

Best Rock Song: "Scar Tissue," Red Hot Chili Peppers

Best Pop Album: *Brand New Day,* Sting

Best Rhythm-and-Blues Song: "No Scrubs," TLC

Best Rap Solo Performance: Eminem

Best Rap Album: *The Slim Shady LP,* Eminem

Best Country Album: *Fly,* Dixie Chicks

Best Contemporary Folk Album: *Mule Variations,* Tom Waits

Best Musical Album for Children: *The Adventures of Elmo in Grouchland,* various artists

THE TONYS

The Antoinette Perry Awards, known as the "Tonys," are annual awards given to the best Broadway plays and to those who write them, act in them, and direct them. Winners for the 1998–1999 season were:

Best Play: *Side Man*

Best Revival of a Play: *Death of a Salesman*

Best Musical: *Fosse*

Best Musical Revival: *Annie Get Your Gun*

Leading Actor in a Play: Brian Dennehy

Leading Actress in a Play: Judi Dench

Leading Actor in a Musical: Martin Short

Leading Actress in a Musical: Bernadette Peters

AMERICAN THEATRE WING

TONY AWARD

CONTESTS

If you have a special talent or interest and you like to compete, why not consider entering a contest? From writing poems and short stories to creating complicated inventions, contests can be challenging and fun. Some appear in books, magazines, or newspapers, and you can enter on your own. Others are run only through schools; you need to ask your teacher about these.

DO YOU LIKE TO WRITE?

CHILDREN'S CREATIVE WRITING CAMPAIGN

Everyone's a winner because everyone who enters this contest gets an award certificate. Students up to age twelve can write about any subject they want, as long as it's totally original—not based on movies, books, or TV shows.

The entries are judged by professional authors, and children as young as five have been finalists. Finalists receive a $100 U.S. savings bond, and their school libraries get $100. In past years, finalists have also received "Creativity" software donated by Microsoft.

Get in touch with the Children's Creative Writing Campaign in the fall for more details and an official entry form. Write to: Creative Director; P.O. Box 999; Cooper Station; New York, NY 10276. Phone: 212-228-3041; fax: 212-228-6574.

ANN ARLYS BOWLER POETRY PRIZE

Every year, *READ* magazine invites students in grades six through twelve to enter this poetry contest. Poems can be about anything, and can be up to one page long. Winners get $100 each, a medal of honor, a certificate of excellence, national publicity, and publication in *READ* magazine. Semifinalists will receive $50 each and special certificates, and they are eligible for publication in *READ*.

Entries must be sent by April 1 of each year (no fooling).

WEB SITE *http://www.weeklyreader.com*

AMERICAN HISTORY ESSAY CONTEST

The Daughters of the American Revolution (DAR) are the descendants of soldiers who fought in the Revolutionary War. They run an essay contest every year for fifth- through eighth-graders. You or your teacher can contact your local DAR chapter to see if it is taking part and find out the topic, which changes every year.

Local contest winners receive certificates and pins. National winners get cash prizes, and their essays are published in *DAR Magazine*.

Log on to www.dar.org for information on how to contact the DAR chapter in your area, or look it up in the phone book.

THE NEWSCURRENTS STUDENT EDITORIAL CARTOON CONTEST

invites kids in grades K–12 to send in their original and creative editorial cartoons. You can enter as many cartoons as you wish. Winners receive U.S. savings bonds. The best 100 cartoons are published in the book *Editorial Cartoons by Kids*. (If your cartoon is published, you receive a free copy of the book.) The deadline is usually in March.

WEB SITE *http://www.ku.com/carcontest.html*

RUBE GOLDBERG MACHINE CONTESTS

Rube Goldberg was a Pulitzer Prize-winning cartoonist who invented—just for fun—complicated machinery to do ordinary tasks, such as sharpening a pencil or toasting a slice of bread.

The object of these contests is to use your imagination to make something much more complicated than it needs to be. Contestants build wacky machines (which actually work!) that use twenty or more steps to do something simple. (In 2000, a contest at the University of Kentucky required people to come up with an elaborate way to turn on a light switch.)

The best known contest is a national event for college students held each year by an engineering fraternity at Purdue University, in Indiana. The Argonne National Laboratory holds a competition for high school students in the Chicago area. Other universities have their own contests and sometimes include categories for middle grade students. Many are held in spring. You could call a nearby engineering department to find out if it has such a contest.

Even if you don't enter a contest, it can be fun to read about Rube Goldberg machines. To see what one looks like, and get more information on contests, visit the Rube Goldberg Web site at

WEB SITE *http://www.rube-goldberg .com*

NATIONAL SPELLING BEE

Fourteen-year-old Nupur Lala from Tampa, Florida, was the 1999 winner of the National Spelling Bee. If you're a good speller, you could follow in her footsteps. Newspapers across the country run spelling bees for kids ages 15 years old and under. Winners may qualify for the Scripps Howard National Spelling Bee in Washington, D.C. The competition is usually held in late May or early June. For information, ask your school principal to contact your local newspaper.

WEB SITE *http://www.spellingbee.com*

Nupur had to spell the following words correctly to win the 1999 National Spelling Bee. (None of them are easy to spell!)

ROUND	SPELLING WORD	ROUND	SPELLING WORD
1	ailanthus	7	cabotinage
2	extraordinaire	8	trianon
3	corollary	9	bouchon
4	palimpsest	10	poimenics
5	balbriggan	11	nociceptor
6	akropodion	12	logorrhea

TOP OF THE WORLD!

David Beihl was thirteen when he won the 1999 National Geographic Bee. It was the second try for this home schooler. He also represented his home state of South Carolina in 1998.

Among David's prizes was a $25,000 college scholarship. What did he have to do to win?

He had to correctly answer this question:

The condition characterized by unusually cold ocean temperature in the equatorial region of the eastern Pacific Ocean is known by what Spanish name?

The winning answer: La Niña.

If you want to enter this contest, sponsored by The National Geographic Society, you must be a fourth- through eighth-grader. You must compete on local, state, and national levels by answering oral and written questions about geography.

For more information, ask your school principal to write to: National Geographic Bee; National Geographic Society; 1145 17th St., NW; Washington, D.C. 20036. The registration deadline every year is October 15.

WEB SITE *http://www. nationalgeographic.com*

Other PRIZES and AWARDS

NOBEL PRIZES

The Nobel Prizes are named after Alfred B. Nobel (1833–1896), a Swedish scientist who invented dynamite, and left money to be given every year to people who have helped humankind. Albert Einstein, the world-famous German-born physicist, won the physics prize in 1921. The Polish-French scientist Marie Curie won two Nobel Prizes—one in physics in 1903 (with Pierre Curie, her husband, and Henry Becquerel) and one in chemistry in 1911. Prizes are also given for medicine-physiology, literature, economics, and peace.

The Nobel Peace Prize goes to people who the judges think did the most during the past year to help achieve peace. In 1999, the prize went to Doctors Without Borders, a group that volunteers to help people in dangerous places.

THE MEDAL OF HONOR

The Medal of Honor is given by the United States government for bravery in war against an enemy. The first medals were awarded in 1863. Since that time, nearly 3,400 people have received the award.

In 2000, Medals of Honor were awarded to 21 World War II soldiers, all Asian-Americans, for "heroic actions."

PULITZER PRIZES

The Pulitzer Prizes are named after Joseph Pulitzer (1847–1911), a journalist and publisher, who gave the money to set them up. The prizes are given yearly in the United States for journalism, drama, literature, and music.

All About... ROSA PARKS

In 1955, in Montgomery, Alabama, a black woman named Rosa Parks was arrested for not giving a white man her seat on the bus, as required by segregation laws. The result: Black people in the city stayed off the buses for 382 days, until the law was struck down by the Supreme Court. This boycott, led by Martin Luther King Jr., started the U.S. civil rights movement.

SPINGARN MEDAL

The Spingarn Medal was set up in 1914 by Joel Elias Spingarn, leader of the National Association for the Advancement of Colored People (NAACP). It is awarded every year by the NAACP for achievement by a black American. Here are some winners.

1999: Publisher Earl Graves

1998: Civil rights activist Myrlie Evers-Williams

1994: Writer and poet Maya Angelou

1991: General Colin Powell

1985: Actor Bill Cosby

1979: Civil rights activist Rosa Parks

1975: Baseball player Hank Aaron

1957: Martin Luther King, Jr.

Religion

? What belief do Christians, Jews, and Muslims have in common? *You can find the answer on pages 191 - 192.*

WORLD RELIGIONS

How did the universe begin? Why are we here on Earth? What happens to us after we die? For many people, religion is a way of answering questions like these. Believing in a God or gods, or in a Divine Being, is one way of making sense of the world around us. Religions can also help guide people's lives.

About six billion people all over the world belong to some group. Different religions have different beliefs. For example, Christians, Jews, and Muslims all believe in one God, while Hindus believe in many gods. On this page and the next are some facts about the world's major religions.

BUDDHISM

Who Started Buddhism? Gautama Siddhartha (the Buddha), around 525 B.C.

What Do Buddhists Believe? Buddha taught that life is filled with suffering. In order to be free of that suffering, believers have to give up worldly possessions and worldly goals and try to achieve a state of perfect peace known as *nirvana.*

How Many Are There? In 2000, there were more than 350 million Buddhists, mostly in Asia.

What Kinds Are There? There are two main kinds of Buddhists. **Theravada** ("Path of the Elders") **Buddhism,** the older kind, is more common in the southern part of Asia. **Mahayana** ("Great Vessel") **Buddhism** is more common in northern Asia.

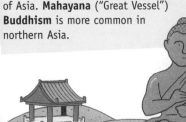

CHRISTIANITY

Who Started Christianity? Jesus Christ, in the first century. He was born in Bethlehem between 8 B.C. and 4 B.C. and died about A.D. 29.

What Do Christians Believe? That there is one God. That Jesus Christ is the Son of God, who came on Earth, died to save humankind, and rose from the dead.

How Many Are There? Christianity is the world's biggest religion. In 2000 there were almost two billion Christians, in nearly all parts of the world. More than one billion of the Christians were **Roman Catholics**, who follow the leadership of the pope in Rome. Other groups of Christians include **Orthodox Christians**, who accept most of the same teachings as Roman Catholics but follow different leadership, and **Protestants**, who often disagree with Catholic teachings. Protestants rely especially on the Bible itself. They belong to many different groups.

HINDUISM

Who Started Hinduism?
Aryan beliefs spread into India, around 1500 B.C. These beliefs were mixed with the beliefs of the people who already lived there.

What Do Hindus Believe?
That there are many gods and many ways of worshipping. That people die and are reborn many times as other living things. That there is a universal soul or principle known as *Brahman*. That the goal of life is to escape the cycle of birth and death and become part of the *Brahman*. This is achieved by leading a pure and good life.

How Many Are There?
In 2000, there were nearly 800 million Hindus, mainly in India and places where people from India have gone to live.

What Kinds Are There?
There are many kinds of Hindus, who worship different gods or goddesses.

ISLAM

Who Started Islam?
Muhammad, the Prophet, in A.D. 610.

What Do Muslims Believe?
People who believe in Islam are known as Muslims. The word "Islam" means submission to God. Muslims believe that there is no other god than the one God; that Muhammad is the prophet and lawgiver of his community; that they should pray five times a day, fast during the month of Ramadan, give to the poor, and once during their life make a pilgrimage to Mecca in Saudi Arabia if they can afford it.

How Many Are There?
In 2000, there were about one billion Muslims, mostly in parts of Africa and Asia. The two main branches are: **Sunni Muslims**, who make up over 80 percent of all Muslims today, and **Shiite Muslims**, who broke away in a dispute over leadership after Muhammad died in 632.

JUDAISM

Who Started Judaism?
Abraham is considered to be the founder of Judaism. He lived around 1300 B.C.

What Do Jews Believe?
That there is one God who created the universe and rules over it. That they should be faithful to God and carry out God's commandments.

How Many Are There?
In 2000, there were about 14 million Jews living around the world. Many live in Israel or the United States.

What Kinds Are There?
In the United States there are three main kinds: **Orthodox**, **Conservative**, and **Reform**. Orthodox Jews are the most traditional. Traditional means that they follow strict laws about how they dress, what they can eat, and how they conduct their lives. Conservative Jews follow many of the traditions. Reform Jews are the least traditional.

RELIGIOUS MEMBERSHIP in the United States

Did you know that Protestants are the largest religious group in the United States, and that Catholics are the second largest? The pie chart below shows how many people belong to the major religious groups. These numbers are recent estimates; no one knows exactly how many people belong to each group.

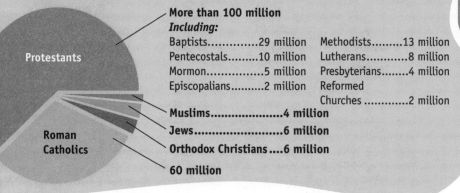

Protestants

Roman Catholics

More than 100 million
Including:

Baptists	29 million	Methodists	13 million
Pentecostals	10 million	Lutherans	8 million
Mormon	5 million	Presbyterians	4 million
Episcopalians	2 million	Reformed Churches	2 million

Muslims .... **4 million**

Jews .... **6 million**

Orthodox Christians .... **6 million**

60 million

RELIGIOUS WRITINGS

Every religion has its writings or sacred texts that set out its laws and beliefs. Among them are:

THE BIBLE

The Old Testament
Also known as the Hebrew Bible, this is a collection of laws, history, and other writings that are holy books for Jews and also for Christians. The first five books of the Old Testament are known by Jews as the Torah. These contain the stories of creation and the beginnings of human life, as well as the laws handed down by the prophet Moses.

The New Testament
A collection of Gospels (stories about Jesus), epistles (letters written to guide the early Christians), and other writings. The Old Testament and New Testament together make up the Bible that is read by Christians.

THE KORAN

The Koran (al-Qur'an in Arabic) sets out the main beliefs and practices of Islam, the religion of Muslims. Muslims believe that the Koran was revealed by God to the prophet Muhammad through the angel Gabriel.

THE BHAGAVAD GHITA

The Bhagavad Ghita is one of several Hindu religious writings. Part of a long poem about war, it is familiar to almost every Hindu. In it the god Krishna, in the form of a man, drives the chariot of Prince Arjuna into battle and teaches him about how to live.

MAJOR HOLY DAYS
FOR CHRISTIANS, JEWS, AND MUSLIMS

CHRISTIAN HOLY DAYS

	2000	2001	2002
Ash Wednesday	March 8	February 28	February 13
Good Friday	April 21	April 13	March 29
Easter Sunday	April 23	April 15	March 31
Easter for Orthodox Churches	April 30	April 15	May 5
Christmas	December 25	December 25	December 25

JEWISH HOLY DAYS The Jewish holy days begin at sundown the previous night. The dates listed below are the first full day of the observance.

	2000 (5760–5761)	2001 (5761–5762)	2002 (5762–5763)
Passover	April 20	April 8	March 28
Rosh Hashanah (New Year)	September 30	September 18	September 7
Yom Kippur	October 9	September 27	September 16
Hanukkah	December 22	December 10	November 30

ISLAMIC (MUSLIM) HOLY DAYS

	2000–2001 (1421)	2001–2002 (1422)	2002–2003 (1423)
Muharram 1 (New Year)	April 6	March 26	March 15
Mawlid (Birthday of Muhammad)	June 14	June 4	May 24
Ramadan 1	November 27	November 16	November 6
Id al-Adha Dhu al-Hijjah 10	March 5	February 22	February 11

? What major cure for infectious diseases was discovered by accident?
You can find the answer on page 199.

WHAT EVERYTHING IS MADE OF

Everything we see and use is made up of basic ingredients called elements. There are at least 112 elements. Most have been found in nature. Some are created by scientists in labs.

Elements Found in Earth's Crust
(percent by weight)

Iron, Calcium, Sodium, Potassium, Others

Aluminum

17%

8%

Oxygen 47%

Silicon 28%

Elements Found in the Atmosphere
(percent by volume)

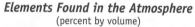
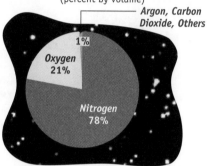

Argon, Carbon Dioxide, Others

1%

Oxygen 21%

Nitrogen 78%

IT ALL STARTS WITH AN ATOM

The smallest possible piece of an element that has all the properties of the original element is called an **atom**. Each tiny atom is made up of even smaller particles called **protons**, **neutrons**, and **electrons**.

To tell one element from another, scientists count the number of protons in an atom. The total number of protons is called the element's **atomic number**. All of the atoms of an element have the same number of protons and electrons, but some atoms have a different number of neutrons. For example, carbon-12 has six protons and six neutrons, and carbon-13 has six protons and seven neutrons.

We call the amount of matter in an atom its **atomic mass**. Carbon-13 has a greater atomic mass than carbon-12. The average atomic mass of all of the different atoms of the same element is called the element's **atomic weight**. Every element has a different atomic number and a different atomic weight.

CHEMICAL SYMBOLS ARE SCIENTIFIC SHORTHAND

When scientists write the names of elements, they often use a symbol instead of spelling out the full name. The symbol for each element is one or two letters. Scientists write O for oxygen and He for helium. The symbols usually come from the English name for the element (C for carbon). The symbols for some of the elements come from the element's Latin name. For example, the symbol for gold is Au, which is short for *Aurum,* the Latin word for gold.

HOW ELEMENTS ARE NAMED

How many of these elements have you encountered today?

NAME	SYMBOL	WHAT IT IS	WHEN FOUND	NAMED FOR
Berkelium	Bk	radioactive metal	1949	University of California, Berkeley
Bohrium	Bh	radioactive metal	1981	scientist Niels Bohr
Helium	He	gas	1868	the Greek word *helios*, meaning sun
Hydrogen	H	gas	1766	the Greek word *hydro*, water, and *gen*, forming
Krypton	Kr	gas	1898	the Greek word *kryptos*, hidden
Magnesium	Mg	metal	1829	Latin for Magnesia, a district in Asia Minor
Mercury	Hg	liquid metal	B.C.	the Roman god Mercury
Polonium	Po	metal	1898	Poland, native land of chemist Marie Curie; she and her husband discovered it

The elements 110-112 were discovered in recent years and have not yet been named. Reports of the discoveries of elements 114, 116, and 118 were made in 1999, but have not yet been confirmed. Discoveries of elements 113 and 115 have not yet been reported. Elements are usually named after people, places, and things. But no element gets a new name until the International Union of Pure and Applied Chemistry (IUPAC) accepts it. Do you have any suggestions for the nameless elements?

All About... COMPOUNDS

Carbon, hydrogen, nitrogen, and oxygen are the most common chemical elements in the human body. Many other elements may be found in small amounts. These include calcium, iron, phosphorous, potassium, and sodium.

When elements join together, they form *compounds*. Water is a compound made up of hydrogen and oxygen. Salt is a compound made up of sodium and chlorine.

Common Name	Contains the Compound	Contains the Elements
Vinegar	Acetic acid	carbon, hydrogen, oxygen
Chalk	Calcium carbonate	calcium, carbon, oxygen
Soda bubbles	Carbon dioxide	carbon, oxygen
Rust	Iron oxide	iron, oxygen
Baking soda	Sodium bicarbonate	sodium, hydrogen, carbon, oxygen
Toothpaste	Sodium fluoride	sodium, fluorine

MINERALS, ROCKS, and GEMS

WHAT ARE MINERALS?

Minerals are solid materials in the soil that were never alive. All the land on our planet—even the ocean floor—rests on a layer of rock made up of minerals. Minerals have also been found on other planets, on our moon, and in meteorites that landed on Earth. Some minerals, such as **gold** and **silver,** are made up entirely of one element. But most are formed from two or more elements joined together.

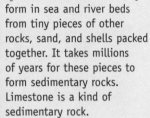
Quartz

The most common mineral is **quartz,** which is made of silicon and oxygen and is found all over the world. **Sand** is made up mostly of quartz. **Graphite,** which is used in pencils, is another common mineral. Other minerals, like **diamonds,** are very rare and valuable. Oddly enough, diamonds and graphite are different forms of the same element—carbon.

WHAT ARE ROCKS?

Rocks are combinations of minerals. The three kinds of rocks are:

❶ **Igneous rocks**—rocks that form from melted minerals in the Earth that cool and become solid. Granite is an igneous rock made from quartz, feldspar, and mica.

❷ **Sedimentary rocks**—rocks that usually form in sea and river beds from tiny pieces of other rocks, sand, and shells packed together. It takes millions of years for these pieces to form sedimentary rocks. Limestone is a kind of sedimentary rock.

❸ **Metamorphic rock**—Over millions of years, the heat and pressure inside Earth can change the minerals in igneous and sedimentary rocks. When the minerals in a rock change, the new rock is called a **metamorphic rock.** Marble is a metamorphic rock formed from limestone.

WHAT ARE GEMS?

Most **gems** are minerals that have been cut and polished to be used as jewelry or other kinds of decoration. Some gems are not minerals. A pearl is a gem that is not a mineral, because it comes from an oyster, which is a living thing. The most valued gems—diamonds, emeralds, rubies, and sapphires—are minerals called **precious stones.** Below are some popular gems, the kind of mineral each one is, the elements each is made up of, and the usual colors for the gem.

GEM NAME	MINERAL	ELEMENT IT IS MADE OF	USUAL COLORS
Amethyst	quartz	silicon, oxygen	purple
Diamond	carbon	carbon	bluish white
Emerald	beryl	beryllium, silicon, aluminum, oxygen	green
Opal	opal	silicon, oxygen	red, green, blue
Ruby	corundum	aluminum, oxygen	red
Sapphire	corundum	aluminum, oxygen	blue

DID YOU KNOW?

*Some minerals glow in the dark. Those that change color under ultraviolet light—like diamonds, opals, and rubies—are called **fluorescent minerals.** Fluorescent minerals that glow in the dark even after ultraviolet light is taken away are called **phosphorescent minerals.***

WHAT IS DNA?

DNA (deoxyribonucleic acid) contains the information that shapes all living things (organisms). Lengths of DNA, called genes, determine what each organism is like.

Genes are like tiny pieces of a secret code. They are passed on from parents to children. They determine how we look and grow. Many things about us, from the color of our eyes to the size of our feet, depend on the genes we inherited from our parents.

DNA DETECTIVES

In each cell of your blood, saliva, hair follicles, and skin, the DNA is the same. No one else has a pattern exactly like it. That's why DNA is useful in crime cases. It can link an accused person to the scene of the crime.

With DNA as evidence, police are looking again at some unsolved cases. In 1979, a man in New York state was suspected of a woman's murder. But there wasn't strong proof to charge him. Now the man's DNA has been matched with that found on evidence that had been in storage for 21 years.

Some suspects have been freed based on DNA testing. In 1996, four Chicago men were freed after spending eighteen years in prison, when DNA tests showed they were innocent.

All About... MAGNETS

► Magnets have strange powers! They can pull objects toward them or push away other magnets.

► The first magnets were pieces of lodestone. This black mineral was used by early mariners to find magnetic north. It is frequently called a natural magnet.

► Magnets make it possible for TVs, CD players, and radios to make sound.

► Computers use magnets to store information.

How Do Magnets React to Other Magnets? Magnets have two poles. One is called the north pole and the other is called the south pole. The north pole of one magnet will attract the south pole of another magnet—in other words, opposites attract. But when the north poles of two magnets are brought near each other, they will push away (repel) each other. Magnets can have different shapes and can be made of different materials.

SOME FAMOUS SCIENTISTS

Benjamin Banneker (1731–1806), a self-taught clockmaker and astronomer, who was the grandson of a slave. He is also known for his work as an architect and a designer of Washington, D.C.

George Washington Carver (1864–1943), onetime slave in Mississippi who became world-famous for his agricultural research. He found new and nutritious uses for peanuts and sweet potatoes, and taught farmers in the South to rotate their crops in order to increase their yield.

Nicolaus Copernicus (1473–1543), a Polish scientist known as the founder of modern astronomy. He believed all planets revolved around the sun.

Gertrude Belle Elion (1918–1999), a chemist who won a Nobel Prize for her research. It led to the development of many drugs, including those to fight leukemia, malaria, and the HIV virus that causes AIDS.

Sir Isaac Newton (1642–1727), a British scientist famous for discovering the laws of gravity. He also discovered that sunlight is made up of all the colors of the rainbow.

Edward Jenner (1749–1823), a British doctor who discovered a way to prevent smallpox by injecting healthy people with cowpox vaccine. Today's vaccines work in a similar way.

Michael Faraday (1791–1867), a British scientist who discovered that magnets can be used to create electricity in copper wires. Faraday's discoveries enable us to produce massive amounts of electricity.

Charles Darwin (1809–1882), a British scientist best known for his theory of evolution. According to this theory, living creatures slowly develop over millions of years.

Gregor Johann Mendel (1822–1884), an Austrian monk who discovered the laws of heredity by showing how characteristics are passed from one generation of plants to the next.

Louis Pasteur (1822–1895), a French chemist who discovered a process called pasteurization, in which heat is used to kill germs in milk.

Marie Curie (1867–1934), a Polish-French physical chemist known for discovering radium, which is used to treat certain diseases.

Albert Einstein (1879–1955), a German-American physicist who developed a revolutionary theory about the relationships between time, space, matter, and energy.

Francis Crick (born 1916) and **Maurice Wilkins** (born 1916) of England and **James D. Watson** (born 1928) of the United States, who worked out the structure of DNA, the basic chemical that controls inheritance in all living cells.

DID YOU KNOW?

Alexander Fleming, a Scottish scientist who lived from 1881 to 1955, discovered penicillin quite by accident! He happened to leave a dish with bacteria growing in it when he went on vacation. While he was gone the dish became contaminated with the Penicillium mold spore. When Fleming returned to his lab he noticed the mold had stopped the growth of the germs. This discovery, made in 1928, has saved millions of lives. Penicillin is one of the most effective drugs used to fight infectious diseases.

LIGHT AND SOUND

WHAT IS A SONIC BOOM?

It is the sound of a plane traveling faster than the speed of sound (breaking the sound barrier). People on the ground hear a thunderous boom. It is actually the sound caused by a sharp rise in air pressure in front and back of the aircraft. The pilot doesn't hear the boom.

WHAT ARE SHADOWS?

Shadows form because light rays, which can travel only in straight lines, do not bend around an object. Instead the light rays leave a dark area with the same shape as the object in their path.

CAN CREATURES GLOW IN THE DARK?

Yes, they can. Fireflies "blink" on and off during mating season. Some fish that live deep in the sea make their own light. Certain plankton often cast a blue glow on the upper levels of the ocean. It is so dark that they must glow in order to attract one another. This is called **bioluminescence**. It is caused by a chemical reaction within the organism that lights it up.

DO LIGHT AND SOUND CAUSE POLLUTION?

Yes, and they are two of the most ignored pollution problems. **Light pollution** is caused by the excessive use of lighting from industry, commercial signs, and streetlights at night. It causes birds that migrate at night to lose their way. Sea turtles that migrate toward the sea at night become confused and move toward streetlights. **Noise pollution** is excessive noise from airplanes, traffic, and humans. It can affect the way humans behave.

HOW LOUD ARE THOSE SOUNDS?

The loudness of a sound (called volume) is measured in **decibels**. The volume depends on how many air molecules are vibrating and how strongly they are vibrating. The quietest sound that can be heard has a value of zero decibels.

30 decibels
library, soft whisper

70 decibels
vacuum cleaner; freeway traffic

120 decibels
thunderclap

180 decibels
rocket engine

30 dB

180 dB

60 decibels
ordinary conversation

80 decibels
garbage disposal, hair dryer, alarm clock

150 decibels
jet taking off

SCIENCE MUSEUMS

If you like hands-on exhibits and like to learn about science, here are a few museums that you might visit. Look in the Index under Museums to find out about museums with exhibits on natural history and computers.

▲ *Museum of Science and Industry, Chicago*

California Museum of Science and Industry,

Los Angeles, California. Includes a giant electromagnet activated by visitors, plus exhibits on electricity, earthquakes, computer-assisted design, aerospace, and health sciences.

WEB SITE *http://www.casciencectr.org*

The Center of Science and Industry, Columbus, Ohio.

Here you can see a shipwreck, watch an underwater robot, and learn about early civilizations—just for starters.

WEB SITE *http://www.cosi.org*

Exploratorium, San Francisco, California.

Has interactive hands-on exhibits.

WEB SITE *http://www.exploratorium.edu*

The Franklin Institute Science Museum, Philadelphia, Pennsylvania.

Includes an exhibit on the environment called Earth Quest and many hands-on exhibits.

WEB SITE *http://www.sln.fi.edu*

Museum of Science and Industry, Chicago, Illinois.

Features a reproduction of a coal mine, a giant heart people can walk through, as well as displays to help visitors learn more about health, human intelligence, and how people live.

WEB SITE *http://www.msichicago.org*

National Air and Space Museum, Washington, D.C.

Has the Wright brothers' plane, Charles Lindbergh's *Spirit of St. Louis*, *Skylab*, and many other planes and rockets.

WEB SITE *http://www.nasm.si.edu*

The Science Place and TI Founders IMAX Theater, Dallas, Texas.

Includes hands-on science exhibits, water and sound experiments, an exhibit on special effects in movies, mathematical puzzles, and a planetarium.

WEB SITE *http://www.scienceplace.org*

CARNATION MAGIC

You can change the color of a carnation. Is it magic? What do you think?

YOU NEED

- ► one white carnation with a long stem
- ► two heavy paper cups
- ► blue food coloring
- ► clear water
- ► small scissors

WHAT TO DO

1. Split the carnation stem in half. Go about halfway up toward the flower.
2. Fill one cup with clear water.
3. Fill the other cup with blue food coloring.
4. Place one side of the stem in the cup of water and the other side in the cup of blue liquid.
5. Wait several hours and see what happens.

WHAT HAPPENED

Half of the flower should stay white and half should turn blue. The flower "drank" the water and the food coloring through tiny veins in the stem.

SINK or SWIM

Have you noticed how you stay on top of the water in a pool? The ability of people or things to float is called buoyancy. If you push something underwater and it rises back up to the top, it has **buoyancy.**

Here's a demonstration of how it works—and you don't even have to change into a bathing suit!

YOU NEED

▶ a clear glass

▶ a few raisins

▶ clear carbonated soda (seltzer or club soda)

WHAT TO DO

1. Fill the glass halfway with soda.

2. Gently drop two or three raisins into the filled glass.

3. Some of the soda bubbles will begin attaching themselves to the raisins and the raisins will start floating to the top of the soda. Then the raisins will drop down to the bottom . . . and back up . . . and back down . . . and back up. It's almost as if they're dancing.

4. When the soda finally goes flat, so will the raisins. Down they go and down they stay. The raisins no longer have the bubbles to give them buoyancy.

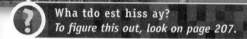

Signs & Symbols

? Wha tdo est hiss ay?
To figure this out, look on page 207.

Signs and symbols give us information at a glance. In the days when most people could not read, simple pictures helped them find their way around. Today, many of the same symbols are used the world over. So, even if you don't understand the native language, you may be able to read the signs!

Handicapped Access

Men's Rest Room

Women's Rest Room

Food

Lodging

Picnic Area

Camping

Swimming

Fishing

Hiking Trail

No Smoking

Flammable

Poison

Radioactive

Explosives

No Bicycles

SYMBOLS IN THE NEWS

Did you know that Democrats and Republicans each have their favorite animals? Democrats use the **donkey** as a symbol of courage, humility, kindness, and intelligence. To Republicans, the **elephant** represents strength, dignity, and intelligence. These political symbols were first used in the 1870s by Thomas Nast, a well-known cartoonist.

All About...
COMANCHE CODE TALKERS

From 1941 to 1945, during World War II, seventeen Comanche Indians—known as Comanche code talkers—helped to keep enemy Germans from learning U.S. military secrets. The code talkers used their own language to send U.S. Army messages over the radio. Since there are no Comanche words for many military terms, they used other words instead. To talk about tanks, for example, the Comanches used their word for turtle. The Germans had no knowledge of the Comanche language to start with, and this sort of double code baffled them even more.

Some Useful Symbols

$\$$	$\cancel{c}$	$\%$	$\&$	R_x
Dollar	Cent	Percent	Ampersand (and)	Prescription

♂	♀	$\pm$	$=$	$\neq$
Male	Female	Plus or minus	Is Equal To	Is Not Equal To

$<$	$>$	( )	©	®
Is Less Than	Is Greater Than	Parentheses	Copyright	Registered Trademark

ROAD SIGNS

 Stop

One Way

No Entry

No U-Turn

No Parking

 Right Turn

 No Left Turn

Hill

Signal Ahead

School Zone

 Pedestrian Crossing

 Deer Crossing

Railroad Crossing

 Road Work Ahead

Cross Road

Winding Road

 Slippery Road

 Divided Highway

 Yield

 Merging Traffic

BRAILLE

Many blind people read with their fingers using a system of raised dots called Braille. Braille was developed by Louis Braille (1809-1852) in France in 1826, when he was a teenager.

The Braille alphabet, numbers, punctuation, and speech sounds are represented by 63 different combinations of 6 raised dots arranged in a grid like this:

❶ ❹
❷ ❺
❸ ❻

All the letters in the basic Braille alphabet are lowercase. Special symbols are added to show that what follows is a capital letter or a number. The white circles on the grid below show the raised dots.

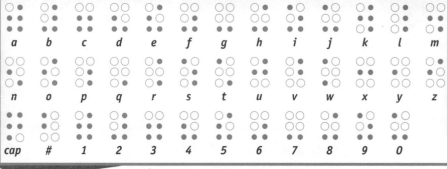

▲ Braille alphabet and numbers

SIGN LANGUAGE

Many people who are deaf or hearing-impaired, and cannot hear spoken words, talk with their fingers instead of their voices. To do this, they use a system of manual signs (the manual alphabet), or finger spelling, in which the fingers are used to form letters and words. Originally developed in France by Abbe Charles Michel De l'Epee in the late 1700s, the manual alphabet was later brought to the United States by Laurent Clerc (1785-1869), a Frenchman who taught people who were deaf.

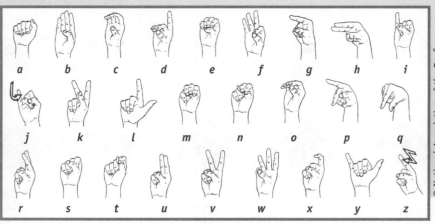

▲ American Manual Alphabet

STERCES EDIH SEDOC

Can you guess what the title of this page says? If you look closely, you will see that it is "codes hide secrets" written backward. This is one simple way to create a secret code. Different kinds of codes have been used since ancient times to keep military plans secret. Secret codes are still used today by the military, by banks for ATM machines, and on the Internet.

CHANGING LETTERS

Ciphers are one kind of code. In a typical cipher, letters are rearranged in different ways or switched for other letters. In the examples below, you can see four ways ciphers are used to hide the same message. Can you figure out what it is?

1 Changing the spaces: YO UCA NU SECO DE STO SEN DSE CR ETM ES SA GEST OY OURFRI ENDS.

2 Writing the sentence backward: SDNEIRF RUOY OT SEGASSEM TERCES DNES OT SEDOC ESU NAC UOY.

3 Writing the sentence using the alphabet from Z to A instead of A to Z, so that A=Z, B=Y, C=X, D=W, and so on: BLF XZM FHV XLWVH GL HVMW HVXIVG NVHHZTVH GL BLFI UIRVMWH.

4 Writing the sentence using an alphabet with the letters rearranged, for example, MQPUWXRDBSVAECNTZFIHOUGKJL (M=A, Q=B, P=C, U=D, and so on): JNO PMC OIW PNUWI HN IWCU IWPFWH EWIIMRWI HN JNOF XFBWCUI.

NUMBERS FOR LETTERS

Numbers can also be used in place of some or all of the letters of the alphabet. If you know that 2=Y, 3=U, 4=T, 5=S, 6=R, 7=O, 8=N, 9=M, 10=I, 11=G, 12=F, 13=E, 14=D, 15=C, 16=A, you can read the message below.

2 7 3   15 16 8   3 5 13   15 7 14 13 5   4 7   5 13 8 14
5 13 15 6 13 4   9 13 5 5 16 11 13 5   4 7   2 7 3 6   12 6 10 13 8 14 5

SECRET MESSAGE PUZZLE

Now use what you learned above to try to decipher (figure out) these codes:

1 Change the spaces: IHA VEAS EC RET.

2 Reverse the sentence: EM DELLAC OHW SSEUG REVEN LLIW UOY

3 Let A=Z, B=Y, C=X, D=W, and so on.

SV HGZIGVW ZH Z IZKKVI ZMW YVXZNV GSV UIVRH KIRMXV.

4 Rearrange the alphabet so that MQPUWXRDBSVAECNTZFIHOUGKJL stands for ABCDEFGHIJKLMNOPQRSTUVWXYZ. That means that M=A, Q=B, P=C, and so on.

FBRDH! GBAA IEBHD!

5 Substitute these numbers for letters: 2=D, 3=E, 4=G, 5=H, 6=I, 7=K, 8=L, 9=N, 10=O, 11=R, 12=S, 13=T, 14=U, 15=W, 16=Y

10 9 8 16   7 6 2 2 6 9 4!   15 6 12 5   6 13   15 3 11 3   13 11 14 3.

Answers are on pages 317-320.

Space

? Where would you look to see Orion, the hunter?
You can find the answer on page 213.

The SOLAR SYSTEM

Nine planets, including Earth, travel around the sun. These planets, together with the sun, form the solar system.

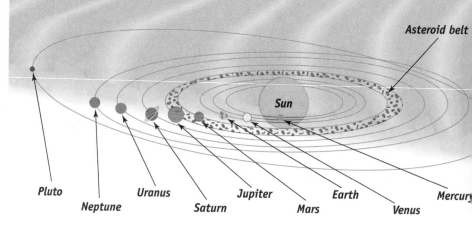

Asteroid belt

Sun

Pluto

Neptune

Uranus

Saturn

Jupiter

Mars

Earth

Venus

Mercury

THE SUN IS A STAR

Did you know that the sun is a star, like the other stars you see at night? It is a typical, medium-size star. But because the sun is much closer to our planet than any other star, we can study it in great detail. The diameter of the sun is 864,000 miles—more than 100 times Earth's diameter. The gravity of the sun is nearly 28 times the gravity of Earth.

How Hot Is the Sun? The surface temperature of the sun is close to 10,000°F, and it is believed that the sun's inner core may reach temperatures near 35 million degrees! The sun provides enough light and heat energy to support all forms of life on our planet.

THE PLANETS ARE IN MOTION

The planets move around the sun along oval-shaped paths called **orbits.** One complete path around the sun is called a **revolution.** Earth takes one year, or 365 ¼ days, to make one revolution around the sun. Planets that are farther away from the sun take longer. Some planets have one or more **moons.** A moon orbits a planet in much the same way that the planets orbit the sun.

Each planet also spins (or rotates) on its axis. An **axis** is an imaginary line running through the center of a planet. The time it takes the planet Earth to rotate one time on its axis equals one day. Here are some other facts about the planets and the symbol for each planet.

The Planets

❶ MERCURY

Average distance from the sun: 36 million miles
Diameter: 3,032 miles
Time to revolve around the sun: 88 days
Time to rotate on its axis: 58 days, 15 hours, 30 minutes
Number of moons: 0
ᴅɪᴅ ʏᴏᴜ ᴋɴᴏᴡ? *Mercury revolves around the sun faster than any other planet. It was named for Mercury, who in ancient Greek myths was the speedy messenger of the gods.*

❷ VENUS

Average distance from the sun: 67 million miles
Diameter: 7,521 miles
Time to revolve around the sun: 224.7 days
Time to rotate on its axis: 243 days
Number of moons: 0
ᴅɪᴅ ʏᴏᴜ ᴋɴᴏᴡ? *Venus is nicknamed the Evening Star because it shines more brightly than any other planet or star. It is also the planet closest to Earth.*

❸ EARTH

Average distance from the sun: 93 million miles
Diameter: 7,926 miles
Time to revolve around the sun: 365 ¹/₄ days
Time to rotate on its axis: 23 hours, 56 minutes, 4.2 seconds
Number of moons: 1
ᴅɪᴅ ʏᴏᴜ ᴋɴᴏᴡ? *Earth is four billion years old and weighs 6,580,000,000,000,-000,000,000 tons (6.58 sextillion tons). About three-fourths of Earth's surface is water. One-fifth of the land surface is mountains.*

❹ MARS

Average distance from the sun: 142 million miles
Diameter: 4,213 miles
Time to revolve around the sun: 687 days
Time to rotate on its axis: 24 hours, 37 minutes, 22 seconds
Number of moons: 2
ᴅɪᴅ ʏᴏᴜ ᴋɴᴏᴡ? *The largest volcano in the solar system is located on Mars. Olympus Mons is 15 miles high, almost three times higher than Mount Everest, the highest mountain on Earth.*

❺ JUPITER

Average distance from the sun: 484 million miles
Diameter: 88,732 miles
Time to revolve around the sun: 11.9 years
Time to rotate on its axis: 9 hours, 55 minutes, 30 seconds
Number of moons: 16
ᴅɪᴅ ʏᴏᴜ ᴋɴᴏᴡ? *When the Galileo spacecraft flew by Jupiter's moon Europa in January 2000, it picked up new evidence that a liquid ocean lies beneath Europa's crust.*

❻ SATURN

Average distance from the sun: 888 million miles
Diameter: 74,975 miles
Time to revolve around the sun: 29.5 years
Time to rotate on its axis: 10 hours, 30 minutes
Number of moons: at least 18
ᴅɪᴅ ʏᴏᴜ ᴋɴᴏᴡ? *The winds on Saturn blow at about 900 miles an hour. That's about six times stronger than hurricane-force winds on Earth.*

Saturn ▶

⑦ URANUS

Average distance from the sun: 1.8 billion miles
Diameter: 31,763 miles
Time to revolve around the sun: 84 years
Time to rotate on its axis: 17 hours, 14 minutes
Number of moons: 18
DiD YOU KNOW? *Unlike other planets, Uranus spins on its side. Its axis is tilted nearly 98 degrees, so its poles sometimes face the sun. When this happens, they are warmer than our Equator.*

⑧ NEPTUNE

Average distance from the sun: 2.8 billion miles
Diameter: 30,603 miles
Time to revolve around the sun: 164.8 years
Time to rotate on its axis: 16 hours, 6 minutes
Number of moons: 8
DiD YOU KNOW? *Since it takes Neptune nearly 165 Earth years to go around the sun, it hasn't completed a full orbit since it was discovered in 1846.*

⑨ PLUTO

Average distance from the sun: 3.6 billion miles
Diameter: 1,413 miles
Time to revolve around the sun: 247.7 years
Time to rotate on its axis: 6 days, 9 hours, 18 minutes
Number of moons: 1
DiD YOU KNOW? *In 1999, Pluto again became the most distant planet. It had been closer to the sun than Neptune for the previous 20 years.*

FACTS About the PLANETS

Largest planet: Jupiter
Smallest planet: Pluto
Planet closest to the sun: Mercury
Planet that comes closest to Earth: Venus (Every 19 months, Venus gets closer to Earth than any other planet ever does.)

Fastest-moving planet: Mercury (107,000 miles per hour)
Slowest planet: Pluto (10,600 mph)
Warmest planet: Venus
Coldest planet: Pluto
Longest days: Mercury
Shortest days: Jupiter

THE MOON

The moon is about 238,900 miles from Earth. It is 2,160 miles in diameter and has no atmosphere. The dusty surface is covered with deep craters. It takes the same time for the moon to rotate on its axis as it does to orbit Earth (27 days, 7 hours, 43 minutes). This is why one side of the moon is always facing Earth. The moon has no light of its own, but reflects light from the sun. The fraction of the lighted part of the moon that we see is called a *phase*. It takes the moon about 29 ½ days to go through all its phases.

PHASES OF THE MOON

New Moon

Crescent Moon

First Quarter

Full Moon

Last Quarter

Crescent Moon

New Moon

DiD YOU KNOW?

At one time, most people who studied the heavens were amateurs. They did it for enjoyment, rather than as a profession. One of the most famous is William Herschel. He was a church organist who found Uranus in 1781.

EXPLORING THE SOLAR SYSTEM

American space exploration began in January 1958, when the Explorer I satellite was launched into orbit. In 1958, NASA (the National Aeronautics and Space Administration) was formed.

SEARCHING FOR LIFE

For years scientists have tried to discover if there is life on other planets in our solar system or elsewhere. They look for signs of what is needed for life on Earth—basics like water and proper temperature.

NASA is searching for signs of life on Mars. The search will continue until 2013. Some spacecraft will fly around Mars taking pictures. Others will land there to study soil and rocks and look for living things. *Mars Pathfinder* and *Mars Global Surveyor*, launched in 1996, reached Mars in 1997. Unfortunately, *Mars Climate Orbiter*, launched in 1998, was apparently lost because of navigation error. Also, all communication attempts with *Mars Polar Lander*, scheduled to land on Mars in December 1999, have failed. Scientists aren't sure what happened to the two spacecraft.

In 1996, two teams of scientists examined two meteorites that may have come from Mars and found evidence that some form of life may have existed there billions of years ago. In January 2000, the spacecraft *Galileo* provided strong evidence there might be life in the icy waters of Europa, one of the 16 moons orbiting Jupiter.

Outside of NASA, another program is looking for life on other worlds. It is called SETI (Search for Extraterrestrial Intelligence). Most often it uses powerful radio telescopes to detect signs of life. Recently, however, astronomers began searching for light signals as signs of extraterrestrial life.

Astronomers have actually found evidence of several planets around stars other than the sun. In 1999, astronomers reported the first evidence of a group of planets orbiting one star, a star not very different from our sun. Perhaps there could be a form of life on one of those planets, or on a planet we have not found yet.

UNMANNED SPACE MISSIONS

1962 — Mariner 2 *First successful flyby of Venus.*

1964 — Mariner 4 *First probe to reach Mars, 1965.*

1972 — Pioneer 10 *First probe to reach Jupiter, 1973.*

1973 — Mariner 10 *Only U.S. probe to Mercury, 1974.*

1975 — Viking 1 and 2 *Landed on Mars in 1976.*

1977 — Voyager 1 *Reached Jupiter in 1979 and Saturn in 1980.*

1977 — Voyager 2 *Reached Jupiter in 1979, Saturn in 1981, Uranus in 1986, Neptune in 1989.*

1978 — Pioneer Venus 1 *Operated in Venus orbit 14 years.*

1989 — Magellan *Orbited and mapped Venus.*

1989 — Galileo *Reached Jupiter, 1995.*

1996 — Mars Pathfinder *Landed on Mars, sent a roving vehicle (Sojourner) to explore the surface.*

1997 — Cassini *Expected to reach Saturn in 2004.*

1998 — Lunar Prospector *Began yearlong orbit.*

1998 — Mars Climate Orbiter *Had been expected to reach Mars September 1999, to study surface and climate. Was apparently lost.*

2001 — 2001-Mars Surveyor 2001 Orbiter *Scheduled to launch in March and arrive in October to take thermal images of the planet's surface. Mars 2001 Lander, expected to launch in April and land on Mars in January 2002, will also take pictures of surrounding terrain.*

COMETS, ASTEROIDS, and SATELLITES

What else is in the solar system?

COMETS are fast-moving chunks of ice, dust, and rock that form huge gaseous heads as they move nearer to the sun. One of the most well-known is **Halley's Comet**. It can be seen about every 76 years and will appear in the sky again in the year 2061.

ASTEROIDS (or minor planets) are solid chunks of rock or metal that range in size from very small, like grains of sand, to very large. **Ceres**, the largest, is about 600 miles across. Thousands of asteroids orbit the sun between Mars and Jupiter.

Comet Hale-Bopp ▲

SATELLITES are objects that move in an orbit around a planet. Moons are natural satellites. Satellites made by humans are used as space stations and astronomical observatories. They are also used to photograph Earth's surface and to transmit communications signals.

DID YOU KNOW?

In January 2000, the Hubble Space Telescope provided stunning new photos of remote galaxies and a dying sun-like star 5,000 light-years away.

What Is an Eclipse?

A **solar eclipse** occurs when the moon moves between the sun and Earth, casting a shadow over part of Earth. When the moon completely blocks out the sun, it is called a total solar eclipse. When this happens, a halo of gas can be seen around the sun. This halo of gas is called the corona.

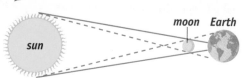

moon   Earth

sun

Sometimes Earth casts a shadow on the moon. This is called a **lunar eclipse**. Usually, a lunar eclipse lasts longer than a solar eclipse. The moon remains visible, but becomes dark, often with a reddish tinge (from sunlight that is bent through Earth's atmosphere).

Earth

sun

moon

UPCOMING TOTAL SOLAR ECLIPSES

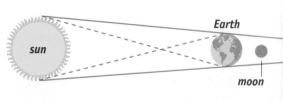

June 21, 2001
Will be seen over the Atlantic Ocean, Africa, and Madagascar.

December 4, 2002
Will be seen in southern Africa, over the Indian Ocean, and in Australia.

August 21, 2017
Will be seen from Oregon to South Carolina.

Constellations

Thousands of years ago, astronomers grouped stars together to form pictures. These groupings, or the areas of sky that they cover, are known as **constellations.** Astronomers all over the world named the constellations after animals or mythological figures or tools.

Most of the constellations we use today were named by the people living in ancient Greece and Rome. But the southernmost parts of the sky could not be seen from that part of the world. Most southern constellations were named only later by European people, when they began traveling more in Earth's southern hemisphere.

In 1930, the International Astronomical Union established a standard set of 88 constellations. They cover the entire sky that is visible from Earth. Astronomers use constellations as a quick way to locate other objects. For example, from Earth, the other planets moving around the sun appear in different constellations at different times.

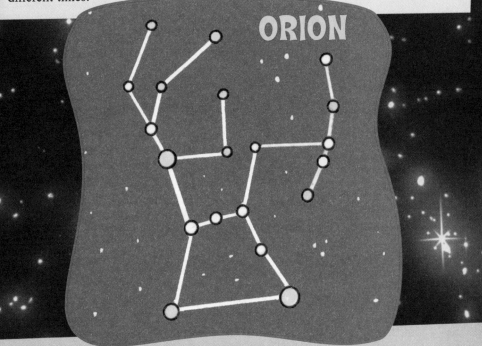

ORION

Constellations are often named because of what they look like. For example, from our viewpoint on Earth, the stars in the constellation of Orion above seem to trace a picture of a hunter. (Orion in Greek mythology was a giant hunter killed by the goddess Artemis.) Three stars form Orion's belt. Betelgeuse (pronounced bet tell juice), a bright red star, is his left shoulder. Rigel, a bright blue-white star, is his right foot.

Two other very well-known constellations are the Great Bear (Ursa Major is its Latin name) and the Little Bear (Ursa Minor).

HEAVENS ABOVE!

IS THERE A MAN ON THE MOON?
No, but there are a man's footprints. When Neil Armstrong walked on the moon, July 20, 1969, he left the first human footprints on the moon's surface. There is no wind or rain on the moon, so his footprints, along with those who came after him, can still be seen.

HOW HIGH IS THE SKY?
It depends on the weather. The sky we see is really the atmosphere. The atmosphere is a layer of gases made up of carbon dioxide, nitrogen, oxygen, and water vapor. It extends about 40 or 50 miles. The clouds we see are much lower, only about nine miles high. When clouds or fog don't get in the way, you can see the stars, and they're billions of miles away.

WHAT IS THE AURORA BOREALIS?
Also called the Northern Lights, it is a night light display. Sometimes the aurora is a quiet glow, almost like a fog. Other times, it may be colorful vertical streamers that wave or arc. The Aurora Borealis has been seen as far south as Key West, Florida. But it is more usually seen along the northern coast of North America and the eastern part of Europe's northern coast.

WHAT IS A GALAXY?
A **galaxy** is a group of billions of stars held together by gravity. Galaxies also contain interstellar gas and dust. The universe may have about 50 billion galaxies. The one we live in is called the **Milky Way**. The sun and the stars we see at night are just a few of the 200 billion stars in the Milky Way. Light from a star along one edge of the galaxy would take about 100,000 years to reach the other edge. Astronomers measure the distance between stars and between galaxies in light-years. One **light-year** is the distance light travels in one year—about 5.9 trillion miles.

DID YOU KNOW?

► One **light-year** is the distance light travels in one year—about 5.9 trillion miles.

► About 50,000 years ago a huge meteorite crash-landed in Arizona. It left a crater 575 feet deep and 4,150 feet wide. Named the Barrington Meteor Crater, it has been used as a training ground for Apollo astronauts.

► In 1999, NASA launched Stardust, a space probe, to collect samples of interstellar dust beginning in 2004. Stardust will come back toward Earth in 2006 and release its dust collection capsule, which will descend by parachute to a site in Utah. This dust may tell us more about the origin of solar systems, planets, and life.

WHAT ARE METEORS, METEORITES, AND METEOR SHOWERS?
On a clear night, you may see a sudden streak of light in the sky. It may be caused by chunks of rock or metal called **meteoroids** speeding through space. When a meteoroid enters Earth's atmosphere, friction with air molecules causes it to burn brightly. The streak we see is called a **meteor**, or **shooting star**.

Many meteoroids follow in the path of a comet as it orbits the sun. As these meteoroids enter Earth's atmosphere, large numbers can be seen coming from about the same area. These streaks are called **meteor showers**. If a meteoroid is big enough to land without burning up completely, it is called a **meteorite**.

ASTRONAUTS in OUTER SPACE

The rapid entry of the United States into space in 1958 was in response to the Soviet Union's launching of its satellite *Sputnik I* into orbit on October 4, 1957. In 1961, three years after NASA was formed, President John F. Kennedy promised Americans that the United States would land a person on the moon by the end of the 1960s. As promised, NASA landed a human on the moon in July 1969. Since then, many astronauts have made trips into outer space. This time line gives some of the major flights of astronauts into space.

1961 — On April 12, Soviet cosmonaut Yuri Gagarin, in *Vostok 1*, became the **first human to orbit Earth**. On May 5, U.S. astronaut Alan B. Shepard Jr. of the *Mercury 3* mission became the **first American in space**.

1962 — On February 20, U.S. astronaut John H. Glenn Jr. of *Mercury 6* became the **first American to orbit Earth**.

1963 — From June 16 to 19, the Soviet spacecraft *Vostok 6* carried the **first woman in space**, Valentina V. Tereshkova.

1965 — On March 18, Soviet cosmonaut Aleksei A. Leonov became the **first person to walk in space**. He spent 10 minutes outside the spaceship. On December 15, U.S. *Gemini 6A* and *7* (with astronauts) became the **first vehicles to rendezvous** (approach and see each other) **in space**.

1966 — On March 16, U.S. *Gemini 8* became the **first craft to dock with** (become attached to) **another vehicle** (an unmanned *Agena* rocket).

1967 — On January 27, a fire in a U.S. *Apollo* spacecraft on the ground killed astronauts Virgil I. Grissom, Edward H. White, and Roger B. Chaffee. On April 23, *Soyuz 1* crashed to the Earth, killing Soviet cosmonaut Vladimir Komarov.

1969 — On July 20, after successful flights of *Apollo 8, 9,* and *10,* U.S. *Apollo 11's* **lunar module** *Eagle* **landed on the moon's surface** in the area known as the Sea of Tranquility. Neil Armstrong became the **first person ever to walk on the moon.**

1970 — In April, *Apollo 13* astronauts returned safely to Earth after an explosion damaged their spacecraft and prevented them from landing on the moon.

1971 — In July and August, U.S. *Apollo 15* astronauts tested the **Lunar Rover** on the moon.

1972 — In December, *Apollo 17* was the sixth and **final U.S. space mission to land successfully on the moon.**

1973 — On May 14, the U.S. put its **first space station, Skylab, into orbit**. Crews worked in Skylab until January 1974, when the last crew left.

1975 — On July 15, the U.S. launched *Apollo 18* and the U.S.S.R. launched *Soyuz 19*. Two days later, the **American and Soviet spacecraft docked**, and for several days their crews worked and spent time together in space. This was NASA's last space mission with astronauts until the space shuttle.

SHUTTLES and SPACE STATIONS

In the 1970s, NASA developed the space shuttle program. Earlier space capsules could not be used again after returning to Earth.

In 1986, the Soviet Union launched its *Mir* space station. By the mid-1990s, the United States and Russia were sharing projects in space. By the late 1990s, the United States and Russia had joined other nations in planning an International Space Station. By 2000 *Mir* was very old, and plans for its future were uncertain.

1977 — The first shuttle, **Enterprise**, took off from the back of a 747 jet airliner.

1981 — **Columbia** was launched and became the first shuttle to reach Earth's orbit.

1983 — In April, NASA began using a third shuttle, **Challenger**. Two more **Challenger** flights in 1983 included astronauts Sally K. Ride and Guion S. Bluford Jr., the first American woman and first African-American man in space. In November, **Columbia** was launched carrying Spacelab, a European scientific laboratory.

1984 — In August, the shuttle **Discovery** was launched for the first time.

1985 — In October, the shuttle **Atlantis** was launched for the first time.

1986 — On January 28, after 24 successful missions, **Challenger** exploded 73 seconds after takeoff. Astronauts Dick Scobee, Michael Smith, Ellison Onizuka, Judith Resnik, Greg Jarvis, and Ron McNair, and teacher Christa McAuliffe died. In February, the Soviet space station **Mir** was launched into orbit.

1988 — In September, more than two years after the **Challenger** disaster, new safety procedures led to a successful launch of **Discovery**.

1990 — On April 24, the **Hubble Space Telescope** was launched from **Discovery**, but the images sent back to Earth were fuzzy.

1992 — In May, NASA launched a new shuttle, **Endeavour**.

1993 — In December, a crew aboard **Endeavour** repaired the Hubble telescope.

1995 — In March, astronaut Norman Thagard became the first American to travel in a Russian spacecraft; he joined cosmonauts on **Mir**. In June, **Atlantis** docked with **Mir** for the first time.

1996 — In March, Shannon Lucid joined the **Mir** crew. She spent 188 days in space, setting the record for all American and all female astronauts.

1998 — Astronaut Andrew Thomas in January became the last U.S. astronaut to join the **Mir** crew. In October astronaut John Glenn was launched into space a second time, aboard the shuttle **Discovery**. In December, **Endeavour** was launched with **Unity**, a U.S.-built part of the International Space Station. The crew attached it to the Russian-built **Zarya** control module.

1999 — In June, **Discovery** astronauts successfully docked with the International Space Station and unloaded 2 tons of supplies. In July, Eileen Collins became the first woman to command a shuttle, the **Columbia**. In December, space shuttle astronauts repaired the **Hubble Space Telescope**.

2000 — By year's end, astronauts were scheduled to be living aboard the International Space Station.

INTERNATIONAL SPACE STATION

After years of research and planning, a permanent space research laboratory is being built in orbit around the Earth. Three astronauts were scheduled to go aboard the station in the summer of 2000 to help build it. The United States, Russia, and 14 other countries hope to complete this International Space Station by 2004. Then seven crew members will call the station home. They will figure out how to live and work safely in space for long periods. Their experiments will also help scientists plan future space travel.

When it is completed, the space station will have a mass of about 500 tons. It will be as long as a football field, including the end zones. The living space for the crew will match the inside of a 747 jumbo jet. Four windows will allow the crew to observe the Earth and other objects in space. A solar array with a surface area of about half an acre will provide electricity for the station. Fifty-two computers will control the systems and the six scientific laboratories on the station.

THE ZODIAC

The zodiac is an imaginary belt (or path) that goes around the sky. The orbits of the sun, the moon, and most of the planets are within the zodiac. The zodiac crosses parts of 21 different constellations. Below are the symbols for the 12 constellations most commonly associated with the zodiac.

ARIES (Ram)
March 21–April 19

TAURUS (Bull)
April 20–May 20

GEMINI (Twins)
May 21–June 21

CANCER (Crab)
June 22–July 22

LEO (Lion)
July 23–August 22

VIRGO (Maiden)
August 23–Sept. 22

LIBRA (Balance)
Sept. 23–Oct. 23

SCORPIO (Scorpion)
Oct. 24–Nov. 21

SAGITTARIUS
(Archer)
Nov. 22–Dec. 21

CAPRICORN (Goat)
Dec. 22–Jan. 19

AQUARIUS
(Water Bearer)
Jan. 20–Feb. 18

PISCES (Fishes)
Feb. 19–March 20

All About... ASTRONOMERS

Astronomers are scientists who study the sky, including stars, planets, moons, comets, asteroids, and meteors, to discover what they are made of, and how they behave. **Astrologers** are not scientists. They believe that the positions and movements of the sun, moon, and planets influence the lives of people on Earth.

Sports & Games

? What two new sports are included in the 2000 Summer Olympic Games in Sydney, Australia? *You can find the answer on page 230.*

Baseball

In 1999 the New York Yankees swept the Atlanta Braves in four straight games to win their second championship in a row. It was their third World Series win in the past four years, and their 25th overall. The Yankees have won more championships than any other major pro sports franchise in North America.

Many individual players also had big success. Yankee pitcher David Cone threw a 6-0 perfect game July 18 against Montreal. St. Louis's Mark McGwire and the Chicago Cubs' Sammy Sosa thrilled fans with their record-breaking home runs. Mark hit 65 and Sammy hit 63. They were the only two players ever to hit 60 or more two seasons in a row. Two other hitters passed the 400 career home-run mark: Tampa Bay's Jose Canseco (431) and Baltimore's Cal Ripken Jr. (402).

FINAL 1999 STANDINGS

AMERICAN LEAGUE

EASTERN DIVISION	WON	LOST
New York Yankees	98	64
Boston Red Sox*	94	68
Toronto Blue Jays	84	78
Baltimore Orioles	78	84
Tampa Bay Devil Rays	69	93

CENTRAL DIVISION	WON	LOST
Cleveland Indians	97	65
Chicago White Sox	75	86
Detroit Tigers	69	92
Kansas City Royals	64	97
Minnesota Twins	63	97

WESTERN DIVISION	WON	LOST
Texas Rangers	95	67
Oakland Athletics	87	75
Seattle Mariners	79	83
Anaheim Angels	70	92

NATIONAL LEAGUE

EASTERN DIVISION	WON	LOST
Atlanta Braves	103	59
New York Mets*[1]	97	66
Philadelphia Phillies	77	85
Montreal Expos	68	94
Florida Marlins	64	98

CENTRAL DIVISION	WON	LOST
Houston Astros	97	65
Cincinnati Reds	96	67
Pittsburgh Pirates	78	83
St. Louis Cardinals	75	86
Milwaukee Brewers	74	87
Chicago Cubs	67	95

WESTERN DIVISION	WON	LOST
Arizona Diamondbacks	100	62
San Francisco Giants	86	76
Los Angeles Dodgers	77	85
San Diego Padres	74	88
Colorado Rockies	72	90

*Wild card team. (1) New York beat Cincinnati (5-0) in a one-game playoff to win the wild card spot.

PLAYOFF RESULTS

AL DIVISION SERIES
New York defeated Texas, 3-0
Boston defeated Cleveland, 3-2

AL CHAMPIONSHIP SERIES
New York defeated Boston, 4-1

NL DIVISION SERIES
Atlanta defeated Houston, 3-1
New York defeated Arizona, 3-1

NL CHAMPIONSHIP SERIES
Atlanta defeated New York, 4-2

1999 WORLD SERIES
New York defeated Atlanta, 4-0

1999 MAJOR LEAGUE LEADERS

MOST VALUABLE PLAYERS
American League: Ivan Rodriguez, Texas Rangers
National League: Chipper Jones, Atlanta Braves

CY YOUNG AWARD WINNERS (TOP PITCHER)
American League: Pedro Martinez, Boston Red Sox
National League: Randy Johnson, Arizona Diamondbacks

ROOKIES OF THE YEAR
American League: Carlos Beltran, Kansas City Royals
National League: Scott Williamson, Cincinnati Reds

BATTING CHAMPS
American League: Nomar Garciaparra, Boston Red Sox, .357
National League: Larry Walker, Colorado Rockies, .379

HOME RUN LEADERS
American League: Ken Griffey Jr., Seattle Mariners, 48
National League: Mark McGwire, St. Louis Cardinals, 65

RUNS BATTED IN (RBI) LEADERS
American League: Manny Ramirez, Cleveland Indians, 165
National League: Mark McGwire, St. Louis Cardinals, 147

MOST PITCHING VICTORIES
American League: Pedro Martinez, Boston Red Sox, 23
National League: Mike Hampton, Houston Astros, 22

▲ *Pedro Martinez*

LITTLE LEAGUE

Little League Baseball is the largest youth sports program in the world. It began in 1939 in Williamsport, Pennsylvania, with 45 boys playing on three teams. Now nearly three million boys and girls ages 5 to 18 play on 200,000 Little League teams in more than 80 countries.

WEB SITE *http://www.littleleague.org*

Baseball Hall of Fame

The National Baseball Hall of Fame and Museum opened in 1939, in Cooperstown, New York. To be nominated for membership, players must be retired from baseball for five years.

Address: 25 Main Street, PO Box 590, Cooperstown, NY 13326.

Phone: (607) 547-7200; toll-free: (888) 425-5633
WEB SITE *http://www.baseballhalloffame.org*

DID YOU KNOW?

▶ *Fernando Tatis of the St. Louis Cardinals became the first player in major league history to hit two grand slams in an inning, on April 23, 1999.*

▶ *1999 American League MVP Ivan Rodriguez of the Texas Rangers became the first catcher in major league history to hit 20 home runs and steal 20 bases in a season.*

WEB SITE *http://www.majorleaguebaseball.com*

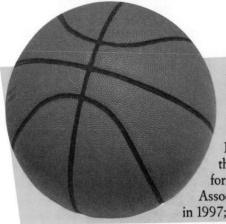

BASKETBALL

Basketball began in 1891 in Springfield, Massachusetts, when Dr. James Naismith invented it, using peach baskets as hoops. At first, each team had nine players instead of five. Big-time pro basketball started in 1949, when the National Basketball Association (NBA) was formed. The Women's National Basketball Association (WNBA) began play with eight teams in 1997; by 2000 it had doubled to sixteen.

MEN'S PROFESSIONAL BASKETBALL
Final 1999-2000 NBA Standings

EASTERN CONFERENCE

ATLANTIC DIVISION	WON	LOST
Miami Heat	52	30
New York Knicks	50	32
Philadelphia 76ers	49	33
Orlando Magic	41	41
Boston Celtics	35	47
New Jersey Nets	31	51
Washington Wizards	29	53

CENTRAL DIVISION	WON	LOST
Indiana Pacers	56	26
Charlotte Hornets	49	33
Toronto Raptors	45	37
Detroit Pistons	42	40
Milwaukee Bucks	42	40
Cleveland Cavaliers	32	50
Atlanta Hawks	28	54
Chicago Bulls	17	65

WESTERN CONFERENCE

MIDWEST DIVISION	WON	LOST
Utah Jazz	55	27
San Antonio Spurs	53	29
Minnesota Timberwolves	50	32
Dallas Mavericks	40	42
Denver Nuggets	35	47
Houston Rockets	34	48
Vancouver Grizzlies	22	60

PACIFIC DIVISION	WON	LOST
Los Angeles Lakers	67	15
Portland Trail Blazers	59	23
Phoenix Suns	53	29
Seattle SuperSonics	45	37
Sacramento Kings	44	38
Golden State Warriors	19	63
Los Angeles Clippers	15	67

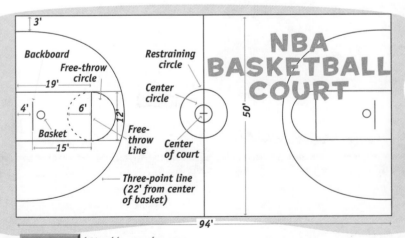

NBA BASKETBALL COURT

3'
Backboard
Free-throw circle
19'
Restraining circle
Center circle
4'
6'
12'
Basket
15'
Free-throw Line
Center of court
50'
Three-point line (22' from center of basket)
94'

WEB SITE http://www.nba.com

HIGHLIGHTS OF THE 1999-2000 NBA SEASON

MVP & SCORING LEADER: Shaquille O'Neal, Los Angeles Lakers
Games: 79   **Points:** 2,344   **Average:** 29.7

REBOUNDING LEADER: Dikembe Mutombo, Atlanta Hawks
Games: 82   **Rebounds:** 1,157   **Average:** 14.1

ASSISTS LEADER: Jason Kidd, Phoenix Suns
Games: 67   **Assists:** 678   **Average:** 10.l

STEALS LEADER: Eddie Jones, Charlotte Hornets
Games: 72   **Steals:** 192   **Average:** 2.67

BLOCKED SHOTS LEADER: Alonzo Mourning, Miami Heat
Games: 79   **Blocks:** 294   **Average:** 3.72

NBA HALL OF FAME

The Naismith Memorial Basketball Hall of Fame was founded in 1959 to honor great basketball players, coaches, referees, and others important to the history of the game.

Address: 1150 W. Columbus Ave., Springfield, MA 01105.

Phone: (413) 781-6500.

WEB SITE *http://www.hoophall.com*

A REAL SPORTSMAN

Wilt Chamberlain, the "Big Dipper," died in October 1999. Here are just a few of his amazing records in the NBA: 55 rebounds in a game (1960), 100 points in one game (1962), averaged 50.4 points-per-game in a season (1961-62), 23,924 career rebounds. He's second on the list of all-time leading scorers (31,419). And he played fair, too—in his 1,045-game career, he never fouled out of a single game!

▲ *Wilt Chamberlain*

WOMEN'S PROFESSIONAL BASKETBALL
Final 1999 WNBA Standings

EASTERN CONFERENCE	WON	LOST	WESTERN CONFERENCE	WON	LOST
New York Liberty	18	14	Houston Comets	26	6
Charlotte Sting	15	17	Los Angeles Sparks	20	12
Detroit Shock	15	17	Sacramento Monarchs	19	13
Orlando Miracle	15	17	Phoenix Mercury	15	17
Washington Mystics	12	20	Minnesota Lynx	15	17
Cleveland Rockers	7	25	Utah Starzz	15	17

WNBA PLAYOFFS
Eastern Conference:
Charlotte Sting defeated Detroit Shock.
New York Liberty defeated Charlotte Sting, 2 games to 1.

Western Conference:
Los Angeles Sparks defeated Sacramento Monarchs.
Houston Comets defeated Los Angeles Sparks, 2 games to 1.

WNBA CHAMPIONSHIP
Houston Comets defeated New York Liberty, 2 games to 1.

Four new teams joined the WNBA in 2000: the Indiana Fever, Miami Sol, Portland Fire, and Seattle Storm.

WEB SITE *http://www.wnba.com*

DiD You KNOW?

Michael Jordan may have hung up his basketball sneakers for good in 1999, but in January 2000, "His Airness" became president of basketball operations and part owner of the Washington Wizards, plus a part-owner of hockey's Washington Capitals.

COLLEGE BASKETBALL

College basketball has become a huge sport. The National Collegiate Athletic Association (NCAA) Tournament began in 1939. Today, it is a spectacular 64-team extravaganza. The Final Four weekend, when the semi-finals and finals are played, is one of the most watched sports events in the United States. The NCAA Tournament for women's basketball began in 1982. Since then, the popularity of the women's game has grown by leaps and bounds.

THE 2000 NCAA TOURNAMENT RESULTS

MEN'S FINAL FOUR RESULTS

SEMI-FINALS:
Michigan State 53, Wisconsin 41
Florida 71, North Carolina 59

CHAMPIONSHIP GAME:
Michigan State 89, Florida 76

The only top-seeded team to make it to the Final Four, the Michigan State Spartans beat the Florida Gators, 89-76, in the NCAA championship game. It was their first title since 1979, when Earvin "Magic" Johnson led the Spartans to victory over Larry Bird's Indiana State Sycamores in the most-watched NCAA final of all time. In 2000, the Spartans were led by "The Flintstones"—Mateen Cleaves, Morris Peterson, and Charlie Bell—who grew up playing basketball together in Flint, Michigan. Mateen, a senior point guard and the team's leader, hurt his ankle early in the second half and had to leave the game. Limping, he came back to play the final 11:51 and was named the Final Four's Most Outstanding Player. Morris led the Spartans with 21 points, Mateen had 18, and Charlie added nine. Florida's Udonis Haslem led all scorers with 27.

WOMEN'S FINAL FOUR RESULTS

SEMI-FINALS:
Connecticut 89, Penn State 67
Tennessee 64, Rutgers 54

CHAMPIONSHIP GAME:
Connecticut 71, Tennessee 52

The University of Connecticut trampled Tennessee, 71-52, to win the national championship. It was the second NCAA title for the Huskies, who finished the season with a record of 36-1. The Lady Vols, who have won six national titles, finished with a record of 33-6 and were the only team to beat the Huskies all season. Final Four MVP Shea Ralph led UConn with 15 points, seven assists, six steals, and one blocked shot. Defensively, Kelly Schumacher led the Huskies with nine blocked shots, a record for the NCAA finals. Tamika Catchings of Tennessee, the national Player of the Year, took only one shot in the first 11 minutes of the game, but finished with 16 points. Winning the title in Philadelphia was doubly sweet for national Coach of the Year Geno Auriemma, who grew up in the Philadelphia suburb of Norristown.

▼ Mateen Cleaves

NAISMITH AWARD WINNERS 1999-2000

MEN
Player of the Year: Kenyon Martin, Cincinnati
Coach of the Year: Mike Montgomery, Stanford

WOMEN
Player of the Year: Tamika Catchings, Tennessee
Coach of the Year: Geno Auriemma, Connecticut

FOOTBALL

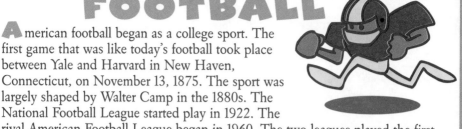

American football began as a college sport. The first game that was like today's football took place between Yale and Harvard in New Haven, Connecticut, on November 13, 1875. The sport was largely shaped by Walter Camp in the 1880s. The National Football League started play in 1922. The rival American Football League began in 1960. The two leagues played the first Super Bowl in 1967. In 1970, the AFL merged with the NFL. Teams were divided into the American and National Football Conferences.

PROFESSIONAL FOOTBALL

The NFL went topsy-turvy in 1999. Many of last season's finest teams didn't even make the playoffs. The biggest surprise of all was the St. Louis Rams and their quarterback Kurt Warner. The Rams, who won only four games in 1998, finished with an NFC-best 13–3 record. Warner, who had never started an NFL game before 1999, became the only player besides Dan Marino to throw more than 40 touchdown passes in a season. Rams running back Marshall Faulk set a new NFL record of 2,429 combined yards (1,381 rushing and 1,048 receiving).

In Super Bowl XXXIV, the NFC's Rams faced off against the AFC's Tennessee Titans. With the score tied 16-16 and less than two minutes left, Warner connected with wide receiver Isaac Bruce for a 72-yard touchdown, but the game wasn't over yet. On the final play, the Rams stopped the Titans one yard shy of a game-tying touchdown to hold on to a 23-16 victory!

Final NFL Standings for the 1999 Season

NATIONAL FOOTBALL CONFERENCE

EASTERN DIVISION	WON	LOST	TIED
Washington Redskins	10	6	0
Dallas Cowboys*	8	8	0
New York Giants	7	9	0
Arizona Cardinals	6	10	0
Philadelphia Eagles	5	11	0
CENTRAL DIVISION	**WON**	**LOST**	**TIED**
Tampa Bay Buccaneers	11	5	0
Minnesota Vikings*	10	6	0
Detroit Lions*	8	8	0
Green Bay Packers	8	8	0
Chicago Bears	6	10	0
WESTERN DIVISION	**WON**	**LOST**	**TIED**
St. Louis Rams	13	3	0
Carolina Panthers	8	8	0
Atlanta Falcons	5	11	0
San Francisco 49ers	4	12	0
New Orleans Saints	3	13	0

Wild card team

AMERICAN FOOTBALL CONFERENCE

EASTERN DIVISION	WON	LOST	TIED
Indianapolis Colts	13	3	0
Buffalo Bills*	11	5	0
Miami Dolphins*	9	7	0
New York Jets	8	8	0
New England Patriots	8	8	0
CENTRAL DIVISION	**WON**	**LOST**	**TIED**
Jacksonville Jaguars	14	2	0
Tennessee Titans*	13	3	0
Baltimore Ravens	8	8	0
Pittsburgh Steelers	6	10	0
Cincinnati Bengals	4	12	0
Cleveland Browns	2	14	0
WESTERN DIVISION	**WON**	**LOST**	**TIED**
Seattle Seahawks	9	7	0
Kansas City Chiefs	9	7	0
San Diego Chargers	8	8	0
Oakland Raiders	8	8	0
Denver Broncos	6	10	0

Wild card team

1999 CONFERENCE CHAMPIONSHIP GAMES
National Football Conference: St. Louis Rams 11, Tampa Bay Buccaneers 6
American Football Conference: Tennessee Titans 33, Jacksonville Jaguars 14

SUPER BOWL XXXIV, JANUARY 30, 2000, GEORGIA DOME, ATLANTA, GEORGIA
St. Louis Rams 23, Tennessee Titans 16

TOP NFL PLAYERS, 1999

RUSHING LEADER: Edgerrin James, Indianapolis Colts
Carries: 369 **Yards:** 1,553 **Average:** 4.2

PASSING LEADER: Kurt Warner, St. Louis Rams
Passing Attempts: 499 **Passing Completions:** 325
Passing Yards: 4,353
Passing Completion Percentage: 65.1
Touchdown Passes: 41 **Passes Intercepted:** 13
Quarterback Rating: 109.2

PASS RECEIVING LEADER: Jimmy Smith, Jacksonville Jaguars
Catches: 116 **Yards:** 1,636 **Average:** 14.1

1999 ASSOCIATED PRESS AWARDS
Most Valuable Player: Kurt Warner, St. Louis Rams
Offensive Player of the Year: Marshall Faulk, St. Louis Rams
Defensive Player of the Year: Warren Sapp, Tampa Bay Buccaneers
Coach of the Year: Dick Vermeil, St. Louis Rams
Offensive Rookie of the Year: Edgerrin James, Indianapolis Colts
Defensive Rookie of the Year: Jevon Kearse, Tennessee Titans
Comeback Player of the Year: Bryant Young, San Francisco 49ers
Super Bowl Most Valuable Player: Kurt Warner, St. Louis Rams

◀ *Edgerrin James*   **WEB SITE** *http://www.nfl.com*

DiD You KNOW?

Quarterback Dan Marino of the Miami Dolphins announced his retirement in March 2000, at the age of 38. At the end of the 1999 season, he held these major NFL records: most career touchdown passes (420), most career passing yards (61,361), most career completions (4,967), most touchdown passes in a season (48 in 1984), most passing yards in a season (5,084 in 1984).

PRO FOOTBALL HALL OF FAME

Football's Hall of Fame was founded in 1963 by the National Football League to honor outstanding players, coaches, and contributors. **Address:** Pro Football Hall of Fame, 2121 George Halas Drive NW, Canton, OH 44708. **Phone:** (330) 456-8207.

WEB SITE *http://www.profootballhof.com*

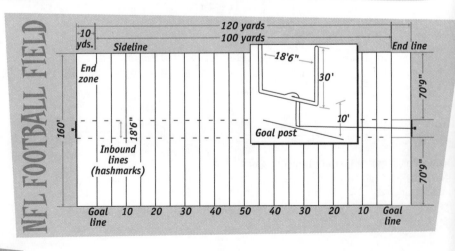

College Football

College football is one of America's most colorful and exciting sports. The National Collegiate Athletic Association (NCAA), founded in 1906, oversees college football today.

On January 4, 2000, the Florida State Seminoles became national champions by beating the Virginia Tech Hokies 46-29 in the Sugar Bowl.

1999 TOP 10 COLLEGE TEAMS
Chosen by the Associated Press Poll and the USA Today/ESPN Poll

RANK	AP	USA TODAY/ESPN POLL
1	Florida State	Florida State
2	Virginia Tech	Nebraska
3	Nebraska	Virginia Tech
4	Wisconsin	Wisconsin
5	Michigan	Michigan
6	Kansas State	Kansas State
7	Michigan State	Michigan State
8	Alabama	Alabama
9	Tennessee	Tennessee
10	Marshall	Marshall

THE BOWL GAMES

The Bowl Championship Series (BCS) now determines the national champion. It consists of the Fiesta, Rose, Sugar, and Orange Bowls. After the 1999 regular season, the Sugar Bowl winner became national champion. The Orange Bowl will determine the national champion after the 2000 season. After the 2001 season, the Rose Bowl, oldest of all the bowls (first played in 1902), will decide the champion.

SOME 1999 SEASON BOWL RESULTS

Rose Bowl (Pasadena, California):
Wisconsin 17, Stanford 9

Orange Bowl (Miami, Florida):
Michigan 35, Alabama 34 (OT)

Cotton Bowl (Dallas, Texas):
Arkansas 27, Texas 6

Fiesta Bowl (Tempe, Arizona):
Nebraska 31, Tennessee 21

Sugar Bowl (New Orleans):
Florida State 46, Virginia Tech 29

COLLEGE FOOTBALL HALL OF FAME

The College Football Hall of Fame was established in 1955. To be nominated, a player must be out of college ten years and have been a first team All-American pick by a major selector. Coaches must be retired three years. Address: 111 South St. Joseph Street, PO Box 11146, South Bend, IN 46601. Phone: (219) 235-9999.

WEB SITE http://collegefootball.org

▼ Ron Dayne

HEISMAN TROPHY

The Heisman Trophy goes to the most outstanding college football player in the U.S. The 1999 winner was running back Ron Dayne of the University of Wisconsin. He set a new all-time career rushing record of 6,397 yards, breaking the mark of 6,279 set by Texas running back Ricky Williams in 1998. As a senior, the 5'10", 254-pound Dayne scored 19 touchdowns and was the nation's second leading rusher, with 1,834 yards.

Dayne also won the Associated Press College Player of the Year Award, the Doak Walker Award for outstanding running back, and the Maxwell Award for best all-around player.

All About...
CHESS

Chess is a game of skill for two players. The aim is to checkmate, or trap, the opponent's king. Chess was probably invented around the 6th or 7th century A.D. in India. From there it moved into Persia (now Iran); the word *chess* comes from the Persian word *shah*, which means king. Today, there are national chess contests for children, and many schools have chess clubs. For further information, contact the U.S. Chess Federation, 3054 NYS Route 9W, New Windsor, NY 12553. Phone: 914-562-8350.

WEB SITE *http://www.uschess.org*

THE BOARD AND THE CHESSMEN

Chess is played on a chessboard divided into 64 squares, alternately light and dark in color, arranged in 8 rows of 8. No matter what colors the squares and chessmen really are, they are always called white and black. White always moves first, then black and white take turns, moving only one piece at a time. Each player begins with 16 chessmen: 8 pieces (the king, the queen, 2 bishops, 2 knights, and 2 rooks) and 8 pawns. When a chessman lands on a space taken by an opponent's piece or pawn, that piece or pawn is captured and removed from the board.

QUEEN: moves any number of open squares in any direction—forward or backward, side to side, or diagonally

ROOK: moves any number of open squares forward or backward, or side to side

KNIGHT: moves in an L-shape, two squares forward or backward and one square to either side, or one forward or backward and two to the side, always landing on a square of the opposite color from its old square (the knight is the only chessman that can jump over others)

BISHOP: moves any number of open squares diagonally

PAWN: moves one or two open squares straight ahead, then one at a time, except when moving diagonally to capture a piece

KING: moves one square in any direction, but cannot move into a position attacked by an opponent's piece

When a player moves a chessman into position to capture the opponent's king, he or she says "check" and the opponent must block the move or must move the king to safety; otherwise, the king is "checkmated" and the game is over.

queen   rook

knight   bishop

pawn   king

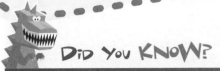

DID YOU KNOW?

World chess champion Garry Kasparov played two tournaments against an IBM computer, Deep Blue. He defeated Deep Blue in 1996. But in 1997, an improved version of the computer beat 12-time world champ Kasparov.

SHARPEN YOUR SKILLS!

Board games are fun, but they go beyond that. They sharpen our mental skills. Some games are based on skill. Others depend only on the throw of dice. For most, winning takes a mixture of skill and luck. That's why games can teach us how to win without gloating and how to lose without being too disappointed.

Games like chess, checkers, Monopoly®, and Scrabble® are played all over the world by both kids and adults. Many board games can also be played on the computer. In fact, computers may be the toughest competitors ever.

BACKGAMMON, a game for two players, was played in ancient Egypt, Greece, and Rome. Each player has 15 pieces to move around the board, and the skill is in deciding which pieces to move. Getting the right numbers when you throw the dice can also help make you a winner. To win the game, you must be the first to get all your pieces off the board.

CHECKERS is a game of skill. A form of checkers was played in ancient Egypt and Greece. The game is played by two players on a board with alternating light and dark squares. The goal is to capture all the opponent's pieces by jumping. To do so, you have to think ahead and take advantage of your opponent's mistakes.

DiD YoU KNoW? *Marion Tinsley is considered the greatest checkers player in history. He lost only 22 games over a 67-year period. Tinsley was a world checkers champion, but lost his title in 1994 to a computer program called Chinook, now considered to be the World Man-Machine Checkers Champion.*

MONOPOLY, a game for two or more players, is one of the best-selling games of the 20th century. It involves both skill and luck. The skill is in making choices. Should you buy Water Works? How many houses should you put on Boardwalk? The luck is in throwing the dice and landing on the right places.

Monopoly was created in the 1930s by Charles P. Darrow, who took the names for places in the game from streets in Atlantic City, New Jersey.

DiD YoU KNoW?

► *The longest Monopoly game ever played took 1,680 hours.*

► *Matt Gissel, a college student from St. Albans, Vermont, was the 1999 national Monopoly champion. Gissel built a railroad monopoly and accumulated $14,098 in assets by the end of the game.*

SCRABBLE is a crossword game for two, three, or four players, played on a board with tiles that are letters. It had its beginnings in the 1930s with a game called Criss-Cross Words, which was invented by Alfred Butts.

To win at Scrabble, it helps to be a good speller, have a big vocabulary, and figure out the best places for your letters. The lucky part is picking up the letters you need at the right time.

DiD YoU KNoW? *JAZY is the four-letter Scrabble word with the highest score. It means "a worsted wig" and is worth 23 points.*

227

GOLF

Golf began in Scotland as early as the 1400s. The first golf course in the U.S. opened in 1888. The sport has grown to include both men's and women's professional tours. And millions play golf just for fun.

The men's tour is run by the Professional Golf Association (PGA). The four major championships (with the year first played) are:

British Open (1860)
United States Open (1895)
PGA Championship (1916)
Masters Tournament (1934)

The women's tour is guided by the Ladies Professional Golf Association (LPGA). The four major championships are:

United States Women's Open (1946)
McDonalds LPGA Championship (1955)
Nabisco Championship (1972)
du Maurier Classic (1973)

All About... TIGER WOODS

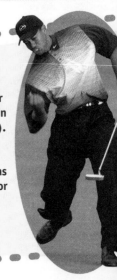

Eldrick "Tiger" Woods has been a professional golfer for only three years, but he's already being counted as one of the sport's all-time greats. He was the youngest-ever winner of the U.S. Junior Amateur Championship (15, in 1991), the U.S. Amateur Championship (18 in 1994), and the Masters (21 years, 3 months, and 14 days, in 1997). By age 23 he had won 21 tournaments, setting the record for the most victories at his age. His PGA Tour earnings of $6.6 million in 1999 were more than double the previous single-year record. He was named Male Athlete of the Year by the Associated Press that year for the second time in three years, becoming only the second golfer to earn the award twice. Tiger lives in Orlando, Florida.

WEB SITE http://tigerwoods.com • http://www.pga.com

GYMNASTICS

It takes strength, coordination, and grace to become a top gymnast. Although the sport goes back to ancient Greece, modern-day gymnastics began in Sweden in the early 1800s. The sport has been part of the Olympics since 1896. There is also an annual World Gymnastics Championship meet.

GYMNASTIC EVENTS

FOR WOMEN

1 All-Around
2 Vault
3 Uneven Parallel Bars
4 Balance Beam
5 Floor Exercises
6 Team Combined Exercises
7 Rhythmic All-Around
8 Rope
9 Hoop
10 Ball
11 Clubs
12 Ribbon

FOR MEN

1 All-Around
2 Horizontal Bar
3 Parallel Bars
4 Rings
5 Vault
6 Pommel Horse
7 Floor Exercises
8 Team Combined Exercises

ICE HOCKEY

Ice hockey began in Canada in the mid-1800s. The National Hockey League (NHL) was formed in 1916.

In 1999-2000, the NHL had twenty-eight teams, twenty-two in the United States and six in Canada. The Atlanta Thrashers joined the NHL's Southeast Division for the 1999-2000 season. Two more expansion teams are scheduled to join the NHL for 2000-2001, the Minnesota Wild and Columbus (Ohio) Blue Jackets.

▲ *The league's leading scorer was Jaromir Jagr of Pittsburgh, with 96 points.*

FINAL 1999-2000 STANDINGS

EASTERN CONFERENCE

Atlantic Division	W	L	T	Pts*
Philadelphia Flyers	45	25	12	105
New Jersey Devils	45	29	8	103
Pittsburgh Penguins	37	37	8	88
New York Rangers	29	41	12	73
New York Islanders	24	49	9	58

Northeast Division	W	L	T	Pts
Toronto Maple Leafs	45	30	7	100
Ottawa Senators	41	30	11	95
Buffalo Sabres	35	36	11	85
Montreal Canadiens	35	38	9	83
Boston Bruins	24	39	19	73

Southeast Division	W	L	T	Pts
Washington Capitals	44	26	12	102
Florida Panthers	43	33	6	98
Carolina Hurricanes	37	35	10	84
Tampa Bay Lightning	19	54	9	54
Atlanta Thrashers	14	61	7	39

WESTERN CONFERENCE

Central Division	W	L	T	Pts
St. Louis Blues	51	20	11	114
Detroit Red Wings	48	24	10	108
Chicago Blackhawks	33	39	10	78
Nashville Predators	28	47	7	70

Northwest Division	W	L	T	Pts
Colorado Avalanche	42	29	11	96
Edmonton Oilers	32	34	16	88
Vancouver Canucks	30	37	15	83
Calgary Flames	31	41	10	77

Pacific Division	W	L	T	Pts
Dallas Stars	43	29	10	102
Los Angeles Kings	39	31	12	94
Phoenix Coyotes	39	35	8	90
San Jose Sharks	35	37	10	87
Anaheim Mighty Ducks	34	36	12	83

Includes points received for regulation tie games.

WEB SITE http://www.nhl.com

DiD YOU KNOW?

▶ *The NHL changed the scoring of regular-season games at the start of the 1999-2000 season, introducing the regulation tie (RT). Now, teams that are tied at the end of regulation time (after three 20-minute periods) both automatically get one point. If one team scores during the five-minute overtime period, it gets an additional point for winning the game.*

▶ *Pittsburgh Penguins superstar Mario Lemieux, who retired in 1997 due to health problems, became the owner of the team in 1999.*

▶ *Since 1981 only three players have led the NHL in scoring (goals plus assists): Wayne Gretzky, Mario Lemieux, and Jaromir Jagr. With the retirement of Lemieux in 1997 and Gretzky in 1999, Jagr is now considered the game's outstanding offensive player.*

HOCKEY HALL OF FAME

The Hockey Hall of Fame was opened in 1961 to honor hockey greats. It moved to its current location in 1993. **Address:** BCE Place, 30 Yonge Street, Toronto, Ontario, Canada M5E 1X8. **Phone:** (416) 360-7735

WEB SITE http://www.hhof.com

THE OLYMPIC GAMES

The first Olympic Games were held in Greece more than 2,500 years ago. They began in 776 B.C. and featured just one event—a footrace. The Greeks later added boxing, wrestling, chariot racing, and the pentathlon (which consists of five different events). The Olympic Games were held every four years for more than 1,000 years, until A.D. 393, when a Roman emperor stopped them. The Olympic Games were revived in modern times largely through the efforts of a French educator named Baron Pierre de Coubertin.

SOME OLYMPIC FIRSTS

1896 The first modern Olympic Games were held in Athens, Greece. A total of 312 athletes from 13 nations participated in nine sports.

1900 Women competed in the Olympic Games for the first time.

1908 For the first time, medals were awarded to the first three people to finish each event—a gold medal for first place, a silver medal for second, and a bronze medal for third.

1920 The Olympic flag was raised for the first time, and the Olympic oath was introduced. The five interlaced rings of the flag represent: Africa, America, Europe, Asia, and Australia.

1924 The Winter Olympics, featuring skiing and skating events, were held for the first time.
The Olympic flame was introduced at the Olympic Games. A relay of runners carries a torch with the flame from Olympia, Greece, to the site of each Olympics.

1994 Starting with the 1994 Winter Olympics, the winter and summer Games have been held two years apart, instead of in the same year.

SYDNEY: THE OLYMPIC CITY

Welcome to Sydney, Australia, host city for the games of the 27th Olympiad, from September 15 to October 1, 2000. That's early spring in Australia. Temperatures in the daytime range from 60 to 68 degrees Fahrenheit, and the weather is usually good. Two new medal sports have been added—taekwondo and the triathlon. Taekwondo has four men's and four women's weight classes. Both men and women compete in the grueling triathlon, which includes swimming, biking, and running. Other new events include trampoline, added to the gymnastics program, and women's water polo. Women are also competing in the modern pentathlon for the first time. In total, the Games have 296 events—166 for men, 118 for women, and 12 mixed. The Sydney Olympics has three official mascots—all of these animals native to Australia. They are Olly, the kookaburra bird; Syd, the duck-billed platypus; and Millie, the echidna.

AFTER 2000:
WHERE TO GO FOR THE OLYMPICS

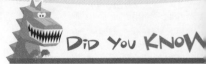

DID YOU KNOW

WINTER GAMES:
2002—Salt Lake City, Utah
2006—Turin, Italy

SUMMER GAMES:
2004—Athens, Greece

The Olympic motto is a Latin phase: "Citius, altus, fortius." It means "Swifter, higher, stronger."

OLYMPIC SPORTS

2000 Summer Olympic Sports

Archery
Badminton
Baseball
Basketball
Boxing
Canoe/Kayak
 (slalom, sprint)
Cycling
 (road, mountain bike,
 track)
Diving
Equestrian
 (dressage, jumping,
 3-day event)

Fencing
Field Hockey
Football (Soccer)
Gymnastics
 (artistic, rhythmic, trampoline)
Handball
Judo
Modern Pentathlon
 (show jumping, running, fencing,
 pistol shooting, swimming—one
 event per day for 5 days)
Rowing
Sailing
Shooting

Softball
Swimming
Synchronized Swimming
Table Tennis
 (Ping-Pong)
Taekwondo
Tennis
Track and Field
Triathlon
Volleyball (beach,
 indoor)
Water Polo
Weightlifting
Wrestling

2002 Winter Olympic Sports

Alpine Skiing
 (downhill, slalom,
 giant slalom, super-G,
 Alpine combined)
Biathlon
 (cross-country
 skiing, rifle
 marksmanship)
Bobsled

Curling
Figure Skating
Freestyle Skiing
 (moguls, aerials)
Ice Hockey
Luge

Nordic Skiing
 (cross-country skiing, ski
 jumping, Nordic combined)
Skeleton
Snowboarding
 (giant slalom, halfpipe)
Speed Skating
 (long track, short track)

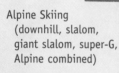

DiD You KNOW?

Before the Atlanta Olympics, no one had ever won both the 200- and the 400-meter dashes at the same games. In 1996, this feat was accomplished by two athletes—first by Marie-José Pérec of France, and several minutes later by Michael Johnson of the U.S. Michael now owns the world record in both events. His time of 19.32 in the 200 meters in Atlanta was a record. And at the 1999 World Championships in Seville, Spain, he added the 400-meter record with a time of 43.18.

◀ *Michael Johnson*

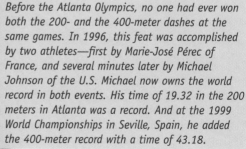

SKATING

The first ice skates were crude runners carved from animal bones and were used for transportation. Recreational skating began with highly waxed wooden blades. Wooden skates with iron and steel blades appeared later, in the Netherlands. The first all-steel skate was invented by E.W. Bushnell of Philadelphia around 1850. There are two types of competitive ice skating today: figure skating and speed skating.

FIGURE SKATING

Figure skating, which is almost like ballet, is judged by the way the skaters perform certain turns and jumps and by the creative difficulty of their programs. There are singles competitions for both men and women, pairs skating, and ice dancing.

2000 World Championships

	WOMEN'S SINGLES	MEN'S SINGLES
Gold Medal:	Michelle Kwan, United States	Alexei Yagudin, Russia
Silver Medal:	Irina Slutskaya, Russia	Elvis Stojko, Canada
Bronze Medal:	Maria Butyrskaya, Russia	Michael Weiss, United States

All About...
MICHELLE KWAN

Michelle Kwan took the skating world by storm in 1996 when she won the World Championship at the age of 15. She won her fourth U.S. championship in February 2000—her third in a row. (The silver and bronze medalists at the U.S. nationals were Sasha Cohen and Sarah Hughes, just 15 and 14 years old, respectively.) Kwan has plenty of experience dealing with youngsters. At the 1998 Winter Olympics, Kwan was beaten for the gold by Tara Lipinski, age 15.

Kwan, a freshman at UCLA, was born in Torrance, California. She trains in nearby Lake Arrowhead with legendary coach John Carroll.

WEB SITE *http://www.usfsa.org http://www.usspeedskating.org*

AMERICA'S OLYMPIC CHAMPIONS *(for figure skating in singles competition)*

MEN: Dick Button (1948, 1952), Hayes Alan Jenkins (1956), David Jenkins (1960), Scott Hamilton (1984), Brian Boitano (1988)

WOMEN: Tenley Albright (1956), Carol Heiss (1960), Peggy Fleming (1968), Dorothy Hamill (1976), Kristi Yamaguchi (1992), Tara Lipinski (1998)

SPEED SKATING

Speed skating is divided into two types: long track and short track. In long track, competitors race the clock skating around a 400-meter oval. This became an Olympic sport for men in 1942, for women in 1960. Short track skating only became an official Olympic sport in 1992. The track is much smaller (111 meters), with a pack of four to six skaters racing against each other instead of the clock.

SOCCER

Soccer, which is called football in many countries, is the number one sport worldwide. It's played by more than 100 million people in some 150 countries. The first rules for the game were published in 1863 by the London Football Association. Since then, the sport has spread rapidly from Europe to almost every part of the world.

More than 18 million children (6 years old and up) and adults play soccer in the U.S., according to the 1999 Soccer Industry Council of America survey. Nearly 14 million are under the age of 18—the sport is growing fastest among young people between the ages of 12 and 17.

THE WOMEN'S WORLD CUP

On July 10, 1999, the U.S. women's soccer team defeated China to win the 1999 Women's World Cup. The game was held at the Rose Bowl in Pasadena, California, in front of a crowd of 90,185, the largest to ever attend a women's sporting event in the United States. The contest was tied 0-0 at the end of regulation time, so the winner had to be decided by penalty kicks. China missed one of their five kicks, while the U.S. team made their first four. It was up to Brandi Chastain to bring home victory for the U.S. Brandi sent a shot high into the net to seal the win 5-4 to the delight of the crowd and her teammates. The Women's World Cup has been held three times (1991, 1995, 1999), and the U.S. has won twice (1991, 1999). The next tournament is scheduled for 2003.

THE WORLD CUP

The men's World Cup, the biggest soccer tournament in the world, was last held in France in 1998. On July 11, in St. Denis, a crowd of 80,000 watched the home country, France, upset 1994 champions Brazil, 3-0, to win their first World Cup. The French gave up just two goals in seven matches, the lowest number ever for a winner. The next Cup will be held in 2002, hosted by Japan and South Korea.

MAJOR LEAGUE SOCCER

On November 21, 1999, Washington D.C. United won its third Major League Soccer championship in four years. In a rematch of the first MLS Cup (1996), the United defeated the Los Angeles Galaxy, 2-0, in Foxboro, Massachusetts. D.C.'s Ben Olsen scored the game's final goal and was chosen the MLS Cup Most Valuable Player (MVP). His teammate, Jaime Moreno, scored the first goal and became the all-time leading scorer in the MLS playoffs. Dallas Burn forward Jason Kreis was the league's leading scorer and MVP for the regular season, while the L.A. Galaxy's Kevin Hartman was named Goalkeeper of the Year.

Jaime Moreno ▶

 **DID YOU KNOW?**

The first men's World Cup was won by Uruguay in 1930. Brazil has won the most World Cup tournaments (four), followed by Germany and Italy (three), Uruguay and Argentina (two), and England and France (one).

SPECIAL OLYMPICS

The Special Olympics is the world's largest program of sports training and athletic competition for children and adults with mental retardation. Founded in 1968, Special Olympics International has offices in all 50 U.S. states and Washington, D.C., and throughout the world. The organization offers training and competition to 1.5 million athletes in 150 countries.

The first Special Olympics competition took place in Chicago in 1968. After national events in individual countries, Special Olympics International holds World Games. These alternate between summer and winter sports every two years. About 2,000 athletes from 85 nations are expected to compete at the 2001 World Winter Games in Alaska.

SPECIAL OLYMPICS OFFICIAL SPORTS

▶ **Winter:** alpine and cross-country skiing, figure and speed skating, floor hockey, snowshoeing

▶ **Summer:** aquatics (swimming and diving), athletics (track and field), basketball, bowling, cycling, equestrian, golf, gymnastics, powerlifting, roller skating, soccer, softball, tennis, volleyball

▶ **Demonstration sports:** badminton, bocce, sailing, snowboarding

For more information, contact Special Olympics International Headquarters, 1325 G Street NW, Suite 500, Washington, D.C. 20005. Phone: (202) 628-3630.

WEB SITE *http://www.specialolympics.org*

Swimming

Competitive swimming as an organized sport began in the second half of the 19th century. When the modern Olympic Games began in Athens, Greece, in 1896, the only racing stroke was the breaststroke. Today, men and women at the Olympics swim the backstroke, breaststroke, butterfly, and freestyle, in events ranging from 50 meters to 1,500 meters.

SOME GREAT U.S. OLYMPIC SWIMMERS

▶ **Mark Spitz** won two gold medals in relays at the 1968 Games. He returned in 1972 to make Olympic swimming history by winning seven gold medals.

▶ **Matt Biondi** won seven medals at the 1998 Olympics, including five golds. He has eight total golds, won from 1984 to 1992.

▶ **Amy Van Dyken** won four gold medals at the 1996 Games in Atlanta, the most a U.S. woman has ever won in a single Olympics.

▶ **Janet Evans**, at age 17, won three gold medals at the 1988 Olympics in Seoul, South Korea. In 1992, she won another gold and a silver in Barcelona, Spain.

All About... JENNY THOMPSON

Jenny Thompson splashed into swimming fame at age 14, when she qualified for the national A-team. Now 26, she has qualified for more national teams than any other swimmer in U.S. history. A two-time USA Swimming Swimmer of the Year, Thompson owns the most career U.S. national titles (23) of any active swimmer and holds the world record in the 100-meter butterfly. She has won six Olympic medals, including five golds.

TENNIS

Modern tennis began in 1873 when a British officer, Major Walter Wingfield, developed it from court tennis. In 1877 the first championships were held in Wimbledon, near London. In 1881 the first official U.S. men's championships were held at Newport, Rhode Island. Six years later, the first women's championships took place, in Philadelphia.

GRAND SLAM TOURNAMENTS

The four most important contests today, called the grand slam tournaments, are the Australian Open, the French Open, the All-England (Wimbledon) Championships, and the U.S. Open. There are separate competitions for men and women in singles and doubles. There are also mixed doubles, where men and women team together.

SINGLES CHAMPIONS

2000 AUSTRALIAN OPEN FINALS
Andre Agassi (USA) defeated Yevgeny Kafelnikov (Russia), 3-6, 6-3, 6-2, 6-4.

Lindsay Davenport (USA) defeated Martina Hingis (Switzerland), 6-1, 7-5.

1999 WIMBLEDON FINALS
Pete Sampras (USA) defeated Andre Agassi (USA), 6-3, 6-4, 7-5.

Lindsay Davenport (USA) defeated Steffi Graf (Germany), 6-4, 7-5.

Andre Agassi ▲

1999 UNITED STATES OPEN FINALS
Andre Agassi (USA) defeated Todd Martin (USA), 6-4, 6-7 (7-5), 6-7 (7-2), 6-3, 6-2.

Serena Williams (USA) defeated Martina Hingis (Switzerland), 6-3, 7-6 (7-4).

1999 FRENCH OPEN FINALS
Andre Agassi (USA) defeated Andrei Medvedev (Ukraine), 1-6, 2-6, 6-4, 6-3, 6-4.

Steffi Graf (Germany) defeated Martina Hingis (Switzerland), 4-6, 7-5, 6-2.

RANKINGS

The Association of Tennis Professionals (ATP) and the Women's Tennis Association (WTA) keep computer rankings of all the players on the tour. The top five men and women at the end of 1999 were:

MEN
1. **Andre Agassi**, USA
2. **Yevgeny Kafelnikov**, Russia
3. **Pete Sampras**, USA
4. **Thomas Enqvist**, Sweden
5. **Gustavo Kuerten**, Brazil

WOMEN
1. **Martina Hingis**, Switzerland
2. **Lindsay Davenport**, USA
3. **Venus Williams**, USA
4. **Serena Williams**, USA
5. **Mary Pierce**, France

All About... THE WILLIAMS SISTERS

The future of women's tennis has braided and brightly beaded hair—and a booming serve (Venus once had a serve clocked at 127 mph!). They are Venus and Serena Williams, the youngest of five sisters, who grew up on the tough streets of Compton, California, playing on the public courts. They're both tall and strong—Venus is 6-foot-1, Serena is 5-foot-10—and they practice against each other. Their father acts as their manager and coach. Venus turned pro in 1995, and Serena followed in 1997. But Serena was the first to win a grand slam tournament, the 1999 U.S. Open singles. Sometimes they play together, and in 1999 they won the doubles titles at both French and U.S. Opens. They live in Palm Beach Gardens, Florida.

Transportation

? Why should bike riders thank Kirkpatrick Macmillan?
You can find the answer on page 237.

Can you imagine life without bikes, buses, cars, planes, trains, or boats? Can you imagine a time when people could go only as fast and far as their legs or their animals' legs could carry them?

A SHORT HISTORY OF TRANSPORTATION
BEFORE MACHINES

1450s
Portuguese build fast ships with three masts. These plus the compass usher in an age of exploration.

3200 BC
Egyptians create the first sailboat. Before this, people made rafts or canoes and paddled them with poles or their hands.

5000 BC
People discover animal-muscle power. Oxen and donkeys carry heavy loads.

1730s
Stagecoach service begins in the U.S.

5000 B.C.

3500 BC
In Mesopotamia (modern-day Iraq), people invent vehicles with wheels. But the first wheels are made of heavy wood, and the roads are terrible.

1100 BC
Chinese invent the magnetic compass. It allows them to sail long distances.

1660s
Horse-drawn stagecoaches begin running in France. They stop at stages to switch horses and passengers—the first mass transit system.

1737
Jouffroy d'Abbans builds the first steamboat. Robert Fulton built an improved version in 1807.

HOW LONG DID IT TAKE?

1492 Christopher Columbus's first trip across the Atlantic Ocean took 70 days. (Part of it was spent on the Canary Islands waiting for good winds.)

1650s It took 50 days to sail across the Atlantic Ocean from London, England, to Boston, Massachusetts.

1819 The first Atlantic Ocean crossing by a ship powered in part by steam (*Savannah*, from Savannah, Georgia, to Liverpool, England) took 27 days.

1927 Charles Lindbergh flew from New York to Paris in 33½ hours. It was the first nonstop flight made across the Atlantic Ocean by one person.

1986 Richard Rutan and Jeana Yeager piloted the airplane *Voyager* on the first nonstop, unfueled flight around the world, in 9 days, 3 minutes.

1999 Bertrand Piccard and Brian Jones, in the *Breitling Orbiter 3*, completed the first around-the-world balloon flight, in 19 days, 21 hours, 55 minutes.

AGE OF MACHINES

1769
James Watt patents the steam engine.

1829
Passenger rail service begins in England with the *Rocket*, a steam train built by George Stephenson. It goes about 24 miles an hour.

1903
At Kitty Hawk, North Carolina, Orville Wright pilots the first powered heavier-than-air machine on a 12-second flight.

1939
The first practical helicopter and first jet plane are invented. The jet flies up to 434 miles an hour. Passenger jet service began in 1958.

1769
Nicholas Cugnot builds a vehicle powered by steam. Made to carry guns for the French army, it goes about two miles an hour.

1852
Henri Giffard of France invents an airship using a bag of hydrogen and a steam-powered propeller.

1908
Henry Ford builds the first Model T, a practical car for the general public. Millions were soon being made on assembly lines.

1947
Flying at 700 mph, U.S. Air Force Capt. Charles "Chuck" Yeager breaks the sound barrier in the jet-powered Bell X-1.

1783
Etienne and Joseph Montgolfier build a hot-air balloon.

1839
Kirkpatrick Macmillan of Scotland invents the first pedaled bicycle.

1864
Siegfried Marcus of Austria builds a horseless carriage, the first gasoline-powered automobile.

1926
Robert Goddard launches the first successful liquid-fuel rocket.

1934
Diesel passenger trains begin operating in the U.S.

1961
Russian cosmonaut Yuri Gagarin orbits the earth in a spaceship.

1969
U.S. astronauts aboard the *Apollo 11* land on the Moon.

All About... NAVIGATION SYSTEMS

Suppose you and your family are on the road, driving to somewhere you've never been. And you left your map at home! It's no problem if you have an on-board navigation system. This new system can tell you how to get to where you want to go. A built-in computer receives information from the Global Positioning System (GPS), a network of 24 satellites orbiting the earth that uses radio waves to pinpoint your location. When the driver enters an address on a keypad, a map shows up on a dashboard computer screen. It lights up, showing which streets to take. More advanced systems can even "speak" the directions!

TRANSPORTATION TODAY

Land

Japanese bullet trains, **Shinkansen**, travel up to 190 miles per hour and carry almost a million passengers a day. A trip from Tokyo to Osaka (321 miles) takes only three hours. The French **Train à Grande Vitesse**, or **TGV**, can go 238 mph but usually travels about 190 mph. At the latter speed it takes two miles to come to a full stop.

Environmental concerns have led to the development of cars with **gas-electric motors**. An on-board computer chooses the most efficient power source for the driving conditions. These cars can get up to 70 miles per gallon and emit much less pollution than regular cars. In 2000, the first hybrid cars became available to the public.

Also available is the **Solar Flair** electric car. It absorbs sunlight through 900 solar energy cells and turns it into electricity, which powers the car up to 40 mph.

Sport Utility Vehicles (SUVs) have four-wheel drive so they can easily climb steep hills and go over rocky, sandy, snowy, or muddy surfaces. Developed in World War II, the Jeep was the original SUV. Today, the SUV is a popular luxury car even though the larger ones get poor gas mileage. In 1998, Americans bought about three million SUVs.

DID YOU KNOW?

*Powered by jet or rocket engines, **land-speed vehicles** are the fastest cars. In 1997 British Royal Air Force pilot Andy Green set a world land-speed record by driving the jet-powered **Thrust SSC** 767 miles per hour across a desert area in Nevada.*

TOP-SELLING PASSENGER CARS IN THE U.S. (FOR 1999)	
NAME OF CAR	NUMBER SOLD
❶ Toyota Camry	448,162
❷ Honda Accord	404,192
❸ Ford Taurus	368,327
❹ Honda Civic	318,308
❺ Chevrolet Cavalier	272,122

MOST POPULAR CAR COLORS (FOR 1999)		
COMPACT/ SPORTS CARS	FULL-SIZE CARS	LUXURY CARS
❶ Silver	White	White Metallic
❷ Black	Silver	Silver
❸ White	Light Brown	Light Brown
❹ Med./Dark Green	Med./Dark Green	White
❺ Med./Dark Blue	Black	Black

Sea

The Navy's largest **submarines** are powered by nuclear energy. They carry missiles that can hit targets 4,000 miles away. They make their own drinking water out of seawater and can stay under for months at a time.

A **hydrofoil** is a boat with wing-like fins called "foils" that lift the hull out of the water at high speeds, so the boat looks like it's flying. Staying above the water creates a smoother, faster ride.

Jet skis are small boats which can carry one or two people. They are designed to handle fast turns without tipping over—but they make a lot of noise.

Air

The Concorde, the first **supersonic passenger plane**, can fly as fast as 1,370 miles per hour, or about twice the speed of sound. Although it runs from New York to London in about 3½ hours, it raises controversy because of its deafening boom. Its engines may damage the ozone layer.

TRANSPORTATION IN THE FUTURE

Land

Paul Moller, inventor of Skycar, hopes his **flying car** will be ready for sale by 2002. It is designed to take off like a helicopter and fly up to 350 miles an hour. With the Skycar, computers do the piloting while passengers enjoy the ride.

Also possibly down the road:

► The Futura, a car that parks itself.

► Cars driven entirely by computers.

► Sensors on roads and autos that prevent cars from driving too close to each other.

The **Maglev** (MAGnetic LEVitation Vehicle) can provide high-speed, clean, and energy-efficient **train** service. There are some in Japan already, and they should become increasingly popular. Huge magnetic forces lift the train above the track and send it forward on electrical currents. Because there is no friction between train and track, it can travel up to 300 miles per hour.

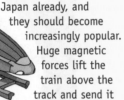

CHALLENGE: What kinds of cars would you like to see in your lifetime? What will they look like? What will they be able to do? How fast will they go?

Sea

Sea vessels will be even larger and made of **aluminum** or another material that can hold up better in ocean water. More ships may be powered by **nuclear energy**, and even very large ships will have crews of fewer than twenty people, since computers will do everything from setting the course to running the engines.

Air

Scientists are working on a **hypersonic** (at least five times the speed of sound) **aircraft** that would run on hydrogen and oxygen, giving off water vapor rather than harmful pollutants. The Orient Express—a **Trans-Atmospheric Vehicle** (TAV)—would fly 10,000 miles per hour, taking only two hours to travel from New York to Japan.

People may one day be able to strap individual **rocket packs** onto their backs and fly wherever they want to go. Such packs have already been designed and flown at 40 miles an hour.

Tiltrotors will take off and land like helicopters, straight up and down, even in small places, and fly like an airplane at speeds over 300 miles per hour.

TRANSPORTATION PUZZLE

How many words can you find in the word **TRANSPORTATION**? The words must have at least three letters. Plurals don't count.

Answers are on pages 317-320.

United Nations

What is special about stamps bought from the UN post office? You can find the answer below.

A COMMUNITY OF NATIONS

The United Nations (UN) was established in 1945 after World War II. The first members of the UN were 50 nations that met in San Francisco, California. They signed an agreement known as the UN Charter. In 2000, the UN had 188 countries as members. Only four independent nations—Switzerland, Taiwan, Tuvalu, and Vatican City—were not members.

The UN Charter lists these purposes:

- to keep worldwide peace and security
- to develop friendly relations among countries
- to help countries cooperate in solving economic and social problems
- to promote respect for human rights and basic freedoms
- to be a center that helps countries achieve their goals

▲ Flags fly at the UN

Fast Facts About the UN

▶ The Secretary General is the chief officer of the UN. He or she is appointed by the General Assembly to serve a five-year term. The current secretary general is Kofi Annan of Ghana. His term began in 1997.

▶ The United States representative to the UN is Richard C. Holbrooke. He began serving in 1999.

▶ The UN has its own fire department, security force, and postal service. The UN post office sells stamps that can be used only to send mail from the UN.

▶ Although UN Headquarters is located on 18 acres of land in New York City, the land and buildings are not part of the United States. They belong to the UN member nations.

▶ The flags of all 188 member nations fly in front of UN headquarters. The flags are arranged in alphabetical order beginning with Afghanistan and ending with Zimbabwe.

▶ The budget for the UN's main operations is $1.25 billion a year. The money is paid by member countries. The United States, which has higher dues than any other country, sometimes falls behind in its dues because of disagreement in Congress with some UN policies.

DID YOU KNOW?

The emblem of the United Nations (pictured at right) shows a map of the world as seen from the North Pole. Around the map are olive branches that stand for peace.

UN PEACEKEEPERS

Keeping peace is one of the UN's main purposes. The Security Council sets up UN peacekeeping missions, to try to stop people from fighting while the countries or groups involved try to work out their differences. Member nations volunteer troops and equipment. UN peacekeepers are easily recognized by their blue helmets or berets with white UN letters.

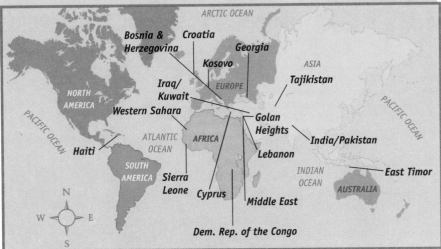

How the UN is ORGANIZED

The work of the UN is done through five main organizations:

GENERAL ASSEMBLY **What It Does:** discusses world problems, admits new members, appoints the secretary-general, decides the UN budget **Members:** All members of the UN belong to the General Assembly; each country has one vote

SECURITY COUNCIL **What It Does:** discusses questions of peace and security **Members:** Five permanent members (China, France, Great Britain, Russia, and the United States), and ten members elected by the General Assembly for two-year terms

ECONOMIC AND SOCIAL COUNCIL **What It Does:** deals with issues related to trade, economic development, industry, population, children, food, education, health, and human rights **Members:** Fifty-four member countries elected for three-year terms

INTERNATIONAL COURT OF JUSTICE (WORLD COURT) located at The Hague, Netherlands **What It Does:** highest court of law for legal disputes between countries; countries that come before the court promise to obey the court's decisions **Members:** Fifteen judges, each from a different country, elected to nine-year terms

SECRETARIAT **What It Does:** carries out day-to-day operations of the UN, such as doing research and helping implement UN decisions **Members:** UN staff, headed by the secretary-general

For more information about the UN, you can write to:
Public Inquiries Unit, Room GA57, United Nations, NY 10017.

WEB SITE http://www.un.org

United States

? When did U.S. women get the right to vote?
You can find the answer on page 245.

UNITED STATES: FACTS & FIGURES

AREA:	LAND	WATER	TOTAL
(50 states and Washington, D.C.)	3,536,278 square miles	181,518 square miles	3,717,796 square miles

POPULATION (2000): 274,943,496   **CAPITAL:** Washington, D.C.

LARGEST, HIGHEST, AND OTHER STATISTICS

Largest state:	Alaska (615,230 square miles)
Smallest state:	Rhode Island (1,231 square miles)
Northernmost city:	Barrow, Alaska (71°17' north latitude)
Southernmost city:	Hilo, Hawaii (19°44' north latitude)
Easternmost city:	Eastport, Maine (66°59'05" west longitude)
Westernmost city:	Atka, Alaska (174°12' west longitude)
Highest settlement:	Climax, Colorado (11,360 feet)
Lowest settlement:	Calipatria, California (184 feet below sea level)
Oldest national park:	Yellowstone National Park (Idaho, Montana, Wyoming), 2,219,791 acres, established 1872
Largest national park:	Wrangell-St. Elias, Alaska (8,323,618 acres)
Longest river system:	Mississippi-Missouri-Red Rock (3,710 miles)
Deepest lake:	Crater Lake, Oregon (1,932 feet)
Highest mountain:	Mount McKinley, Alaska (20,320 feet)
Lowest point:	Death Valley, California (282 feet below sea level)
Rainiest spot:	Mount Waialeale, Hawaii (average annual rainfall, 460 inches)
Tallest building:	Sears Tower, Chicago, Illinois (1,450 feet)
Tallest structure:	TV tower, Blanchard, North Dakota (2,063 feet)
Longest bridge span:	Verrazano-Narrows Bridge, New York (4,260 feet)
Highest bridge:	Royal Gorge, Colorado (1,053 feet above water)

INTERNATIONAL BOUNDARY LINES OF THE U.S.

U.S.-Canadian border . . . . . . 3,987 miles
(excluding Alaska)
Alaska-Canadian border . . . . . 1,538 miles
U.S.-Mexican border . . . . 1,933 miles
(Gulf of Mexico to Pacific Ocean)

Atlantic coast . . . . 2,069 miles
Gulf of Mexico coast . . . . 1,631 miles
Pacific coast . . . . 7,623 miles
Arctic coast, Alaska . . . . 1,060 miles

TERRITORIAL SEA OF THE U.S.
The territorial sea of the United States is the surrounding waters that the country claims as its own. A proclamation made by President Ronald Reagan on December 27, 1988, said that the territorial sea of the United States extends 12 nautical miles from the shores of the country.

SYMBOLS of the United States

THE U.S. NATIONAL MOTTO

The U.S. motto, "In God We Trust," was originally put on coins during the Civil War (1861-1865). It disappeared and reappeared on various coins until 1955, when Congress ordered it placed on all paper money and coins.

THE GREAT SEAL OF THE UNITED STATES

The Great Seal of the United States shows an American bald eagle with a ribbon in its mouth bearing the Latin words "e pluribus unum" (one out of many). In its talons are the arrows of war and an olive branch of peace. On the back of the Great Seal is an unfinished pyramid with an eye (the eye of Providence) above it. The seal was approved by Congress on June 20, 1782.

THE FLAG

The flag of the United States has 50 stars (one for each state) and 13 stripes (one for each of the original 13 states). It is called unofficially the "Stars and Stripes."

The first U.S. flag was commissioned by the Second Continental Congress in 1777 but did not exist until 1783, after the American Revolution. Historians are not certain who designed the Stars and Stripes. Many different flags are believed to have been used during the American Revolution.

The flag of 1777 was used until 1795. In that year Congress passed an act ordering that a new flag have 15 stripes, alternate red and white, and 15 stars on a blue field. In 1818, Congress directed that the flag have 13 stripes and that a new star be added for each new state of the Union. The last star was added in 1960 for the state of Hawaii.

| 1777 | 1795 | 1818 |

PLEDGE OF ALLEGIANCE TO THE FLAG

"I pledge allegiance to the flag of the United States of America and to the republic for which it stands, one nation under God, indivisible, with liberty and justice for all."

NATIONAL ANTHEM: "THE STAR-SPANGLED BANNER"

"The Star-Spangled Banner" was a poem written in 1814 by Francis Scott Key as he watched British ships bombard Fort McHenry, Maryland, during the War of 1812. It became the National Anthem by an act of Congress in 1931. Although it has four stanzas, the one most commonly sung is the first one. The music to "The Star-Spangled Banner" was originally a tune called "Anacreon in Heaven."

THE U.S. CONSTITUTION:
The Foundation of American Government

The Constitution is the document that created the present government of the United States. It was written in 1787 and went into effect in 1789. It establishes the three branches of the U.S. government, which are the executive (headed by the president), the legislative (the Congress), and the judicial (the Supreme Court and other federal courts). The first 10 amendments to the Constitution (the **Bill of Rights**) explain the basic rights of all American citizens.

You can find the constitution on-line at:

WEB SITE *http://www.nara.gov/exhall/charters/constitution/conmain.html*

The Preamble to the Constitution

The Constitution begins with a short statement called the Preamble. The Preamble states that the government of the United States was established by the people.

"We, the people of the United States, in order to form a more perfect Union, establish justice, insure domestic tranquility, provide for the common defense, promote the general welfare, and secure the blessings of liberty to ourselves and our posterity do ordain and establish this Constitution for the United States of America."

The Articles

The original Constitution contained seven articles. The first three articles of the Constitution establish the three branches of the U.S. government.

Article 1, Legislative Branch
Creates the Senate and House of Representatives and describes their functions and powers.

Article 2, Executive Branch
Creates the office of the President and the Electoral College and lists their powers and responsibilities.

Article 3, Judicial Branch
Creates the Supreme Court and gives Congress the power to create lower courts. The powers of the courts and certain crimes are defined.

Article 4, The States
Discusses the relationship of the states to one another and to the citizens. Defines the states' powers.

Article 5, Amending the Constitution
Describes how the Constitution can be amended (changed).

Article 6, Federal Law
Makes the Constitution the supreme law of the land over state laws and constitutions.

Article 7, Ratifying the Constitution
Establishes how to ratify (approve) the Constitution.

AMENDMENTS TO THE CONSTITUTION

The writers of the Constitution understood that it might need to be amended, or changed, in the future. Article 5 describes how the Constitution can be amended. In order to pass, an amendment must be approved by a two-thirds majority in the House of Representatives and a two-thirds majority in the Senate. The amendment must then be approved by three-fourths of the states (38 states). So far, the Constitution has been amended 27 times.

The Bill of Rights: The First Ten Amendments

The first ten amendments were adopted in 1791 and contain the basic freedoms Americans enjoy as a people. These amendments are known as the Bill of Rights. They are summarized below.

1 Guarantees freedom of religion, speech, and the press

2 Guarantees the right of the people to have firearms

3 Guarantees that soldiers cannot be lodged in private homes unless the owner agrees

4 Protects citizens against being searched or having their property searched or taken away by the government without a good reason

5 Protects rights of people on trial for crimes

6 Guarantees people accused of crimes the right to a speedy public trial by jury

7 Guarantees people the right to a trial by jury for other kinds of cases

8 Prohibits "cruel and unusual punishments"

9 Says that specific rights listed in the Constitution do not take away rights that may not be listed

10 Establishes that any powers not given specifically to the federal government belong to states or the people

Other Important Amendments

13 (1865): Ends slavery in the United States

14 (1868): Establishes the Bill of Rights as protection against actions by a state government; guarantees equal protection under the law for all citizens

15 (1870): Guarantees that a person cannot be denied the right to vote because of race or color

19 (1920): Gives women the right to vote

22 (1951): Limits the president to two four-year terms of office

24 (1964): Outlaws the poll tax (a tax people had to pay before they could vote) in federal elections. (The poll tax had been used to keep African Americans in the South from voting.)

25 (1967): Gives the president the power to appoint a new vice president, with the approval of Congress, if a vice president dies or leaves office in the middle of a term

26 (1971): Lowers the voting age to eighteen

THE EXECUTIVE BRANCH:
The PRESIDENT and the CABINET

The executive branch of the federal government is headed by the president. It also includes the vice president, people who work for the president or vice president, the major departments of the federal government, and special agencies. The cabinet is made up of the vice president, heads of the major departments, and other top officials. It meets when the president asks for its advice. As head of the executive branch, the president is responsible for enforcing the laws passed by Congress and is commander in chief of U.S. armed forces. The chart at right shows cabinet departments in the order in which they were created.

PRESIDENT

VICE PRESIDENT

CABINET DEPARTMENTS

State	Commerce	Energy
Treasury	Labor	Education
Defense	Housing and Urban Development	Health and Human Services
Justice		
Interior	Transportation	Veterans Affairs
Agriculture		

▲ The White House, home of the U.S. president

How Long Does the President Serve?

The president serves a four-year term, starting on January 20. No president can be elected more than twice.

What Happens If the President Dies?

If the president dies in office or cannot complete the term, the vice president becomes president. If the president is disabled, the vice president can become acting president until the president is able to work again. The next person to become president after the vice president would be the Speaker of the House of Representatives. A person who finishes more than two years of a president's term can be elected to only one more term.

The White House has an address on the World Wide Web especially for kids. It is:

WEB SITE http://www.whitehouse.gov/WH/kids/html/home.html

You can send e-mail to the president at:

EMAIL president@whitehouse.gov

DiD You KNOW?

You can use the site at left to "tour" the White House and learn about the First Family.

THE JUDICIAL BRANCH:
The SUPREME COURT

The highest court in the United States is the Supreme Court. It has nine justices who are appointed for life by the president with the approval of the Senate. Eight of the nine members are called associate justices. The ninth is the chief justice, who presides over the Court's meetings.

What Does the Supreme Court Do? The Supreme Court's major responsibilities are to judge cases that involve reviewing federal laws, actions of the president, treaties of the United States, and laws passed by state governments to be sure that they do not conflict with the U.S. Constitution. The Supreme Court carries out these responsibilities by deciding cases that come before it. This process is known as **judicial review.** If the Supreme Court finds that a law or action violates the Constitution, the justices declare it unconstitutional.

The Supreme Court's Decision Is Final. Most cases must go through other federal courts or state courts before they go to the Supreme Court. The Supreme Court is the final court for a case, and the justices usually decide which cases they will review. After the Supreme Court hears a case, it may agree or disagree with the decision by a lower court. When the Supreme Court makes a ruling, its decision is final, and all people involved in the case must abide by it.

Who Is on the Supreme Court? Below are the nine justices who were on the Supreme Court at the beginning of its 1999-2000 session.

Back row *(from left to right): Ruth Bader Ginsburg, David H. Souter, Clarence Thomas, Stephen Breyer.* **Front row** *(from left to right): Antonin Scalia, John Paul Stevens, Chief Justice William H. Rehnquist, Sandra Day O'Connor, Anthony M. Kennedy.*

DiD You KNOW?

Marbury v. Madison *in 1803 was an especially important case. The justices decided the Supreme Court was allowed to declare laws unconstitutional (not fitting in with the U.S. Constitution). That decision has affected almost every case that has since come before the Supreme Court.*

THE LEGISLATIVE BRANCH: CONGRESS

The Congress of the United States is the legislative branch of the federal government. Congress's major responsibility is to pass the laws that govern the country and determine how money collected in taxes is spent. It is the president's responsibility to enforce the laws. Congress consists of two parts—the Senate and the House of Representatives.

The Capitol, where Congress meets ▶

THE SENATE

The Senate has 100 members, two from each state. The Constitution says that the Senate will have equal representation (the same number of representatives) from each state. Thus, small states have the same number of senators as large states. Senators are elected for six-year terms. There is no limit on the number of terms a senator can serve.

The Senate also has the responsibility of approving people the president appoints for certain jobs, for example, cabinet members and Supreme Court justices. The Senate must approve all treaties by at least a two-thirds vote. It also has the responsibility under the Constitution of putting on trial high-ranking federal officials who have been impeached (see next page) by the House of Representatives.

THE HOUSE OF REPRESENTATIVES

The House of Representatives has 435 members. The number for each state depends on its population. But each state has at least one representative, no matter how small its population. The first House of Representatives in 1789 had 65 members. As the country's population grew, the number of representatives increased.

Since the 1910 census, however, the total membership has been kept at 435. After the results of Census 2000 has been added up, the number of representatives from each state may go up or down.

You can reach the Senate and the House on-line at:

WEB SITE *http://www.senate.gov*
http://www.house.gov

THE HOUSE OF REPRESENTATIVES, BY STATE

Each state has the following number of representatives in the House:

Alabama	7	Montana	1
Alaska	1	Nebraska	3
Arizona	6	Nevada	2
Arkansas	4	New Hampshire	2
California	52	New Jersey	13
Colorado	6	New Mexico	3
Connecticut	6	New York	31
Delaware	1	North Carolina	12
Florida	23	North Dakota	1
Georgia	11	Ohio	19
Hawaii	2	Oklahoma	6
Idaho	2	Oregon	5
Illinois	20	Pennsylvania	21
Indiana	10	Rhode Island	2
Iowa	5	South Carolina	6
Kansas	4	South Dakota	1
Kentucky	6	Tennessee	9
Louisiana	7	Texas	30
Maine	2	Utah	3
Maryland	8	Vermont	1
Massachusetts	10	Virginia	11
Michigan	16	Washington	9
Minnesota	8	West Virginia	3
Mississippi	5	Wisconsin	9
Missouri	9	Wyoming	1

The District of Columbia (Washington, D.C.), Puerto Rico, American Samoa, Guam, and the Virgin Islands each have one nonvoting member of the House of Representatives.

WHAT IMPEACHMENT MEANS

"Impeachment" means charging a high-ranking U.S. government official (such as a president or federal judge) with serious crimes — "high crimes and misdemeanors" — in order to possibly remove the person from office. Only the House of Representatives can vote to impeach officials. Once it does, there is a trial in the Senate.

The chief justice of the Supreme Court presides. A two-thirds vote is needed to remove the person from office.

In 1868, President Andrew Johnson (above) was impeached. He was found not guilty in a Senate trial. In 1974, a House committee recommended the impeachment of President Richard Nixon, but he resigned before the whole House could vote. On December 19, 1998, the House voted to impeach President Bill Clinton (left) for perjury and obstructing justice. On February 12, 1999, after a Senate trial, he was found not guilty of perjury, 55-45, and of obstructing justice, by a 50-50 vote.

How a Bill Becomes a Law

STEP 1. Senators and Representatives Propose a Bill.

A proposed law is called a **bill**. Any member of Congress may propose (introduce) a bill. A bill is introduced in each house of Congress. The House of Representatives and the Senate consider a bill separately. A member of Congress who introduces a bill is known as the bill's **sponsor**. Bills to raise money always begin in the House of Representatives.

STEP 2. House and Senate Committees Consider the Bill.

The bill is then sent to appropriate committees for consideration. A bill relating to agriculture, for example, would be sent to the agriculture committees in the House and in the Senate. A committee is made up of a small number of members of the House or Senate. Whichever party has a majority in the House or Senate has a majority on each committee. When committees are considering a bill, they hold **hearings** at which people can speak for or against it.

STEP 3. Committees Vote on the Bill.

The committees can change the bill as they see fit. Then they vote on it.

STEP 4. The Bill Is Debated in the House and Senate.

If the committees vote in favor of the bill, it goes to the full House and Senate, where it is debated and may be changed further. The House and Senate can then vote on it.

STEP 5. From the House and Senate to Conference Committee.

If the House and the Senate pass different versions of the same bill, the bill must go to a **conference committee,** where differences between the two versions must be worked out. A conference committee is a special committee made up of both Senate and House members.

STEP 6. Final Vote in the House and Senate.

The House and the Senate then vote on the conference committee version. In order for this version to become a law, it must be approved by a majority of members of both houses of Congress and signed by the president.

STEP 7. The President Signs the Bill Into Law.

If the bill passes both houses of Congress, it goes to the president for his signature. Once the president signs a bill, it becomes law.

STEP 8. What If the President Doesn't Sign the Bill?

Sometimes the president does not approve of a bill and decides not to sign it. This is called **vetoing** it. A bill that has been vetoed goes back to Congress, where the members can vote again. If the House and the Senate pass the bill with a two-thirds majority vote, it becomes law. This is called **overriding** the veto.

Major GOVERNMENT AGENCIES

Government agencies have a variety of functions. Some set rules and regulations or enforce laws. Others investigate or gather information. Some major agencies are listed below, along with what they try to do.

Central Intelligence Agency (CIA)
Gathers secret information on other countries and their leaders.

Consumer Product Safety Commission
Examines the products that people buy to see that they are safe.

Environmental Protection Agency (EPA)
Enforces laws on clean air and water and is responsible for cleaning up hazardous waste sites.

Equal Employment Opportunity Commission (EEOC)
Makes sure that people are not discriminated against when they apply for a job and when they are at work.

Federal Aviation Administration (FAA)
Watches over the airline industry and establishes safety rules.

Federal Bureau of Investigation (FBI)
Investigates federal crimes and collects statistics on crime in the United States.

Federal Communications Commission (FCC)
Gives out licenses to radio and TV stations and makes broadcasting rules.

Federal Emergency Management Agency (FEMA)
Helps local communities recover from disasters such as hurricanes, earthquakes, and floods.

Federal Trade Commission (FTC)
Makes sure that businesses operate fairly and that they obey the law.

Library of Congress
The main library of the United States. Collects most of the books published in the United States. It also has many historic documents and photographs.

National Endowment for the Arts (NEA)
National Endowment for the Humanities (NEH)
Gives government money to museums, artists, writers, and many creative projects.

Occupational Safety and Health Administration (OSHA)
Makes sure that places where people work are safe and will not harm workers' health.

Peace Corps
Sends American volunteers to foreign countries for two years to help with special projects such as teaching and farming.

Securities and Exchange Commission (SEC)
Makes sure that the stock market operates fairly and obeys the laws.

ELECTIONS
Electing the President and Vice President

Every four years the first Tuesday after the first Monday in November is an important date for Americans. That's when voters go to the polls and elect a president and vice president. Right? Well, sort of.

The president and vice president are the only elected U.S. officials who are not actually chosen by a direct vote of the people. They are really elected by the 538 members of the Electoral College.

The Electoral College is not what we think of as a college, but just a group of people chosen in each state. In 1787 the men writing the Constitution did not agree on how a president should be selected. Some did not trust ordinary people to make a good choice. So they compromised and agreed to have the Electoral College do it.

In the early days before political parties became important, electors voted for whomever they wanted. In modern times the political parties hold primary elections and conventions to choose candidates for president and vice president. When voters pull a lever for the candidates of a particular party, they are actually choosing electors from that party. The electors have agreed to vote for their party's candidate, and except in very rare cases this is what they do.

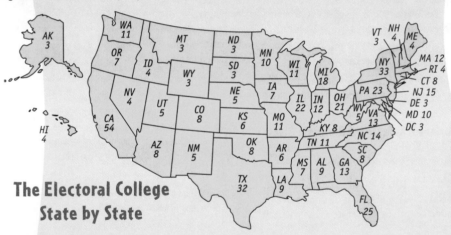

The Electoral College
State by State

The number of electors for each state and the District of Columbia is equal to the total number of senators and representatives each has in Congress. For example, Minnesota has eight representatives and two senators, for a total of ten. The electors chosen in November meet in state capitals in December. In almost all states, the party that got the most votes in November wins all the electors and electoral votes for the state. This would happen even if the results of the election in the state were very close.

In early January the electors' votes are finally opened during a special session of Congress—though everybody already knows what they are. If no presidential candidate wins a majority (at least 270) of the electoral votes, the House of Representatives chooses the president. This happened in 1800 and 1824.

Can a candidate who didn't win the most popular votes still win a majority of electoral votes? Yes. That's what happened in the elections of 1876 and 1888. It could still happen today.

PRESIDENTS and VICE PRESIDENTS of the UNITED STATES

PRESIDENT VICE PRESIDENT	YEARS IN OFFICE	PRESIDENT VICE PRESIDENT	YEARS IN OFFICE
1 George Washington	**1789–1797**	**22 Grover Cleveland**	**1885–1889**
John Adams	1789–1797	Thomas A. Hendricks	1885
2 John Adams	**1797–1801**	**23 Benjamin Harrison**	**1889–1893**
Thomas Jefferson	1797–1801	Levi P. Morton	1889–1893
3 Thomas Jefferson	**1801–1809**	**24 Grover Cleveland**	**1893–1897**
Aaron Burr	1801–1805	Adlai E. Stevenson	1893–1897
George Clinton	1805–1809	**25 William McKinley**	**1897–1901**
4 James Madison	**1809–1817**	Garret A. Hobart	1897–1899
George Clinton	1809–1812	Theodore Roosevelt	1901
Elbridge Gerry	1813–1814	**26 Theodore Roosevelt**	**1901–1909**
5 James Monroe	**1817–1825**	Charles W. Fairbanks	1905–1909
Daniel D. Tompkins	1817–1825	**27 William Howard Taft**	**1909–1913**
6 John Quincy Adams	**1825–1829**	James S. Sherman	1909–1912
John C. Calhoun	1825–1829	**28 Woodrow Wilson**	**1913–1921**
7 Andrew Jackson	**1829–1837**	Thomas R. Marshall	1913–1921
John C. Calhoun	1829–1832	**29 Warren G. Harding**	**1921–1923**
Martin Van Buren	1833–1837	Calvin Coolidge	1921–1923
8 Martin Van Buren	**1837–1841**	**30 Calvin Coolidge**	**1923–1929**
Richard M. Johnson	1837–1841	Charles G. Dawes	1925–1929
9 William H. Harrison	**1841**	**31 Herbert Hoover**	**1929–1933**
John Tyler	1841	Charles Curtis	1929–1933
10 John Tyler	**1841–1845**	**32 Franklin D. Roosevelt**	**1933–1945**
No Vice President		John Nance Garner	1933–1941
11 James Knox Polk	**1845–1849**	Henry A. Wallace	1941–1945
George M. Dallas	1845–1849	Harry S. Truman	1945
12 Zachary Taylor	**1849–1850**	**33 Harry S. Truman**	**1945–1953**
Millard Fillmore	1849–1850	Alben W. Barkley	1949–1953
13 Millard Fillmore	**1850–1853**	**34 Dwight D. Eisenhower**	**1953–1961**
No Vice President		Richard M. Nixon	1953–1961
14 Franklin Pierce	**1853–1857**	**35 John F. Kennedy**	**1961–1963**
William R. King	1853	Lyndon B. Johnson	1961–1963
15 James Buchanan	**1857–1861**	**36 Lyndon B. Johnson**	**1963–1969**
John C. Breckinridge	1857–1861	Hubert H. Humphrey	1965–1969
16 Abraham Lincoln	**1861–1865**	**37 Richard M. Nixon**	**1969–1974**
Hannibal Hamlin	1861–1865	Spiro T. Agnew	1969–1973
Andrew Johnson	1865	Gerald R. Ford	1973–1974
17 Andrew Johnson	**1865–1869**	**38 Gerald R. Ford**	**1974–1977**
No Vice President		Nelson A. Rockefeller	1974–1977
18 Ulysses S. Grant	**1869–1877**	**39 Jimmy Carter**	**1977–1981**
Schuyler Colfax	1869–1873	Walter F. Mondale	1977–1981
Henry Wilson	1873–1875	**40 Ronald Reagan**	**1981–1989**
19 Rutherford B. Hayes	**1877–1881**	George Bush	1981–1989
William A. Wheeler	1877–1881	**41 George Bush**	**1989–1993**
20 James A. Garfield	**1881**	Dan Quayle	1989–1993
Chester A. Arthur	1881	**42 Bill Clinton**	**1993–**
21 Chester A. Arthur	**1881–1885**	Al Gore	1993–
No Vice President			

PRESIDENTS
of the United States

1 **GEORGE WASHINGTON** Federalist Party   **1789-1797**
Born: Feb. 22, 1732, at Wakefield, Westmoreland County, Virginia
Married: Martha Dandridge Custis (1731-1802); no children
Died: Dec. 14, 1799; buried at Mount Vernon, Fairfax County, Virginia
Early Career: Soldier; head of the Virginia militia; commander of the
   Continental Army; chairman of Constitutional Convention (1787)

2 **JOHN ADAMS** Federalist Party   **1797-1801**
Born: Oct. 30, 1735, in Braintree (now Quincy), Massachusetts
Married: Abigail Smith (1744-1818); 3 sons, 2 daughters
Died: July 4, 1826; buried in Quincy, Massachusetts
Early Career: Lawyer; delegate to Continental Congress; signer of the
   Declaration of Independence; first vice president

3 **THOMAS JEFFERSON** Democratic-Republican Party   **1801-1809**
Born: Apr. 13, 1743, at Shadwell, Albemarle County, Virginia
Married: Martha Wayles Skelton (1748-1782); 1 son, 5 daughters
Died: July 4, 1826; buried at Monticello, Albemarle County, Virginia
Early Career: Lawyer; member of the Continental Congress; author of the
   Declaration of Independence; governor of Virginia; first secretary of
   state; author of the Virginia Statute on Religious Freedom

4 **JAMES MADISON** Democratic-Republican Party   **1809-1817**
Born: Mar. 16, 1751, at Port Conway, King George County, Virginia
Married: Dolley Payne Todd (1768-1849); no children
Died: June 28, 1836; buried at Montpelier Station, Virginia
Early Career: Member of the Virginia Constitutional Convention (1776);
   member of the Continental Congress; major contributor to the U.S.
   Constitution; writer of the *Federalist Papers*; secretary of state

5 **JAMES MONROE** Democratic-Republican Party   **1817-1825**
Born: Apr. 28, 1758, in Westmoreland County, Virginia
Married: Elizabeth Kortright (1768-1830); 2 daughters
Died: July 4, 1831; buried in Richmond, Virginia
Early Career: Soldier; lawyer; U.S. senator; governor of Virginia;
   secretary of state

6 **JOHN QUINCY ADAMS** Democratic-Republican Party   **1825-1829**
Born: July 11, 1767, in Braintree (now Quincy), Massachusetts
Married: Louisa Catherine Johnson (1775-1852); 3 sons, 1 daughter
Died: Feb. 23, 1848; buried in Quincy, Massachusetts
Early Career: Diplomat; U.S. senator; secretary of state

ANDREW JACKSON Democratic Party   **1829-1837**
Born: Mar. 15, 1767, in Waxhaw, South Carolina
Married: Rachel Donelson Robards (1767-1828); 1 son
Died: June 8, 1845; buried in Nashville, Tennessee
Early Career: Lawyer; U.S. representative and senator; soldier in the
    U.S. Army

MARTiN VAN BUREN Democratic Party   **1837-1841**
Born: Dec. 5, 1782, at Kinderhook, New York
Married: Hannah Hoes (1783-1819); 4 sons
Died: July 24, 1862; buried at Kinderhook, New York
Early Career: Governor of New York; secretary of state; vice president

WiLLiAM HENRY HARRiSON Whig Party   **1841**
Born: Feb. 9, 1773, at Berkeley, Charles City County, Virginia
Married: Anna Symmes (1775-1864); 6 sons, 4 daughters
Died: Apr. 4, 1841; buried in North Bend, Ohio
Early Career: First governor of Indiana Territory; superintendent of
    Indian affairs; U.S. representative and senator

JOHN TYLER Whig Party   **1841-1845**
Born: Mar. 29, 1790, in Greenway, Charles City County, Virginia
Married: Letitia Christian (1790-1842); 3 sons, 5 daughters
    Julia Gardiner (1820-1889); 5 sons, 2 daughters
Died: Jan. 18, 1862; buried in Richmond, Virginia
Early Career: U.S. representative and senator; vice president

JAMES KNOX POLK Democratic Party   **1845-1849**
Born: Nov. 2, 1795, in Mecklenburg County, North Carolina
Married: Sarah Childress (1803-1891); no children
Died: June 15, 1849; buried in Nashville, Tennessee
Early Career: U.S. representative; Speaker of the House; governor
    of Tennessee

ZACHARY TAYLOR Whig Party   **1849-1850**
Born: Nov. 24, 1784, in Orange County, Virginia
Married: Margaret Smith (1788-1852); 1 son, 5 daughters
Died: July 9, 1850; buried in Louisville, Kentucky
Early Career: Indian fighter; general in the U.S. Army

MiLLARD FiLLMORE Whig Party   **1850-1853**
Born: Jan. 7, 1800, in Cayuga County, New York
Married: Abigail Powers (1798-1853); 1 son, 1 daughter
    Caroline Carmichael McIntosh (1813-1881); no children
Died: Mar. 8, 1874; buried in Buffalo, New York
Early Career: Farmer; lawyer; U.S. representative; vice president

FRANKLIN PIERCE Democratic Party   1853-1857
Born: Nov. 23, 1804, in Hillsboro, New Hampshire
Married: Jane Means Appleton (1806-1863); 3 sons
Died: Oct. 8, 1869; buried in Concord, New Hampshire
Early Career: U.S. representative, senator

JAMES BUCHANAN Democratic Party   1857-1861
Born: Apr. 23, 1791, Cove Gap, near Mercersburg, Pennsylvania
Never Married
Died: June 1, 1868, buried in Lancaster, Pennsylvania
Early Career: U.S. representative; secretary of state

ABRAHAM LINCOLN Republican Party   1861-1865
Born: Feb. 12, 1809, in Hardin County, Kentucky
Married: Mary Todd (1818-1882); 4 sons
Died: Apr. 15, 1865; buried in Springfield, Illinois
Early Career: Lawyer; U.S. representative

ANDREW JOHNSON Democratic Party   1865-1869
Born: Dec. 29, 1808, in Raleigh, North Carolina
Married: Eliza McCardle (1810-1876); 3 sons, 2 daughters
Died: July 31, 1875; buried in Greeneville, Tennessee
Early Career: Tailor; member of state legislature; U.S. representative;
    governor of Tennessee; U.S. senator; vice president

ULYSSES S. GRANT Republican Party   1869-1877
Born: Apr. 27, 1822, in Point Pleasant, Ohio
Married: Julia Dent (1826-1902); 3 sons, 1 daughter
Died: July 23, 1885; buried in New York City
Early Career: Army officer; commander of Union forces during Civil War

RUTHERFORD B. HAYES Republican Party   1877-1881
Born: Oct. 4, 1822, in Delaware, Ohio
Married: Lucy Ware Webb (1831-1889); 5 sons, 2 daughters
Died: Jan. 17, 1893; buried in Fremont, Ohio
Early Career: Lawyer; general in Union Army; U.S. representative;
    governor of Ohio

JAMES A. GARFIELD Republican Party   1881
Born: Nov. 19, 1831, in Orange, Cuyahoga County, Ohio
Married: Lucretia Rudolph (1832-1918); 5 sons, 2 daughters
Died: Sept. 19, 1881; buried in Cleveland, Ohio
Early Career: Teacher; Ohio state senator; general in Union Army;
    U.S. representative

21 **CHESTER A. ARTHUR** Republican Party   **1881-1885**
Born: Oct. 5, 1829, in Fairfield, Vermont
Married: Ellen Lewis Herndon (1837-1880); 2 sons, 1 daughter
Died: Nov. 18, 1886; buried in Albany, New York
Early Career: Teacher; lawyer; vice president

22 **GROVER CLEVELAND** Democratic Party   **1885-1889**
Born: Mar. 18, 1837, in Caldwell, New Jersey
Married: Frances Folsom (1864-1947); 2 sons, 3 daughters
Died: June 24, 1908; buried in Princeton, New Jersey
Early Career: Lawyer; mayor of Buffalo; governor of New York

23 **BENJAMIN HARRISON** Republican Party   **1889-1893**
Born: Aug. 20, 1833, in North Bend, Ohio
Married: Caroline Lavinia Scott (1832-1892); 1 son, 1 daughter
          Mary Scott Lord Dimmick (1858-1948); 1 daughter
Died: Mar. 13, 1901; buried in Indianapolis, Indiana
Early Career: Lawyer; general in Union Army; U.S. senator

24 **GROVER CLEVELAND**   **1893-1897**
See 22, above

25 **WILLIAM MCKINLEY** Republican Party   **1897-1901**
Born: Jan. 29, 1843, in Niles, Ohio
Married: Ida Saxton (1847-1907); 2 daughters
Died: Sept. 14, 1901; buried in Canton, Ohio
Early Career: Lawyer; U.S. representative; governor of Ohio

26 **THEODORE ROOSEVELT** Republican Party   **1901-1909**
Born: Oct. 27, 1858, in New York City
Married: Alice Hathaway Lee (1861-1884); 1 daughter
          Edith Kermit Carow (1861-1948); 4 sons, 1 daughter
Died: Jan. 6, 1919; buried in Oyster Bay, New York
Early Career: Assistant secretary of the Navy; cavalry leader in
          Spanish-American War; governor of New York; vice president

27 **WILLIAM HOWARD TAFT** Republican Party   **1909-1913**
Born: Sept. 15, 1857, in Cincinnati, Ohio
Married: Helen Herron (1861-1943); 2 sons, 1 daughter
Died: Mar. 8, 1930; buried in Arlington National Cemetery, Virginia
Early Career: Reporter; lawyer; judge; secretary of war

28 **WOODROW WILSON** Democratic Party   **1913-1921**
Born: Dec. 28, 1856, in Staunton, Virginia
Married: Ellen Louise Axson (1860-1914); 3 daughters
          Edith Bolling Galt (1872-1961); no children
Died: Feb. 3, 1924; buried in Washington, D.C.
Early Career: College professor and president; governor of New Jersey

WARREN G. HARDING Republican Party   1921-1923
Born: Nov. 2, 1865, near Corsica (now Blooming Grove), Ohio
Married: Florence Kling De Wolfe (1860-1924); 1 daughter
Died: Aug. 2, 1923; buried in Marion, Ohio
Early Career: Ohio state senator; U.S. senator

CALVIN COOLIDGE Republican Party   1923-1929
Born: July 4, 1872, in Plymouth, Vermont
Married: Grace Anna Goodhue (1879-1957); 2 sons
Died: Jan. 5, 1933; buried in Plymouth, Vermont
Early Career: Massachusetts state legislator; lieutenant governor and
governor; vice president

HERBERT HOOVER Republican Party   1929-1933
Born: Aug. 10, 1874, in West Branch, Iowa
Married: Lou Henry (1875-1944); 2 sons
Died: Oct. 20, 1964; buried in West Branch, Iowa
Early Career: Mining engineer; secretary of commerce

FRANKLIN DELANO ROOSEVELT Democratic Party   1933-1945
Born: Jan. 30, 1882, in Hyde Park, New York
Married: Anna Eleanor Roosevelt (1884-1962); 4 sons, 1 daughter
Died: Apr. 12, 1945; buried in Hyde Park, New York
Early Career: Lawyer; New York state senator; assistant secretary of the
Navy; governor of New York

HARRY S. TRUMAN Democratic Party   1945-1953
Born: May 8, 1884, in Lamar, Missouri
Married: Elizabeth Virginia "Bess" Wallace (1885-1982); 1 daughter
Died: Dec. 26, 1972; buried in Independence, Missouri
Early Career: Farmer, haberdasher (ran men's clothing store); judge; U.S.
senator; vice president

DWIGHT D. EISENHOWER Republican Party   1953-1961
Born: Oct. 14, 1890, in Denison, Texas
Married: Mary "Mamie" Geneva Doud (1896-1979); 2 sons
Died: Mar. 28, 1969; buried in Abilene, Kansas
Early Career: Commander, Allied landing in North Africa and later
Supreme Allied Commander in Europe during World War II; president of
Columbia University

JOHN FITZGERALD KENNEDY Democratic Party   1961-1963
Born: May 29, 1917, in Brookline, Massachusetts
Married: Jacqueline Lee Bouvier (1929-1994); 2 sons, 1 daughter
Died: Nov. 22, 1963; buried in Arlington National Cemetery, Virginia
Early Career: U.S. naval commander; U.S. representative and senator

LYNDON BAINES JOHNSON Democratic Party   1963-1969

Born: Aug. 27, 1908, near Stonewall, Texas
Married: Claudia "Lady Bird" Alta Taylor (b. 1912); 2 daughters
Died: Jan. 22, 1973; buried in Johnson City, Texas
Early Career: U.S. representative and senator; vice president

RICHARD MILHOUS NIXON Republican Party   1969-1974

Born: Jan. 9, 1913, in Yorba Linda, California
Married: Thelma "Pat" Ryan (1912-1993); 2 daughters
Died: Apr. 22, 1994; buried in Yorba Linda, California
Early Career: Lawyer; U.S. representative and senator; vice president

GERALD R. FORD Republican Party   1974-1977

Born: July 14, 1913, in Omaha, Nebraska
Married: Elizabeth "Betty" Bloomer (b. 1918); 3 sons, 1 daughter
Early Career: Lawyer; U.S. representative; vice president

JIMMY (JAMES EARL) CARTER Democratic Party   1977-1981

Born: Oct. 1, 1924, in Plains, Georgia
Married: Rosalynn Smith (b. 1927); 3 sons, 1 daughter
Early Career: Peanut farmer; Georgia state senator; governor
of Georgia

RONALD REAGAN Republican Party   1981-1989

Born: Feb. 6, 1911, in Tampico, Illinois
Married: Jane Wyman (b. 1914); 1 son, 1 daughter
Nancy Davis (b. 1923); 1 son, 1 daughter
Early Career: Film and television actor; governor of California

GEORGE BUSH Republican Party   1989-1993

Born: June 12, 1924, in Milton, Massachusetts
Married: Barbara Pierce (b. 1925); 4 sons, 2 daughters
Early Career: U.S. Navy pilot; businessman; U.S. representative; U.S.
ambassador to the United Nations; vice president

BILL (WILLIAM JEFFERSON) CLINTON Democratic Party   1993-

Born: Aug. 19, 1946, in Hope, Arkansas
Married: Hillary Rodham (b. 1947); 1 daughter
Early Career: College professor; Arkansas state attorney general;
governor of Arkansas

PRESIDENTIAL FACTS, FAMILIES, AND FIRST LADIES

PRESIDENTIAL FACTS

First president to live in White House: John Adams

Three presidents who all died on July 4: John Adams, Thomas Jefferson, James Monroe

President with the most children: John Tyler, who had 15 children with two wives

Only president who was unmarried: James Buchanan

Only president to resign: Richard Nixon, who resigned because of the Watergate scandal

Presidents who were impeached: Andrew Johnson (1868), Bill Clinton (1998); both were acquitted in a Senate trial.

Presidents who died in office: Eight U.S. presidents have died while they served as president. Four of them were assassinated: Abraham Lincoln, James Garfield, William McKinley, and John F. Kennedy. The other four were William Henry Harrison, Zachary Taylor, Warren G. Harding, and Franklin D. Roosevelt.

FAMOUS FIRST FAMILIES

Adams family: John Adams was the second president, and his son, John Quincy Adams, became the sixth president.

Harrison family: Benjamin Harrison, the 23rd president, was the great-grandson of Benjamin Harrison, a signer of the Declaration of Independence, and the grandson of William Henry Harrison, the ninth president of the United States.

Roosevelt family: Theodore Roosevelt was the 26th president and his fifth cousin, Franklin Delano Roosevelt, the 32nd. Franklin's wife, Eleanor Roosevelt, was also Theodore Roosevelt's niece.

First Ladies make news

Lucy Hayes, wife of Rutherford B. Hayes, was the first president's wife to earn a college degree. When she and her husband went to the West Coast, she became the first First Lady to travel across North America.

Edith Wilson, wife of Woodrow Wilson, was controversial. She took charge when her husband became very ill. She said she never made any key decisions, but for several weeks she decided who could see the President.

Lou Henry Hoover, wife of Herbert Hoover, spoke several languages, including Chinese. She had a degree in geology, which was unusual for a woman of her time. As First Lady, she worked to involve all children in sports.

Eleanor Roosevelt, wife of Franklin D. Roosevelt, was an important public figure. She urged her husband to support civil rights and the rights of workers. After his death she served as a delegate to the United Nations.

Lady Bird Johnson, wife of Lyndon Johnson, turned a love of the outdoors into a campaign. An environmentalist, she has encouraged Americans to beautify their country by planting flowers in many places, even along highways.

Hillary Rodham Clinton, wife of Bill Clinton, became a lawyer and active First Lady. In 2000, she became a candidate for the U.S. Senate from New York.

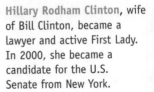

THE FIRST PEOPLE IN NORTH AMERICA: BEFORE 1492

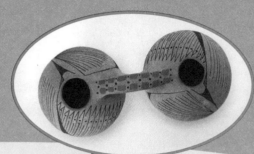

14,000 B.C.–11,000 B.C.
Paleo-Indians use stone points attached to spears to hunt big mammoths in northern parts of North America.

11,000 B.C.
Big mammoths disappear and Paleo-Indians begin to gather plants for food.

AFTER A.D. 500
Anasazi peoples in the Southwestern United States live in homes on cliffs, called cliff dwellings. Anasazi pottery and dishes are well known for their beautiful patterns.

AFTER A.D. 700
Mississippian Indian people in Southeastern United States develop farms and build burial mounds.

000 B.C.

40,000 B.C.–11,000 B.C.
First people (called Paleo-Indians) cross from Siberia to Alaska and begin to move into North America.

8000 B.C.–1000 B.C.
North American Indians begin using stone to grind food and to hunt bison and smaller animals.

1000 B.C.–A.D. 500
Woodland Indians, who lived east of the Mississippi River, bury people who have died under large burial mounds (which can still be seen today).

700–1492
Many different Indian cultures develop throughout North America.

COLONIAL AMERICA AND THE AMERICAN REVOLUTION: 1492-178[9]

St. Augustine

1492

1492
Christopher Columbus sails across the Atlantic Ocean and reaches an island in the Bahamas in the Caribbean Sea.

1513
Juan Ponce de León explores the Florida coast.

1524
Giovanni da Verrazano explores the coast from Carolina north to Nova Scotia, enters New York harbor.

1540
Francisco Vásquez de Coronado explores the Southwest.

1565
St. Augustine, Florida, the first town established by Europeans in the United States, is founded by the Spanish. Later burned by the English in 1586.

BENJAMIN FRANKLIN (1706-1790)

was a great American leader, printer, scientist, and writer. In 1732, he began publishing a magazine called *Poor Richard's Almanack*. Poor Richard was a make-believe person who gave advice about common sense and honesty. Many of Poor Richard's sayings are still known today. Among the most famous are "God helps them that help themselves" and "Early to bed, early to rise, makes a man healthy, wealthy, and wise."

1634

1634
Maryland is founded as a Catholic colony, with religious freedom for all granted in 1649.

1664
The English seize New Amsterdam from the Dutch. The city is renamed New York.

1699
French settlers move into Mississippi and Louisiana.

1732
Benjamin Franklin begins publishing *Poor Richard's Almanack*.

1754-1763
French and Indian War between England and France. The French are defeated and lose their lands in Canada and the American Midwest.

1764-1766
England places taxe[s] on sugar that come[s] from their North American colonies. England also requires colonists t[o] buy stamps to help pay for royal troops[.] Colonists protest, and the Stamp Act is repealed in 1766[.]

1607
Jamestown, Virginia, the first English settlement in North America, is founded by Captain John Smith.

1609
Henry Hudson sails into New York Harbor, explores Hudson River. Spaniards settle Santa Fe, New Mexico.

1619
The first African slaves are brought to Jamestown. (Slavery is made legal in 1650.)

1620
Pilgrims from England arrive at Plymouth, Massachusetts, on the *Mayflower*.

1626
Peter Minuit buys Manhattan island for the Dutch from Man-a-hat-a Indians for goods worth $24. The island is renamed New Amsterdam.

1630
Boston is founded by Massachusetts colonists led by John Winthrop.

PORTION OF THE DECLARATION OF INDEPENDENCE, JULY 4, 1776

"We hold these truths to be self-evident, that all men are created equal, that they are endowed by their Creator with certain unalienable rights, that among these are life, liberty, and the pursuit of happiness."

770
oston Massacre: English oops fire on a group people protesting glish taxes.

1773
Boston Tea Party: English tea is thrown into the harbor to protest a tax on tea.

1775
Fighting at Lexington and Concord, Massachusetts, marks the beginning of the American Revolution.

1776
The Declaration of Independence is approved July 4 by the Continental Congress (made up of representatives from the American colonies).

1781
British General Cornwallis surrenders to the Americans at Yorktown, Virginia, ending the fighting in the Revolutionary War.

THE NEW NATION: 1783-1900

WHO ATTENDED THE CONVENTION?

The Constitutional Convention met in Philadelphia in the hot summer of 1787. Most of the great founders of America attended. Among those present were George Washington, James Madison, and John Adams. They met to form a new government that would be strong and, at the same time, protect the liberties that were fought for in the American Revolution. The Constitution they created is still the law of the United States.

THE LOUISIANA PURCHASE (1803)

1784

1784
The first successful daily newspaper, the *Pennsylvania Packet & General Advertiser*, is published.

1787
The Constitutional Convention meets to write a Constitution for the U.S.

1789
The new Constitution is approved by the states. George Washington is chosen as the first president.

1800
The federal government moves to a new capital, Washington, D.C.

1803
The U.S. makes the Louisiana Purchase from France. The Purchase doubled the area of the U.S.

The Trail of Tears

UNCLE TOM'S CABIN

Harriet Beecher Stowe's novel about the sufferings of slaves was an instant bestseller in the North and banned in most of the South. When President Abraham Lincoln met Stowe, he called her "the little lady who started this war" (the Civil War).

"THE TRAIL OF TEARS"

The Cherokee Indians living in Georgia were forced, by the state government of Georgia, to leave in 1838. They were sent to Oklahoma. On the long march, thousands died because of disease and the cold weather.

1836

1836
Texans fighting for independence from Mexico are defeated at the Alamo.

1838
Cherokee Indians are forced to move to Oklahoma, along "The Trail of Tears."

1844
The first telegraph line connects Washington and Baltimore.

1846–1848
U.S. war with Mexico: Mexico is defeated and the United States takes control of the Republic of Texas and of Mexican territories in the West.

1848
The discovery of gold in California leads to a "rush" of 80,000 people to the West in search of gold.

1852
Uncle Tom's Cabin is published.

1804
Lewis and Clark explore what is now the northwestern United States.

1812–1814
War of 1812 with Great Britain: British forces burn the Capitol and White House. Francis Scott Key writes the words to "The Star-Spangled Banner."

1820
The Missouri Compromise bans slavery west of the Mississippi River and north of 36°30' latitude, except in Missouri.

1823
The Monroe Doctrine warns European countries not to interfere in the Americas.

1825
The Erie Canal opens and links New York City with the Great Lakes.

1831
The Liberator, a newspaper opposing slavery, is published in Boston.

CIVIL WAR DEAD AND WOUNDED

The U.S. Civil War between the North and South lasted four years (1861-1865) and resulted in the death or wounding of more than 600,000 people. Little was known at the time about the spread of diseases. As a result, many casualties were also the result of illnesses such as influenza, measles, and infections from battle wounds.

1898
Spanish-American War: The U.S. defeats Spain, gains control of the Philippines, Puerto Rico, and Guam.

858
braham incoln and tephen ouglas ebate about lavery during heir Senate ampaign n Illinois.

1860
Abraham Lincoln is elected president.

1861
The Civil War begins.

1863
President Lincoln issues the Emancipation Proclamation, freeing most slaves.

1865
The Civil War ends as the South surrenders. President Lincoln is assassinated.

1869
The first railroad connecting the East and West coasts is completed.

1890
Battle of Wounded Knee is fought in South Dakota—the last major battle between Indians and U.S. troops.

UNITED STATES IN THE 20ᵗʰ CENTURY

WORLD WAR I

In World War I the United States fought with Great Britain, France, and Russia (the Allies) against Germany and Austria-Hungary. The Allies won the war in 1918.

1900

1903

The United States begins digging the Panama Canal. The canal opens in 1914, connecting the Atlantic and Pacific oceans.

1908

Henry Ford introduces the Model T car, priced at $850.

1916

Jeannette Rankin of Montana becomes the first woman elected to Congress.

1917-1918

The United States joins World War I on the side of the Allies against Germany.

1927

Charles A. Lindbergh becomes the first person to fly alone nonstop across the Atlantic Ocean.

SCHOOL SEGREGATION

The U.S. Supreme Court ruled that separate schools for black students and white students were not equal. The Court said such schools were against the U.S. Constitution. The ruling also applied to other forms of segregation—separation of the races that were supported by some states.

1954

1954

The U.S. Supreme Court forbids racial segregation in public schools.

1963

President John Kennedy is assassinated.

1964

Congress passes the Civil Rights Act, which outlaws discrimination in voting and jobs.

1965

The United States sends large numbers of soldiers to fight in the Vietnam War.

1968

Civil rights leader Martin Luther King Jr. is assassinated in Memphis. Senator Robert F. Kennedy is assassinated in Los Angeles.

1969

U.S. Astronaut Neil Armstrong becomes the first person to walk on the moon.

1973

U.S. participation in the Vietnam War ends.

THE GREAT DEPRESSION

The stock market crash of October 1929 led to a period of severe hardship for the American people—the Great Depression. As many as 25 percent of all workers could not find jobs. The Depression lasted until the early 1940s. The Depression also led to a great change in politics. In 1932, Franklin D. Roosevelt, a Democrat, was elected president. He served as president for 12 years, longer than any other president.

1929
A stock market crash marks the beginning of the Great Depression.

1933
President Franklin D. Roosevelt's New Deal increases government help to people hurt by the Depression.

1941
Japan attacks Pearl Harbor, Hawaii. The United States enters World War II.

1945
Germany and Japan surrender, ending World War II. Japan surrenders after the U.S. drops atomic bombs on Hiroshima and Nagasaki.

1947
Jackie Robinson becomes the first black baseball player in the major leagues when he joins the Brooklyn Dodgers.

1950–1953
U.S. armed forces fight in the Korean War.

WATERGATE

In June 1972, five men were arrested in the Watergate building in Washington, D.C., for trying to bug telephones in the offices of the Democratic National Committee. Some of those arrested worked for the committee to reelect President Richard Nixon. Later it was discovered that Nixon was helping to hide information about the break-in.

1985
U.S. President Ronald Reagan and Soviet leader Mikhail Gorbachev begin working together to improve relations between their countries.

1991
The Persian Gulf War: The United States and its allies defeat Iraq.

1998
The federal government announces that, for the first time in many years, it will begin receiving more money than it spends.

1999
After an impeachment trial, the Senate finds President Clinton not guilty.

1974
President Richard Nixon resigns because of the Watergate scandal.

1979
U.S. hostages are taken in Iran, beginning a 444-day crisis that ends with their release in 1981.

1981
Sandra Day O'Connor becomes the first woman on the U.S. Supreme Court.

1992
Bill Clinton, a Democrat, is elected president, defeating George Bush.

1994
The Republican Party wins majorities in both houses of Congress for the first time in 40 years.

2000
The U.S. government returns 84,000 acres of land in northern Idaho to the Ute Indian tribe.

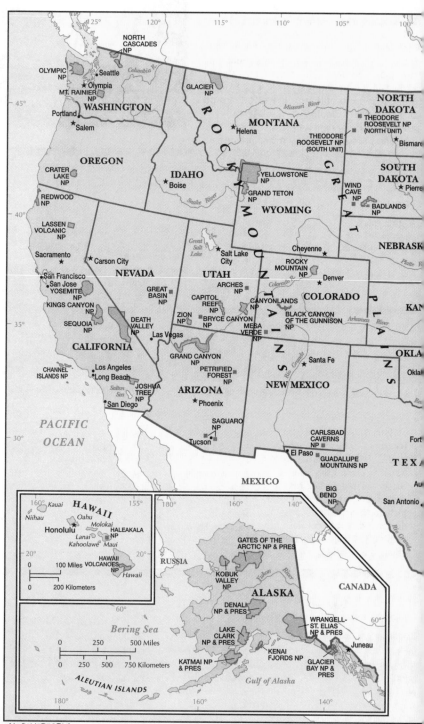

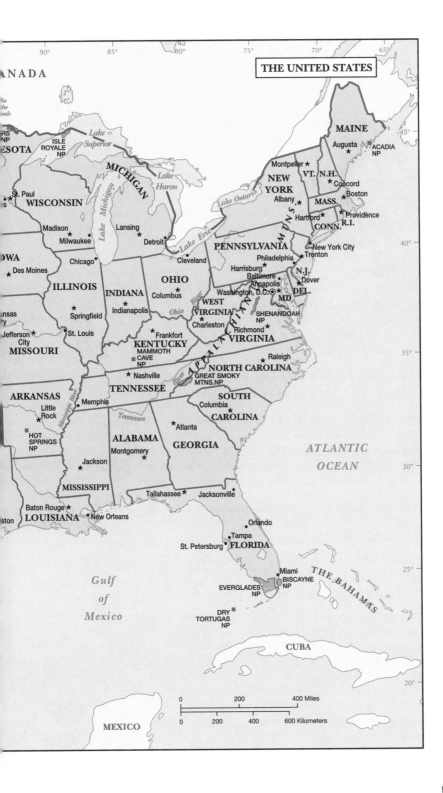

THE UNITED STATES

90° 85° 80° 75° 70° 65°

CANADA

MAINE
Augusta ★ ACADIA NP

MINNESOTA
ISLE ROYALE NP
Lake Superior

St. Paul

MICHIGAN
Lake Huron
Lake Michigan

WISCONSIN

Montpelier ★
NEW YORK
VT. N.H.
Concord

Albany ★
MASS.
Boston

Madison
Lansing

Hartford ★
CONN. R.I.
Providence ★

Milwaukee
Detroit
Lake Erie

IOWA
Chicago
Cleveland

PENNSYLVANIA
New York City
Trenton

Des Moines

ILLINOIS
INDIANA
OHIO
Columbus

Harrisburg ★
Philadelphia
N.J.
Dover

Baltimore
Annapolis
DEL.

Springfield
Indianapolis

Washington, D.C.
WEST VIRGINIA
MD

Kansas City

St. Louis
Ohio River

Charleston ★
SHENANDOAH NP

Jefferson City

Frankfort
KENTUCKY
MAMMOTH CAVE NP

Richmond ★
VIRGINIA

MISSOURI

Raleigh ★

Nashville ★
NORTH CAROLINA

ARKANSAS
TENNESSEE
GREAT SMOKY MTNS.NP

Little Rock ★
Memphis
Tennessee River

Columbia ★
SOUTH CAROLINA

HOT SPRINGS NP

ALABAMA
Atlanta ★

Jackson ★
Montgomery ★
GEORGIA

ATLANTIC OCEAN

MISSISSIPPI

Baton Rouge ★
Tallahassee ★
Jacksonville

LOUISIANA
New Orleans

Orlando

Tampa
St. Petersburg
FLORIDA

Miami
BISCAYNE NP

Gulf
of
Mexico

EVERGLADES NP

THE BAHAMAS

DRY TORTUGAS NP

CUBA

MEXICO

APPALACHIAN MTNS.

Mississippi River

45°
40°
35°
30°
25°
20°

0   200   400 Miles
0   200   400   600 Kilometers

FRED FABULOUS and the FAB FLYER

Fred Fabulous, the almost-famous inventor, has just built Fred's Fabulous Flying Machine, known as the Fab Flyer. Use the map on pages 268-269 to help you fill in the blanks in the journal Fred kept as he flew around the U.S.

1 The Fab Flyer and I started our trip in the capital of Texas, which is _____. We buzzed west to the longest state on the coast of the _____ Ocean. That state is _____.

2 Next we zipped across the ocean to the island state. Crowds cheered as we landed on its biggest island, _____.

3 Then it was back in the air zooming east across the ocean to the state north of Oregon, which is _____. We were way ahead of schedule so we flew to all three national parks in that state. They are _____, _____, and _____.

NATIONAL PARK

4 Then we headed three states east to North _____. Crowds cheered as we made a perfect landing in its capital, _____.

5 I was hungry, but it was time to take off for the capital of Iowa. That city is _____. TV cameras greeted us at the airport. The Fab Flyer and I did a few tricks in the air just to show off. I ate three sandwiches—no baloney—after I landed.

6 I was so full, I wasn't sure we would even get off the ground. But my Fab Flyer didn't let me down. We had another great take-off and headed three states east to _____.

7 I checked the time on my Wonder Winder Watch. (I invented that, too.) Last chance to show off the Fab Flyer before heading home! We headed two states south, where I waved to the wonderful folks in Nashville. That's the capital of _____.

8 It was getting dark so I pressed the zoom button. About five minutes later we landed back at our starting place in _____, the capital of Texas. What a fabulous trip!

9 Like all excellent flyers, I will be back in the air again tomorrow. Maybe the Fab Flyer and I will visit the states on the east coast along the _____ Ocean. Zooming here, zooming there! Zooming, zooming everywhere!

Answers are on pages 317-320.

FACTS About the STATES

After every state name is the postal abbreviation for the state. The Area includes both land and water. It is given in square miles (sq. mi.) and square kilometers (sq. km.). Numbers in parentheses after Population, Area, and Entered Union show the state's rank compared with other states. For example, Alabama is the 23rd largest state in population.

ALABAMA (AL)

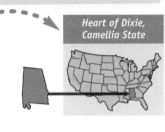

Heart of Dixie, Camellia State

Population (1999): 4,369,862 (23rd)
Area: 52,237 sq. mi. (30th) (135,294 sq. km.)
Entered Union: December 14, 1819 (22nd)
Flower: Camellia   **Bird:** Yellowhammer
Tree: Southern longleaf pine   **Song:** "Alabama"
Capital: Montgomery
Largest Cities (with population): Birmingham, 252,997;
Mobile, 202,181; Montgomery, 197,014; Huntsville, 175,979
Important Products: clothing and textiles, metal products, transportation equipment, paper, industrial machinery, food products, lumber, coal, oil, natural gas, livestock, peanuts, cotton
Places to Visit: Alabama Space and Rocket Center, Huntsville; Carver Museum, Tuskegee

WEB SITE *http://alaweb.asc.edu • http://www.touralabama.org*

DID YOU KNOW? *Montgomery, Alabama, was the first capital of the Confederate States of America (1861). Alabama is a major center for rocket and space research.*

ALASKA (AK)

The Last Frontier

Population (1999): 619,500 (48th)
Area: 615,230 sq. mi. (1st) (1,593,444 sq. km.)
Entered Union: January 3, 1959 (49th)
Flower: Forget-me-not   **Bird:** Willow ptarmigan
Tree: Sitka spruce   **Song:** "Alaska's Flag"
Capital: Juneau (population, 30,191)
Largest Cities (with population): Anchorage, 254,982; Fairbanks, 33,295
Important Products: oil, natural gas, fish, food products, lumber and wood products, fur
Places to Visit: Glacier Bay and Denali national parks, Mendenhall Glacier, Mount McKinley

WEB SITE *http://www.state.ak.us • http://www.commerce.state.ak.us/tourism*

DID YOU KNOW? *Mount McKinley is the highest mountain in the United States. Alaska has more than 5,000 glaciers covering 100,000 square miles.*

ARIZONA (AZ)

Grand Canyon State

Population (1999): 4,778,332 (20th)
Area: 114,006 sq. mi. (6th) (295,276 sq. km.)
Entered Union: February 14, 1912 (48th)
Flower: Blossom of the Saguaro cactus   **Bird:** Cactus wren
Tree: Paloverde   **Song:** "Arizona"
Capital and Largest City: Phoenix (population, 1,198,064)
Other Large Cities (with population): Tucson, 460,466; Mesa, 360,076; Glendale, 193,482;
Scottsdale, 195,394; Tempe, 167,622
Important Products: electronic equipment, transportation and industrial equipment, instruments, printing and publishing, copper and other metals
Places to Visit: Grand Canyon, Painted Desert, Petrified Forest, Navajo National Monument

WEB SITE *http://www.state.az.us • http://www.arizonaguide.com*

DID YOU KNOW? *The Grand Canyon is the largest land gorge in the world and one of the world's natural wonders. It is 277 miles long and 6,000 feet deep at its deepest point.*

ARKANSAS (AR)

Population (1999): 2,551,373 (33rd)
Area: 53,182 sq. mi. (28th) (137,741 sq. km.)
Flower: Apple blossom   **Bird:** Mockingbird
Tree: Pine   **Song:** "Arkansas"
Entered Union: June 15, 1836 (25th)
Capital and Largest City: Little Rock (population, 175,303)
Other Large Cities (with population): North Little Rock, 59,184; Pine Bluff, 52,968
Important Products: food products, paper, electronic equipment, industrial machinery, metal products, lumber and wood products, livestock, soybeans, rice, cotton, natural gas
      Places to Visit: Hot Springs National Park; Ozark Folk Center, near Mountain View

WEB SITE *http://www.state.ar.us • http://www.arkansas.com*

DID YOU KNOW? *Arkansas has the only working diamond mine in North America. President Bill Clinton was born in Arkansas and served as one of its governors.*

CALIFORNIA (CA)

Population (1999): 33,145,121 (1st)
Area: 158,869 sq. mi. (3rd) (411,471 sq. km.)
Flower: Golden poppy   **Bird:** California valley quail
Tree: California redwood   **Song:** "I Love You, California"
Entered Union: September 9, 1850 (31st)
Capital: Sacramento (population, 404,168)
Largest Cities (with population): Los Angeles, 3,597,556; San Diego, 1,220,666; San Jose, 861,284; San Francisco, 745,774
Important Products: transportation and industrial equipment, electronic equipment, oil, natural gas, motion pictures, milk, cattle, fruit, vegetables
Places to Visit: Yosemite Valley, Lake Tahoe, Palomar Observatory, Disneyland, San Diego Zoo, Hollywood, Sequoia National Park

WEB SITE *http://www.state.ca.us • http://www.gocalif.ca.gov*

DID YOU KNOW? *California has more people, more cars, more schools, and more businesses than any other state in the United States. The oldest living things on earth are believed to be the bristlecone pine trees in California's Inyo National Forest, estimated to be 4,700 years old. The world's tallest tree, 365 feet tall and 44 feet around, is a redwood tree in Redwoods State Park.*

COLORADO (CO)

Population (1999): 4,056,133 (24th)
Area: 104,100 sq. mi. (8th) (269,619 sq. km.)
Flower: Rocky Mountain columbine   **Bird:** Lark bunting
Tree: Colorado blue spruce   **Song:** "Where the Columbines Grow"
Entered Union: August 1, 1876 (38th)
Capital and Largest City: Denver (population, 491,055)
Other Large Cities (with population): Colorado Springs, 344,887; Aurora, 250,604; Lakewood, 136,883
Important Products: instruments and industrial machinery, food products, printing and publishing, metal products, electronic equipment, oil, coal, cattle
Places to Visit: Rocky Mountain National Park, Mesa Verde National Park, Dinosaur National Monument, old mining towns

WEB SITE *http://www.state.co.us • http://www.colorado.com*

DID YOU KNOW? *The Grand Mesa in Colorado is the world's largest flat-top mountain. The world's highest bridge (1,053 feet) is in Colorado—it's the suspension bridge over the Royal Gorge of the Arkansas River. Colorado has more mountains over 14,000 feet and more elk than any other state.*

CONNECTICUT (CT)

Constitution State, Nutmeg State

Population (1999): 3,282,031 (29th)
Area: 5,544 sq. mi. (48th) (14,359 sq. km.)
Flower: Mountain laurel   **Bird:** American robin
Tree: White oak   **Song:** "Yankee Doodle"
Entered Union: January 9, 1788 (5th)
Capital: Hartford
Largest Cities (with population): Bridgeport, 137,425; Hartford, 131,523; New Haven, 123,189; Waterbury, 105,346; Stamford, 110,689
Important Products: aircraft parts, helicopters, industrial machinery, metals and metal products, electronic equipment, printing and publishing, medical instruments, chemicals, dairy products, stone
Places to Visit: Mystic Seaport and Marine Life Aquarium, in Mystic; P. T. Barnum Circus Museum, Bridgeport; Peabody Museum, New Haven

WEB SITE *http://www.state.ct.us • http://www.state.ct.us/tourism*

DID YOU KNOW? *The first library for children opened in Salisbury, in 1803, and the first permanent school for the deaf opened in Hartford in 1817. The first woman to receive an American patent was Mary Kies of South Killingly, in 1809, for a machine to weave straw and silk or thread.*

DELAWARE (DE)

First State, Diamond State

Population (1999): 753,538 (45th)
Area: 2,396 sq. mi. (49th) (6,206 sq. km.)
Flower: Peach blossom   **Bird:** Blue hen chicken
Tree: American holly   **Song:** "Our Delaware"
Entered Union: December 7, 1787 (1st)
Capital: Dover
Largest Cities (with population): Wilmington, 71,529; Dover, 30,369; Newark, 28,000
Important Products: chemicals, transportation equipment, food products, chickens
Places to Visit: Rehoboth Beach, Henry Francis du Pont Winterthur Museum near Wilmington

WEB SITE *http://www.state.de.us • http://www.state.de.us/tourism/intro.htm*

DID YOU KNOW? *Delaware was the first state to agree to the Constitution and thus became the first state of the United States. Delaware also had the first log cabins in America.*

FLORIDA (FL)

Sunshine State

Population (1999): 15,111,244 (4th)
Area: 59,928 sq. mi. (23rd) (155,213 sq. km.)
Flower: Orange blossom   **Bird:** Mockingbird
Tree: Sabal palmetto palm   **Song:** "Old Folks at Home"
Entered Union: March 3, 1845 (27th)
Capital: Tallahassee (population, 136,628)
Largest Cities (with population): Jacksonville, 693,630; Miami, 368,624; Tampa, 289,156; Saint Petersburg, 236,029
Important Products: electronic and transportation equipment, industrial machinery, printing and publishing, food products, citrus fruits, vegetables, livestock, phosphates, fish
Places to Visit: Walt Disney World and Universal Studios, near Orlando; Sea World, Orlando; Busch Gardens, Tampa; Spaceport USA, at Kennedy Space Center, Cape Canaveral; Everglades National Park

WEB SITE *http://www.state.fl.us • http://www.flausa.com*

DID YOU KNOW? *St. Augustine, Florida, is the oldest permanent European settlement in the United States. From any point in Florida, a beach is no more than 60 miles away. Orange juice is the official state beverage.*

GEORGIA (GA)

Empire State of the South, Peach State

Population (1999): 7,788,240 (10th)
Area: 58,977 sq. mi. (24th) (152,750 sq. km.)
Flower: Cherokee rose   **Bird:** Brown thrasher
Tree: Live oak   **Song:** "Georgia on My Mind"
Entered Union: January 2, 1788 (4th)
Capital and Largest City: Atlanta (population, 403,219)
Other Large Cities (with population): Columbus, 182,219; Savannah, 131,674; Macon, 114,336
Important Products: clothing and textiles, transportation equipment, food products, paper, chickens, peanuts, peaches, clay
Places to Visit: Stone Mountain Park; Six Flags Over Georgia; Martin Luther King, Jr., Natl. Historic Site, Atlanta

WEB SITE *http://www.state.ga.us • http://www.georgia.org*

DID YOU KNOW? *The first U.S. gold rush took place in Georgia. The first American Indian newspaper was published in Georgia by a Cherokee in 1828. The first radio station owned and operated by African Americans started in Atlanta in 1949. Civil rights leader Martin Luther King, Jr. (1929-1968) and baseball player Jackie Robinson (1919-1972) were born in Georgia.*

HAWAII (HI)

Aloha State

Population (1999): 1,185,497 (42nd)
Area: 6,459 sq. mi. (47th) (16,728 sq. km.)
Flower: Yellow hibiscus   **Bird:** Hawaiian goose
Tree: Kukui   **Song:** "Hawaii Ponoi"
Entered Union: August 21, 1959 (50th)
Capital and Largest City: Honolulu (population, 395,789)
Other Large Cities (with population): Hilo, 37,808; Kailua, 36,818; Kaneohe, 35,448
Important Products: food products, pineapples, sugar, printing and publishing, fish, flowers
Places to Visit: Hawaii Volcanoes National Park; Haleakala National Park, Maui; U.S.S. *Arizona* Memorial, Pearl Harbor; Polynesian Cultural Center, Laie

WEB SITE *http://www.state.hi.us • http://www.gohawaii.com*

DID YOU KNOW? *Hawaii is the only state made up entirely of islands. (People live on seven of the islands.) Hawaii's Mauna Loa is the biggest volcano in the world. It has not erupted since 1984.*

IDAHO (ID)

Gem State

Population (1999): 1,251,700 (40th)
Area: 83,574 sq. mi. (14th) (216,456 sq. km.)
Flower: Syringa   **Bird:** Mountain bluebird
Tree: White pine   **Song:** "Here We Have Idaho"
Entered Union: July 3, 1890 (43rd)
Capital and Largest City: Boise (population, 157,452)
Other Large Cities (with population): Pocatello, 53,074; Idaho Falls, 48,122
Important Products: potatoes, hay, wheat, cattle, milk, lumber and wood products, food products
Places to Visit: Sun Valley; Hells Canyon; Craters of the Moon, near Arco; World Center for Birds of Prey, Boise; ghost towns

WEB SITE *http://www2.state.id.us • http://www.visitid.com*

DID YOU KNOW? *The first hydroelectric power plant built by the federal government was the Minidoka Dam on the Snake River in Idaho; the first unit started in 1909. Idaho grows more potatoes than any other U.S. growing region — 14 billion pounds a year.*

ILLINOIS (IL)

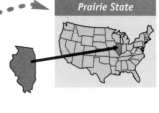

Prairie State

Population (1999): 12,128,370 (5th)
Area: 57,918 sq. mi. (25th) (150,007 sq. km.)
Flower: Native violet   **Bird:** Cardinal
Tree: White oak   **Song:** "Illinois"
Entered Union: December 3, 1818 (21st)
Capital: Springfield
Largest Cities (with population): Chicago, 2,802,079;
Rockford, 143,656; Peoria, 111,148; Aurora, 124,736; Springfield, 117,098
Important Products: industrial machinery, metals and metal products, printing and publishing,
electronic equipment, food products, corn, soybeans, hogs
Places to Visit: Lincoln Park Zoo, Adler Planetarium, Field Museum of Natural History, and Museum
of Science and Industry, all in Chicago; Abraham Lincoln's home and burial site, Springfield;
New Salem Village

WEB SITE *http://www.state.il.us • http://www.enjoyillinois.com*

DID YOU KNOW? *Illinois has one of the world's busiest airports (O'Hare) and the tallest
building in the U.S. (the Sears Tower in Chicago). The world's first skyscraper was built in Chicago, in
1885. Abraham Lincoln lived and worked in Illinois and is buried there.*

INDIANA (IN)

Hoosier State

Population (1999): 5,942,901 (14th)
Area: 36,420 sq. mi. (38th) (94,328 sq. km.)
Flower: Peony   **Bird:** Cardinal
Tree: Tulip poplar   **Song:** "On the Banks of the Wabash,
                        Far Away"
Entered Union: December 11, 1816 (19th)
Capital and Largest City: Indianapolis (population, 741,304)
Other Large Cities (with population): Fort Wayne, 185,716; Evansville, 122,779; Gary, 108,469;
South Bend, 99,417
Important Products: transportation equipment, electronic equipment, industrial machinery, iron and
steel, metal products, corn, soybeans, livestock, coal
Places to Visit: Children's Museum, Indianapolis; Conner Prairie Pioneer Settlement, Noblesville;
Lincoln Boyhood Memorial, Lincoln City; Wyandotte Cave

WEB SITE *http://www.state.in.us/.tourism • http://www.ai.org*

DID YOU KNOW? *The first city to be lit with electricity was Wabash. Indiana's Lost River travels
22 miles underground. Indiana is home of the famous Indianapolis 500 auto race.*

IOWA (IA)

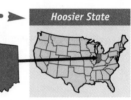

Hawkeye State

Population (1999): 2,869,413 (30th)
Area: 56,276 sq. mi. (26th) (145,754 sq. km.)
Flower: Wild rose   **Bird:** Eastern goldfinch
Tree: Oak   **Song:** "The Song of Iowa"
Entered Union: December 28, 1846 (29th)
Capital and Largest City: Des Moines (population, 191,293)
Other Large Cities (with population): Cedar Rapids, 114,653; Davenport, 96,852; Sioux City, 82,697
Important Products: corn, soybeans, hogs, cattle, industrial machinery, food products
Places to Visit: Effigy Mounds National Monument, Marquette; Herbert Hoover Birthplace, West
Branch; Living History Farms, Des Moines; Adventureland; the Amana Colonies; Fort Dodge
Historical Museum

WEB SITE *http://www.state.ia.us • http://www.state.ia.us/tourism/index.html*

DID YOU KNOW? *The bridge built in 1856 between Davenport, Iowa, and Rock Island, Illinois,
was the first bridge to span the Mississippi River. Buffalo Bill Cody (1846-1917), a frontiersman and
head of a famous Wild West show, was born in Iowa.*

KANSAS (KS) · · · · · · · · · · · · · · · · ·

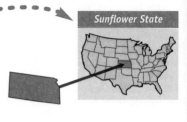

Sunflower State

Population (1999): 2,654,052 (32nd)
Area: 82,282 sq. mi. (15th) (213,110 sq. km.)
Flower: Native sunflower   **Bird:** Western meadowlark
Tree: Cottonwood   **Song:** "Home on the Range"
Entered Union: January 29, 1861 (34th)
Capital: Topeka
Largest Cities (with population): Wichita, 329,211;
Kansas City, 147,297; Overland Park, 139,685; Topeka, 118,977
Important Products: cattle, aircraft and other transportation equipment, industrial machinery, food products, wheat, corn, hay, oil, natural gas
Places to Visit: Dodge City; Fort Scott and Fort Larned national historical sites; Eisenhower Center, Abilene; Kansas Cosmosphere and Space Discovery Center, Hutchinson

WEB SITE *http://www.ink.org • http://www.kansas.commerce.com*

DiD YoU KNOW? *Kansas is at the geographical center of the United States (excluding Alaska and Hawaii). The first newspaper in Kansas was written in the Shawnee Indian language.*

KENTUCKY (KY) · · · · · · · · · · · · · · · · ·

Bluegrass State

Population (1999): 3,960,825 (25th)
Area: 40,411 sq. mi. (37th) (104,665 sq. km.)
Flower: Goldenrod   **Bird:** Cardinal
Tree: Tulip poplar   **Song:** "My Old Kentucky Home"
Entered Union: June 1, 1792 (15th)
Capital: Frankfort (population, 26,418)
Largest Cities (with population): Louisville, 225,045; Lexington 241,749
Important Products: coal, industrial machinery, electronic equipment, transportation equipment, metals, tobacco, cattle
Places to Visit: Mammoth Cave National Park; Lincoln's Birthplace, Hodgenville; Cumberland Gap National Historical Park, Middlesboro

WEB SITE *http://www.state.ky.us • http://www.kentuckytourism.com*

DiD YoU KNOW? *Kentucky has the longest group of caves in the world (Mammoth Caves). Abraham Lincoln was born in Kentucky. Kentucky is home of the Kentucky Derby, the most famous horse race in America.*

LOUISIANA (LA) · · · · · · · · · · · · · · · · ·

Pelican State

Population (1999): 4,372,035 (22nd)
Area: 49,651 sq. mi. (31st) (128,596 sq. km.)
Flower: Magnolia   **Bird:** Eastern brown pelican
Tree: Cypress   **Song:** "Give Me Louisiana"
Entered Union: April 30, 1812 (18th)
Capital: Baton Rouge
Largest Cities (with population): New Orleans, 465,538;
Baton Rouge, 211,551; Shreveport, 188,319
Important Products: natural gas, oil, chemicals, transportation equipment, paper, food products, cotton, fish
Places to Visit: Aquarium of the Americas, Audubon Zoo and Gardens, both New Orleans

WEB SITE *http://www.state.la.us • http://www.louisianatravel.com*

DiD YoU KNOW? *The busiest port in the United States is located in the state. Louisiana is the second-biggest mining state (after Alaska). The state's biggest city is New Orleans, known for its jazz and the colorful Mardi Gras festival.*

MAINE (ME)

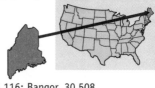

Pine Tree State

Population (1999): 1,253,040 (39th)
Area: 33,741 sq. mi. (39th) (87,389 sq. km.)
Flower: White pine cone and tassel   **Bird:** Chickadee
Tree: Eastern white pine   **Song:** "State of Maine
Entered Union: March 15, 1820 (23rd)   Song"
Capital: Augusta (population, 19,978)
Largest Cities (with population): Portland, 62,786; Lewiston, 36,116; Bangor, 30,508
Important Products: paper, transportation equipment, wood and wood products, electronic equipment, footwear, clothing, potatoes, milk, eggs, fish, and seafood
Places to Visit: Acadia National Park, Bar Harbor; Booth Bay Railway Museum; Portland Headlight Lighthouse, near Portland

WEB SITE   *http://www.state.me.us • http://www.visitmaine.com*

DID YOU KNOW? *Over 90 percent of the nation's lobsters are caught off the coast of Maine. Mount Katahdin, the highest spot in Maine (5,267 feet), is the first place in the United States that the sun hits in the morning.*

MARYLAND (MD)

Old Line State, Free State

Population (1999): 5,171,634 (19th)
Area: 12,297 sq. mi. (42nd) (31,849 sq. km.)
Flower: Black-eyed susan   **Bird:** Baltimore oriole
Tree: White oak   **Song:** "Maryland, My Maryland"
Entered Union: April 28, 1788 (7th)
Capital: Annapolis (population, 33,585)
Largest Cities (with population): Baltimore, 645,593; Frederick, 47,468; Rockville, 46,788; Gaithersburg, 46,980
Important Products: printing and publishing, food products, transportation equipment, electronic equipment, chickens, soybeans, corn, stone
Places to Visit: Antietam National Battlefield; Fort McHenry National Monument, in Baltimore Harbor; U.S. Naval Academy in Annapolis

WEB SITE   *http://www.state.md.us • http://www.mdisfun.org*

DID YOU KNOW? *The American flag on Fort McHenry during the War of 1812 inspired Francis Scott Key to write "The Star-Spangled Banner," the national anthem. In 1791, Maryland donated land for the new U.S. capital, Washington, D.C.*

MASSACHUSETTS (MA)

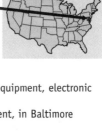

Bay State, Old Colony

Population (1999): 6,175,169 (13th)
Area: 9,241 sq. mi. (45th) (23,934 sq. km.)
Flower: Mayflower   **Bird:** Chickadee
Tree: American elm   **Song:** "All Hail to Massachusetts"
Entered Union: February 6, 1788 (6th)
Capital and Largest City: Boston (population: 555,447)
Other Large Cities (with population): Worcester, 166,535; Springfield, 148,144; Lowell, 101,075
Important Products: industrial machinery, electronic equipment, instruments, printing and publishing, metal products, fish, flowers and shrubs, cranberries
Places to Visit: Plymouth Rock; Minute Man National Historical Park; Children's Museum, Boston; Basketball Hall of Fame, Springfield; Old Sturbridge Village; Martha's Vineyard; Cape Cod; historical sites in Boston

WEB SITE   *http://www.state.ma.us • http://www.mass-vacation.com*

DID YOU KNOW? *The Pilgrims settled in Massachusetts and celebrated the first Thanksgiving there. Massachusetts had America's first printing press (1639) and first college (Harvard, 1636). The American Revolution began in Massachusetts.*

MICHIGAN (MI)

Great Lakes State, Wolverine State

Population (1999): 9,863,775 (8th)
Area: 96,705 sq. mi. (11th) (250,465 sq. km.)
Flower: Apple blossom   Bird: Robin
Tree: White pine   Song: "Michigan, My Michigan"
Entered Union: January 26, 1837 (26th)
Capital: Lansing (population, 127,825)
Largest Cities (with population): Detroit, 970,196;
Grand Rapids, 185,437; Warren, 142,455; Flint, 131,668
Important Products: automobiles, industrial machinery, metal products, office furniture, plastic products, chemicals, food products, milk, corn, natural gas, iron ore, blueberries
Places to Visit: Greenfield Village and Henry Ford Museum, Dearborn; Mackinac Island; Kalamazoo Aviation History Museum; Motown Historical Museum, Detroit

WEB SITE *http://www.migov.state.mi.us • http://www.michigan.org*

DID YOU KNOW? *Michigan is known for manufacturing automobiles. Lake Michigan is the largest lake entirely in the United States.*

MINNESOTA (MN)

North Star State, Gopher State

Population (1999): 4,775,508 (21st)
Area: 86,943 sq. mi. (12th) (225,182 sq. km.)
Flower: Pink and white lady's-slipper   Bird: Common loon
Tree: Red pine   Song: "Hail! Minnesota"
Entered Union: May 11, 1858 (32nd)
Capital: St. Paul
Largest Cities (with population): Minneapolis, 351,731;
St. Paul, 257,284
Important Products: industrial machinery, printing and publishing, computers, food products, scientific and medical instruments, milk, hogs, cattle, corn, soybeans, iron ore
Places to Visit: Voyageurs National Park; Minnesota State Fair, Fort Snelling; U.S. Hockey Hall of Fame, Eveleth; Walker Art Center, Minneapolis

WEB SITE *http://www.state.mn.us • http://www.exploreminnesota.com*

DID YOU KNOW? *Minnesota is sometimes called the Land of 10,000 Lakes—it has more than 15,000 lakes. Minnesota is the second coldest state (Alaska is the coldest). The Mall of America, in Bloomington, is the largest shopping mall in the U.S. Snowmobiles were invented in Minnesota.*

MISSISSIPPI (MS)

Magnolia State

Population (1999): 2,768,619 (31st)
Area: 48,286 sq. mi. (32nd) (125,061 sq. km.)
Flower: Magnolia   Bird: Mockingbird
Tree: Magnolia   Song: "Go, Mississippi!"
Entered Union: December 10, 1817 (20th)
Capital and Largest City: Jackson (population, 188,319)
Other Large Cities (with population): Biloxi, 47,316; Greenville, 42,042
Important Products: transportation equipment, furniture, electrical machinery, lumber and wood products, cotton, rice, chickens, cattle
Places to Visit: Vicksburg National Military Park; Natchez Trace Parkway; Old Capitol, Jackson; Old Spanish Fort and Museum, Pascagoula

WEB SITE *http://www.state.ms.us • http://www.mississippi.org*

DID YOU KNOW? *Mississippi was the first state to celebrate Memorial Day (originally called Decoration Day) as a holiday, in 1866. Mississippi opened the first state-run college for women in Columbus in 1884. Jefferson Davis, president of the Confederate States of America, was born in Mississippi.*

MISSOURI (MO) · · · · · · · · · · · · · · ·

Show Me State

Population (1999): 5,468,338 (17th)
Area: 69,709 sq. mi. (21st) (180,546 sq. km.)
Flower: Hawthorn   **Bird:** Bluebird
Tree: Dogwood   **Song:** "Missouri Waltz"
Entered Union: August 10, 1821 (24th)
Capital: Jefferson City (population, 34,911)
Largest Cities (with population): Kansas City, 441,574; St. Louis, 339,316; Springfield, 142,898; Independence, 116,832
Important Products: transportation equipment, electrical and electronic equipment, printing and publishing, food products, cattle, hogs, milk, soybeans, corn, hay, lead
Places to Visit: Gateway Arch, St. Louis; Mark Twain Area, Hannibal; Harry S. Truman Museum, Independence; George Washington Carver Birthplace, Diamond; Pony Express Museum, St. Joseph

WEB SITE   *http://www.ecodev.state.mo.us • http://www.missouritourism.org*

DID YOU KNOW? *Missouri is a major center for shipping and railroads. President Harry S. Truman, agricultural scientist George Washington Carver, and poet Langston Hughes were born in Missouri. It has been said that the ice cream cone was first sold at a World's Fair in St. Louis, in 1904. The stainless steel Gateway Arch (630 feet high) is the internationally known symbol of St. Louis.*

MONTANA (MT) · · · · · · · · · ·

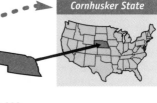

Treasure State

Population (1999): 882,779 (44th)
Area: 147,046 sq. mi. (4th) (380,850 sq. km.)
Flower: Bitterroot   **Bird:** Western meadowlark
Tree: Ponderosa pine   **Song:** "Montana"
Entered Union: November 8, 1889 (41st)
Capital: Helena (population, 27,982)
Largest Cities (with population): Billings, 91,750; Great Falls, 56,395; Missoula, 52,239; Butte, 33,994
Important Products: cattle, copper, gold, wheat, barley, wood and paper products
Places to Visit: Yellowstone and Glacier national parks; Little Bighorn Battlefield National Monument; Museum of the Rockies (in Bozeman); Museum of the Plains Indian, Blackfeet Reservation (near Browning)

WEB SITE   *http://www.mt.gov • http://www.state.mt.us*

DID YOU KNOW? *Montana is the fourth-biggest state, after Alaska, Texas, and California. The most famous Indian battle in history took place in Montana, at Little Bighorn in 1876.*

NEBRASKA (NE) · · · · · · · · · · · ·

Cornhusker State

Population (1999): 1,666,028 (38th)
Area: 77,358 sq. mi. (16th) (200,358 sq. km.)
Flower: Goldenrod   **Bird:** Western meadowlark
Tree: Cottonwood   **Song:** "Beautiful Nebraska"
Entered Union: March 1, 1867 (37th)
Capital: Lincoln
Largest Cities (with population): Omaha, 371,291; Lincoln, 213,088
Important Products: cattle, hogs, milk, corn, soybeans, hay, wheat, sorghum, food products, industrial machinery
Places to Visit: Oregon Trail landmarks; Stuhr Museum of the Prairie Pioneer, Grand Island; Agate Fossil Beds National Monument; Boys Town, near Omaha

WEB SITE   *http://www.state.ne.us • http://www.visitnebraska.org*

DID YOU KNOW? *Nebraska is the only state whose nickname comes from a college football team—the popular University of Nebraska Cornhuskers.*

NEVADA (NV)

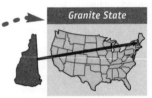

Population (1999): 1,809,253 (35th)
Area: 110,567 sq. mi. (7th) (286,368 sq. km.)
Flower: Sagebrush
Trees: Single-leaf piñon, bristlecone pine
Bird: Mountain bluebird
Song: "Home Means Nevada"
Entered Union: October 31, 1864 (36th)
Capital: Carson City (population, 49,301)
Largest Cities (with population): Las Vegas, 404,288; Reno, 163,334; Henderson, 152,717
Important Products: gold, silver, cattle, hay, food products, plastics, chemicals
Places to Visit: Great Basin National Park, including Lehman Caves; Nevada State Museum, Carson City; Hoover Dam, Lake Tahoe, Pony Express Territory.

WEB SITE *http://www.state.nv.us* • *http://www.travelnevada.com*

DiD You KNOW? *It usually rains less in Nevada than in any other state. Between 1980 and 1990 the population of Nevada increased by more than one half, making it the fastest-growing state. It also has the most wild horses.*

NEW HAMPSHIRE (NH)

Granite State

Population (1999): 1,201,134 (41st)
Area: 9,283 sq. mi. (44th) (24,043 sq. km.)
Flower: Purple lilac
Tree: White birch
Bird: Purple finch
Song: "Old New Hampshire"
Entered Union: June 21, 1788 (9th)
Capital: Concord
Largest Cities (with population): Manchester, 102,524; Nashua, 82,169; Concord, 37,444
Important Products: industrial machinery, electric and electronic equipment, metal products, plastic products, dairy products, maple syrup and maple sugar
Places to Visit: White Mountain National Forest; Mount Washington; Old Man in the Mountain, Franconia Notch; Canterbury Shaker Village; Flume gorge and aerial tramway

WEB SITE *http://www.state.nh.us* • *http://www.visitnh.gov*

DiD You KNOW? *Mount Washington is the highest mountain in the northeast. Its peak is said to be the windiest spot on Earth. The first town-supported, free public library in the United States opened in New Hampshire, in 1833. New Hampshire has the first-in-the-nation presidential primary every four years.*

NEW JERSEY (NJ)

Garden State

Population (1999): 8,143,412 (9th)
Area: 8,215 sq. mi. (46th) (21,277 sq. km.)
Flower: Purple violet
Tree: Red oak
Bird: Eastern goldfinch
Song: none
Entered Union: December 18, 1787 (3rd)
Capital: Trenton (population, 84,494)
Largest Cities (with population): Newark, 267,823; Jersey City, 232,429; Paterson, 148,212; Elizabeth, 110,661
Important Products: chemicals, pharmaceuticals/drugs, electronic equipment, nursery and greenhouse products, food products, tomatoes, blueberries and peaches
Places to Visit: ocean beaches; Edison National Historical Site, West Orange; Liberty State Park; Pine Barrens wilderness area; Revolutionary War sites

WEB SITE *http://www.state.nj.us* • *http://www.state.nj.us/travel*

DiD You KNOW? *The electric light bulb was invented in New Jersey by Thomas Edison in 1879. The first ferryboat just for cars was built in New Jersey and placed in service in 1926. New Jersey manufactures more flags than any other state.*

NEW MEXICO (NM)

Land of Enchantment

Population (1999): 1,739,844 (37th)
Area: 121,598 sq. mi. (5th) (314,939 sq. km.)
Flower: Yucca   **Bird:** Roadrunner
Tree: Piñon   **Song:** "O, Fair New Mexico"
Entered Union: January 6, 1912 (47th)
Capital: Santa Fe
Largest Cities (with population): Albuquerque, 419,311; Las Cruces, 76,102; Santa Fe, 67,879
Important Products: electronic equipment, foods, machinery, clothing, lumber, transportation equipment, hay, onions, chiles
Places to Visit: Carlsbad Caverns National Park; Palace of the Governors and Mission of San Miguel, Santa Fe; Chaco Culture Natl. Historical Park; cliff dwellings

WEB SITE *http://www.state.nm.us • http://www.newmexico.org*

DID YOU KNOW? *The oldest capital city in the United States is Santa Fe, New Mexico. Pueblo Indians had an advanced civilization in New Mexico a thousand years ago. The largest natural underground chamber in the world is in New Mexico's Carlsbad Caverns. The first atom bomb was exploded in New Mexico, in a test on July 16, 1945.*

NEW YORK (NY)

Empire State

Population (1999): 18,196,601 (3rd)
Area: 53,989 sq. mi. (27th) (139,831 sq. km.)
Flower: Rose   **Bird:** Bluebird
Tree: Sugar maple   **Song:** "I Love New York"
Entered Union: July 26, 1788 (11th)
Capital: Albany (population, 94,305)
Largest Cities (with population): New York, 7,420,166; Buffalo, 300,717; Rochester, 216,887; Yonkers, 190,153
Important Products: books and magazines, automobile and aircraft parts, toys and sporting goods, electronic equipment, machinery, clothing and textiles, metal products, milk, cattle, hay, apples
Places to Visit: In New York City, museums, Empire State Building, United Nations, Bronx Zoo, Statue of Liberty and Ellis Island; Niagara Falls; National Baseball Hall of Fame, Cooperstown; Fort Ticonderoga; Franklin D. Roosevelt National Historical Site, Hyde Park

WEB SITE *http://www.state.ny.us • http://www.iloveny.state.ny.us*

DID YOU KNOW? *New York City is the largest city (in population) in the United States and was the nation's first capital. The first pizza restaurant in the United States opened in New York City in 1895.*

NORTH CAROLINA (NC)

Tar Heel State, Old North State

Population (1999): 7,650,789 (11th)
Area: 52,672 sq. mi. (29th) (136,420 sq. km.)
Flower: Dogwood   **Bird:** Cardinal
Tree: Pine   **Song:** "The Old North State"
Entered Union: November 21, 1789 (12th)
Capital: Raleigh
Largest Cities (with population): Charlotte, 504,637; Raleigh, 259,473; Greensboro, 197,910; Winston-Salem, 164,316; Durham, 153,513
Important Products: clothing and textiles, tobacco and tobacco products, industrial machinery, electronic equipment, furniture, cotton, soybeans, peanuts
Places to Visit: Great Smoky Mountains National Park; Cape Hatteras National Seashore; Wright Brothers National Memorial, at Kitty Hawk

WEB SITE *http://www.state.nc.us • http://www.visitnc.com*

DID YOU KNOW? *The Wright Brothers took the first airplane ride in history, in North Carolina. This state has more miles of paved roads than any other state—about 80,000.*

NORTH DAKOTA (ND)

Peace Garden State

Population (1999): 633,666 (47th)
Area: 70,704 sq. mi. (18th) (183,123 sq. km.)
Flower: Wild prairie rose   **Bird:** Western meadowlark
Tree: American elm   **Song:** "North Dakota Hymn"
Entered Union: November 2, 1889 (39th)
Capital: Bismarck
Largest Cities (with population): Fargo, 86,718; Grand Forks, 47,327; Bismarck, 54,040; Minot, 35,286
Important Products: wheat, barley, hay, sunflowers, sugar beets, cattle, sand and gravel, food products, farm equipment, high-tech electronics
Places to Visit: Theodore Roosevelt National Park; Bonanzaville, near Fargo; Dakota Dinosaur Museum, Dickinson; International Peace Garden

WEB SITE   *http://www.state.nd.us • http://www.glness.com/tourism*

DID YOU KNOW? *North Dakota is one of the two biggest wheat-growing states in the United States (the other is Kansas). Theodore Roosevelt was a rancher here before he became president.*

OHIO (OH)

Buckeye State

Population (1999): 11,256,654 (7th)
Area: 44,828 sq. mi. (34th) (116,103 sq. km.)
Flower: Scarlet carnation   **Bird:** Cardinal
Tree: Buckeye   **Song:** "Beautiful Ohio"
Entered Union: March 1, 1803 (17th)
Capital and Largest City: Columbus (population, 670,234)
Other Large Cities (with population): Cleveland, 495,817; Cincinnati, 336,400; Toledo, 312,174; Akron, 215,712; Dayton, 167,475
Important Products: metal and metal products, transportation equipment, industrial machinery, rubber and plastic products, electronic equipment, printing and publishing, chemicals, food products, corn, soybeans, livestock, milk
Places to Visit: Mound City Group National Monuments, Indian burial mounds; Neil Armstrong Air and Space Museum; homes of and memorials to 8 U.S. presidents who lived here

WEB SITE   *http://www.state.oh.us • http://www.ohiotourism.com*

DID YOU KNOW? *Seven American presidents were born in Ohio (Garfield, Grant, Harding, B. Harrison, Hayes, McKinley, Taft). Ohio was the home of the first professional baseball team, the Cincinnati Red Stockings, and the birthplace of the hot dog.*

OKLAHOMA (OK)

Sooner State

Population (1999): 3,358,044 (27th)
Area: 69,903 sq. mi. (20th) (181,049 sq. km.)
Flower: Mistletoe   **Bird:** Scissor-tailed flycatcher
Tree: Redbud   **Song:** "Oklahoma!"
Entered Union: November 16, 1907 (46th)
Capital and Largest City: Oklahoma City (population, 472,221)
Other Large Cities (with population): Tulsa, 381,393; Norman, 93,019; Lawton, 81,109
Important Products: natural gas, oil, cattle, nonelectrical machinery, transportation equipment, metal products, wheat, hay
Places to Visit: Indian City U.S.A., near Anadarko; Fort Gibson Stockade; National Cowboy Hall of Fame; White Water Bay and Frontier City theme parks; Cherokee Heritage Center

WEB SITE   *http://www.state.ok.us • http://www.otrd.state.ok.us*

DID YOU KNOW? *The American Indian nations called The Five Civilized Tribes (Cherokee, Chickasaw, Choctaw, Creek, and Seminole) settled in Oklahoma. Today, more Native Americans live in Oklahoma than in any other state.*

OREGON (OR)

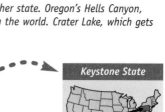

Beaver State

Population (1999): 3,316,154 (28th)
Area: 97,132 sq. mi. (10th) (251,572 sq. km.)
Flower: Oregon grape   **Bird:** Western meadowlark
Tree: Douglas fir   **Song:** "Oregon, My Oregon"
Entered Union: February 14, 1859 (33rd)
Capital: Salem
Largest Cities (with population): Portland, 503,891; Eugene, 128,240; Salem, 126,702
Important Products: lumber and wood products, electronics and semiconductors, food products, paper, cattle, hay, vegetables, Christmas trees
Places to Visit: Crater Lake National Park; Oregon Caves National Monument; Fort Clatsop National Memorial; Oregon Museum of Science and Industry, Portland

WEB SITE   *http://www.state.or.us • http://www.traveloregon.com*

DiD YoU KNoW? *Oregon produces more timber than any other state. Oregon's Hells Canyon, 7,900 feet deep at its maximum, is one of the deepest canyons in the world. Crater Lake, which gets as deep as 1,932 feet, is the deepest lake in the United States.*

PENNSYLVANIA (PA)

Keystone State

Population (1999): 11,994,016 (6th)
Area: 46,058 sq. mi. (33rd) (119,290 sq. km.)
Flower: Mountain laurel   **Bird:** Ruffed grouse
Tree: Hemlock   **Song:** "Pennsylvania"
Entered Union: December 12, 1787 (2nd)
Capital: Harrisburg (population, 49,502)
Largest Cities (with population): Philadelphia, 1,436,287; Pittsburgh, 340,520; Erie, 102,640; Allentown, 100,757
Important Products: iron and steel, coal, industrial machinery, printing and publishing, food products, electronic equipment, transportation equipment, stone, clay and glass products
Places to Visit: Independence Hall and other historic sites in Philadelphia; Franklin Institute Science Museum, Philadelphia; Valley Forge; Gettysburg; Hershey; Pennsylvania Dutch country, Lancaster County

WEB SITE   *http://www.state.pa.us • http://www.state.pa.us/visit*

DiD YoU KNoW? *Pennsylvania is known for the Liberty Bell in Philadelphia, which first rang after the signing of the Declaration of Independence. Philadelphia was also the U.S. capital for ten years. The first hospital in the United States was built there.*

RHODE ISLAND (RI)

Little Rhody, Ocean State

Population (1999): 980,819 (43rd)
Area: 1,231 sq. mi. (50th) (3,188 sq. km.)
Flower: Violet   **Bird:** Rhode Island red
Tree: Red maple   **Song:** "Rhode Island"
Entered Union: May 29, 1790 (13th)
Capital and Largest City: Providence (population, 150,890)
Other Large Cities (with population): Warwick, 84,094; Cranston, 74,521; Pawtucket, 68,169
Important Products: costume jewelry, toys, textiles, machinery, electronic equipment, fish
Places to Visit: Block Island; mansions, old buildings, and harbor in Newport; International Tennis Hall of Fame, Newport

WEB SITE   *http://www.state.ri.us • http://www.visitrhodeisland.com*

DiD YoU KNoW? *Rhode Island is the smallest state. The bluffs and islands of Rhode Island attract many tourists who like fishing and swimming. The oldest synagogue in the United States (Touro Synagogue, 1763) is in Newport.*

SOUTH CAROLINA (SC)

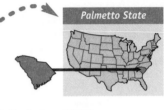

Population (1999): 3,885,736 (26th)
Area: 31,189 sq. mi. (40th) (80,779 sq. km.)
Flower: Yellow jessamine   **Bird:** Carolina wren
Tree: Palmetto   **Song:** "Carolina"
Entered Union: May 23, 1788 (8th)
Capital and Largest City: Columbia (population, 110,840)
Other Large Cities (with population): Charleston, 87,044; North Charleston, 68,072; Greenville, 56,436
Important Products: clothing and textiles, chemicals, industrial machinery, metal products, livestock, tobacco, Portland cement
Places to Visit: Grand Strand and Hilton Head Island beaches; Revolutionary War battlefields; historic sites in Charleston; Fort Sumter; Charleston Museum

WEB SITE *http://www.state.sc.us • http://www.sccsi.com/sc*

DID YOU KNOW? *More battles of the American Revolution took place in South Carolina than in any other state. The first shots of the Civil War were fired in South Carolina. Charleston Museum, opened in 1773, is the oldest U.S. museum.*

SOUTH DAKOTA (SD)

Population (1999): 733,133 (46th)
Area: 77,121 sq. mi. (17th) (199,743 sq. km.)
Flower: Pasqueflower   **Bird:** Chinese ring-necked pheasant
Tree: Black Hills spruce   **Song:** "Hail, South Dakota"
Entered Union: November 2, 1889 (40th)
Capital: Pierre (population, 13,267)
Largest Cities (with population): Sioux Falls, 116,762; Rapid City, 57,513
Important Products: food and food products, machinery, electric and electronic equipment, corn, soybeans
Places to Visit: Mount Rushmore National Memorial; Crazy Horse Memorial; Jewel Cave; Badlands and Wind Caves national parks; Wounded Knee battlefield; Homestake Gold Mine

WEB SITE *http://www.state.sd.us • http://www.state.sd.us/tourism*

DID YOU KNOW? *South Dakota is best known for the faces of presidents carved on Mount Rushmore (Presidents Washington, Jefferson, Lincoln, and T. Roosevelt). Famous South Dakotans include Crazy Horse, Sitting Bull, and Wild Bill Hickok.*

TENNESSEE (TN)

Population (1999): 5,483,535 (16th)
Area: 42,146 sq. mi. (36th) (109,158 sq. km.)
Flower: Iris   **Bird:** Mockingbird
Tree: Tulip poplar   **Song:** "The Tennessee Waltz"
Entered Union: June 1, 1796 (16th)
Capital: Nashville
Largest Cities (with population): Memphis, 603,507; Nashville, 510,274; Knoxville, 165,540; Chattanooga, 147,790
Important Products: chemicals, machinery, vehicles, food products, metal products, publishing, electronic equipment, paper products, rubber and plastic products, tobacco
Places to Visit: Great Smoky Mountains National Park; the Hermitage, home of President Andrew Jackson, near Nashville; Civil War battle sites; Grand Old Opry and Opryland, USA theme park, Nashville; Graceland, home of Elvis Presley, in Memphis

WEB SITE *http://www.state.tn.us • http://www.state.tn.us/tourdev*

DID YOU KNOW? *Tennessee can claim Nashville as the country music capital of the world. Frontiersman Davy Crockett was born in Tennessee. Elvis Presley and President Andrew Jackson are among the famous people who lived in Tennessee.*

TEXAS (TX)

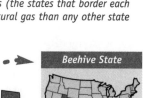

Lone Star State

Population (1999): 20,044,141 (2nd)
Area: 267,277 sq. mi. (2nd) (692,247 sq. km.)
Flower: Bluebonnet   **Bird:** Mockingbird
Tree: Pecan   **Song:** "Texas, Our Texas"
Entered Union: December 29, 1845 (28th)
Capital: Austin
Largest Cities (with population): Houston, 1,786,691; San Antonio, 1,114,130; Dallas, 1,075,894;
El Paso, 615,032; Austin, 552,434; Fort Worth, 491,801
Important Products: oil, natural gas, cattle, milk, eggs, transportation equipment, chemicals,
clothing, industrial machinery, electrical and electronic equipment, cotton, grains
Places to Visit: Guadalupe Mountains and Big Bend national parks; the Alamo, in San Antonio;
Lyndon Johnson National Historic Site, near Johnson City; George Bush Presidential Library,
College Station

WEB SITE *http://www.state.tx.us • http://www.traveltex.com*

DiD YoU KNoW? *Texas is the largest of the contiguous 48 states (the states that border each
other) and is second in size only to Alaska. Texas has more oil and natural gas than any other state
and the most farmland. It is the only state with five major ports.*

UTAH (UT)

Beehive State

Population (1999): 2,129,836 (34th)
Area: 84,904 sq. mi. (13th) (219,902 sq. km.)
Flower: Sego lily   **Bird:** Seagull
Tree: Blue spruce   **Song:** "Utah, We Love Thee"
Entered Union: January 4, 1896 (45th)
Capital and Largest City: Salt Lake City (population, 174,348)
Other Large Cities (with population): Provo, 110,419; West Valley City, 99,372
Important Products: transportation equipment, medical instruments, electronic parts, food
products, steel, copper, cattle, corn, hay, wheat, barley
Places to Visit: Arches, Canyonlands, Bryce Canyon, Zion, and Capitol Reef national parks; Great
Salt Lake; Temple Square (Mormon Church headquarters) in Salt Lake City; Indian cliff dwellings

WEB SITE *http://www.state.ut.us • http://www.utah.com*

DiD YoU KNoW? *Utah's Great Salt Lake, which contains 6 billion tons of salt, is the largest lake in
the United States outside of the Great Lakes. Rainbow Bridge in Utah is the largest natural arch or rock
bridge in the world; it is 200 feet high and 270 feet wide.*

VERMONT (VT)

Green Mountain State

Population (1999): 593,740 (49th)
Area: 9,615 sq. mi. (43rd) (24,903 sq. km.)
Flower: Red clover   **Bird:** Hermit thrush
Tree: Sugar maple   **Song:** "Hail, Vermont!"
Entered Union: March 4, 1791 (14th)
Capital: Montpelier (population, 7,734)
Largest Cities (with population): Burlington, 38,453; Rutland, 17,348
Important Products: machine tools, furniture, scales, books, computer parts, foods, dairy products,
apples, maple syrup
Places to Visit: Green Mountain National Forest; Maple Grove Maple Museum, St. Johnsbury

WEB SITE *http://www.state.vt.us • http://www.travelvermont.com*

DiD YoU KNoW? *Vermont is famous for its granite, marble, scenery, and maple syrup. Vermont
passed the first constitution (1777) to prohibit slavery and to allow all men to vote. The first ski tow
in the United States was established in Vermont in 1934.*

VIRGINIA (VA)

Population (1999): 6,872,912 (12th)
Area: 42,326 sq. mi. (35th) (109,391 sq. km.)
Flower: Dogwood **Bird:** Cardinal
Tree: Dogwood **Song:** "Carry Me Back to Old Virginia"
Entered Union: June 25, 1788 (10th)
Capital: Richmond
Largest Cities (with population): Virginia Beach, 432,380; Norfolk, 215,215; Chesapeake, 199,564; Richmond, 194,173; Newport News, 178,615
Important Products: transportation equipment, textiles, chemicals, printing, machinery, electronic equipment, food products, coal, livestock, tobacco, wood products, furniture
Places to Visit: Colonial Williamsburg; Arlington National Cemetery; Mount Vernon (George Washington's home); Monticello (Thomas Jefferson's home); Shenandoah National Park

WEB SITE *http://www.state.va.us • http://www.virginia.org*

DID YOU KNOW? *Virginia was the birthplace of eight presidents (Presidents W. H. Harrison, Jefferson, Madison, Monroe, Taylor, Tyler, Washington, Wilson), more than any other state. The first permanent English settlement in the New World was in Virginia.*

WASHINGTON (WA)
Evergreen State

Population (1999): 5,756,361 (15th)
Area: 70,637 sq. mi. (19th) (182,950 sq. km.)
Flower: Western rhododendron **Bird:** Willow goldfinch
Tree: Western hemlock **Song:** "Washington, My Home"
Entered Union: November 11, 1889 (42nd)
Capital: Olympia (population, 39,188)
Largest Cities (with population): Seattle, 536,978; Spokane, 184,058; Tacoma, 179,814
Important Products: aircraft, lumber and plywood, pulp and paper, machinery, electronics, computer software, aluminum, processed fruits and vegetables
Places to Visit: Mount Rainier, Olympic, and North Cascades national parks; Mount St. Helens; Seattle Center, with Space Needle and monorail

WEB SITE *http://www.access.wa.gov • http://www.tourism.wa.gov*

DID YOU KNOW? *Grand Coulee Dam, on the Columbia River, is the world's largest concrete dam. Mount Rainier is the tallest volcano in the contiguous 48 states (those that border each other). Washington is known for its apples, timber, and fishing fleets.*

WEST VIRGINIA (WV)
Mountain State

Population (1999): 1,806,928 (36th)
Area: 24,231 sq. mi. (41st) (62,759 sq. km.)
Flower: Big rhododendron **Bird:** Cardinal
Tree: Sugar maple **Songs:** "The West Virginia Hills"; "This Is My West Virginia"; "West Virginia, My Home Sweet Home"
Entered Union: June 20, 1863 (35th)
Capital and Largest City: Charleston (population, 55,056)
Other Large Cities (with population): Huntington, 52,571; Wheeling, 32,541
Important Products: coal, natural gas, fabricated metal products, chemicals, automobile parts, aluminum, steel, machinery, cattle, hay, apples, peaches, tobacco
Places to Visit: Harpers Ferry National Historic Park; Exhibition Coal Mine, Beckley; Monongahela National Forest

WEB SITE *http://www.state.wv.us • http://wvweb.com/www/travel_recreation*

DID YOU KNOW? *West Virginia's mountain scenery and mineral springs attract many tourists. The state is one of the biggest coal mining states. West Virginia was part of Virginia until West Virginians decided to secede (break away) in 1861.*

WISCONSIN (WI)

Badger State

Population (1999): 5,250,446 (18th)
Area: 65,499 sq. mi. (22nd) (169,642 sq. km.)
Flower: Wood violet   **Bird:** Robin
Tree: Sugar maple   **Song:** "On, Wisconsin!"
Entered Union: May 29, 1848 (30th)
Capital: Madison
Largest Cities (with population): Milwaukee, 578,364; Madison, 209,306; Green Bay, 97,789; Kenosha, 87,849; Racine, 81,095
Important Products: paper products, printing, milk, butter, cheese, foods, food products, motor vehicles and equipment, medical instruments and supplies, plastics, corn, hay, vegetables
Places to Visit: Wisconsin Dells; Cave of the Mounds, near Blue Mounds; Milwaukee Public Museum; Circus World Museum, Baraboo; National Railroad Museum, Green Bay

WEB SITE *http://www.state.wi.us • http://www.tourism.state.wi.us*

DID YOU KNOW? *Wisconsin is known as America's Dairyland; more recently it has also become a major manufacturing state. The first kindergarten in America was opened in Wisconsin in 1856.*

WYOMING (WY)

Cowboy State

Population (1999): 479,602 (50th)
Area: 97,818 sq. mi. (9th) (253,349 sq. km.)
Flower: Indian paintbrush   **Bird:** Western meadowlark
Tree: Plains cottonwood   **Song:** "Wyoming"
Entered Union: July 10, 1890 (44th)
Capital and Largest City: Cheyenne (population, 53,640)
Other Large Cities (with population): Casper, 48,283; Laramie, 25,035
Important Products: oil, natural gas, petroleum (oil) products, cattle, wheat, beans
Places to Visit: Yellowstone and Grand Teton national parks; Fort Laramie; Buffalo Bill Historical Center, Cody; pioneer trails

WEB SITE *http://www.state.wy.us • http://www.state.wy/us/state/tourism/tourism/html*

DID YOU KNOW? *Wyoming is the home of the first U.S. national park (Yellowstone). Established in 1872, Yellowstone has 10,000 geysers, including the world's tallest active geyser (Steamboat Geyser).*

COMMONWEALTH OF PUERTO RICO (PR)

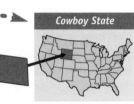

Puerto Rico

History: Christopher Columbus landed in Puerto Rico in 1493. Puerto Rico was a Spanish colony for centuries, then was ceded (given) to the United States in 1898 after the Spanish-American War. In 1952, still associated with the United States, Puerto Rico became a commonwealth with its own constitution.
Population (1998): 3,860,091
Area: 3,508 sq. mi. (9,086 sq. km.)
Flower: Maga   **Bird:** Reinita   **Tree:** Ceiba
National Anthem: "La Borinqueña"
Capital and Largest City: San Juan (population, 439,427)
Other Large Cities (with population): Bayamón, 233,797; Ponce, 191,469; Carolina, 190,469
Important Products: chemicals, food products, electronic equipment, clothing and textiles, industrial machinery, coffee, sugarcane, fruit, hogs
Places to Visit: San Juan National Historic Site; beaches and resorts

WEB SITE *http://www.fortaleza.govpr.org http://www.discoverpuertorico.com*

DID YOU KNOW? *Puerto Ricans have most of the rights of American citizens, but cannot vote in U.S. presidential elections and do not pay federal income tax. That would change if Puerto Rico becomes a state. In 1998, Puerto Rico voted to remain a commonwealth.*

ALABAMA comes from an Indian word for "tribal town."

ALASKA comes from *alakshak*, the Aleutian (Eskimo) word meaning "peninsula" or "land that is not an island."

ARIZONA comes from a Pima Indian word meaning "little spring place," or the Aztec word *arizuma*, meaning "silver-bearing."

ARKANSAS is a variation of *Quapaw*, the name of an Indian tribe. *Quapaw* means "south wind."

CALIFORNIA is the name of an imaginary island in a Spanish story. It was named by Spanish explorers of Baja California, a part of Mexico.

COLORADO comes from a Spanish word meaning "red." It was first given to the Colorado River because of its reddish color.

CONNECTICUT comes from an Algonquin Indian word meaning "long river place."

DELAWARE is named after Lord De La Warr, the English governor of Virginia in colonial times.

FLORIDA, which means "flowery" in Spanish, was named by the explorer Ponce de Leon, who landed there during Easter.

GEORGIA was named after King George II of England, who granted the right to create a colony there in 1732.

HAWAII probably comes from *Hawaiki*, or *Owhyhee*, the native Polynesians' word for "homeland."

IDAHO'S name is of uncertain origin, but it may come from a Kiowa Apache name for the Comanche Indians.

ILLINOIS is the French version of *Illini*, an Algonquin Indian word meaning "men" or "warriors."

INDIANA means "land of the Indians."

IOWA comes from the name of an American Indian tribe that lived on the land that is now the state.

KANSAS comes from a Sioux Indian word that possibly meant "people of the south wind."

KENTUCKY comes from an Iroquois Indian word, possibly meaning "meadowland."

LOUISIANA, which was first settled by French explorers, was named after King Louis XIV of France.

MAINE means "the mainland." English explorers called it that to distinguish it from islands nearby.

MARYLAND was named after Queen Henrietta Maria, wife of King Charles I of England, who granted the right to establish an English colony there.

MASSACHUSETTS comes from an Indian word meaning "large hill place."

MICHIGAN comes from the Chippewa Indian words *mici gama*, meaning "great water" (referring to Lake Michigan).

MINNESOTA got its name from a Dakota Sioux Indian word meaning "cloudy water" or "sky-tinted water."

MISSISSIPPI is probably from Chippewa Indian words meaning "great river" or "gathering of all the waters," or from an Algonquin word.

MISSOURI comes from an Algonquin Indian term meaning "river of the big canoes."

MONTANA comes from a Latin or Spanish word meaning "mountainous."

GOT THEIR NAMES

NEBRASKA comes from "flat river" or "broad water," an Omaha or Otos Indian name for the Platte River.

NEVADA means "snow-clad" in Spanish. Spanish explorers gave the name to the Sierra Nevada Mountains.

NEW HAMPSHIRE was named by an early settler after his home county of Hampshire, in England.

NEW JERSEY was named for the English Channel island of Jersey.

NEW MEXICO was given its name by 16th-century Spaniards in Mexico.

NEW YORK, first called New Netherland, was renamed for the Duke of York and Albany after the English took it from Dutch settlers.

NORTH CAROLINA, the northern part of the English colony of Carolana, was named for King Charles I.

NORTH DAKOTA comes from a Sioux Indian word meaning "friend" or "ally."

OHIO is the Iroquois Indian word for "fine or good river."

OKLAHOMA comes from a Choctaw Indian word meaning "red man."

OREGON may have come from *Ouaricon-sint,* a name on an old French map that was once given to what is now called the Columbia River. That river runs between Oregon and Washington.

PENNSYLVANIA, meaning "Penn's woods," was the name given to the colony founded by William Penn.

RHODE ISLAND may have come from the Dutch "Roode Eylandt" (red island) or may have been named after the Greek island of Rhodes.

SOUTH CAROLINA, the southern part of the English colony of Carolana, was named for King Charles I.

SOUTH DAKOTA comes from a Sioux Indian word meaning "friend" or "ally."

TENNESSEE comes from "Tanasi," the name of Cherokee Indian villages on what is now the Little Tennessee River.

TEXAS comes from a word meaning "friends" or "allies," used by the Spanish to describe some of the American Indians living there.

UTAH comes from a Navajo word meaning "upper" or "higher up."

VERMONT comes from two French words, *vert* meaning "green" and *mont* "mountain."

VIRGINIA was named in honor of Queen Elizabeth I of England, who was known as the Virgin Queen because she was never married.

WASHINGTON was named after George Washington, the first president of the United States. It is the only state named after a president.

WEST VIRGINIA got its name from the people of western Virginia, who formed their own government during the Civil War.

WISCONSIN comes from a Chippewa name that is believed to mean "grassy place." It was once spelled *Ouisconsin* and *Mesconsing.*

WYOMING comes from Algonquin Indian words that are said to mean "at the big plains," "large prairie place," or "on the great plain."

WASHINGTON, D.C.
The Capital of the United States

Land Area: 61 square miles
Population: 523,124
Flower: American beauty rose
Bird: Wood thrush

WEB SITE http://www.washington.org

HISTORY Washington, D.C., became the capital of the United States in 1800, when the federal government moved there from Philadelphia. The city of Washington was designed and built to be the capital. It was named after George Washington. Many of its major sights are on the Mall, an open grassy area that runs from the Capitol to the Potomac River.

Capitol, which houses the U.S. Congress, is at the east end of the Mall, on Capitol Hill. The Capitol's dome can be seen from far away.

Franklin Delano Roosevelt Memorial, honoring the 32nd president of the United States, and his wife, Eleanor, was dedicated in 1997. In a parklike setting, it has sculptures showing events during the president's years of service.

Jefferson Memorial, a circular marble building located near the Potomac River. Its design is partly based on one by Thomas Jefferson for the University of Virginia.

Korean War Veterans Memorial, dedicated in 1995, is at the west end of the Mall. It shows a group of 19 troops ready for combat.

Lincoln Memorial, at the west end of the Mall, is built of white marble and styled like a Greek temple. Inside is a large, seated statue of Abraham Lincoln. His Gettysburg Address is carved on a nearby wall.

National Archives, on Constitution Avenue, holds the Declaration of Independence, Constitution, and Bill of Rights.

National Gallery of Art, on the Mall, is one of the world's great art museums. Older paintings and sculptures are housed in the West Building, while 20th-century art is housed in the newer East Building.

Smithsonian Institution has 14 museums, including the National Air and Space Museum and the Museum of Natural History. The National Zoo is part of the Smithsonian.

U.S. Holocaust Memorial Museum presents the history of the Nazis' murder of more than six million Jews and millions of other people from 1933 to 1945. The exhibit *Daniel's Story* tells the story of the Holocaust from a child's point of view.

Vietnam Veterans Memorial has a black-granite wall shaped like a V. Names of the Americans killed or missing in the Vietnam War are inscribed on the wall.

Washington Monument, a white marble pillar, or obelisk, standing on the Mall and rising to over 555 feet. From the top, there are wonderful views of the city.

White House, at 1600 Pennsylvania Avenue, has been the home of every U.S. president except George Washington.

Women in Military Service for America Memorial, near the entrance to Arlington National Cemetery. It honors the 1.8 million women who have served in the U.S. armed forces.

NATIONAL PARKS

The world's first national park was Yellowstone, established in 1872. Since then, the U.S. government has set aside a total of 55 national parks. The 53 parks in the United States are listed below.

Two are outside the United States—one in the U.S. Virgin Islands and one in American Samoa.

You can find out more about national parks by writing to the National Park Service, Department of the Interior, 1849 C Street NW, Washington, D.C. 20240.

For information on-line, go to **WEB SITE** *http://www.nps.gov/parks.html*

ACADIA (Maine) 47,738 acres; established 1929. Rugged coast and granite cliffs; seals, whales, and porpoises; highest land along the East Coast of the U.S.

ARCHES (Utah) 73,379 acres; established 1971. Giant natural sandstone arches, including Landscape Arch, over 100 feet high and 291 feet long

BADLANDS (South Dakota) 242,756 acres; established 1978. A prairie where, over centuries, the land has been formed into many odd shapes with a variety of colors

BIG BEND (Texas) 801,163 acres; established 1935. Desert land and rugged mountains, on the Rio Grande River; dinosaur fossils

BISCAYNE (Florida) 172,924 acres; established 1980. A water-park on a chain of islands in the Atlantic Ocean, south of Miami, with beautiful coral reefs

BLACK CANYON OF THE GUNNISON (Colorado) 30,300 acres; established 1999. Newest national park, features the dramatic Black Canyon carved out by the Gunnison River

BRYCE CANYON (Utah) 35,835 acres; established 1928. Odd and very colorful rock formations carved by centuries of erosion

CANYONLANDS (Utah) 337,598 acres; established 1964. Sandstone cliffs above the Colorado River; rock carvings from an ancient American Indian civilization

CAPITOL REEF (Utah) 241,904 acres; established 1971. Sandstone cliffs cut into by gorges with high walls; old American Indian storage huts

CARLSBAD CAVERNS (New Mexico) 46,766 acres; established 1930. A huge cave system, not fully explored, with the world's largest underground chamber, called "the Big Room"

CHANNEL ISLANDS (California) 249,354 acres; established 1980. Islands off the California coast, with sea lions, seals, and sea birds

CRATER LAKE (Oregon) 183,224 acres; established 1902. The deepest lake in the United States, carved in the crater of an inactive volcano; lava walls up to 2,000 feet high

DEATH VALLEY (California, Nevada) 3,367,628 acres; established 1994. Largest national park outside Alaska. Vast hot desert, rocky slopes and gorges, huge sand dunes; hundreds of species of plants, some unique to the area; variety of wildlife, including desert foxes, bobcats, coyotes

DENALI (Alaska) 4,740,907 acres; established 1980. Huge park, containing America's tallest mountain, plus caribou, moose, sheep

DRY TORTUGAS (Florida) 64,700 acres; established 1992. Colorful birds and fish; a 19th-century fort, Fort Jefferson

EVERGLADES (Florida) 1,508,607 acres; established 1934. The largest subtropical wilderness within the U.S.; swamps with mangrove trees, rare birds, alligators

GATES OF THE ARCTIC (Alaska) 7,224,813 acres; established 1984. One of the largest national parks; huge tundra wilderness, with rugged peaks and steep valleys

GLACIER (Montana) 1,013,572 acres; established 1910. Rugged mountains, with glaciers, lakes, sheep, bears, and bald eagles

GLACIER BAY (Alaska) 3,224,794 acres; established 1986. Glaciers moving down mountainsides to the sea; seals, whales, bears, eagles

GRAND CANYON (Arizona) 1,217,403 acres; established 1919. Mile-deep expanse of multicolored layered rock, a national wonder

GRAND TETON (Wyoming) 309,993 acres; established 1929. Set in the Teton Mountains; a winter feeding ground for elks

GREAT BASIN (Nevada) 77,180 acres; established 1986. From deserts to meadows to tundra; caves; ancient pine trees

GREAT SMOKY MOUNTAINS (North Carolina, Tennessee) 521,621 acres; established 1934. Forests with deer, fox, and black bears; streams with trout and bass

GUADALUPE MOUNTAINS (Texas) 86,416 acres; established 1966. Remains of a fossil reef formed 225 million years ago

HALEAKALA (Hawaii) 28,350 acres; established 1960. The largest crater of any inactive volcano in the world

HAWAII VOLCANOES (Hawaii) 209,695 acres; established 1961. Home of two large volcanoes, Mauna Loa and Kilauea, along with a desert and a tree fern forest

HOT SPRINGS (Arkansas) 5,549 acres; established 1921. 47 hot springs that provide warm waters for drinking and bathing

ISLE ROYALE (Michigan) 571,790 acres; established 1931. On an island in Lake Superior; woods, lakes, many kinds of animals—and no roads

JOSHUA TREE (California) 1,022,976 acres; established 1994. Large desert with rock formations and unusual desert plants, including many Joshua trees; fossils from prehistoric times; wildlife, including desert bighorn

KATMAI (Alaska) 3,674,530 acres; established 1980. Contains the Valley of Ten Thousand Smokes, which was filled with ash when Katmai Volcano erupted in 1912

KENAI FJORDS (Alaska) 669,983 acres; established 1980. Fjords, rain forests, the Harding Icefield; sea otters, seals; a breeding place for many birds

KINGS CANYON (California) 461,901 acres; established 1940. Mountains and woods; the highest canyon wall in the U.S.

KOBUK VALLEY (Alaska) 1,750,698 acres; established 1980. Located north of the Arctic Circle, with caribou and black bears; archeological sites indicate humans have lived there for over 10,000 years

LAKE CLARK (Alaska) 2,619,859 acres; established 1980. Lakes, waterfalls, glaciers, volcanoes, fish and wildlife

LASSEN VOLCANIC (California) 106,372 acres; established 1916. Contains Lassen Peak, a volcano that began erupting in 1914, after being dormant for 400 years

MAMMOTH CAVE (Kentucky) 52,830 acres; established 1941. The world's longest known cave network, with 144 miles of mapped underground passages

MESA VERDE (Colorado) 52,122 acres; established 1906. A plateau covered by woods and canyons; the best preserved ancient cliff dwellings in the U.S.

MOUNT RAINIER (Washington) 235,613 acres; established 1899. Home of the Mount Rainier volcano; thick forests, glaciers

NORTH CASCADES (Washington) 504,781 acres; established 1968. Rugged mountains and valleys, with deep canyons, lakes and glaciers

OLYMPIC (Washington) 922,651 acres; established 1938. Rain forest, with woods and mountains, glaciers, and rare elk

PETRIFIED FOREST (Arizona) 93,533 acres; established 1962. A large area of woods which have petrified, or turned into stone; American Indian pueblos and rock carvings

REDWOOD (California) 112,430 acres; established 1968. Groves of ancient redwood trees, and the world's tallest trees

ROCKY MOUNTAIN (Colorado) 265,723 acres; established 1915. Located in the Rockies, with gorges, alpine lakes, and mountain peaks

SAGUARO (Arizona) 91,444 acres; established 1994. Forests of saguaro cacti, some 50 feet tall and 200 years old

SEQUOIA (California) 402,510 acres; established 1890. Groves of giant sequoia trees; Mount Whitney (14,494 feet)

SHENANDOAH (Virginia) 198,182 acres; established 1926. Located in the Blue Ridge Mountains, overlooking the Shenandoah Valley

THEODORE ROOSEVELT (North Dakota) 70,447 acres; established 1978. Scenic badlands and a part of the old Elkhorn Ranch that belonged to Theodore Roosevelt

VOYAGEURS (Minnesota) 218,200 acres; established 1971. Forests with wildlife and many scenic lakes for canoeing and boating

WIND CAVE (South Dakota) 28,295 acres; established 1903. Limestone caverns in the Black Hills; bison herds

WRANGELL-SAINT ELIAS (Alaska) 8,323,618 acres; established 1980. The biggest national park, with mountain peaks over 16,000 feet high

YELLOWSTONE (Idaho, Montana, Wyoming) 2,219,791 acres; established 1872. The first national park and world's greatest geysers; bears and moose

YOSEMITE (California) 761,266 acres; established 1890. Yosemite Valley; highest waterfall in North America; mountain scenery

ZION (Utah) 146,592 acres; established 1919. Deep, narrow Zion Canyon and other canyons in different colors; Indian cliff dwellings over 1,000 years old

UNITED STATES PUZZLES

STATE OF TRIVIA

The left column is a list of state trees, birds, flowers, songs, and sites of interest. The column on the right has state abbreviations. Can you match the items at the left that belong to the states at the right? You can find the information in this chapter.

1. orange blossom
2. sugar maple
3. "Yankee Doodle"
4. Baltimore oriole
5. cactus wren
6. Baseball Hall of Fame
7. Hollywood
8. Mount Vernon
9. Lincoln home and tomb
10. Mark Twain's home

a. CT
b. IL
c. VA
d. CA
e. MD
f. VT
g. FL
h. MO
i. NY
j. AZ

HIDDEN CITIES

The Word Box below lists 12 state capitals and major cities. Can you fill in the state abbreviation for each? Can you find all 12 city names hidden in the puzzle below the Word Box? The names go across, up, down, or backward. Some letters are used more than once. Spots marked X are not used.

WORD BOX

JUNEAU, _____   ALBANY, _____   BOSTON, _____

DENVER, _____   BOISE, _____   BANGOR, _____

HELENA, _____   JACKSON, _____   PIERRE, _____

DOVER, _____   HILO, _____   SALEM, _____

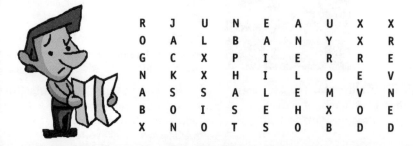

R	J	U	N	E	A	U	X	X
O	A	L	B	A	N	Y	X	R
G	C	X	P	I	E	R	R	E
N	K	X	H	I	L	O	E	V
A	S	S	A	L	E	M	V	N
B	O	I	S	E	H	X	O	E
X	N	O	T	S	O	B	D	D

Answers are on pages 317–320.

Weather

? What place once had the hottest temperature on record?
You can find the answer on page 297.

WEATHER WORDS

front Boundary between two air masses.

humidity Amount of water vapor (water in the form of a gas) in the air.

jet stream Long band of winds moving rapidly from west to east 20,000 to 40,000 feet above Earth.

El Niño Condition characterized by unusually warm temperatures in the Pacific Ocean near South America.

La Niña Condition characterized by unusually cold temperatures in the Pacific Ocean off South America.

meteorologist A person who studies the atmosphere, weather, and weather forecasting.

wind chill How much colder it feels when there is a wind. When it is 35 degrees F and the wind is 15 miles an hour, it will feel like 16 degrees F.

PRECIPITATION

precipitation Water that falls from clouds as rain, snow, hail, or sleet.

rain Water falling in drops.

freezing rain Water that freezes as it hits the ground.

sleet Drops of water that freeze in cold air and reach the ground as ice pellets or a mixture of snow and rain.

hail Frozen raindrops that are kept in the air by air currents. Water keeps freezing on the hailstone until it is so heavy that it falls to the ground.

snow Ice crystals that form in clouds and fall.

STORMS

blizzard A heavy snowstorm with strong winds.

cyclone A storm with winds rotating around a center. Also the name for a hurricane in the Indian Ocean.

hurricane Large tropical cyclone with winds more than 73 mph; called a typhoon in the western Pacific Ocean.

monsoon A system of winds that changes direction between seasons; often brings heavy rains in summer.

tornado Violently circulating winds of more than 200 mph form a dark funnel reaching from the cloud to the ground.

THE SPEED OF WIND

This Beaufort Scale at right is used to measure the speed of wind. The U.S. Weather Service also uses the numbers 13 to 17 for winds of hurricane speed.

0 Calm   *4 Moderate Breeze*   *8 Gale*   *12 Hurricane*

0	Calm	(under 1 mph)
1	Light Air	(1-3 mph)
2	Light Breeze	(4-7 mph)
3	Gentle Breeze	(8-12 mph)
4	Moderate Breeze	(13-18 mph)
5	Fresh Breeze	(19-24 mph)
6	Strong Breeze	(25-31 mph)
7	Near Gale	(32-38 mph)
8	Gale	(39-46 mph)
9	Strong Gale	(47-54 mph)
10	Storm	(55-63 mph)
11	Violent Storm	(64-72 mph)
12	Hurricane	(over 73 mph)

WILD WINDS

For many years, violent storms have been given names. Until early in the 20th century, people named storms after saints. Then, in 1953, the U.S. government began to use women's names for hurricanes. Men's names began to be used in 1978.

WHAT IS A HURRICANE?

Hurricanes are the largest storms. They form over warm, usually tropical, oceans. As the warm seawater evaporates into the air, the pressure drops and winds begin to circulate, creating a huge wall of clouds and rain, wrapped around a calm center. As warm, moist air continues to feed the storm, it gets stronger and can spread out to an area 300 miles wide. Winds up to 250 miles an hour can rip trees out by their roots and tear roofs off buildings. Torrential rains and giant waves caused by the fierce wind can cause flooding and massive damage before the storm finally moves out over land and dies down. This usually takes between three days and two weeks.

HURRICANE Names for 2001

Hurricanes in the North Atlantic: Allison, Barry, Chantal, Dean, Erin, Felix, Gabrielle, Humberto, Iris, Jerry, Karen, Lorenzo, Michelle, Noel, Olga, Pablo, Rebekah, Sebastien, Tanya, Van, and Wendy

Hurricanes in the Eastern Pacific: Adolph, Barbara, Cosme, Dalilia, Erick, Flossie, Gil, Henriette, Israel, Juliette, Kiko, Lorena, Manuel, Narda, Octave, Priscilla, Raymond, Sonia, Tico, Velma, Wallis, Xina, York, and Zelda

TORNADOES

Tornadoes, also called "twisters," are violent winds that spin in the shape of a funnel at speeds up to 250 miles per hour or more. A tornado can suck up and destroy anything in its path! The flying debris causes many deaths and injuries. Tornadoes form when winds change direction, speed up, and spin around before a thunderstorm. When this happens, the National Weather Service issues a tornado watch. A tornado warning is announced when a tornado has actually been seen in the area.

You can read more about tornadoes at

WEB SITE *http://www.nsw.noaa.gov/om/tornado.htm*

TAKING TEMPERATURES

HOW TO MEASURE TEMPERATURE Two systems for measuring temperature are used in weather forecasting. One is Fahrenheit (abbreviated F). The other is Celsius (abbreviated C). Another word for Celsius is Centigrade. Zero degrees (0°) Celsius is equal to 32 degrees (32°) Fahrenheit.

To Convert Fahrenheit Temperatures to Celsius:

1 Subtract 32 from the Fahrenheit temperature value.

2 Then multiply by 5.

3 Then divide the result by 9. **Example:**
To convert 68 degrees Fahrenheit to Celsius,
68 − 32 = 36; 36 × 5 = 180; 180 ÷ 9 = 20

To Convert Celsius Temperatures to Fahrenheit:

1 Multiply the Celsius temperature by 9.

2 Then divide by 5.

3 Then add 32 to the result. **Example:** To convert
20 degrees Celsius to Fahrenheit, 20 × 9 = 180; 180 ÷ 5 = 36; 36 + 32 = 68

F		C
122°		50°
95°	**Normal Room Temperature** 68°F 20°C	35°
68°		20°
32°	**Freezing Point of Water** 32°F 0°C	0°
−4°		−20°
−22°		−30°
−40°		−40°

The HOTTEST and COLDEST Places in the World

CONTINENT	HIGHEST TEMPERATURE	LOWEST TEMPERATURE
Africa	El Azizia, Libya, 136°F (58°C)	Ifrane, Morocco, −11°F (−24°C)
Antarctica	Vanda Station, 59°F (15°C)	Vostok, −129°F (−89°C)
Asia	Tirat Tsvi, Israel, 129°F (54°C)	Verkhoyansk, Russia, and Oimekon, Russia, −90°F (−68°C)
Australia	Cloncurry, Queensland, 128°F (53°C)	Charlotte Pass, New South Wales, −9°F (−23°C)
Europe	Seville, Spain, 122°F (50°C)	Ust'Shchugor, Russia, −67°F (−55°C)
North America	Death Valley, California, 134°F (57°C)	Snag, Yukon Territory, −81°F (−63°C)
South America	Rivadavia, Argentina, 120°F (49°C)	Sarmiento, Argentina, −27°F (−33°C)

Hottest Places in the U.S.

State	Temperature	Year
California	134°F	(1913)
Arizona	128°F	(1994)*
Nevada	125°F	(1994)*

Coldest Places in the U.S.

State	Temperature	Year
Alaska	-80°F	(1971)
Montana	-70°F	(1954)
Utah	-69°F	(1985)

Tied with a record set earlier

To read more about the weather try the Weather Channel at

WEB SITE http://www.weather.com

Weights & Measures

Which is longer, a kilometer or a mile?
You can find the answer on page 300.

The Earliest MEASUREMENTS

We use weights and measures all the time—you can measure how tall you are, or how much gasoline a car needs. People who lived in ancient times—more than 1,000 years ago—developed measurements to describe the amounts or sizes of things. The first measurements were based on the human body and on everyday activities.

Ancient measure			
	1 foot = length of a person's foot	**1 yard =** from nose to fingertip	**1 acre =** land an ox could plow in a day
Modern measure	12 inches	3 feet or 36 inches	43,560 square feet or 4,840 square yards

Measurements We Use Today

The system of measurement used in the United States is called the U.S. customary system. Most other countries use the metric system. A few metric measurements are also used in the United States, such as for soda, which comes in 1-liter and 2-liter bottles. In the tables below, abbreviations are given in parentheses the first time they are used.

LENGTH, HEIGHT, AND DISTANCE

The basic unit of **length** in the U.S. system is the **inch.** Length, width, depth, thickness, and the distance between two points all use the inch or larger related units.

1 foot (ft.) = 12 inches (in.)

1 yard (yd.) = 3 feet or 36 inches

1 rod (rd.) = 5½ yards

1 furlong (fur.) = 40 rods or 220 yards or 660 feet

1 mile (mi.) (also called statute mile) = 8 furlongs or 1,760 yards or 5,280 feet

1 league = 3 miles

AREA

Area is used to measure a section of a flat surface like the floor or the ground. Most area measurements are given in **square units.** Land is measured in **acres.**

1 square foot (sq. ft.) = 144 square inches (sq. in.)

1 square yard (sq. yd.) = 9 square feet or 1,296 square inches

1 square rod (sq. rd.) = 30¼ square yards

1 acre = 160 square rods or 4,840 square yards or 43,560 square feet

1 square mile (sq. mi.) = 640 acres

CAPACITY

Units of **capacity** are used to measure how much of something will fit into a container. **Liquid measure** is used to measure liquids, such as water or gasoline. **Dry measure** is used with large amounts of solid materials, like grain or fruit.

Dry Measure. Although both liquid and dry measures use the terms "pint" and "quart," they mean different amounts and should not be confused. Look at the lists below for examples.

1 quart (qt.) = 2 pints (pt.)

1 peck (pk.) = 8 quarts

1 bushel (bu.) = 4 pecks

Liquid Measure. Although the basic unit in liquid measure is the **gill** (4 fluid ounces), you are more likely to find liquids measured in pints or larger units.

1 gill = 4 fluid ounces

1 pint (pt.) = 4 gills or 16 ounces

1 quart (qt.) = 2 pints or 32 ounces

1 gallon (gal.) = 4 quarts = 128 ounces

For measuring most U.S. liquids,
   1 barrel (bbl.) = 31½ gallons

For measuring oil,
   1 barrel (bbl.) = 42 gallons

Cooking measurements. Cooking measure is used to measure amounts of solid and liquid foods used in cooking. The measurements used in cooking are based on the **fluid ounce**.

1 teaspoon (tsp.) = ⅙ fluid ounce (fl. oz.)

1 tablespoon (tbsp.) = 3 teaspoons or
                          ½ fluid ounce

1 cup = 16 tablespoons or 8 fluid ounces

1 pint = 2 cups

1 quart = 2 pints

1 gallon = 4 quarts

VOLUME

The amount of space taken up by an object (or the amount of space available within an object) is measured in **volume**. Volume is usually expressed in **cubic units**. If you wanted to buy a room air conditioner and needed to know how much space there was to be cooled, you could measure the room in cubic feet.

1 cubic foot (cu. ft.) = 1,728 cubic inches
                          (cu. in.)

1 cubic yard (cu. yd.) = 27 cubic feet

DEPTH

Some measurements of length are used to measure ocean depth and distance.

1 fathom = 6 feet

1 cable = 120 fathoms or 720 feet

1 nautical mile = 6,076.1 feet or
                   1.15 statute miles

WEIGHT

Although 1 cubic foot of popcorn and 1 cubic foot of rock take up the same amount of space, they wouldn't feel the same if you tried to lift them. We measure heaviness as **weight**. Most objects are measured in **avoirdupois weight** (pronounced a-ver-de-POIZ), although precious metals and medicines use different systems.

1 dram (dr.) = 27.344 grains (gr.)

1 ounce (oz.) = 16 drams or 437.5 grains

1 pound (lb.) = 16 ounces

1 hundredweight (cwt.) =
   100 pounds

1 ton = 2,000 pounds
   (also called short ton)

THE METRIC SYSTEM

Do you ever wonder how much soda you are getting when you buy a bottle that holds 1 liter? Or do you wonder how long a 50-meter swimming pool is? Or how far away from Montreal, Canada, you would be when a map says "8 kilometers"?

Every system of measurement uses a basic unit for measuring. In the U.S. customary system, the basic unit for length is the inch. In the metric system, the basic unit for length is the **meter**. The metric system also uses **liter** as a basic unit of volume or capacity and the **gram** as a basic unit of mass. The related units are made by adding a prefix to the basic unit. The prefixes and their meanings are:

milli- = $^1/_{1,000}$	**deci-** = $^1/_{10}$	**hecto-** = 100
centi- = $^1/_{100}$	**deka-** = 10	**kilo-** = 1,000

FOR EXAMPLE:

millimeter (mm)	= $^1/_{1,000}$ of a meter		milligram (mg)	= $^1/_{1,000}$ of a gram
centimeter (cm)	= $^1/_{100}$ of a meter		centigram (cg)	= $^1/_{100}$ of a gram
decimeter (dm)	= $^1/_{10}$ of a meter		decigram (dg)	= $^1/_{10}$ of a gram
dekameter (dm)	= 10 meters		dekagram (dg)	= 10 grams
hectometer (hm)	= 100 meters		hectogram (hg)	= 100 grams
kilometer (km)	= 1,000 meters		kilogram (kg)	= 1,000 grams

To get a rough idea of what measurements equal in the metric system, it helps to know that a liter is a little more than a quart. A meter is a little over a yard. And a kilometer is less than a mile.

A bottle of soda that holds 2 liters holds a little more than 2 quarts (2.1 quarts to be exact).

A football field is 100 yards long. It is a little more than 90 meters (91.4 meters to be exact).

METRIC MATH MISTAKE COSTS MILLIONS

Question: How did NASA, the U.S. space agency, lose a spacecraft worth $125 million?

Answer: Two teams of workers doing math calculations didn't use the same system of measurements.

The *Mars Climate Orbiter* was supposed to be the first interplanetary weather satellite. The spacecraft was entering orbit around Mars, but stopped sending information back to Earth when it passed behind the planet.

Before the craft began its journey, one team of workers had programmed its navigation data using the metric system. Not realizing this, another team of workers used U.S. customary units. The mission failed because the craft could not convert the two systems of measurement—a costly misunderstanding that could easily have been prevented.

How to Convert Measurements

Do you want to convert feet to meters or miles to kilometers? You first need to know how many meters are in one foot or how many kilometers are in one mile. The tables below show how to convert units in the U.S. customary system to units in the metric system and how to convert metric units to U.S. customary units.

If you want to convert numbers from one system to the other, a calculator would be helpful for doing the multiplication.

Converting U.S. Customary Units to Metric Units

If you know the number of	Multiply by	To get the number of
inches	2.5400	centimeters
inches	.0254	meters
feet	30.4800	centimeters
feet	.3048	meters
yards	.9144	meters
miles	1.6093	kilometers
square inches	6.4516	square centimeters
square feet	.0929	square meters
square yards	.8361	square meters
acres	.4047	hectares
cubic inches	16.3871	cubic centimeters
cubic feet	.0283	cubic meters
cubic yards	.7646	cubic meters
quarts (liquid)	.9464	liters
ounces	28.3495	grams
pounds	.4536	kilograms

Converting Metric Units to U.S. Customary Units

If you know the number of	Multiply by	To get the number of
centimeters	.3937	inches
centimeters	.0328	feet
meters	39.3701	inches
meters	3.2808	feet
meters	1.0936	yards
kilometers	.621	miles
square centimeters	.1550	square inches
square meters	10.7639	square feet
square meters	1.1960	square yards
hectares	2.4710	acres
cubic centimeters	.0610	cubic inches
cubic meters	35.3147	cubic feet
cubic meters	1.3080	cubic yards
liters	1.0567	quarts (liquid)
grams	.0353	ounces
kilograms	2.2046	pounds

? Which ancient people invented democracy?
You can find the answer on page 310.

Highlights of WORLD HISTORY

The section on World History is divided into five parts. Each part is a major region of the world: the Middle East, Africa, Asia, Europe, and the Americas. Major events from ancient times to the present are described under the headings for each region.

THE ANCIENT MIDDLE EAST 4000 B.C.–1 B.C.

4000–3000 B.C.
▶ The world's first cities are built by the Sumerian peoples in Mesopotamia, now southern Iraq.
▶ Egyptians develop a kind of writing called hieroglyphics.
▶ Sumerians develop a kind of writing called cuneiform.

Great Pyramid ▶ of Cheops, Giza, Egypt

2700 B.C. Egyptians begin building the great pyramids in the desert. The pharaohs' (kings') bodies are buried in them.

1792 B.C. First written laws are created in Babylonia. They are called the Code of Hammurabi.

ACHIEVEMENTS OF THE ANCIENT MIDDLE EAST
Early peoples of the Middle East:
❶ Studied the stars (astronomy).
❷ Invented the wheel.
❸ Created alphabets from picture drawings (hieroglyphics and cuneiform).
❹ Established the 24-hour day.
❺ Studied medicine and mathematics.

1200 B.C. Hebrew people settle in Canaan in Palestine after escaping from slavery in Egypt. They are led by the prophet Moses.

THE TEN COMMANDMENTS
Unlike most early peoples in the Middle East, the Hebrews believed in only one God (monotheism). They believed their faith was given to Moses in the Ten Commandments on Mount Sinai when they fled Egypt.

▲ *Trail to top of Mount Sinai*

1000 B.C. King David unites the Hebrews in one strong kingdom.

ANCIENT PALESTINE
Palestine was invaded by many different peoples after 1000 B.C., including the Babylonians, the Egyptians, the Persians, and the Romans. It came under Arab Muslim control in the 600s and remained mainly under Muslim control until the 1900s.

336 B.C. Alexander the Great, King of Macedonia, builds an empire from Egypt to India.

63 B.C. Romans conquer Palestine and make it part of their empire.

AROUND 4 B.C. Jesus Christ, the founder of the Christian religion, is born in Bethlehem. He is crucified about A.D. 29.

All About...
EGYPTIAN MUMMIES

Ancient Egypt brings to mind pyramids and mummies. They belong together in many ways.

The pyramids were built beginning around 2700 B.C. to protect the eternal souls of the pharaohs who ruled the kingdom. The remains of about 70 pyramids still exist. The famous pyramids at Giza are among the Seven Wonders of the Ancient World; the largest is composed of 2.3 million blocks, weighing an average of 2.5 metric tons each. Building these pyramids took back-breaking labor by large numbers of workers.

Egyptians also believed that the souls of the pharaohs would need their bodies in the next life. The dry, sandy conditions in Egypt were perfect for preserving dead bodies, and the Egyptians developed advanced techniques for embalming and drying out bodies—so that they could last for thousands of years. Embalmers removed almost all the internal organs and replaced them with cloth, mud, or sawdust. Then they used chemicals to dry out the rest of the body. The entire process took more than two months.

The Egyptian art of embalming peaked around 1600 to 1100 B.C. It was an expensive process, so most of the people who had their bodies mummified were rich, in many cases royalty. Over time, though, ordinary Egyptians joined in the practice. Mummy-making finally came to an end around the A.D. 300s. At that time, many Egyptians were becoming Christians, and preserving bodies after death became less important. (A form of embalming is widely practiced today, but it is not long-lasting.)

In the centuries that followed, many mummies were destroyed. From about 1200 to 1600, Europeans often ground them up and put them in medicines. But by the 1800s, scientists were studying mummies to see what clues they gave about the past. For instance, we know from them that tooth decay was a big problem for ancient Egyptians. Apparently, desert sand got into their bread and wore down their teeth, leading to infections that weakened their health. The Egyptians suffered from many kinds of illnesses that struck at all ages, keeping the average life span at only around 35 to 40 years.

Perhaps the most famous mummy belongs to an unimportant Egyptian pharaoh named Tutankhamen. King Tut, as he's called, ruled for less than ten years, in the late 1300s B.C.,

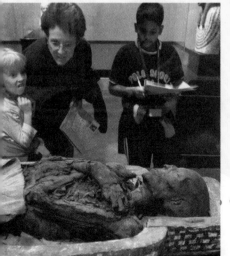

when he was still a boy. He died of unknown causes when he was only around 16 years old. King Tut's burial place is the only royal Egyptian tomb uncovered so far that was not emptied by grave robbers.

Thanks to the discovery of Tut's tomb in 1922, we have an idea of how much wealth was buried along with the mummified bodies of pharaohs. "Can you see anything?" asked one of the men who discovered the tomb as he stood at an opening. "Yes," came the reply from his fellow explorer. "Yes, wonderful things!"

THE MIDDLE EAST A.D. 1-1940s

ISLAM: A RELIGION GROWS IN THE MIDDLE EAST

570-632 Muhammad is born in Mecca in Arabia. In 610, as a prophet, he proclaims and teaches Islam, a religion which spreads from Arabia to all the neighboring regions in the Middle East and North Africa. His followers are called Muslims.

THE KORAN The holy book of Islam is the Koran. It was related by Muhammad beginning in 611. The Koran gives Muslims a program they must follow. For example, it gives rules about how one should treat one's parents and neighbors.

632 Muhammad dies. By now, Islam is accepted in Arabia as a religion.

641 Arab Muslims conquer the Persians.

LATE 600s Islam begins to spread to the west into Africa and Spain.

711-732 Umayyads invade Europe but are defeated by Frankish leader Charles Martel in France. This defeat halts the spread of Islam into Western Europe.

1071 Muslim Turks conquer Jerusalem.

1095-1291 Europeans try to take back Jerusalem and other parts of the Middle East for Christians during the Crusades.

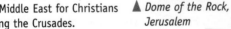
▲ Dome of the Rock, Jerusalem

THE SPREAD OF ISLAM

The Arab armies that went across North Africa brought great change:

❶ The people who lived there were converted to Islam.

❷ The Arabic language replaced many local languages as an official language. North Africa is still an Arabic-speaking region today, and Islam is the major faith.

ACHIEVEMENTS OF THE UMAYYAD AND ABBASID DYNASTIES

The Umayyads (661-750) and the Abbasids (750-1256) were the first two Muslim-led dynasties. Both empires stretched across northern Africa across the Middle East and into Asia. Both were known for great achievements. They:

❶ Studied math and medicine.

❷ Translated the works of other peoples, including Greeks and Persians.

❸ Spread news of Chinese inventions like paper and gunpowder.

❹ Wrote great works on religion and philosophy.

1300-1900s The Ottoman Turks, who were Muslims, created a huge empire, covering the Middle East, North Africa, and part of Eastern Europe. The Ottoman Empire fell apart gradually, and European countries took over portions of it beginning in the 1800s.

1914-1918 World War I begins in 1914. The Ottoman Empire has now broken apart. Most of the Middle East falls under British or French control.

1921 Two new Arab kingdoms are created: Transjordan and Iraq. The French take control of Syria and Lebanon.

1922 Egypt becomes independent from Britain.

JEWS MIGRATE TO PALESTINE

Jewish settlers from Europe began migrating to Palestine in the 1880s. They wanted to return to the historic homeland of the Hebrew people.

In 1945, after World War II, many Jews who survived the Holocaust migrated to Palestine. Arabs living in the region opposed the Jewish immigration. In 1948, after the British left, war broke out between the Jews and the Arabs.

THE MIDDLE EAST 1948-1990s

1948 The state of Israel is created.

THE ARAB-ISRAELI WARS Arab countries near Israel (Egypt, Iraq, Jordan, Lebanon, and Syria) attack the new country in 1948 but fail to destroy it. Israel and its neighbors fight wars again in 1956, 1967, and 1973. Israel wins each war. In the 1967 war, Israel captures the Sinai Desert from Egypt, the Golan Heights from Syria, and the area known as the West Bank from Jordan.

1979 Egypt and Israel sign a peace treaty. Israel returns the Sinai to Egypt.

THE MIDDLE EAST AND OIL Much of the oil we use to drive our cars, heat our homes, and run our machines comes from the Arabian peninsula in the Middle East. For a brief time in 1973-1974, Arab nations would not let their oil be sold to the United States because of its support of Israel. After that, the United States tried not to rely so much on oil imports.

THE 1990s

▶ In 1991, the United States and its allies go to war with Iraq after Iraq invades neighboring Kuwait. The conflict, known as the Persian Gulf War, results in the defeat of Iraq's army. Iraq signs a peace agreement but is accused by the United States and others of violating the peace terms, especially of making weapons for chemical and germ warfare.

▶ Israel and the Palestine Liberation Organization (PLO) agree to work toward peace (1993). In 1995, Prime Minister Yitzhak Rabin of Israel is assassinated. Benjamin Netanyahu, a critic of Rabin's peace policies, becomes prime minister. Negotiations continue, but go slowly. In 1999, Netanyahu loses office and Ehud Barak becomes prime minister. Barak has been more active in seeking peace.

ANCIENT AFRICA 3500 B.C.—A.D. 900

ANCIENT AFRICA In ancient times, northern Africa was dominated, for the most part, by the Egyptians, Greeks, and Romans. However, we know very little about the lives of ancient people in Africa south of the Sahara Desert (sub-Saharan Africa).

The people of Africa south of the Sahara did not have written languages in ancient times. What we learn about them comes from such things as weapons, tools, and other items from their civilization that have been found in the earth.

2000 B.C. The Kingdom of Kush arises just south of Egypt. It becomes a major center of art, learning, and trade. Kush dies out around A.D. 350.

500 B.C. The Nok culture becomes strong in Nigeria, in West Africa. The Nok use iron for tools and weapons. They are also known for their fine terra-cotta ▼ sculptures of heads.

AROUND A.D. 1 Bantu-speaking peoples in West Africa begin to move into eastern and southern Africa.

50 The Kingdom of Axum in northern Ethiopia, founded by traders from Arabia, becomes a wealthy trading center for ivory.

400 Ghana, the first known African state south of the Sahara Desert, rules the upper Senegal and Niger river region. It controls the trade in gold that is being sent from the southern parts of Africa north to the Mediterranean Sea.

660s-900 The Islamic religion begins to spread across North Africa and into Spain. The Arabic language takes root in North Africa, replacing local languages.

AFRICA 900s-1990s

900 Arab Muslims begin to settle along the coast of East Africa. Their contact with Bantu people produces the Swahili language, which is still spoken today.

1050 The Almoravid Kingdom in Morocco, North Africa, is powerful from Ghana to as far north as Spain.

1230 The Mali Kingdom begins in North Africa. Timbuktu, a center for trade and learning, is its main city.

1464 The Songhai Empire becomes strong in West Africa. By 1530, it has destroyed Mali. The Songhai are remembered for their bronze sculptures.

1505-1575 Portuguese settlement begins in Africa. Portuguese people settle in Angola and Mozambique.

THE AFRICAN SLAVE TRADE

Once Europeans began settling in the New World, they needed people to harvest their sugar. The first African slaves were taken to the Caribbean. Later, slaves were taken to South America and the United States. The slaves were crowded onto ships and many died during the long journey. Shipping of African slaves to the United States lasted until the early 1800s.

1652-1835

❶ Dutch settlers arrive in southern Africa. They are known as the Boers.

❷ Shaka the Great forms a Zulu Empire in eastern Africa. The Zulus are warriors.

❸ The "Great Trek" (march) of the Boers north takes place. They defeat the Zulus at the Battle of Bloody River.

 ▼ Zulu doll

1880S: EUROPEAN COLONIES IN AFRICA European settlers start moving into the interior of Africa and forming colonies in the mid-1800s. The major European countries with colonies in Africa were:

❶ **Great Britain:** East and Central Africa, from Egypt to South Africa.
❷ **France:** Most of West Africa and North Africa.
❸ **Spain:** Parts of Northwest Africa.
❹ **Portugal:** Mozambique (East Africa) and Angola (West Africa).
❺ **Italy:** Libya (North Africa) and Somalia (East Africa).
❻ **Germany:** East and Southwest Africa.
❼ **Belgium:** South Central Africa.

1899: BOER WAR The South African War between Great Britain and the Boers begins. It is also called the Boer War. The Boers accept British rule but are allowed a role in government.

1948 The white South African government creates the policy of apartheid, the total separation of blacks and whites. Blacks are banned from restaurants, theaters, schools, and jobs considered "white." Apartheid sparked protests, many of which ended in bloodshed.

1950S: AFRICAN INDEPENDENCE African colonies begin to receive their independence in the 1950s from Britain, France, Spain, and other European countries.

1983 Droughts (water shortages) lead to starvation over much of Africa.

THE 1990S Apartheid is ended in South Africa. Nelson Mandela, a black freedom fighter, becomes South Africa's first black president in 1994. Warfare between two groups, the Hutus and Tutsis, breaks out in Rwanda and Burundi in the mid-1990s. About 500,000 people, mainly Tutsi, are killed, and approximately two million refugees flee.

ANCIENT ASIA 4000 B.C.–1 B.C.

4000 B.C. Communities of people settle in the Indus River Valley of India and Pakistan and the Yellow River Valley of China.

2500 B.C. Cities of Mohenjo-Daro and Harappa in Pakistan become centers of trade and farming.

 1600 B.C. Shang peoples in China build walled towns and use a kind of writing based on pictures. This writing develops into the writing Chinese people use today.

1500 B.C. The Hindu religion (Hinduism) begins to spread throughout India.

1027 B.C. Chou peoples in China overthrow the Shang and control large territories.

700 B.C. In China, a 500-year period begins in which many warring states fight one another.

563 B.C. Gautama Siddhartha is born in India. He becomes known as the Buddha—which means the "Enlightened One"—and is the founder of the Buddhist religion (Buddhism).

551 B.C. The Chinese philosopher Confucius is born. His teachings—especially the rules and morals about how people should treat each other and get along—spread throughout China and are still followed today.

TWO IMPORTANT ASIAN RELIGIONS
Many of the world's religions began in Asia. Two of the most important were:
1. **Hinduism.** Hinduism began in India and has spread to other parts of southern Asia and to parts of the Pacific region.
2. **Buddhism.** Buddhism also began in India and spread to China, Japan, and Southeast Asia.

Today, both religions have millions of followers all over the world.

320-232 B.C.: INDIA
1. Northern India is united under the emperor Chandragupta Maurya.
2. Asoka, emperor of India, begins to send Buddhist missionaries throughout southern Asia to spread the Buddhist religion.

221 B.C. The Chinese ruler Shih Huang Ti makes the Chinese language the same throughout the country. Around the same time, the Chinese begin building the Great Wall of China. It is 1,500 miles long and is meant to keep invading peoples from the north out of China.

202 B.C. The Han people in China won control of China.

ACHIEVEMENTS OF THE ANCIENT CHINESE
1. Invented paper.
2. Invented gunpowder.
3. Studied astronomy.
4. Studied engineering.
5. Invented acupuncture to treat illnesses.

The Great Wall of China ▼

ASIA A.D. 1-1700s

320 The Gupta Empire controls northern India. The Guptas are Hindus. They drive the Buddhist religion out of India. The Guptas are well known for their many advances in the study of mathematics and medicine.

618 The Tang dynasty begins in China. The Tang are famous for inventing the compass and for advances in surgery and the arts. They trade silk, spices, and ivory as far away as Africa.

960 The Northern Sung Dynasty in China makes advances in banking and paper money. China's population of 50 million doubles over 200 years, thanks to improved ways of farming that lead to greater food production.

1000 The Samurai, a warrior people, become powerful in Japan. They live by a code of honor known as Bushido.

1180 The Angkor Empire is powerful in Cambodia. The empire became widely known for its beautiful temples.

1206 The Mongol people of Asia are united under the ruler Genghis Khan. He builds a huge army and creates an empire that stretches all the way from China to India, Russia, and Eastern Europe.

▼ *Detail of Angkor Wat temple, Cambodia*

1264 Kublai Khan, the grandson of Genghis Khan, rules China as emperor from his new capital at Beijing.

1368 The Ming Dynasty comes to power in China. The Ming drive the Mongols out of the country.

THE SILK ROAD Around 100 B.C., only the Chinese knew how to make silk. Europeans were willing to pay high prices for the light, comfortable material. To get it, they sent fortunes in glass, gold, jade, and other items to China. The exchanges between Europeans and Chinese created one of the greatest trading routes in history—the Silk Road. Chinese inventions such as paper and gunpowder were also spread over the Silk Road. Europeans found out how to make silk around A.D. 500, but trade continued until about 1400.

1467-1603: WAR AND PEACE IN JAPAN
❶ Civil war breaks out in Japan. The conflicts last more than 100 years.
❷ Peace comes to Japan under the military leader Hideyoshi.
❸ The Shogun period begins in Japan, and lasts until 1868. Europeans are driven out of the country and Christians are persecuted.

1526-1556: THE MUGHALS IN INDIA
❶ The Mughal Empire in India begins under Babur. The Mughals are Muslims who invade and conquer India.
❷ Akbar, the grandson of Babur, becomes Mughal emperor of India. He attempts to unite Hindus and Muslims but does not succeed.

1644 The Ming Dynasty in China is overthrown by the Manchu peoples. They allow more Europeans to trade in China.

1739 Nadir Shah, a Persian warrior, conquers parts of western India and captures the city of Delhi.

MODERN ASIA 1800s-1990s

1839 The Opium War takes place in China between the Chinese and the British. The British and other Western powers want to control trade in Asia. The Chinese want the British to stop selling opium to the Chinese. Britain wins the war.

1858 The French begin to take control of Indochina (Southeast Asia).

1868 The Shogunate dynasty ends in Japan. The new ruler is Emperor Meiji. Western ideas begin to influence the Japanese.

THE JAPANESE IN ASIA Japan became a powerful country during the early 20th century. It was a small country with few raw materials of its own. For example, Japan had to buy oil from other countries. The Japanese army and navy took control of the government during the 1930s. Japan soon began to invade some of its neighbors. In 1941, the United States and Japan went to war after Japan attacked the U.S. Navy at Pearl Harbor, Hawaii.

1945 Japan is defeated in World War II after the U.S. drops atomic bombs on the Japanese cities of Hiroshima and Nagasaki.

1947 India and Pakistan become independent from Great Britain, which had ruled them as colonies since the mid-1800s.

1949 China comes under the rule of the Communists led by Mao Zedong.

CHINA UNDER THE COMMUNISTS The Communists brought great changes to China. Private property was abolished, and the government took over all businesses and farms. Religions were persecuted. China became more isolated from other countries.

1950-1953: THE KOREAN WAR North Korea, a Communist country, invades South Korea. The U.S. and other nations join to fight the invasion. China joins North Korea. The Korean War ends in 1953. Neither side wins.

1954-1975: THE VIETNAM WAR The French are defeated in Indochina in 1954 by the Vietminh. The Vietminh are Vietnamese fighters under the leadership of the Communists headed by Ho Chi Minh. The U.S. sends troops to fight in the Vietnam War in 1965 on the side of South Vietnam against Ho Chi Minh and Communist North Vietnam. The U.S. withdraws from the war in 1973. In 1975, South Vietnam is defeated and taken over by North Vietnam.

1972 President Richard Nixon visits Communist China. Relations between China and the United States improve.

1989 Chinese students protest for democracy, but the protests are crushed by the army in Tiananmen Square.

THE 1990s The economies of Japan, South Korea, Taiwan, and some other Asian countries show great growth in the early 1990s. But during the late 1990s, several Asian nations have serious financial trouble. The British, rulers of Hong Kong, return it to China in 1997. Macao becomes part of China in 1999. China builds its economy, but is accused of violating human rights.

▼ *Hong Kong*

ANCIENT EUROPE 4000 B.C.–300 B.C.

4000 B.C. People in many parts of Europe start building monuments out of large stones called megaliths. Examples can still be seen today, including Stonehenge in England.

2500 B.C.–1200 B.C.: THE MINOANS AND THE MYCENAEANS

❶ People on the island of Crete (Minoans) in the Mediterranean Sea built great palaces and became sailors and traders.

❷ People in the city of Mycenae in Greece built stone walls and a great palace.

❸ Mycenaean people invaded Crete and destroyed the power of the Minoans.

THE TROJAN WAR The Trojan War was a conflict between invading Greeks and the people of Troas (Troy) in Southwestern Turkey around the year 1200 B.C. Although little is known today about the real war, it has become a part of Greek poetry and mythology. According to a famous legend, a group of Greek soldiers hid inside a huge wooden horse. The horse was pulled into the city of Troy. Then the soldiers jumped out of the horse and conquered Troy.

900–600 B.C. Celtic peoples in Northern Europe settle on farms and in villages and learn to mine for iron ore.

700 B.C. Etruscan peoples rule most of Italy until 400 B.C. They build many cities and become traders.

▼ Stonehenge

SOME ACHIEVEMENTS OF THE GREEKS
The early Greeks were responsible for:

❶ The first governments that were elected by people. Greeks invented democratic government.

❷ Great poets such as Homer, who composed the *Iliad,* a long poem about the Trojan War and the *Odyssey,* an epic poem about the travels of Odysseus.

❸ Great philosophers such as Socrates, Plato, and Aristotle.

❹ Great architecture, like the Parthenon in Athens, which can still be seen (*see below*).

431 B.C. The Peloponnesian Wars begin between the Greek cities of Athens and Sparta. The wars end in 404 B.C. when Sparta wins.

338 B.C. King Philip II of Macedonia in northern Greece conquers all the cities of Greece.

336 B.C. Philip's son Alexander becomes king. He conquers lands and makes an empire from the Mediterranean Sea to India. He is known as Alexander the Great. For the next 300 years, Greek culture dominates this vast area.

EUROPE 300 B.C.–A.D. 800s

264 B.C.-A.D. 476: ROMAN EMPIRE The city of Rome in Italy begins to expand and captures surrounding lands. The Romans gradually build a great empire and control all of the Mediterranean region. At its height, the Roman Empire includes Western Europe, Greece, Egypt, and much of the Middle East. The Roman Empire lasts until A.D. 476.

ROMAN ACHIEVEMENTS

1. Roman law. Many of our laws are based on Roman law.
2. Great roads to connect their huge empire. The Appian Way, south of Rome, is a Roman road that is still in use today.
3. Aqueducts to bring water to the people in large cities.
4. Great sculpture. Roman statues can still be seen in Europe.
5. Great architecture. The Colosseum, which still stands in Rome today, is an example of great Roman architecture.
6. Great writers, such as the poet Vergil, who wrote the *Aeneid*.

49 B.C. A civil war breaks out that destroys Rome's republican form of government.

45 B.C. Julius Caesar becomes the sole ruler of Rome but is murdered one year later by rivals in the Roman army.

27 B.C. Octavian becomes the first emperor of Rome. He takes the name Augustus. A peaceful period of almost 200 years begins.

THE CHRISTIAN FAITH Christians believe that Jesus Christ is the Son of God. The history and beliefs of Christianity are found in the New Testament of the Bible. Christianity spread slowly throughout the Roman Empire. The Romans tried to stop the new religion and persecuted the Christians. They were forced to hold their services in hiding, and some were crucified. Eventually, more and more Romans became Christian.

337 The Roman Emperor Constantine the Great becomes a Christian. He is the first Roman emperor to be a Christian.

410 The Visigoths and other barbarian tribes from northern Europe invade the Roman Empire and begin to take over its lands.

476 The last Roman emperor is overthrown.

THE BYZANTINE EMPIRE, centered in modern-day Turkey, was made up of the eastern half of the old Roman Empire. Byzantine rulers extended their power into western Europe. The great Byzantine Emperor Justinian ruled parts of Spain, North Africa, and Italy. The city of Constantinople (now Istanbul, Turkey) became the capital of the Byzantine Empire in 330.

768 Charlemagne becomes king of the Franks in northern Europe. He rules a kingdom that includes parts of France, Germany and northern Italy.

800 Feudalism becomes important in Europe. Feudalism means that poor farmers are allowed to farm a lord's land in return for certain services to the lord.

▼ *The Colosseum, Rome, Italy*

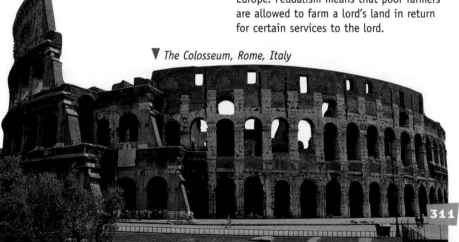

EUROPE 800s–1500s

898 Magyar peoples from lands east of Russia found Hungary.

800s–900s Viking warriors and traders from Scandinavia begin to move into the British Isles, France, and parts of the Mediterranean.

Viking ship ▶

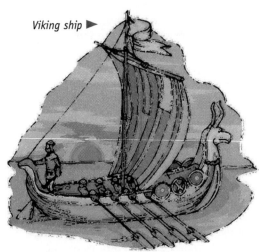

989 The Russian state of Kiev becomes Christian.

1066 William of Normandy, a Frenchman, successfully invades England and makes himself king. He is known as William the Conqueror.

1096–1291: THE CRUSADES
In 1096, Christian European kings and nobles sent a series of armies to the Middle East to try to capture the city of Jerusalem from the Muslims. Between 1096 and 1291 there were about ten Crusades. During the Crusades the Europeans briefly captured Jerusalem. But in the end, the Crusades did not succeed in their aim.

One of the most important results of the Crusades had nothing to do with religion: trade increased greatly between the Middle East and Europe.

1215: THE MAGNA CARTA The Magna Carta is a document agreed to by King John of England and the English nobility. The English king agreed that he did not have absolute power and had to obey the laws of the land. The Magna Carta was an important step toward democracy.

1290 The beginning of the Ottoman Empire. It is controlled by Turkish Muslims who conquer lands in the eastern Mediterranean and the Middle East.

1337–1453: WAR AND PLAGUE IN EUROPE
❶ The Hundred Years' War (1337) begins in Europe between France and England. The war lasts until 1453 when France wins.
❷ The bubonic plague begins in Europe (1348). The plague, also called the Black Death, is a deadly disease caused by the bite of infected fleas. Perhaps as many as one third of the whole population of Europe die from the plague.

1453 The Ottoman Turks capture the city of Constantinople and rename it Istanbul.

1517: THE REFORMATION The Reformation led to the breakup of the Christian church into Protestant and Roman Catholic branches in Europe. It started when the German priest Martin Luther opposed some teachings of the Church. He broke away from the pope (the leader of the Catholic church) and had many followers. He believed and said that God makes himself known especially through the Bible.

1534 King Henry VIII of England breaks away from the Roman Catholic church. He names himself head of the English (Anglican) church.

1558 The reign of King Henry's daughter Elizabeth I begins in England. During her long rule, England's power grows.

1588 The Spanish Armada (fleet of warships) is defeated by the English navy as Spain tries to invade England.

MODERN EUROPE 1600s-1990s

1600 The Ottoman Turks attack central Europe. They take control of territories in the Balkan region of southeastern Europe.

1618 The Thirty Years' War begins in Europe. The war is fought over religious issues. Much of Europe is destroyed in the conflict, which ends in 1648.

1642 The English civil war begins. King Charles I fights against the forces of the Parliament (legislature). The king's forces are defeated, and he is executed in 1649. But his son, Charles II, eventually returns as king in 1660.

1762 Catherine the Great becomes the Empress of Russia. She allows religious freedom and extends the Russian Empire.

1789: THE FRENCH REVOLUTION The French Revolution ended the rule of kings in France and led to democracy there. At first, however, there were wars, much bloodshed, and times when dictators took control. Many people were executed. King Louis XVI and Queen Marie Antoinette were overthrown in the Revolution, and both were executed in 1793.

1799 Napoleon Bonaparte, an army officer, becomes dictator of France. Under his rule, France conquers most of Europe by 1812.

1815 Napoleon's forces are defeated by the British and German armies at Waterloo (in Belgium). Napoleon is exiled to a remote island and dies there in 1821.

1848 Revolutions break out in countries of Europe. People force their rulers to make more democratic changes.

▲ *Napoleon Bonaparte*

1914-1918: WORLD WAR I IN EUROPE At the start of World War I in Europe, Germany and Austria-Hungary opposed England, France, and Russia (the Allies). The United States joined the war in 1917 on the side of the Allies. The Allies won in 1918.

1917 The Russian Revolution takes place. The czar (emperor) is overthrown. The Bolsheviks (Communists) under Vladimir Lenin eventually take control of the government. The country is renamed the Soviet Union.

THE RISE OF HITLER Adolf Hitler became dictator of Germany in 1933. He joined forces with rulers in Italy and Japan to form the Axis powers. By 1939, the Axis had started World War II. They fought against the Allies—Great Britain, the Soviet Union, and the U.S. By 1945, Hitler and the Axis powers were defeated. During his 12-year reign, Hitler persecuted Jews, and killed at least six million (the Holocaust). He also persecuted and killed many political opponents, Gypsies, members of religious minorities, and others.

1945 The Cold War begins. It is a 45-year period of tension between the United States and the Soviet Union. Both countries build up their armies and make nuclear weapons but do not go to war.

THE 1990s Communist governments in Eastern Europe are replaced by democratic ones, and Germany becomes one nation. The Soviet Union breaks up. The European Union (EU), made up of 15 countries, takes steps toward European unity. Poland, Hungary, and the Czech Republic join the North Atlantic Treaty Organization (NATO). NATO bombs Yugoslavia in an effort to protect Albanians driven out of the Kosovo region.

THE AMERICAS 6000 B.C.-A.D. 1600s

6000 B.C. People in South America gather plants for food and hunt animals using stone-pointed spears.

3000 B.C. People in Central America begin farming, growing corn and beans for food.

1500 B.C. Mayan people in Central America begin to live in small villages.

500 B.C. People in North America begin to hunt buffalo to use for meat and for clothing.

100 B.C. The city of Teotihuacán is founded in Mexico. It becomes the center of a huge empire extending from central Mexico to Guatemala. Teotihuacán contains many large pyramids and temples.

A.D. 150 Mayan people in Guatemala build many centers for religious ceremonies. They create a calendar and learn mathematics and astronomy.

▲ *Mayan pyramid, Yucatan Peninsula, Mexico*

900 Toltec warriors in Mexico begin to invade lands of Mayan people. Mayans leave their old cities and move to the Yucatan Peninsula of Mexico.

1000 Native Americans in the southwestern United States begin to live in settlements called pueblos. They learn to farm.

1325 Mexican Indians known as Aztecs create huge city of Tenochtitlán and rule a large empire in Mexico. They are warriors who practice human sacrifice.

1492 Christopher Columbus sails from Europe across the Atlantic Ocean and lands in the Bahamas, in the Caribbean Sea. This marked the first step toward the founding of European settlements in the Americas.

1500 Portuguese explorers reach Brazil and claim it for Portugal.

1519 Spanish conqueror Hernán Cortés travels into the Aztec Empire in search of gold. The Aztecs are defeated in 1521 by Cortés. The Spanish take control of Mexico.

WHY DID THE SPANISH WIN?

How did the Spanish defeat the powerful Aztec Empire in such a short time? One reason is that the Spanish had better weapons. Another is that the Aztecs became sick and died from diseases brought to the New World by the Spanish. The Aztecs had never had these illnesses before and, as a result, did not have immunity to them. Also, many neighboring Indians hated the Aztecs as conquerors. Those Indians helped the Spanish to defeat them.

1534 Jacques Cartier of France explores Canada.

1583 The first English colony in North America is set up in Newfoundland, Canada. It is unsuccessful.

1607 English colonists led by Captain John Smith settle in Jamestown, Virginia. Virginia was the oldest of the Thirteen Colonies that turned into the United States.

1619 First African slaves arrive in English-controlled America.

1682 The French explorer Robert Cavalier sieur de La Salle sails down the Mississippi River. The area is named Louisiana after the French King Louis XIV.

THE AMERICAS 1700s

EUROPEAN COLONIES By 1700, most of the Americas are under the control of Europeans:

Spain: Florida, southwestern United States, Mexico, Central America, western South America.

Portugal: eastern South America.

France: central United States, parts of Canada.

England: eastern U.S., parts of Canada.

Holland: eastern U.S., West Indies, eastern South America.

1700 European colonies in North and South America begin to grow in population and wealth.

1775-1783: AMERICAN REVOLUTION The American Revolution begins in 1775 when the first shot is fired in Lexington, Massachusetts. The thirteen original British colonies in North America become independent under the Treaty of Paris, signed in 1783.

THE AMERICAS 1800s-1990s

SIMÓN BOLÍVAR: LIBERATOR OF SOUTH AMERICA

In 1810, Simón Bolívar began a revolt against Spain. He fought for more than 10 years against the Spanish and became president of the independent country of Greater Colombia in 1824. As a result of his leadership, ten South American countries had become independent from Spain by 1830. However, Bolívar himself was criticized as being a dictator.

SOUTH AMERICAN INDEPENDENCE

COUNTRY	YEAR OF INDEPENDENCE
Argentina	1816
Bolivia	1825
Brazil[1]	1822
Chile	1818
Colombia	1819
Ecuador	1830
Guyana[2]	1966
Mexico	1821
Paraguay	1811
Peru	1824
Suriname[3]	1973
Uruguay	1825
Venezuela	1821

❶ Brazil was governed by Portugal.
❷ Guyana was a British colony.
❸ Suriname was a Dutch colony.

1810-1910: MEXICO'S REVOLUTION In 1846, Mexico and the United States go to war. Mexico loses parts of the Southwest and California to the United States. A revolution in 1910 overthrows Porfirio Díaz.

1867 The Canadian provinces are united as the Dominion of Canada.

1898: THE SPANISH-AMERICAN WAR Spain and the United States fight a brief war in 1898. Spain loses its Caribbean colonies Cuba and Puerto Rico, and the Philippines in the Pacific.

U.S. POWER IN THE 1900s
During the 1900s the United States influenced affairs in Central America and the Caribbean. The United States sent troops to Mexico (1914; 1916–1917), Nicaragua (1912–1933), Haiti (1915–1934; 1994–1995), Dominican Republic (1965), Grenada (1983), and Panama (1989). In 1962, the United States went on alert when the Soviet Union put missiles on Cuba, only 90 miles from Florida.

1990s In 1994, the North American Free Trade Agreement (NAFTA) is signed to increase trade between the United States, Canada, and Mexico. Relations between the United States and Cuba remain hostile.

WORLD HISTORY PUZZLE

The dates give you clues about where you can find specific answers.

ACROSS

1. _____ the Great of Macedonia (336 B.C.)
5. French explorer of the Mississippi (1682)
7. Their empire was destroyed by Cortes (1519)
8. Palestine Liberation Organization (1990s)
9. Launched an armada against England (1588)
11. Ancient Egyptian picture drawing (4000–3000 B.C.)
13. This European city begins to expand in 264 B.C.
15. Turks built the _____ Empire (1300)
16. Cold ___, tension between the U.S. and Soviet Union (1945)
17. English king executed in 1649
19. Dutch settler in South Africa (1770)
20. Changed his name to Augustus (29 B.C.)
22. Ancient Hebrews believed in ___ God (4000–1 B.C.)
24. Name for emperor of Russia (1917)
25. Mexico and the _____ States go to war (1846)

DOWN

1. South Africa's policy of separation of the races begins (1948)
2. _____ Mandela, first president of South Africa (1994)
3. French dictator who lost at Waterloo (1815)
4. They ruled most of Italy until 400 B.C.
6. Grandson of Genghis Khan: _____ Khan (1264)
10. _____ Wars between Athens and Sparta (431 B.C.)
11. Author of the *Iliad* (700s B.C.)
12. Protestants break away from Catholic Church (1517)
14. Name of a Cambodian empire (1180)
17. British document that led to democracy: Magna _____ (1215)
18. The _____ empire fell in A.D. 476
21. Israel and its _____ neighbors fought wars beginning in 1948
23. The European Union is abbreviated this way (1900s)

Answers are on pages 317–320.

PUZZLE ANSWERS

ANIMALS, Page 39 WORD SEARCH

S	D	N	A	L	S	S	A	R	G
P	E	T	U	R	T	L	E	E	B
E	N	D	A	N	G	E	R	E	D
C	T	O	R	R	A	P	A	L	R
I	S	G	O	R	F	A	M	I	A
E	R	U	A	S	O	N	I	D	G
S	R	A	E	B	E	D	N	O	O
W	O	R	C	U	B	A	O	C	N
I	N	S	E	C	T	Z	I	O	F
X	O	D	I	K	R	A	L	R	L
E	K	O	Y	N	O	L	O	C	Y

MATCHING ANIMALS 1. h; 2. j; 3. a; 4. f; 5. b; 6. i; 7. c; 8. d; 9. e; 10. g.

COMPUTERS

Page 60: HERE'S A BL: 1. b; 2. a; 3. a; 4. b; 5. a; 6. a; 7. b; 8. a.

Page 61: FIND THE FACTS a. 38; b. 11; c. 378; d. 46; e. 7.

The formula is: $(38 \times b) - c + d - e = X$

$$(38 \times 11) - 378 + 46 - 7 = 79.$$

Page 61: FIND THE WORDS 1. That bug in the computer is actually a ba**by te**rmite; 2. Is slo **mo use**less in watching TV sports? No way! 3. Turn your mode**m on. It** ordinarily won't work until you do that; 4. If a ghost said **boo t**o me, I'd run; 5. Hey, show-off typists, if you s**print, er**rors will appear on the screen; 6. My floppy disk fell in the dirty clothes b**in. PU!** Throw it away! 7. For a writing **pro, gram**mar is the number one concern; 8. By sending e-mail**s, can ner**ds make more friends?

ENVIRONMENT, Page 76 ENVIRONMENT PUZZLE

Across/Down entries shown in grid:

4. MEDICINES
7. DROUGHT
11. A
12. CLIMATE
13. RATS
14. TREES
15. HABITAT
17. GREENHOUSE

Down words include: 1. B... 2. B... 3. B... 5. BA... 6. H... 8. OX... 9. G... 10. FOSSIL

317

PUZZLE ANSWERS

GEOGRAPHY, Page 85

MATCH THE SIGHT WITH THE SITE
1. b; 2. c; 3. d; 4. e; 5. a

DISCOVER THE CONTINENTS
AUSTRALIA, EUROPE, ANTARCTICA, SOUTH AMERICA, NORTH AMERICA, AFRICA, ASIA

EXPLORERS' PUZZLE

S	A	M	U	E	L	
J	A	C	Q	U	E	S
E	R	I	C	S	O	N
	B	A	L	B	O	A
H	U	D	S	O	N	
P	I	Z	A	R	R	O
	C	O	R	T	E	S

LANGUAGE

Page 104: PICTURE THIS
1. running into each other; 2. cold fish; 3. can of worms

Page 111: PICTURE THESE
1. going in a circle; 2. three degrees below zero; 3. backward glance; 4. far from home; 5. six of one kind, half a dozen of another; 6. Washington crossing the Delaware; 7. three-ring circus; 8. Oval Office; 9. he's beside himself; 10. mixed-up kid; 11. just between friends; 12. crossroads; 13. keep it under your hat; 14. check on your work; 15. leftover chicken

NATIONS, Page 154 NATIONS PUZZLE

Across/Down answers in grid:
- 1 F
- 2 SAINT VINCENT
- 3 TUVIAL... (Down): TUVALU
- 4 CANADA
- 5 CHAD
- 6 DENMARK
- 7 JAPAN
- 8 SPAIN
- 9 AUSTRALIA
- 10 SLOVENIA
- 11 AZERBAIJAN
- 12 ZAMBIA
- 13 GEORGIA
- 14 GUYANA
- 15 AUSTRIA
- 16 ITALY
- 17 TONGA
- 18 ISRAEL
- 19 GABON
- 20 MALAWI

318

NUMBERS

Page 171: ROMAN NUMERALS: MMI

Page 174: THE SPEEDY LETTER CARRIER

Page 174: TOOTHPICKS AND TRIANGLES

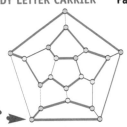

June starts here.

Page 174: WHICH NUMBER COMES NEXT?

a. 9, 11, 13, . . . (These are all odd numbers.)

b. 28, 36, 45, 55, . . . (the triangular numbers, 10 = 6 + 4, 15 = 10 + 5, 21 = 15 + 6, 28 = 21 + 7, 36 = 28 + 8, and so on)

c. 21, 34, 55, . . . (Each number is the sum of the two before it.)

Page 175: CLIP AND GUESS: The actual number of paper clips is 191.

POPULATION, Page 185

A CITIZENSHIP TEST 1. red, white, and blue; 2. the 13 original states; 3. passes the laws that govern the U.S.; 4. 100; 5. Native Americans; 6. Abraham Lincoln; 7. William H. Rehnquist; 8. Answers could include freedom of speech, freedom of religion, or right to vote; 9. Alaska and Hawaii; 10. 27

SIGNS & SYMBOLS, Page 207

CHANGING LETTERS, NUMBERS FOR LETTERS

You can use codes to send secret messages to your friends.

SECRET MESSAGE PUZZLE 1. I HAVE A SECRET; 2. YOU WILL NEVER GUESS WHO CALLED ME; 3. HE STARTED AS A RAPPER AND BECAME THE FRESH PRINCE; 4. RIGHT! WILL SMITH! 5. ONLY KIDDING! WISH IT WERE TRUE.

TRANSPORTATION, Page 239

TRANSPORTATION PUZZLE

Here are some words that can be formed from TRANSPORTATION, not counting plurals. How many of them did you find? Did you find any others?

3 letters: air, ant, apt, art, ion, nap, nip, not, oar, par, pan, pat, pin, pit, pot, ran, rap, rat, rip, rot, sap, sat, sin, sip, sir, sit, tan, tap, tar, tat, tin, tip, ton, top, tot

4 letters: atop, into, noon, onto, pain, pair, pant, part, past, pint, poor, port, post, rain, rant, rapt, rasp, riot, roar, root, snap, snip, soar, soon, soot, sort, span, spar, spat, spin, spit, spot, star, stir, stop, tarp, tart, tint, toot, tort, trap, trio, trip, trot

5 letters: apart, onion, paint, pants, pasta, patio, pinto, point, print, ratio, roast, roost, rotor, saint, satin, snoop, snort, sonar, spoon, sport, stain, stair, start, stint, stoop, strap, strip, taint, toast, train, trait, troop

6 letters: artist, nation, notion, option, orator, parrot, pastor, piston, potion, potato, prison, ration, rattan, sprain, strain, strait, sprint, tartan, torpor

7 letters: artisan, instant, portion, spartan, station, torsion, tortoni, traitor, transit

8 letters: aspirant, notation, portrait, rotation

9 letters: transport

PUZZLE ANSWERS

UNITED STATES

Page 270: FRED FABULOUS AND THE FAB FLYER 1. Austin, Pacific, California; 2. Hawaii; 3. Washington, Mt. Rainier, Olympic, North Cascades; 4. Dakota, Bismarck; 5. Des Moines; 6. Ohio; 7. Tennessee; 8. Austin; 9. Atlantic

Page 294: STATE OF TRIVIA 1. FL; 2. VT; 3. CT; 4. MD; 5. AZ; 6. NY; 7. CA; 8. VA; 9. IL; 10. MO

Page 294: HIDDEN CITIES

Juneau, Alaska
Denver, Colorado
Helena, Montana
Dover, Delaware

Albany, New York
Boise, Idaho
Jackson, Mississippi
Hilo, Hawaii

Boston, Massachusetts
Bangor, Maine
Pierre, South Dakota
Salem, Oregon

R	J	U	N	E	A	U	X	X
O	A	L	B	A	N	Y	X	R
G	C	X	P	I	E	R	R	E
N	K	X	H	I	L	O	E	V
A	S	S	A	L	E	M	V	N
B	O	I	S	E	H	X	O	E
X	N	O	T	S	O	B	D	D

WORLD HISTORY, Page 316

Crossword puzzle grid:

- 1 Across: ALEXANDER
- 5 Across: LASALLE
- 7 Across: AZTECS
- 8 Across: PLO
- 9 Across: S / PAIN
- 11 Across: HIE
- 12 Across: ROGLYPH
- 13 Across: ROME
- 15 Across: OTTOMAN
- 16 Across: WAR
- 17 Across: CHARLES
- 19 Across: BOER
- 20 Across: OCTAVIAN
- 22 Across: ONE
- 24 Across: CZAR
- 25 Across: UNITED

Down clues include: 2 N, 3 NAPOLEON, 4 ETRURUC, 6 KUBLAI, 10 PAINE, 14 ANGKOR, 18 RAMA, 21 ANRB, 23 E

320

INDEX

B

C

E

Earth, 209
  crust of, 82, 195
  hemispheres of, 77
  latitude and longitude, 53, 77
  plates of, 82
Earthquakes, 82–83
Eastern Europe, 80, 160–161
East Timor, 136–137
Eclipse, 212
Ecosystem, 69
Ecuador, 138–139
  Galapagos Islands, 152
  map, 158; flag, 168
Education, U.S. spending on, 116
Egypt, 138–139
  calendar, 52
  Great Sphinx, 152
  Lighthouse of Alexandria, 51
  longest river, 80
  map, 164; flag, 168
  mummies, 303
  pyramids, 51, 152
Einstein, Albert, 199
Eisenhower, Dwight D., 253, 258
Election Day, 96, 252
Elections, 252
Electoral College, 252
Elements, chemical, 195–196
El Salvador, 138–139
  map, 157; flag, 168
E-mail (electronic mail), 55, 59, 102
Emergencies, what to do in, 95
Emmy Awards, 187
Encyclopedia, 48
Endangered species, 34
Endocrine system, 87
Energy, 62–66
  production and use of energy, 65
  renewable resources and conservation, 66
  sources and types of energy, 62–64
England. *See* Great Britain
Entertainment
  awards, 186–187
  inventions, 100
  movies, videos, and TV, 120–123
  museums, 126
Environment, 67–76
  air pollution, 72–73
  biodiversity, 68
  forests, 75
  garbage and recycling, 69, 70–71
  puzzle, 76
  water pollution, 74
Environmental Protection Agency (EPA), 251
Equal Employment Opportunity Commission
  (EEOC), 251
Equator, 77
Equatorial Guinea, 138–139
  map, 165; flag, 168
Eritrea, 138–139
  map, 164; flag, 168

Estonia, 138–139
  map, 161; flag, 168
Ethiopia, 138–139
  map, 164; flag, 168
Europe, 79
  history, 310–313
  map, 160–161
Exchange rates, 113, 133–151
Executive branch, U.S., 244, 246
Exercise, 88
Explorers, 81
Exports, 118
Extraterrestrial life, search for, 211

F

Faces and places, 9–27
Fat, dietary, 90
Father's Day, 97
Federal Aviation Administration (FAA), 251
Federal Bureau of Investigation (FBI), 251
Federal Communications Commission (FCC), 251
Federal Emergency Management Agency
  (FEMA), 251
Federal Trade Commission (FTC), 251
Figure skating. *See* Skating
Fiji, 138–139
  map, 166; flag, 168
Fillmore, Millard, 253, 255
Films. *See* Movies, videos, and TV
Finland, 138–139
  map, 161; flag, 168
First ladies, 254–259, 260
Fish, 29
Flags
  of nations of world, 167–170
  Olympic flag, 230
  of United States, 170, 243
Florida, 273
  map, 269
  national parks, 291–292
  origin of name, 288
Folk dance, 130
Food
  food pyramid, 91
  nutrients, calories and fat, 90
  recycling, 71
  U.S. spending on, 116
  word origins, 105
Football, 223–225
  college football, 225
  halls of fame, 224, 225
  standings for 1999, 223
  Super Bowl, 223
  top performers, 224, 225
Ford, Gerald R., 253, 259
Forests, 32, 75, 178
Fossil fuels, 63–64
Fossils, 32
France, 138–139
  Eiffel Tower, 152
  map, 160; flag, 168
Franklin, Benjamin, 112, 262

G

Gabon, 138–139
    map, 165; flag, 168
Galapagos Islands, 152, 166
Galaxy, 214
Gambia, The, 138–139
    map, 164; flag, 168
Games
    board, 226–227
    computer, 59
Garfield, James A., 253, 256, 260
Gems, 197
Genes, 198
Geography, 77–85
    contest, 189
    continents and oceans, 79
    earthquakes, 82–83
    explorers, 81
    globe, 77
    map reading, 78
    puzzles, 85
    regions of world, 80
    volcanoes, 84
Georgia (nation), 138–139
    map, 162; flag, 168
Georgia (state), 274
    map, 269
    origin of name, 288
Geothermal energy, 66
Germany, 138–139
    map, 160; flag, 168
    Neuschwanstein Castle, 152
Ghana, 138–139
    map, 164; flag, 168
Global warming, 69, 73
Globe, 77
Golf, 19, 228
González, Elián, 23
Gore, Al, 22, 253
Government of United States, 244–251
Grammy Awards, 187
Grand Canyon, 292
Grant, Ulysses S., 112, 253, 256
Grasslands, 32, 179
Great Britain, 15, 138–139
    bridges and tunnels, 50–51
    Buckingham Palace, 153
    map, 160; flag, 170
Great Depression, 266
Great Seal of United States, 243
Great Wall of China, 152, 307
Greece, 138–139
    Acropolis, 153
    earthquake, 83
    map, 161; flag, 168
    wonders of the ancient world, 51
Greenhouse effect, 69, 73
Greenland, 80, 156
Greenwich meridian, 53, 77
Grenada, 138–139
    map, 157; flag, 168
Griffey, Jr., Ken, 19

Guatemala, 138–139
    earthquake, 83
    map, 157; flag, 168
Guinea, 138–139
    map, 164; flag, 168
Guinea-Bissau, 140–141
    map, 164; flag, 168
Guyana, 140–141
    map, 158; flag, 168
Gymnastics, 228

H

Habitats, 32, 34, 69
Haiti, 140–141
    map, 157; flag, 168
Halley's Comet, 212
Halloween, 97
Halls of Fame
    baseball, 219
    basketball, 221
    football, 224, 225
    hockey, 229
    inventors, 100
    rock and roll, 129
Hamilton, Alexander, 112
Hamm, Mia, 18
Hanks, Tom, 13
Harding, Warren G., 253, 258, 260
Harrison, Benjamin, 253, 257, 260
Harrison, William Henry, 253, 255, 260
Harry, Prince (Great Britain), 15
Harry Potter (fictional character), 24, 46
Hawaii, 274
    map, 268
    national parks, 292
    origin of name, 288
Hayes, Lucy, 260
Hayes, Rutherford B., 253, 256
Health, 86–95
    accident prevention, 95
    AIDS, 94
    allergies, 93
    colds, 92
    dreams, 89
    drugs and alcohol, 94
    exercise, 88
    human body, 86–88
    inventions, 98
    nutrition, 90–91
    teeth, 92
Heisman Trophy, 225
Hemispheres of Earth, 77
Hinduism, 192, 193, 307
Hip-hop, 128
Hispanic-Americans, 182
Historic restorations, 125
Hockey. *See* Ice hockey
Holidays, 96–97
    around the world, 97
    legal U.S. holidays, 96–97
    religious holy days, 194
Holocaust Memorial Museum, U.S., 290

ILLUSTRATION AND PHOTO CREDITS

This product/publication includes images from the Corel Stock Photo Library, PhotoDisc Digital Stock Photography, and the ArtToday web site, which are protected by the copyright laws of the U.S., Canada, and elsewhere. Used under license.

ILLUSTRATION: Teresa Anderko: 4, 5, 35, 57, 85, 88, 89, 103, 104, 202, 203, 294; Dolores Bego: 6, 73, 78, 82, 84, 86, 178, 208; Olivia McElroy: 91; Chris Reed: 3, 51, 191, 213, 270.

PHOTOGRAPHY: 5: Sacagawea, Courtesy of the U.S. Mint. 7: Space Station, Courtesy of NASA/HSF. 8: Tornado, © J. Pat Carter/AP/Wide World Photos. 9: Christina Aguilera & Enrique Iglesias, © AP/Wide World Photos/The Walt Disney Company; *Stuart Little*, © AP/Wide World Photos/Sony Pictures/Imageworks; Princes William & Harry, © AP/Wide World Photos; Vince Carter, © AP/Wide World Photos. 10: Christina Aguilera & Enrique Iglesias, © AP/Wide World Photos/The Walt Disney Company. 11: 'N Sync, © Ethan Miller/Corbis; Ricky Martin, © AP/Wide World Photos. 12: Haley Joel Osment, © Reuters Newmedia Inc./Corbis. 13: *Stuart Little*, © AP/Wide World Photos/Sony Pictures/Imageworks; Tim Allen & Tom Hanks, © Pacha/Corbis. 14: Venus & Serena Williams, © AP/Wide World Photos. 15: Princes William & Harry, © AP/Wide World Photos; Coco & Kelly Miller, © AP/Wide World Photos. 16: The Rock, © AP/Wide World Photos/World Wrestling Federation; *Peanuts*, Reprinted with permission of United Features Syndicate, Inc. 17: Pokémon, © AP/Wide World Photos. 18: Mia Hamm, © Jed Jacobsohn/Allsport. 19: Ken Griffey Jr., © AP/Wide World Photos; Tiger Woods, © AP/Wide World Photos. 20: Kurt Warner, © AP/Wide World Photos. 21: Vince Carter, © AP/Wide World Photos; Marion Jones, © Shaun Botterill/Allsport. 22: Al Gore, © AFP/Corbis; George Bush, © AFP/Corbis. 23: Elián González (both), © AP/Wide World Photos. 24: J. K. Rowling, © AP/Wide World Photos; *Who Wants to Be a Millionaire?*, © AP/Wide World Photos/ABC. 41: Boccioni painting, © Scala/Art Resource, NY. 45: *Bud, Not Buddy* by Christopher Paul Curtis, Courtesy of Random House, Inc. 46: *Harry Potter and the Sorcerer's Stone*, Cover, Illustration by Mary GrandPre from HARRY POTTER AND THE SORCERER'S STONE by J. K. Rowling. Published by Arthur Levine Books, an imprint of Scholastic Press, a division of Scholastic Inc. Copyright © 1998 by Mary GrandPre. Reprinted by permission. 50: Petronas Towers, © V. Miladinovic/Sygma. 77: Globe, © Tom Van Sant/The Stock Market. 110: Child laborer, © Riccardo Chot Kifox/AP/Wide World Photos. 112: Sacagawea, Courtesy of the U.S. Mint. 120: *The Sixth Sense*, © GPN. 121: Buzz Lightyear, © AP/Wide World Photos. 123: Frankie Muniz, © Reuters Newmedia Inc./Corbis; Natalie Portman, © David Allen/Corbis. 128: Britney Spears, © AP/Wide World Photos/NBC Photo. 186: Haley Joel Osment, © Reuters Newmedia Inc./Corbis. 187: Santana, © AP/Wide World Photos. 187: Tony Award, © Tony Awards/Courtesy of Keith Sherman & Assoc. 190: Rosa Parks, © AP/Wide World Photos. 201: Exhibit, © Kelly-Mooney Photography/CO. 211: NASA logo, © NASA. 212: Hale-Bopp, Courtesy of NASA/JPL/Caltech. 214: Meteor, Courtesy of NASA/MSF. 217: Space Station, Courtesy of NASA/HSF. 219: Pedro Martinez, © AP/Wide World Photos. 221: Wilt Chamberlain, © Hulton Picture Library/Allsport. 222: Mateen Cleaves, © AP/Wide World Photos. 224: Edgerrin James, © Andy Lyons/Allsport. 225: Ron Dayne, © AP/Wide World Photos. 228: Tiger Woods, © AP/Wide World Photos. 229: Jaromir Jagr, © AP/Wide World Photos. 231: Michael Johnson, © AP/Wide World Photos. 232: Michelle Kwan, © AP/Wide World Photos. 233: Jaime Moreno, © Jamie Squire/Allsport. 234: Jenny Thompson, © AP/Wide World Photos. 235: Andre Agassi, © AP/Wide World Photos. 240: UN Building, Courtesy of the United Nations/A. Brizzi. 247: Supreme Court, Courtesy of the Supreme Court Historical Society. 249: President Johnson, © 1967 by Dover Publications; President Clinton, Courtesy of the White House. 253-259: U.S. Presidents 1–36, © 1967 by Dover Publications. 259: President Nixon, Courtesy of Richard Nixon Library; President Ford, Courtesy of Gerald R. Ford Museum; President Carter, Courtesy of Jimmy Carter Library; President Reagan, Courtesy of Ronald Reagan Library; President Bush, Courtesy of Bush Presidential Material Project; President Clinton, Courtesy of the White House. 260: Lucy Hayes, Edith Wilson, Lou Henry Hoover, Eleanor Roosevelt, Lady Bird Johnson, Hillary Rodham Clinton, Courtesy of Library of Congress Prints and Photographs Division. 266: Model T Ford, Courtesy of The Center for American History, The University of Texas at Austin. 267: Jackie Robinson, Courtesy of Library of Congress Prints and Photographs Division. 289: George Washington, © 1967 by Dover Publications. 296: Hurricane, © AP/Wide World Photos; Tornado, © J. Pat Carter/AP/Wide World Photos. 303: Mummy, AP/Wide World Photos/Richmond Times-Dispatch.

FRONT COVER: Flat Screen TV, Courtesy of Philips Consumer Electronics; Image on TV screen, Courtesy of Sony PlayStation; Paninfarina Minicar, © Rex USA, Ltd.; Delaware State Quarter, Courtesy of the U.S. Mint; Soccer player, © Mike Powell/Allsport.

Calling All Kids!

The editors of *The World Almanac for Kids* would like to hear from you. What you tell us could help us plan the next edition of our book.

► What did you like best in *The World Almanac for Kids*?
► What would you like to read more about in the next edition?
► Who are your favorite stars or sports figures?

Be sure to ask a parent or guardian if it's OK to write us.

If you do send us a letter or e-mail, you could also get your name in the book as a Kid Contributor. Think we're joking? No way!

Just check out the list of editors and consultants near the beginning of this book, just before the Contents pages. Included are the names of real kids who helped us plan *The World Almanac for Kids 2001*. They told us what they liked, and gave us ideas for new things.

If you want to be a Kid Contributor for *The World Almanac for Kids 2002*, tell us, and include your name, complete address, age, and daytime phone number.

If you are picked as a Kid Contributor, we'll ask you for a few more ideas. We'll also send you a free copy of *The World Almanac for Kids 2002*.

I'M THE MASCOT OF **THE WORLD ALMANAC FOR KIDS,** AND I WANT TO HEAR FROM YOU.

You can write to us at:
**The World Almanac for Kids
One International Boulevard, Suite 630
Mahwah, NJ 07495-0017**

Or send us an e-mail at:
Waforkids@waegroup.com

We hope to hear from you!

Are you older than Haley Joel Osment?
⟶ 26

What dinosaurs lived in the Jurassic period?
⟶ 37

How lor does a mouse liv
⟶ 3

How do you spell "love" in sign language?
⟶ 206

Why is Santana celebrating?
⟶ 187

What is the record for the fastest car?
⟶ 238

What materials used to be stuffed inside mummies?
⟶ 303

Wha can we to redu air pollutio

Which three celebrities were born on February 11?
⟶ 26

Where does "Queen Amidala" go to college?
⟶ 123

Where would you find Chichén Itzá?
⟶ 153

Who was the youngest golfer ever to win the Masters?
⟶ 228

Wh countr flag squar

What Polish woman won two Nobel Prizes?
⟶ 190

What does Michelle Kwan do when she's not skating?
⟶ 232

What was the "Trail of Tears"?
⟶ 264

How old are you in Roman numerals?
⟶ 171

Wh we h no hair